Camden Market

Textbook 6

Für Klasse 10

Diesterweg

Camden Market 6

Herausgegeben von:
Otfried Börner, StD a.D. und
Dr. phil. h.c. Christoph Edelhoff, StD a.D.,
Vorsitzender THE ENGLISH ACADEMY

Erarbeitet von:
Katrin Frost (Themes 5 und 6) und
Ulrike Handke (Wordbanks)
sowie: Ruth Barker, Zoe Carroll, Ingrid Gebhard und
Pat Jüngst
Unter Mitwirkung der Redaktion:
Lisa Fast, Julia Mohm und Henriette Vahle

Fachliche Beratung:
Sigrid Boinski, Petra Günther, Ulrike Handke,
Grit Machut, Annette Schade und
Claudia Stammwitz

**Zusatzmaterialien
zum vorliegenden Schülerbuch**
- Workbook 6 mit Audio-CD für Schüler
  (Best.-Nr. 978-3-425-72832-2)
- Workbook 6
  (Best.-Nr. 978-3-425-72818-6)
- Audio-CD für Schüler 6
  (Best.-Nr. 978-3-425-72860-5)

Lehrer-Materialien
- Audio-CD 6 für Lehrer
  (Best.-Nr. 978-3-425-72872-8)
- Teacher's Manual 6 inkl. Copymaster
  und Workbook-Lösungsheft
  (Best.-Nr. 978-3-425-72898-8)
- Lehrer-Software 6
  (Best.-Nr. 978-3-425-72840-7)
- Vorschläge für Lernerfolgskontrollen 6
  mit CD-ROM
  (Best.-Nr. 978-3-425-72868-1)

© 2010 Bildungshaus Schulbuchverlage
Westermann Schroedel Diesterweg Schöningh Winklers GmbH, Braunschweig
www.diesterweg.de

Druck A[9] / Jahr 2018
Alle Drucke der Serie A sind im Unterricht parallel verwendbar.

Redaktion: Lisa Fast, Julia Mohm, Henriette Vahle
Herstellung: Sandra Grünberg
Illustrationen: Ulf Marckwort, Kassel
Umschlaggestaltung: blum design und kommunikation, Hamburg
Satz: Bock Mediengestaltung, Hannover
Vokabelanhang: Lea Gonsior
Druck und Bindung: westermann druck GmbH, Braunschweig

ISBN 978-3-425-**72808**-7

ZIMBABWE

Save

MOZAMBIQUE

Serowe

Limpopo

Polokwane

Kruger
Nat. Park

Maxixe

Limpopo

Molepolole
Gaborone

Nelspruit

Xai-Xai

Rustenburg

Pretoria

Mpumalanga

Maputo

Mafikeng

Krugersdorp

Gauteng

Johannesburg

North West

Mbabane

Swaziland

Vaal River

Welkom

Zululand

Africa

Free State

KwaZulu-
Natal

Richards Bay

Kimberley

Bloemfontein

Maseru

3482 ▲

Pietermaritzburg

Lesotho

Durban

Senqu River

Indian Ocean

Drakensberge

Queenstown

Mthatha

Eastern Cape

Bhisho

East London

Grahamstown

Port Elizabeth

Heights in m

> 3,000
1,500 – 3,000
1,000 – 1,500
500 – 1,000
200 – 500
100 – 200
0 – 100

2505 ▲ Heights in m
Borders between countries
Borders between provinces
Rivers
Wadi, dry valley
National parks

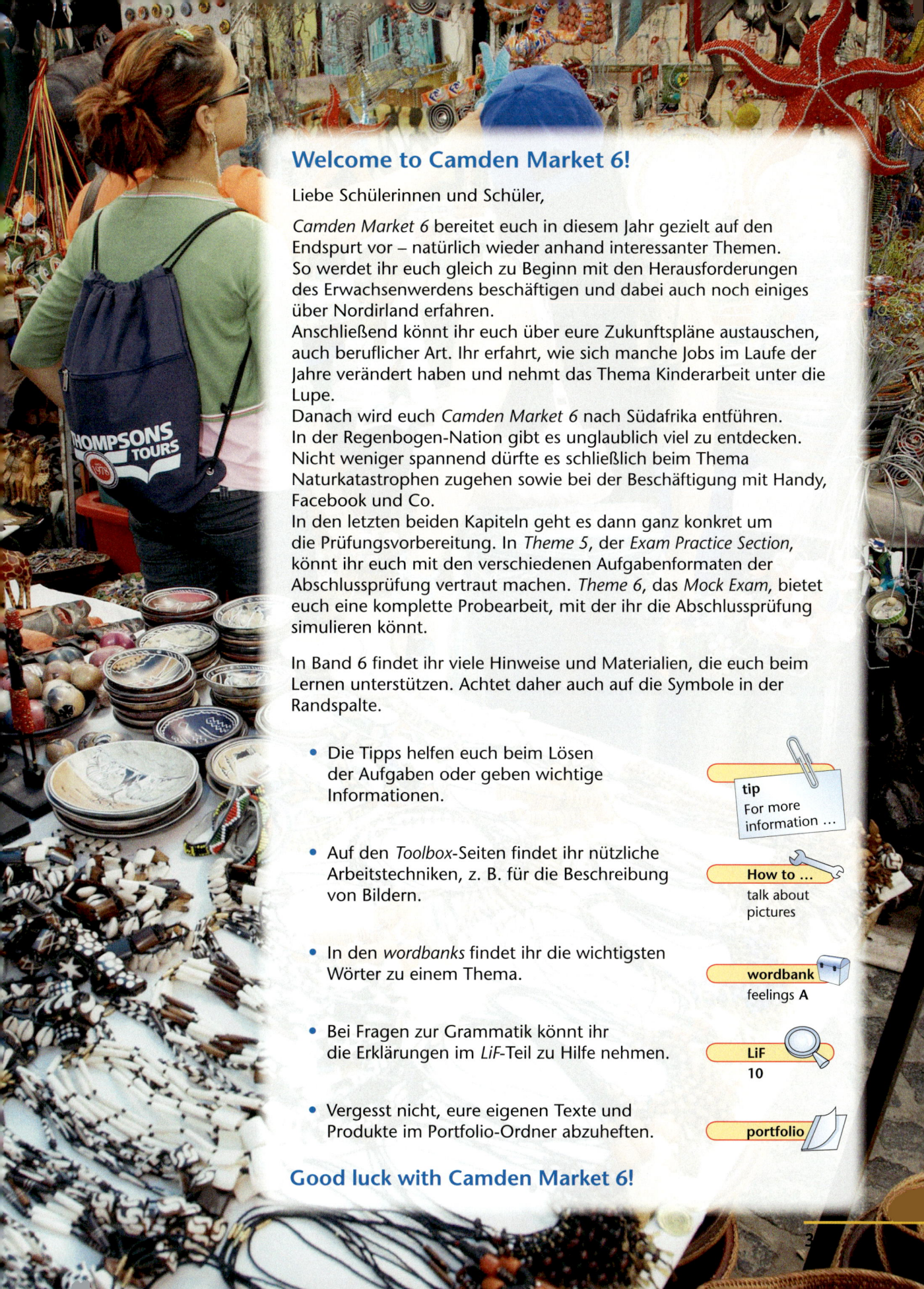

Welcome to Camden Market 6!

Liebe Schülerinnen und Schüler,

Camden Market 6 bereitet euch in diesem Jahr gezielt auf den Endspurt vor – natürlich wieder anhand interessanter Themen. So werdet ihr euch gleich zu Beginn mit den Herausforderungen des Erwachsenwerdens beschäftigen und dabei auch noch einiges über Nordirland erfahren.

Anschließend könnt ihr euch über eure Zukunftspläne austauschen, auch beruflicher Art. Ihr erfahrt, wie sich manche Jobs im Laufe der Jahre verändert haben und nehmt das Thema Kinderarbeit unter die Lupe.

Danach wird euch *Camden Market 6* nach Südafrika entführen. In der Regenbogen-Nation gibt es unglaublich viel zu entdecken. Nicht weniger spannend dürfte es schließlich beim Thema Naturkatastrophen zugehen sowie bei der Beschäftigung mit Handy, Facebook und Co.

In den letzten beiden Kapiteln geht es dann ganz konkret um die Prüfungsvorbereitung. In *Theme 5*, der *Exam Practice Section*, könnt ihr euch mit den verschiedenen Aufgabenformaten der Abschlussprüfung vertraut machen. *Theme 6*, das *Mock Exam*, bietet euch eine komplette Probearbeit, mit der ihr die Abschlussprüfung simulieren könnt.

In Band 6 findet ihr viele Hinweise und Materialien, die euch beim Lernen unterstützen. Achtet daher auch auf die Symbole in der Randspalte.

- Die Tipps helfen euch beim Lösen der Aufgaben oder geben wichtige Informationen.

  tip
  For more information …

- Auf den *Toolbox*-Seiten findet ihr nützliche Arbeitstechniken, z. B. für die Beschreibung von Bildern.

  How to …
  talk about pictures

- In den *wordbanks* findet ihr die wichtigsten Wörter zu einem Thema.

  wordbank
  feelings A

- Bei Fragen zur Grammatik könnt ihr die Erklärungen im *LiF*-Teil zu Hilfe nehmen.

  LiF
  10

- Vergesst nicht, eure eigenen Texte und Produkte im Portfolio-Ordner abzuheften.

  portfolio

Good luck with Camden Market 6!

Inhalt

Methodenkompetenz	Textsorten	Sprachliche Mittel	People & Places
How to work with others How to read How to listen How to write How to talk about pictures How to watch How to help out in English	Song literarischer Text Sachtext Hörtext Bildergeschichte Bilder aus Film Filmkritik Flyer	R: Konjunktionen R: *past perfect* R: Indirekte Rede	Northern Ireland
How to talk about pictures How to listen How to read How to give a talk How to listen How to read How to write	Fotos Hörtext literarische Texte	R: Das Passiv R: Relativsätze mit/ohne Pronomen R: Bedingungssätze (Typ II) R: Konjunktionen	
How to read How to work with others How to write a letter How to listen How to write your opinion How to talk about pictures How to read	Gedicht E-Mail Hörtext Fotos Statistik Zeitungsartikel Sachtext	R: *present perfect* mit *since* und *for* R: Das Passiv R: Adverbien der Art und Weise	UNICEF
How to read How to help out in English How to write a letter How to talk about pictures How to listen How to read How to watch	Hörtext Zeitschriftenartikel Dialog Stellenanzeigen Bewerbungsschreiben Fotos	R: Wortstellung und Fragebildung Partizipien zur Verkürzung von Adverbialsätzen emphatischer Gebrauch von *do*	
How to read How to talk How to listen How to talk about pictures How to read How to listen How to give a talk	Dialog SMS-Nachrichten Bordkarte Seite aus Reiseführer Hörtext Fotos Lexikonauszug Sachtext Song Erfahrungsberichte	R: Die -ing-Form R: Wortstellung und Fragebildung R: Bedingungssätze (Typ II) R: Steigerung von Adjektiven R: Modalverben und ihre Ersatz- formen	South Africa
How to work with others How to help out in English How to read How to write your opinion How to listen How to write a letter How to read How to give a talk	Hörtext Broschüre E-Mail Statistiken Sachtext	Satzadverbien R: Wortstellung und Fragebildung	

R = *revision* (Wiederholung)

Inhalt

Inhalt

Methodenkompetenz	Textsorten	Sprachliche Mittel	People & Places
How to read How to work with others How to help out in English How to write How to work with others How to write your opinion How to listen How to discuss	Fotos Zeitungsartikel Hörtext Zeitschriftenartikel Facebook-Seite Erfahrungsbericht Internet-Chat Sachtext	R: Das Passiv R: Stützwörter: *one/ones* R: Indirekte Rede Steigerung von Adverbien R: Bedingungssätze (Typ III)	Samuel Morse
How to listen How to talk How to read How to write your opinion	Fotos Karte Hörtext Gedicht Werbeanzeigen Internetartikel Statistik	Inversion Das Passiv in der Zukunft R: Verb + Objekt mit Infinitiv	

Aufgabenformat/Inhalt

multiple choice, gap filling, sentence completion, true/false/not given

multiple choice, matching, putting statements in order, answering questions, true/false/not given

form, letter, email, flyer, poster, notice, creative writing, discussing statements

telling someone about the main points of a text, helping out in English

describing and interpreting pictures, suggesting/agreeing/disagreeing, discussing, role cards

multiple choice, gap filling, true/false/not given, sentence completion

multiple choice, matching, true/false/not given

form, poster, flyer, application (email)

telling someone about the main points of a text

describing and interpreting pictures, suggesting/agreeing/disagreeing, discussing, role cards

R = *revision* (Wiederholung)

Inhalt

Die Symbole

CD Dieser Hörtext ist auf der CD für Lehrer und auf der CD für Schüler.

CD Dieser Hörtext ist nur auf der CD für Lehrer.

LiF 9 Hierzu gibt es eine Erklärung im Grammatik-Teil *Language in Focus.*

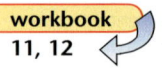
workbook 11, 12 Im Workbook gibt es weitere Übungen.

portfolio Diese Arbeit kannst du in deinem Portfolio-Ordner abheften.

How to … write Auf den *How to*-Seiten findest du Techniken, die dir beim Englischlernen helfen.

tip You can … Tipps oder Hilfen

wordbank feelings A In den *wordbanks* sind die wichtigsten Wörter zu einem Thema zusammengefasst.

Schwierige Texte und Aufgaben im *MORE*-Teil

Der Aufbau

	Der Basis-Teil erfüllt die Grundanforderungen für Klasse 10. Hier werden alle Kompetenzen trainiert.
MORE **M6-M8**	Verknüpfungsmöglichkeit mit dem *MORE*-Teil
	Der *MORE*-Teil bietet Zusatzmaterial zur Differenzierung für mittleres und höheres Niveau.
	Der *Exam*-Teil (*Themes* 5 und 6) bereitet gezielt auf die Abschlussprüfung vor.
	How to-Seiten vermitteln Lern- und Arbeitstechniken, *wordbanks* stellen thematischen Wortschatz zur Verfügung.
	Optionales Zusatzmaterial: *Reading is fun* – Lesestoff ergänzend zu jedem *Theme*.

Diese Arbeitsanweisungen findest du in Camden Market:

Act out the dialogue.	Spielt den Dialog nach.
Add notes to your grid.	Ergänze deine Tabelle.
Collect phrases/arguments/information/…	Sammle Redewendungen/Argumente/Informationen/…
Compare your findings with a partner's.	Vergleiche deine Ergebnisse mit denen eines Partners/einer Partnerin.
Complete the sentences.	Vervollständige die Sätze.
Describe what is happening.	Beschreibe, was passiert.
Find a headline for each paragraph.	Finde eine Überschrift für jeden Absatz.
Find the words that match …	Finde Wörter, die zu … passen.
Find out …	Finde heraus …
Finish the statements/dialogues.	Schreibe die Aussagen/Dialoge zu Ende.
Give each other feedback.	Gebt einander Feedback.
Listen to the song/story/dialogue.	Höre dir das Lied/die Geschichte/den Dialog an.
Listen and take notes.	Höre zu und mache dir Notizen.
Look at the examples/pictures/…	Sieh dir die Beispiele/Bilder/… an.
Make a mindmap/list/fact file/…	Erstelle ein Wortnetz/eine Liste/einen Steckbrief/…
Make up a story.	Denke dir eine Geschichte aus.
Match the pictures/sounds with the texts.	Ordne die Bilder/Geräusche den Texten zu.
Practise your talk/presentation first.	Probe deine Rede/Präsentation zuerst.
Present your findings in class.	Präsentiere der Klasse deine Ergebnisse.
Put the sentences/pictures/events/… in the right order.	Bringe die Sätze/Bilder/Ereignisse/… in die richtige Reihenfolge.
Prepare a short talk/an interview/…	Bereite eine kurze Rede/ein Interview/… vor.
Read the text/article/brochure.	Lies den Text/Artikel/die Broschüre.
Swap your report with a partner.	Tausche deinen Bericht mit einem Partner/einer Partnerin.
Take notes (in a grid).	Mache dir Notizen (in einer Tabelle).
Take turns.	Wechselt euch ab.
Talk to a partner about …	Sprich mit einem Partner/einer Partnerin über …
Watch the film.	Sieh dir den Film an.
Work with a partner/in groups.	Arbeite mit einem Partner/einer Partnerin/in einer Gruppe.
Write a letter/story/poem/…	Schreibe einen Brief/eine Geschichte/ein Gedicht/…
Write down words/phrases/reasons/…	Schreibe Wörter/Ausdrücke/Gründe/… auf.

Diese Sätze helfen dir, wenn du am Computer arbeitest:

Surf the Internet for information on …	Suche im Internet nach Informationen über …
Can I print it out/download it?	Kann ich das ausdrucken/herunterladen?
I've already saved it.	Ich habe es schon gespeichert.
The computer has crashed.	Der Computer ist abgestürzt.
What's your email address?	Wie ist deine E-Mail-Adresse?
You can click on this link.	Du kannst diesen Link anklicken.

GROWING UP

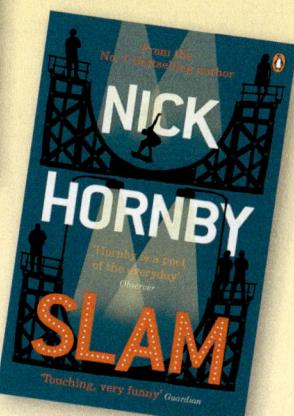

In this Theme …

- you will read about a young couple and their problems.
- you will talk about young people's feelings and give advice.
- you can watch and discuss a film about a pregnant teenager.
- you can think about reasons why to get married.
- you can find out about the difference between an arranged marriage and a love marriage.
- you will be able to read and listen to parts of the book 'SLAM'.

CD

1 Growing up 👂 👄

a) Listen to the song 'Graduation' by Vitamin C about growing up. Do you like the song? Say why/why not.

b) What comes to your mind when you think about growing up? Brainstorm with a partner. Then talk to another pair and share your ideas.

How to ...
work with others (1)

2 Kevin and Sadie 👄 👓

The book 'Across the Barricades' by Joan Lingard deals with growing up in Belfast almost 40 years ago.

a) Look at the information about the two main characters in the book – Kevin and Sadie. Work with a partner and write down what YOU think the book is about.

Catholic 18 years old

unskilled worker

eight brothers and sisters

Kevin McCoy

Belfast, Northern Ireland

Sadie Jackson

shop assistant

16 years old

Protestant

one brother

b) Now read part A from 'Across the Barricades'. Why are Sadie's parents so angry?

A Sadie has spent the afternoon with Kevin. She now returns home.

How to ...
read

[...] Sadie stood with her head up listening to her mother's tirade. At the end of it she said, "All I've done is go for a walk with a boy."
"All?" said her mother.
"You're not seeing him again, do you hear?" said her father.
"I'll see him if I want to." Sadie opened the kitchen door.
"Come you back here," roared her father. [...] "You'll do what I tell you as long as you're living under my roof."
"I don't have to stay under your roof. I'm sixteen, going on seventeen. I can go if I want to. You can't get the police to bring me back."
[...] Sadie [...] walked up the stairs. He made to follow her but his wife said quietly, "Let her be, Jim. She's headstrong, you'll only turn her against you." [...]

workbook
1-2

3 Trouble 👓 👄

wordbank
feelings A

a) Read part B. What do you learn about Kevin? What do you learn about his friend Brian? How do they feel?

B Kevin has just come back from the seaside town of Bangor where he spent the day with Sadie. He meets his friend Brian in the street.

tip
Prods = Protestants

[...] "Hey there, Kevin! [...] Where've you been all day?"
"Bangor."
"You missed it all here. Doyle's pub got burnt down by the Prods. [...] They're going to pay for this. They'd burn us out to the last man if we let them."
"We [Catholics] do a bit of burning ourselves," said Kevin wearily.
Brian seized him by the shoulder and spun him round so that they stood face to face.
"I don't like the sound of that talk."
"What good does burning things do? I'm sick of fires."

"So you take yourself off to Bangor for the day?"

"Why not? It's no crime."

"Could be. Depends on who you were with."

"What do you want to say?" Kevin shoved Brian's hand off his shoulder.

"I met your Uncle Albert on the way home. He was telling me you were with a blonde girl by the name of Sadie."

"So what?"

"I remember a girl called Sadie. Few years back."

"Mind your own business!" Kevin spoke fiercely.

"I don't know that it might not be my business, if it's the same Sadie I'm thinking of."

"You won't tell me what to do, Brian Rafferty."

"No?" Brian smiled and leaned back against the wall of a house.

"No," said Kevin and left him. [...]

b) Work with a partner and read or act out the scene.

workbook
3-4

4 What's next?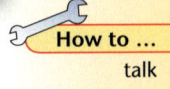

How to …
talk

a) What happened on the following days? Find out by linking the sentence halves with the conjunctions in the box.

but • although • and • because

LiF
24

1 Brian and two other boys beat Kevin up **???** for them he was a traitor.

2 Kevin couldn't escape **???** was badly injured.

3 Without telling Kevin, his sister Brede went to see Sadie **???** she didn't like going into the Protestant streets.

4 Brede asked Sadie not to meet Kevin again **???** she didn't want her brother to be beaten up again.

5 Sadie said she had to think about it **???** she couldn't promise not to see Kevin again.

b) If you were Sadie's best friend, what advice would you give her?

wordbank
giving advice B

PEOPLE & PLACES

Northern Ireland

In 1800 Ireland was made part of the United Kingdom (UK). Life in Ireland was very hard for the Catholic population in the 19th and early 20th century. There was a famine and many people starved or had to leave the country. The resistance against the English, who were mainly Protestant, grew. In the early 20th century the Irish began to fight for their independence from England. In 1948 the southern part of Ireland became the Republic of Ireland. The majority of the population in the Republic is Catholic. Northern Ireland stayed part of the UK. But the Nationalists (who were mainly Catholic) in Northern Ireland wanted to be part of the Republic; the Unionists (who were mainly Protestant) wanted to stay part of the UK. From the 1970s onwards the problems between the Nationalists and the Unionists became more and more violent. Belfast saw some of the worst of these so-called 'Troubles' in Northern Ireland. Paramilitary groups on both sides carried out bombings and attacks. Many innocent people, Catholics and Protestants, died. In 1998 the British government held peace talks with all the different groups. A peaceful solution to the conflict was agreed on. Although the 'Troubles' have ended, there is still mistrust and sometimes violence between the Catholic and Protestant communities.

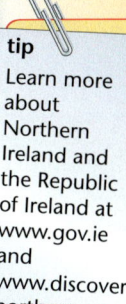

tip
Learn more about Northern Ireland and the Republic of Ireland at www.gov.ie and www.discovernorthernireland.com

13

5 The story goes on

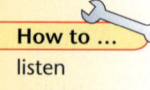
CD

a) Listen to a British school class talking about how the story goes on. Then put the pictures in the right order.

How to …
listen

A

B

C

D

E

F

LiF
4

b) Look at the pictures again. Then write down what happened.

Example: Kevin – arrive at the river / he – wait for Sadie
After Kevin had arrived at the river, he waited for Sadie.

1 Kevin – lean against a tree / an elderly man (Mr Blake) – offer to help him
2 Sadie – finally come to meet Kevin / she – recognize Mr Blake as her former teacher
3 Kevin and Sadie – decide to stay together / they – start seeing each other at Mr Blake's place

workbook
5

4 Sadie – lose her job / she – work as a housekeeper for Mr Blake
5 Mr Blake – get anonymous letters for some time / someone – throw a bomb into his house

6 Leaving

a) Read part C. What does Kevin decide to do?

C After Mr Blake's funeral Kevin and Sadie go for a walk.

[…] Kevin looked down at the hand that held Sadie's and tightened his hold on hers. […]
They walked on Cave Hill, above the city.
"I've been thinking," he began.
"Yes?"
He turned and looked into her face and said quickly, "Sadie, I've got to go away. I can't stay here any longer. I haven't a job and I'm sick of bombs and people getting killed!

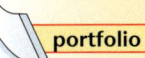

And now that this has happened with Mr Blake ..." He paused, then continued, "It's not a case of running away, you mustn't think that. I just don't want any part of what's going on here. I don't like the way we've got to live. It's not living anyway. Not living the way I want it."
She did not speak for a moment. [...] She swallowed. "When will you go?" she asked.
"Next week."

b) Can you understand Kevin? Write a text and say what you think. Give reasons.

How to ... write your opinion

portfolio

I think ... • I'm sure ... • On the one hand ..., but on the other hand ... • That's why I think ... • All in all, I would say ...

7 A happy ending?

a) Read the last part of the book and find out how the story ends.

D Kevin arrives at the harbour where he will take a ship to Liverpool.

Standing beside the Liverpool shed was Sadie. He ran the last few yards to reach her.
"So you managed to come and see me off?"
"Did you think I wouldn't?"
"No."
"Anyway, I haven't come to see you off. I'm coming with you." He was looking at her in amazement. She added anxiously, "You don't mind, do you?"
"Mind?" He put down his suitcase and lifted her up and whirled her round till she was breathless with laughter. "That's the best news I've had in months. But where's your luggage?"
"I couldn't walk out of the house with a suitcase, could I now? You'll have to take me as I stand. But I've bought a ticket."
She took the piece of paper from her pocket and held it out.
"Come on then," said Kevin. "What are we waiting for?"
"Nothing," said Sadie. [...]
He took her hand and together they walked across the shed to the white, waiting ship.

MORE M1-M6 getting married

tip You can read more about Kevin and Sadie on page 126 or in other books by Joan Lingard.

b) How do you imagine Sadie and Kevin's life ten years later? Talk to your partner.

workbook 6

8 Choose an activity

- **Kevin has just told Sadie about his plans to leave Belfast. Write Sadie's diary entry.**
- **Work in a group. Write a dialogue between Kevin and his parents in which he tells them that he will leave Belfast. Then act out the scene.**
- **Sadie has decided to go to England with Kevin. Write Sadie's farewell letter to her parents.**

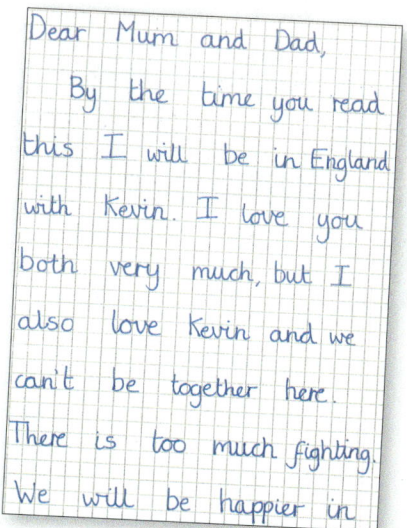

Dear Mum and Dad,
By the time you read this I will be in England with Kevin. I love you both very much, but I also love Kevin and we can't be together here. There is too much fighting. We will be happier in

How to ... write

How to ... talk

How to ... write a letter

portfolio

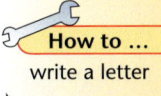

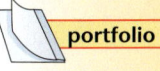

9 Baby blues

a) Look at the stills from the film 'Juno'. Choose one of them and describe it. Talk about the situation and the atmosphere.

How to ...
talk about pictures

wordbank
feelings A

The picture shows … • In the foreground/background there is/are … • The person on the left/right looks as if … • In the middle of the picture there is/are … • Maybe he/ she is thinking/talking about … • The atmosphere seems to be … • I can see … • One person has got …, the other one has … • They are probably … • …

A

B

C

D

E

F

CD

b) Listen to the song 'Dearest' by Buddy Holly from the soundtrack of the film. Which picture does the song fit best? Why?

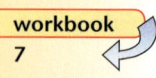
workbook
7

The song is happy/ sad/slow/fast/ … so I think picture … fits best.

The song makes me feel angry/excited/lonely/… so I think …

1

10 A film review

a) Look at the stills in number 9 again. What do you think happens in the film? Talk to a partner and make some notes. Then talk to another pair and share your ideas.

How to ...
work with
others (1)

b) Now read this film review from an English school magazine. Find out if the author likes the film.

JUNO – A TEENAGE COMEDY

When 16-year-old Juno McGuff (Ellen Page) finds herself pregnant after having sex for the first time, she immediately knows that she does not want to keep the baby. After all, she only slept with her classmate Paulie Bleeker (Michael Cera) to find out what it was like and because it had been another boring afternoon. So she makes an appointment for an abortion at the local hospital but when she is there she just cannot do it. Instead she decides to give up the baby for adoption.

After the first shock her parents react quite understandingly. They accept Juno's decision and support her during the pregnancy.

Paulie tells Juno that he is okay with whatever she decides.

Together with her best friend Leah, Juno looks for a family who want to adopt a baby. The couple she finally chooses is rich, they seem to be nice and Juno decides that they are the best parents for her baby. Although there are some unrealistic parts – Juno's understanding and tolerant parents and Juno's calm way of handling the matter – the film manages to show not only the emotional chaos a pregnant teenager faces but also a funny side of things. Most of all, it does not damn abortion or adoption. The film clearly states that women should have a choice when finding themselves in such a situation but it also shows that it is best not to get pregnant in the first place.

The wonderful cast, a really good soundtrack and the great script that won an Oscar make this a very enjoyable movie.

Kirsty Wedderspoon

How to ...
read

MORE
M7-M9
SLAM

c) How close were you with your ideas about the film?

11 Telling the story

Kirsty tells a friend about the film. Look at the statements from the film and write down what the people said.

LiF
12

Example: Juno: "I've done three tests. I'm pregnant."
Juno told Paulie/said that she had done three tests and that she was pregnant.

1 Juno: "Dad, I don't want to keep the baby."
2 Paulie: "I'm okay with whatever you decide."
3 Leah: "What's it like to be pregnant?"
4 Juno's parents: "We'll support you."
5 Juno's dad: "How could you be so stupid?"
6 Paulie's mum: "I never thought you would do anything like that."

I'm pregnant.

workbook
8-9

12 How will it end?

a) Before you watch the film: Write down what YOU think will be the last words or the last scene in the film.

How to ...
watch

b) Watch the film in English. Were you right in a)?

c) After watching the film: Look at the review in number 10 again. Do you think the reviewer is right? Say why/why not.

13 Juno on the screen

CD

How to ...
listen

a) Listen to five people being interviewed after watching 'Juno'. Who liked the film? Who didn't? Why? Copy the grid and take notes.

b) Who do you agree with? Give reasons.

name	liked the film	didn't like the film	reasons
Rob			

14 Getting help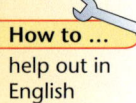

Read this flyer of a helpline. Explain to someone who doesn't speak English who the flyer is for and what the organization offers.

How to ...
help out in
English

american pregnancy helpline

So, your partner has just told you she is pregnant and you need to know how much of the decision-making process involves you.
Call the helpline toll-free at **1-866-942-6466** to get answers to your questions. Take a look at the three options. If you want to know what rights and responsibilities you have as a father, call. We'll put you in touch with professionals who can assist you with your questions. Don't wait, call today.

Parenting — Am I required to pay child support? What if I don't know if I'm the father?

Adoption — Can I take part in choosing the adoptive couple? Can I keep in touch with my child?

Abortion — Do I have to pay anything? What if I don't agree with my partner's decision?

workbook
10

15 Choose an activity

portfolio

• Your English club at school is showing 'Juno'. Design a poster for the event.

How to ...
write

• Imagine you are Paulie and Juno has just told you about her pregnancy. How do you feel? Write a blog entry.

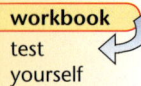
workbook
test
yourself

• Write your own film review. First take notes on what you liked and didn't like about the film, then write a text.

M1 Different ways to get married 👄

a) Look at these wedding pictures. Which is your favourite one? Why?

A

B

C

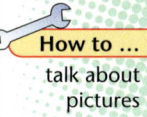
How to …
talk about pictures

D

E

workbook
M1

> I think picture C was taken in …

b) Where and when do you think were the pictures taken?

LiF
9

M2 Why get married? 👄 ✏️

Throughout the centuries people have got married for one reason or another.

a) Here is a list of possible reasons. Can you think of more reasons?

You want to share your lives with each other.

You don't want to be alone.

You believe in romantic, everlasting love.

You want to be free from your parents.

You've always wanted a fancy wedding.

All your friends are married.

Your culture or religion tells you to do so.

Your partner has got money.

You want to have someone around when you're old.

…

You want to help someone get work in your country.

workbook
M2

b) Which reasons do YOU think are the 'right' reasons to get married? Work in small groups and talk quietly about your ideas. One of you takes notes. Then choose a member of your group to present your results in class.

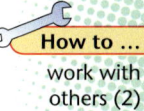
How to …
work with others (2)

M3 Different views

A radio station asked its listeners what they think about getting married.

a) Listen to six statements and take notes. Who thinks getting married is the right thing to do (+)? Who says everyone should make their own decisions (?) and who argues against it (-)?

CD

b) Listen again. Use *who* or *which* to match the sentence parts. Then decide: Where can you leave out the relative pronoun?

LiF
16

1	The man		A was raised to believe in marriage respects it.
2	The place		B ruins love is marriage, says Wendy.
3	The thing	*who* *which*	C Robert leads now will change after he gets married.
4	Alisha		D says that his marriage is great is called Robert.
5	The life		E Jacky went to a year ago is London.

workbook
M3

How to …
write your
opinion

c) Do YOU want to get married one day? Write a text. Give reasons.

M4 (Un)arranged marriage

In some countries and cultures arranged marriages are a common tradition.

a) What do you think an arranged marriage is? What is the difference between an arranged marriage and a love marriage? Talk to your partner.

> In his novel '(Un)arranged marriage' Bali Rai tells the story of Manjit, a British Asian whose family came from India. Manjit was born in Britain and has an English girlfriend, Lisa. Because Manjit feels more British than Indian, he often has problems with his parents.

b) What might Manjit's problems be? Write down your ideas. Then read the following extract from the novel. Are any of your ideas in the extract?

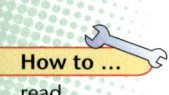

How to …
read

> While we waited for Lisa's mum after school, I talked a little more to Lisa about the whole deal to do with arranged marriages the way my parents saw it. Lisa told me again to say 'no' and keep on saying it until my parents gave up.
> "They can't make you do something you don't want to do." [...]
> "You don't understand, Lisa. It isn't that simple. [...] my old man is threatening to take me to India if I don't agree. My mum just cries every time we talk about it."
> "So what are you going to do? Say yes to keep them happy? What about what *you* want?"
> That was the problem. I knew that I didn't want to get married young to some girl who I didn't even know. [...] I didn't want to spend my life looking after my parents in their old age and having to go to the weddings of distant cousins because it was the right thing to do. [...] And deep down inside I was scared that if I did say no, my dad would kill me and my mum would kill herself [...] because of the shame. How could I do that to them? How?

bali rai
(un)arranged
marriage

And how was I going to explain that to Lisa who was never going to have to choose between what she wanted out of life and her family? She didn't have to fight to be seen as an individual.

"I told you what they've been like. All my mum does is cry, starts slapping her thighs and threatens to kill herself."

"But she did that with your brothers too. And you know she doesn't mean it, don't you?"

"Yeah, but what if she does?"

"She won't, Manny, I promise." She held my hand and squeezed it really hard, trying to reassure me. "It'll be fine after a while. When they've accepted you for you."

"I really don't think that will ever happen, Lisa. They're just too set in their old ways to accept what I want to do with my life." [...]

Lisa kissed me on the cheek and squeezed my hand again. I looked at her and tried to smile. [...]

"On a more selfish level, what about me?"

"You know how I feel about you, Lisa."

"And you know that I love you too. But if you end up having an arranged marriage, provided we're still together at that point, are you going to just cast me aside?"

This time I kissed her on the lips and gave her a big hug. "Never. And we will still be together – I know we will."

"Oh, Manny, what are we going to do?"

c) **Manjit is scared. What would happen to him if he didn't agree to the marriage?**

> If he didn't agree, his father/mother would ...

d) **After the conversation Manjit talks to his father again. Work with a partner. Write and act out the dialogue.**

M5 Things to follow

a) **How might the story in M4 go on? Collect ideas. Think of:**

> • Who? • What? • When? • Where? • Why?

Write down what might happen.

b) **Present your texts. Which one do you like best? Give reasons.**

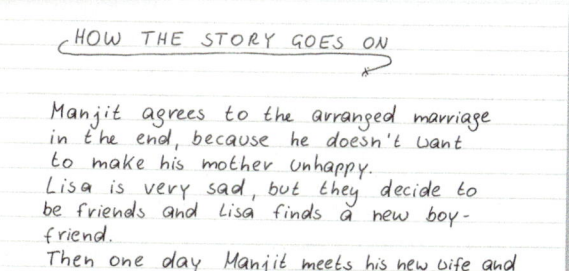

HOW THE STORY GOES ON

Manjit agrees to the arranged marriage in the end, because he doesn't want to make his mother unhappy.
Lisa is very sad, but they decide to be friends and Lisa finds a new boy-friend.
Then one day Manjit meets his new wife and

tip
You can put all the texts on your desks, walk around the classroom and read them.

M6 YOUR talk: Is marriage out of date?

a) **Prepare a two-minute talk about this question: Is marriage out of date? Make notes on some cards.**

b) **Practise your talk before you present it to the class.**

workbook M4

LiF 7

How to ...
talk

How to ...
write

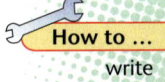
portfolio

workbook M5

How to ...
give a talk

CD

M7 What is it about?

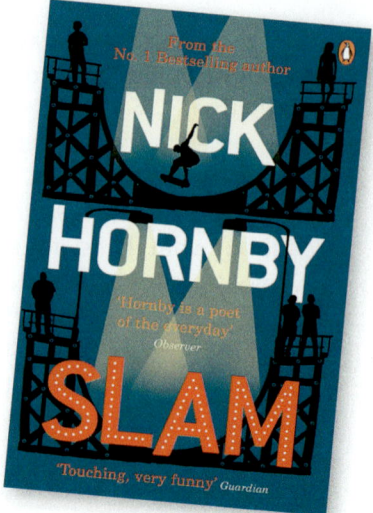

a) Listen to the extract from Nick Hornby's novel 'SLAM'. What can you find out about the plot? Take notes on:

- Who?
- What?
- When?
- Where?
- Why?

How to ...
listen

b) Work with a partner. Use your notes to tell each other what you have found out about the plot.

M8 Sleepless

a) Read the following extract from the novel 'SLAM'. Try to say in five sentences what the situation is.

> I woke up in the middle of the night. I wasn't in my own bed, and there was someone in the bed with me, and there was a baby crying.
> "Oh, shit." I recognized the voice. The person in bed with me was Alicia.
> "Your turn," she said.
> I didn't say anything. I didn't know where I was or even when I was, and I didn't know what 'Your turn' meant. [...]
> "Sam," she said. "Wake up. He's awake. Your turn."
> "Right," I said. I knew what 'my turn' meant now, and I knew where and when I was. Roof was about three weeks old. We couldn't remember a time when he wasn't with us. Every night we slept as though we hadn't slept for months; every night we were woken up after one or two or, if we were lucky, three hours, and we didn't know where we were or what was making the noise, and we had to remember everything all over again. It was weird.
> "He can't need feeding," she said. "He had one about an hour ago, and I've got nothing left. So he either needs winding or he has a dirty nappy. He hasn't been changed for hours."
> "I keep making a mess of it," I said.
> "You're better at it than me."
> [...]
> Alicia put the bedside light on and looked at me to see if I was awake. [...] She looked tired and her hair was greasy, but she'd been like that for a while, and I'd got used to it. She was different, I could see that. But so was everything else. I don't think I'd have liked her so much if she'd stayed the same. It would have been like she wasn't taking Roof seriously. I got out of bed. [...] The baby was sleeping in a little cot at the end of the bed. He was all red in the face from crying.
> I bent down and put my face near him. [...] I put him on the changing table, unbuttoned his sleep suit and his vest, pulled them both back above his bum, opened the nappy and wiped him. Then I folded the nappy up, put it in the bag, put a new one on and buttoned him back up again. Easy. He was crying, so I picked him up and put him against my chest

and jiggled him, and he went quiet. I knew how to hold him without his head jerking about. I sang to him a bit too, just made-up stuff. He liked it, I think. [...]

I put Roof back in his cot and climbed into bed, and Alicia put her arms around me. [...]

"You do love me, Sam, don't you?" Alicia said. [...]

"Yeah," I said. "Of course."

I still didn't know whether that was true. But I did know it was more likely to come true if I said it, because she'd like me more, and I'd like her more, and eventually we might love each other properly, and life would be easier if that happened.

b) Read the extract again. Then complete the sentences with the conjunctions in the box.

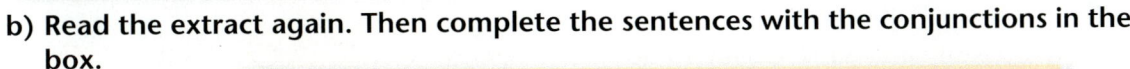

therefore • although • because • when • however • while

1   **???**   Sam woke up, he didn't know where he was.
2   Sam and Alicia didn't get much sleep   **???**   they had to care for their baby every night.
3   **???**   Alicia looked different now, Sam liked her a lot.
4   **???**   Roof was crying, Sam changed his nappy and sang to him.
5   Sam said he loved Alicia.   **???**   , he didn't know whether that was true.
6   Having a child was hard for the two teenagers.   **???**   , Sam hoped that they could really love each other to make things easier.

c) Imagine you are in Alicia's or Sam's position. How would you feel?

d) Now tell someone who hasn't read 'SLAM' what it is about. What has it got in common with 'Juno' and what is different? Name two to three facts.

LiF
24

M9 Choose an activity

- **Tell the story from M8 from Alicia's point of view and write it down.**

- **Find out about the author Nick Hornby. Make a fact file about him and his work to give a talk. You can use the Internet.**

- **Find information about teenage pregnancy. Think about:**
  - how many teenagers get pregnant each year
  - which countries have got the highest/lowest rates
  - what the causes are
  - what is done to reduce the numbers
  - …

Present the most interesting facts to the class.

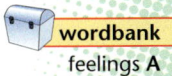
wordbank
feelings A

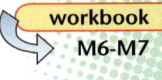
workbook
M6-M7

How to …
write

How to …
give a talk

I woke up in the middle of the night. At first I didn't know where I was. Then I realised that Sam was lying next to me and our baby was crying. I couldn't believe it. He was awake again after only one hour.

tip
You can present your results in a chart.

portfolio

Check it out!

tip
You can quiz your partner!

Did you get it all?

- Who sings about growing up?
- Who wrote the book 'Across the Barricades'?
- Where is 'Across the Barricades' set?
- Who helps Kevin and Sadie?
- Where do Kevin and Sadie decide to go?
- How old is Juno McGuff?
- What is Juno's best friend's name?
- What does Juno decide to do about her baby?

Good to know ...

When going abroad, it's always good to know at least a little about the foreign country's culture and history. You can avoid offending people if you know what might be difficult topics in their culture.

Did you know that ...

... the longest name of a place in Ireland is Muckanagh-eder-dauhaulia?

... Queen Victoria probably started the tradition of getting married in a white dress?

... Ireland is the only country in the world with a musical instrument – the harp – for a national symbol?

Find out about different wedding costumes and traditions. What are the most interesting ones?

Find out the national symbol of YOUR country.

... the Gaelic name of Ireland is Eire?

... in some countries the wedding ring is worn on the left hand?

Find out why.

... newborn babies who are breastfed eat as often as twelve times a day?

... teenage pregnancies cost the United States at least $7 billion per year?

MAKING IT ON YOUR OWN

In this Theme …

- you will talk about the time when school is over.
- you will learn how jobs have changed over the years.
- you will read about children who are forced to do extremely hard work.
- you can learn how to write a letter of application for a job abroad.
- you will get the chance to talk about the film 'Slumdog Millionaire'.

2

1 The start of something new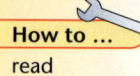

a) Read the poem. What is it about?

How to ...
read

School bell rings for one last time
Oh how quickly seven years go by!
The doors open, at last I'm free
To be whoever I want to be.
Goodbye teachers, goodbye rules
Goodbye lessons, goodbye school.

But now that the future is really here,
All my hopes and dreams turn into fears,
Will I find the right job and make new friends?
So many questions
And who knows how it will end!

Am I ready to face the world alone?
What if things don't go to plan?
Am I ready to leave the safety of my home?
What if the boy isn't ready to be a man ...

Zoe Carroll

How to ...
work with
others (3)

b) What does the person in the poem feel or think about the future? In class, form a double circle and talk to each other about your ideas.

2 School's out

a) Your time at school is almost over now. What are your plans, your dreams, your wishes? Make a mindmap about your future.

wordbank
jobs C

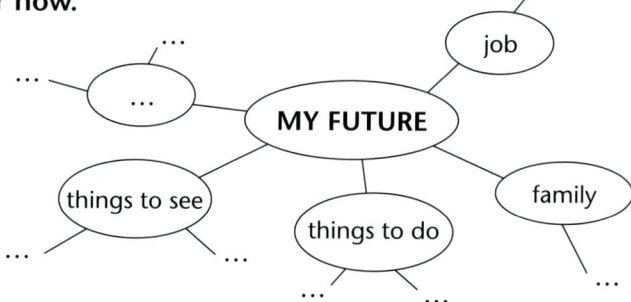

...
...
...
job
MY FUTURE
things to see
things to do
family
...
...
...
...
...

b) Talk about your mindmaps in small groups. Which plans are realistic? Where do you see problems?

workbook
1

3 An email exchange

a) Read this answer from a British school class to their German partner school. What do you think the German school class asked in their email?

How to ...
read

Subject: Hi from the UK

In about two months school will be over for me. I think 10 years is enough.
I'm not sure what my future job will be. On the one hand I'm very interested in
electronics. I might become a programmer or a radio and television mechanic. On
the other hand I like working with tools. I could become a plumber. I wouldn't
like to work in an office all day. And I hate working with chemicals.
I started writing applications about three months ago. I've written about
15 letters of application to find a position as a trainee. I've tried many
different firms but I haven't got all the answers yet. Next week, however, I've
got a job interview with a building company. I think I'll try to find my own
room or a small flat as soon as I know where I'll work and how much I'll earn.
All the best to you,
Ben

I've wanted to become a hairdresser since I was about five. But then, when I did my work experience at a hairdressing salon, I had an allergic reaction to the chemicals in the hair dye that was used. At first I was really sad but now I'm happy that I found out about my allergy before I applied to the hairdressing course. I hope that I can do something similar, like beauty therapy. But I wouldn't mind working in an office either. Looking forward to hearing from you soon,
Kate

Aeroplanes have always fascinated me. When I was little, I started collecting model aeroplanes and now I've got hundreds. Then I began to make model aeroplanes. So it is hardly surprising that I would really like to be an aeroplane mechanic in the future.
Unfortunately, I'm not going to do that well in my GCSE exams. I'm one of the lazier pupils in my class. But not everybody enjoys reading books and studying. So I'm not going to go into the sixth form and do A levels. I'm more practical, I'd rather work with my hands. My dad knows someone who works at the local airfield and he's happy to give me some training. So after school I'll start working there and I can't wait. Best wishes to all of you,
Aaron

I'm feeling down. Everybody in my class already knows what they're going to do after school but I don't know yet. I know I would like to work with cars. I love getting my hands dirty. I've been helping my father to check the car for ages. I've also done small repairs on it. I'd love to become a car mechanic but when I talk to my mum about it, she just gets angry. She says, "Ladies don't get their hands dirty and women normally don't understand engines. You won't like the job." But what does she know? I already did my four-week work experience at our local garage and I did like it a lot. My teacher has been saying we should choose a job we are really interested in. Hope you lot aren't as depressed as I am. Best wishes,
Melinda

MORE
M1–M8
using your English

b) Match the sentence parts. When do you need *since*, when do you need *for*?

Ben has been writing applications		she was about five.
Kate has wanted to become a hairdresser	**for**	he was little.
Aaron has collected model aeroplanes	**since**	a very long time.
Melinda has helped her father with his car		three months.

LiF
2

c) Choose one of the English students and answer him or her.

d) Imagine you are a job counsellor. What would you tell Melinda?

How to …
write a letter

I think it is a good idea to …

If I were you, I would …

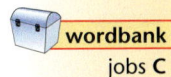
wordbank
giving advice **B**

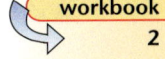
wordbank
jobs **C**

workbook
2

CD

How to …
listen

4 Now and then

a) Listen to Melinda and her grandfather. When did Melinda's grandfather start working?

b) Look at the pictures and listen again. What are the differences between now and then? Take notes in a grid.

c) Did you get all the information? Work with a partner and compare your notes.

5 Modern life

tip
CPhT = certified pharmacy technician

a) Match each picture with the correct job.

b) Now describe how these jobs were done in the past and how they are done today.

butcher • waiter/waitress • carpenter • office administrator • CPhT • cook • taxi driver • welder • receptionist

wordbank
jobs C

LiF
9

Example: In the past, orders were written down on a piece of paper. Today they are typed into a portable computer.

1
orders – written/typed – on paper/into portable computer

2
meat – produced – in small shops/in factories

3
letters – written – on typewriter/on computer

4
medicine – mixed/made – at the chemist's/by large companies

5
route – looked up/worked out – on map/by navigation system

6
metal – welded – with heat and hammer/with a machine

workbook
3-4

6 Choose an activity

How to …
write your opinion

portfolio

• Is working life nicer today or was it better 50 years ago? Write a text and say what you think.

• Look at your mindmap from number 2 again and write about how you imagine your future.

• Write a poem or an acrostic about your future.

2

7 Child labour or doing your chores?

a) Look at the photos. What do they have in common? In what ways are they different from one another? Work with a partner and take notes.

country • age • type of work • reasons for working • ...

How to ...
talk about pictures

tip
Use a dictionary to look up words you don't know.

MORE
M9–M13
Slumdog Millionaire

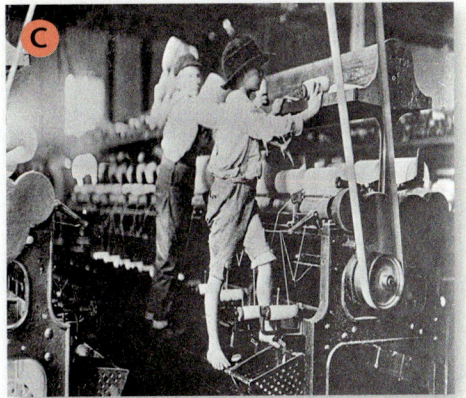

workbook
5-6

b) Write a caption for each photo.

c) Which chores do YOU have to do at home? Do you get paid for helping at home? What do you do with the money you get?

tip
You can make a survey in class.

8 Just a number?

Look at the statistics. What do they tell you? Talk to a partner.

About ... per cent of children work ...

I was really shocked by the number of children working ...

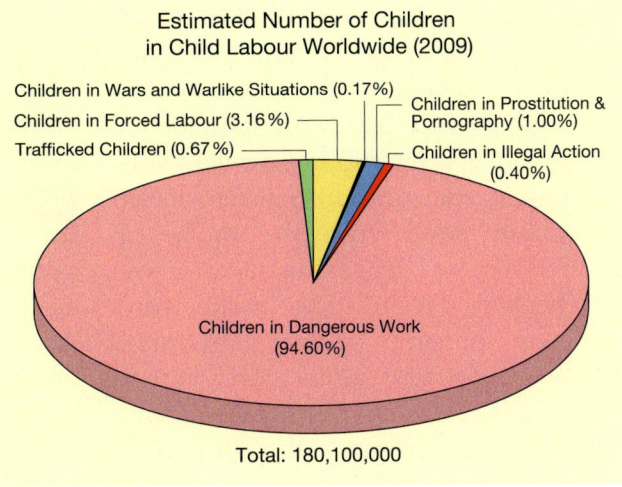

Estimated Number of Children
in Child Labour Worldwide (2009)

Children in Wars and Warlike Situations (0.17%)
Children in Forced Labour (3.16%)
Children in Prostitution & Pornography (1.00%)
Trafficked Children (0.67%)
Children in Illegal Action (0.40%)
Children in Dangerous Work (94.60%)

Total: 180,100,000

wordbank
statistics D

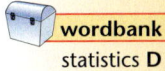

2

CD

How to ...
listen

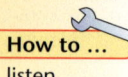

workbook
7

9 Schooling wanted

a) The journalist Bert Robertson wants to write an article about child labour. For his article he interviews some children. Listen to the interview with 13-year-old Ali Akbar from Pakistan. How many brothers and sisters has Ali got?

b) Read the statements. Then listen again. Are they true or false?

1 Ali is the youngest child in the factory.
2 The boss decides how many footballs the children have to sew.
3 Ali can't go to school because he has to work.

4 Yassir can go to school because his parents are rich.
5 Yassir sometimes teaches his friend Ali.
6 Ali's parents don't earn any money.

10 Bad conditions

a) Read Bert Robertson's article. Why is Mira's job dangerous?

How to ...
read

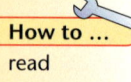

A CHILD'S WORK

tip
Look at the map at the back of your book to find out where Mira and Ali come from.

UNICEF estimates that about 180 million children, between 5 and 14, are forced to work. Most of them come from developing countries like Mira Go, who is 15 years old and works in a clothes factory in Jakarta, Indonesia. "My day starts at 7.00 in the morning, so I get up early and I work very hard for 12 hours every day, 9 on Saturdays," she tells us. "I earn 40 dollars a week. This is less than the minimum wage. I can hardly buy food with the money I make. When we leave the factory, we are checked carefully to make sure that we haven't stolen anything. We have a lot of women here, young girls, 12, 13 years old. We can't refuse to do overtime – they fire you.

And if we don't sew the number of pieces for that day, we have to stay without pay to properly finish them. If you are ill, you are fired. The work can be dangerous – we have no goggles to protect our faces and sometimes needles break and injure us. Once we went on strike for better wages. The management openly refused to give in and the people who they thought had secretly organised the strike were fired."

Ali Akbar, 13, from Pakistan started sewing footballs when he was seven. Like most children in Pakistan he comes from a large family who desperately need the money he earns. Ali would rather go to school but his family cannot easily afford to let him stop working.
Apart from these two there are millions more who work as soldiers, builders, prostitutes, domestic servants and factory workers.

workbook
8

b) Look at the text again and complete the sentences with the right adverbs.

1 Mira works very ??? every day.
2 The factory owner checks his workers ??? .
3 The management ??? refused to listen to the workers.

4 The workers organised the strike ??? .
5 Ali's wages are ??? needed by his family.
6 Ali's family cannot ??? afford to let him go to school.

LiF
21

 PEOPLE & PLACES

UNICEF

You probably know the UN, the *United Nations Organization,* which was founded in 1945 and has about 200 member states today. The aims of the UN are to secure world peace and human rights.
In 1989 the UN published the *Convention on the Rights of the Child* which states basic rights for children.

These basic rights are: the right to life, survival and development, the right to protection and the right to take part in cultural, family and social life.

UNICEF (*United Nations International Children's Emergency Fund*) is an organization of the UN that takes special care of children's rights. UNICEF was founded in 1946 to help children in Europe after the Second World War.

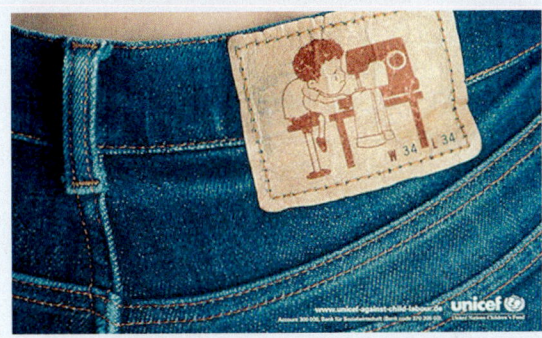

In 1965 the organization won the Nobel Peace Prize.

Today UNICEF is mainly active in developing countries. They support about 160 countries with medical, financial and educational help. Because there are about 180 million children working and a large number of children cannot go to school, there is still a lot to do for UNICEF.

---

11 Choose an activity

• **Make a poster about child labour around the world. Find out:**

  – in which countries children have to work
  – which industries use child labour
  – …

• **Imagine you want to organise a protest against child labour. Design a flyer or a brochure.**

• **Look at the label of your favourite pair of jeans. Use the Internet to find out more about the company and the production. Is child labour involved? Present your findings to the class.**

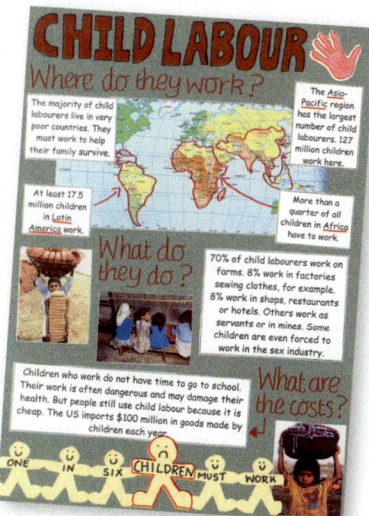

wordbank
jobs C

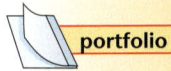
portfolio

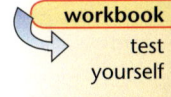
workbook
test yourself

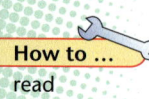

M1 **English spoken**

Listen to the scenes. Which five jobs can you hear where English is needed?

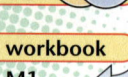

M2 **Jessica and Torge**

For an international youth magazine, young Europeans were asked about their jobs and their English language skills.

a) Read what these two Germans told the magazine. What do they say about their English?

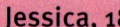

Jessica, 18

I learned English at school. It was one of my favourite subjects. After school I started an apprenticeship as *Restaurantfachfrau*. The lady who owns the restaurant is very successful.

Many people come and book for conferences and family parties. We decorate the rooms and the tables nicely and offer delicious meals and a good service. I have been quite successful in competitions and would like to see other places after I have finished my apprenticeship. In special hotel newspapers and on the Internet I found a lot of adverts in which they look for waitresses in other European countries and for the service on ships. I would love to work on one of the famous cruise ships for one or two years. In my vocational school I learn special English for my job and I can practise my English whenever there are foreign guests in the restaurant. It is fun and helps me to make my dream come true.

Torge, 20

I work as a joiner and I like my job very much. A friend told me that you can work in other countries if you join an organization of craftsmen who call themselves *Rolandsbrüder*. They leave their home town and work in other firms to get more experience. I like this idea and have already spoken to colleagues and have surfed the Internet for more information on this old tradition. Here I am in the special clothes of these craftsmen who travel around the world. I had some young joiners as guests in our house. They came from Ireland, France and Canada. I think that my English is good enough to talk to them. We were taught to speak a lot at school and that helps me. I will have to speak English on my tour through Scandinavia and Ireland. I have to learn the job of a carpenter, too, so that I can travel around the world. I think that is a good thing because I will always find work then.

b) Find words in the texts that match these definitions:

- a school where you learn things for your job
- the time when you are training for a job
- a group of people who share the same interests

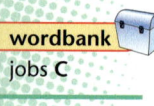

c) Look at Jessica's text again. There is no English word for 'Restaurantfachfrau'. How would you explain it in English?

M3 Question time

Work with a partner and ask and answer questions about Jessica and Torge. Take turns. You want to know …

1 … what Jessica does in her job.
2 … what Jessica's dream is.
3 … what Jessica says about learning English.
4 … what 'Rolandsbrüder' are.
5 … when Torge had to speak English.
6 … which countries Torge wants to visit.
7 …

LiF
13

M4 Another way of saying it

Make these sentences shorter.
Example: After he had talked to the interviewer, Torge went back to work.
        Having talked to the interviewer, Torge went back to work.

1 After she had finished school, Jessica started an apprenticeship.
2 Because she learned English at school, Jessica has no problem using it.
3 After he had heard about 'Rolandsbrüder', Torge wanted to learn more about them.
4 Because he had Irish joiners in his house, Torge knows a lot about Ireland.

LiF
17

workbook
M2

M5 Helping out

Torge and his Irish guest Sean have made an appointment with a small building firm in town. They want to find a job for Sean for the next few weeks.

a) **Read the dialogue. What does Torge say to Sean? What does he say to Herr Braun? Write it into your exercise book.**

How to …
help out in English

Torge: Guten Morgen, Herr Braun. Das hier ist Sean O'Brian aus Irland. Er ist zur Zeit auf der Walz und wohnt für sechs Wochen bei mir. Sean hat in Dublin als Tischler gearbeitet und sucht jetzt einen Job. Haben Sie etwas für ihn?
Herr Braun: Yes, hello, Mr O'Brian. Äh, can you, interessant, … ach, hat er auch schon woanders gearbeitet?
Torge: Sean, Herr Braun wants to know …
Sean: I worked as a joiner in Copenhagen for five weeks.
Torge: Er hat gesagt, dass …
Herr Braun: Klingt interessant, ja. Einer unserer Tischler hat sich den Fuß gebrochen und fällt die nächsten sechs Wochen aus.
Torge: One of …

workbook
M3

Sean: Great. I mean, poor man. Do you think I could start tomorrow?
Torge: Sean fragt …
Herr Braun: Warum nicht? Arbeitsbeginn ist um 7 Uhr.
Torge: …
Sean: Sounds OK to me. And when do we finish?
Torge: …
Herr Braun: Arbeitsende ist um 17 Uhr. Bitte gehen Sie doch jetzt noch zu meiner Sekretärin. Sie muss die Personalien aufnehmen – Namen, Geburtsdatum, Adresse und so weiter.
Torge: …
Sean: Thank you, Herr Braun. Bye.
Torge: Auf Wiedersehen, Herr Braun, und vielen Dank.
Herr Braun: Auf Wiedersehen.

b) **Now listen to the CD and find out what Torge really said.**

c) **Work in groups of three and read or act out the scene.**

CD

How to …
talk

33

MORE

M6 New horizons

Lots of young people would like to spend some time in another country and work there.

a) Read the job adverts. How would you express these phrases from the adverts in German?

embark onto new horizons • we are currently recruiting •
a good command of the English language • previous experience is preferred

workbook
M4

DO YOU WANT TO SEE THE WORLD?

Who hasn't dreamed of working on a cruise ship? This is your chance!

We are looking for candidates who are motivated, dedicated and flexible, and who like adventure. Are you ready to embark onto new horizons? Are you looking for a career change?

We are currently recruiting:

Bakers

Cruise staff

Hair stylists

for cruises in the Caribbean and Mediterranean Seas.

- You should be a team player, be communicative and reliable.
- You will need fluent English and a second language (e.g. German).
- You should have 2 to 5 years of experience (professional qualifications are required for hair stylists and bakers).

For further information or to apply contact Jasmine Mayor at jas.mayor@sevenseas.com

How to ...
read

tip
Rd = Road

We are looking for a

certified welder

to join our team.

We support companies in the UK, in Sweden, Germany and Spain.

- You should have 2 to 3 years of experience and the necessary welding qualifications.
- A good command of the English language is absolutely necessary.
- You need to be flexible and reliable and you should be a team player.

For more information and to apply contact Jamie McHoggart at jamie@industrysupport.co.uk

RECEPTION STAFF WANTED

Family run **B&B in Stirling (Scotland)** is looking for reliable, polite and communicative reception staff.

Previous experience in a hotel environment is preferred. Language skills required: English and German

Contact: Stephen Roper
Home & Dry B&B
15 Kenilworth Rd
Stirling FK8 1JU

b) Read the adverts again. Take notes about what qualifications and soft skills are needed for each job.

wordbank
jobs C

c) Is there a job offered on this page that YOU would like to do? Say why/why not.

M7 A letter of application

a) **Read the letter of application and complete it with the following phrases:**

- enclosing my CV
- have the opportunity
- to hearing from you
- I finished school
- including reception
- to apply for

Hohenzollernstr. 54
66111 Saarbrücken
Germany

Stephen Roper
Home & Dry B&B
15 Kenilworth Rd
Stirling FK8 1JU

20th January 2010

Application for the position of reception staff

Dear Mr Roper,

I am writing ⟋⟍ the position of reception staff as seen on *www.monster.co.uk* on Friday, 15 January.

As you will see from my CV, ⟋⟍ three years ago. I have been working as a trainee in a large hotel since then. I have experience in all areas of hotel work, ⟋⟍. My apprenticeship will be finished in September and I would like to ⟋⟍ of working abroad.

I am reliable and polite and I like communicating with people.

I am ⟋⟍ and the names and addresses of two referees.

I look forward ⟋⟍ .

Yours sincerely,

Rebecca Mertens
Rebecca Mertens

---

b) **Write your own letter of application for one of the jobs offered in M6.**

c) **Swap your letter with your partner's. Edit his/her letter and give each other feedback on layout, information, spelling and grammar.**

M8 YOUR phrase book for spending time abroad

Imagine you are going to spend some time abroad and stay in other people's homes. Work with a partner. Make a little book with phrases, questions and statements that could be useful. Think about:

> meeting people • asking about things and places • talking about food, transport, … • …

How to …
write a letter

workbook
M5

wordbank
travelling E

portfolio

workbook
M6

M9 A place to live

**a) Look at the picture. What would you call an area like this?
What do you think living there is like?**

How to …
talk about
pictures

workbook
M7

How to …
work with
others (4)

**b) Imagine you are one of the people in the picture. What could you do to lead
a better life? Give and take: Write down three things. Then walk around the
classroom and ask several classmates about their ideas.**

M10 From rags to riches

The film 'Slumdog Millionaire' is about Jamal Malik, a boy from the slums.

CD

How to …
listen

a) Listen to a radio interview about the film. Where is the film set?

b) Listen again. Make a mindmap about Jamal.

**c) Look at your mindmap and write a
short portrait of Jamal.**

Salim — Jamal — Latika
background — Jamal — Mumbai

M11 On location

A film magazine interviewed Dawn, the production assistant of 'Slumdog
Millionaire', about filming on location.

**a) Read the extract from the interview.
What was Dawn shocked about?**

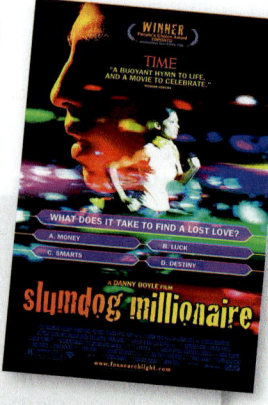

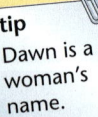
tip
Dawn is a
woman's
name.

tip
mag =
magazine

and we were very happy about that.

mag: I'm sure. So how did you find the actors? What was the
casting process like?

Dawn: Oh we were so happy with our actors. We really did look at
a lot of people but the ones we settled on were just those
with that special something, you know. The kids especially,
they are amazing.

mag: Yes, are they really from Mumbai?

Dawn: Not just from Mumbai, but they are all from the slums. We felt that was
important, to have kids that know what the slums are like. They grew up
there, you know and that was important to us. I was shocked about the many
very poor kids who can't go to school because they have to earn money.

2

So we did want to make sure that the kids in our film can go to school now.

mag: What was filming in Mumbai like?

Dawn: Oh it was absolutely crazy. The noise, the heat, the millions of people … We did film in the streets and not in a studio. So, whenever we set up our camera and equipment, thousands of people would watch. It was sometimes quite difficult for the actors.

mag: Was it very hot?

Dawn: Yes. It was hard to work in the heat. When you're filming you sometimes work 10 or 12 hours a day and the heat and the dust … it was difficult, yeah.

mag: Did you feel safe in the slums?

Dawn: Yeah, actually. We didn't feel threatened or anything. You know, slums aren't like you would expect. I mean it was such a fantastic place. People are poor but they are friendly and curious and interested. They did come out and watch us and it was a very family kind of atmosphere. It was a great experience.

mag: Music is very important in the film. Can you tell us something about that?

Dawn: You're right. The music does play a very important role in the film. The composer A.R. Rahman is very famous in India and …

b) What were the problems and difficulties on location?
Take notes on these points:

> actors • filming • heat • slums

c) Read the interview again. What does Dawn do to stress special points? Look for examples like this:

> The music does play a very important role in the film.

LiF 25

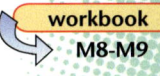
workbook
M8-M9

M12 Watching 'Slumdog Millionaire'

a) Watch the film. What has the director done to make the film special?

b) Do you like the ending of the film? Say why/why not.

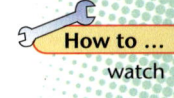
How to …
watch

M13 Project: YOUR research on 'Slumdog Millionaire'

Get together in groups to make a poster, a brochure or a PowerPoint presentation.

> slums • music • Danny Boyle • Mumbai • actors • …

How to …
give a talk

1 PLAN IT In your group think about:

- Which topic interests you most?
- Which information do you need to present your topic?
- Where can you get the information?

2 DO IT Collect information and take notes. Then decide:

- What do you want to present?
- How do you want to present it?

Prepare your poster/presentation/brochure.

3 CHECK IT

- Can you make your presentation more interesting?
- Perhaps you could add some photos, a map, …
- Are the texts correct?

4 PRESENT IT

- Practise your talk first, then present your work to the class.

portfolio

2 Check it out!

Did you get it all?

- Where does Ben have a job interview?
- Where did Kate do her work experience?
- Who does Melinda talk to about work?
- How many children in the world have to work?
- Who interviews Ali?
- Where is Ali from?
- What is Ali's job?
- How many hours a day does Mira have to work?

Good to know ...

In English-speaking countries people often use your first name right from the start. Especially in formal situations like job interviews it is very important to know that this is a common way of addressing people. It does not, however, mean that the situation is less formal.

Did you know that ...

... about 930,000 people graduated from school in Germany in 2009?

... the oldest known American high school graduate, Gustava Bennett Burrus, was 97 when she graduated?

... until 1847 many children under ten had to work in coal mines in England?

Find out how old the youngest person to graduate high school was.

Find out in what year Germany passed a law against child labour.

... Mumbai used to be called Bombay?

... Queen Elizabeth had her own cruise ship – the Britannia – until 1997?

... one in six children in the world today is involved in child labour?

... about 20% of the dialogue from 'Slumdog Millionaire' is in Hindi with English subtitles?

Find out where and what the Britannia is today.

SOUTH AFRICA – THE RAINBOW NATION

3

In this Theme …

- you will read about a young German working in South Africa.
- you will find out about Cape Town's sights and attractions.
- you will learn a lot about South Africa's past and present.
- you will give a presentation about South Africa.
- you can learn about the famous Kruger National Park.
- you can read about the South African music called 'kwaito'.

How to ...
work with others (1)

1 What do you know?

What comes to your mind when you think of South Africa? Brainstorm with a partner. Then talk to another pair and share your ideas.

2 Away from home 👓 👄

Isabel from Leipzig is working as a volunteer animal carer in South Africa.

a) **Read the dialogue between Isabel and her colleague Thabo and find out where exactly Isabel is working.**

How to ...
read

Thabo: You've been here for nearly two months now. I'd really love to know how you feel about living in my home country.

Isabel: As you know, I had problems with my English at first. You and the others here speak so fast and I was afraid of not understanding you and making mistakes. But you were all so friendly and helped me to overcome my fears.

Thabo: Oh, come on, your English has been great right from the start. You even knew all the words to do with the animals here.

Isabel: Well, animals have always been my biggest hobby. I'm fond of looking after and caring for them. I also read lots of English magazines about animal care before I came here. I really enjoy working at the Kruger National Park. For me a dream has come true.

Thabo: That sounds great. I remember when you arrived at Kruger and we took a tour in the park, you were so excited. The landscape, the different mammals and the other animals really fascinated you. But tell me, what do you think of South Africa in general?

Isabel: Well, this is just a very small part of this huge country. I always hear that South Africa is a land of contrasts.

Thabo: Yes, that's true. On the one hand there is this great landscape, the beautiful beaches and the animals. But on the other hand there is a lot of crime and violence.

Isabel: The other day someone told me that South Africa has got the strongest economy on the African continent. But it has got some of the poorest people as well. That really surprised me.

Thabo: Well, that's mainly because of South Africa's past. Even today many black South Africans still live in poverty and are discriminated against.

Isabel: I really need to see more of the country and find out for myself. I'm looking forward to going to places like Durban and Cape Town but also to more traditional areas. I'd like to see a township for example.

Thabo: Travelling is always the best way to get an idea about a foreign country. But don't travel on your own. Some areas are dangerous so it's good to have a local guide who knows the area well. I'll think about your plans ...

tip
Look at the map at the front of your book to see where the Kruger National Park is.

MORE
M2–M5
The Kruger National Park

LiF
18

b) **Read the dialogue again and take notes to answer the following questions:**

1 What were Isabel's fears in the beginning?
2 What does she like doing?
3 What are her plans?

> She enjoys/is fond of ...

> Isabel was afraid of ...

workbook
1

c) **What do you learn about South Africa from the dialogue? Which pieces of information are new to you?**

3 Plans

A few hours later Isabel and Thabo text each other.

a) Read the text messages and put them in the right order. What are Isabel and Thabo planning to do?

A
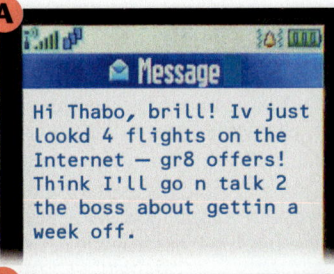
Hi Thabo, brill! Iv just lookd 4 flights on the Internet — gr8 offers! Think I'll go n talk 2 the boss about gettin a week off.

B
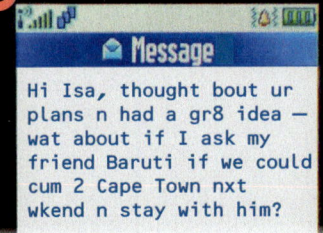
Hi Isa, thought bout ur plans n had a gr8 idea — wat about if I ask my friend Baruti if we could cum 2 Cape Town nxt wkend n stay with him?

C
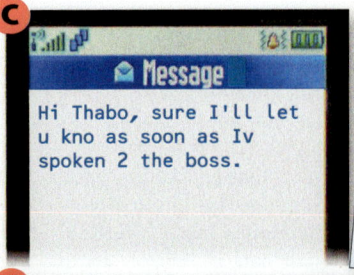
Hi Thabo, sure I'll let u kno as soon as Iv spoken 2 the boss.

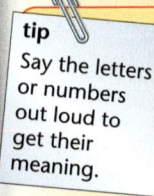
tip
Say the letters or numbers out loud to get their meaning.

D
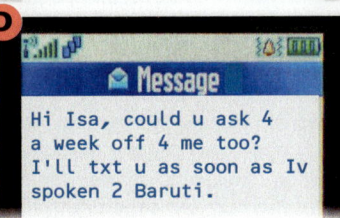
Hi Isa, could u ask 4 a week off 4 me too? I'll txt u as soon as Iv spoken 2 Baruti.

E
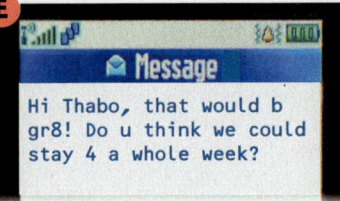
Hi Thabo, that would b gr8! Do u think we could stay 4 a whole week?

F
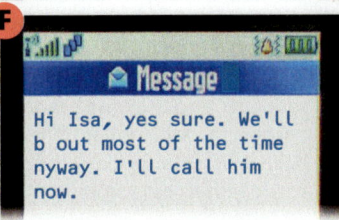
Hi Isa, yes sure. We'll b out most of the time nyway. I'll call him now.

b) Work with a partner and finish the text message conversation. One of you is Thabo, the other one is Isabel.
You can start like this:

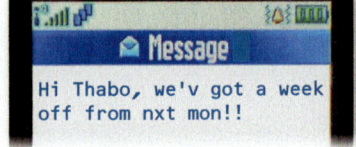
Hi Thabo, we'v got a week off from nxt mon!!

c) Read out your conversation to the class.

How to ...
talk

4 A boarding pass

Look at Isabel's boarding pass. Work with a partner and ask and answer questions. Take turns.

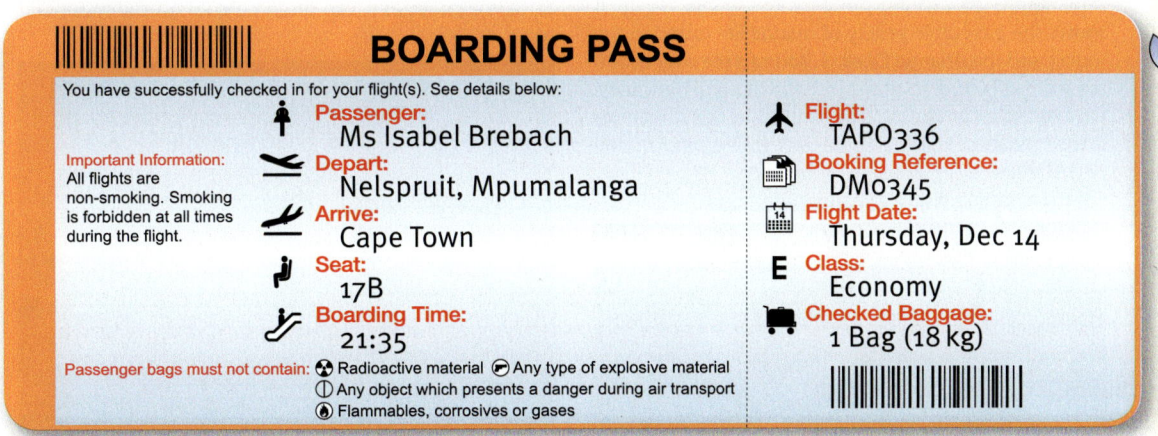

BOARDING PASS

You have successfully checked in for your flight(s). See details below:

Important Information: All flights are non-smoking. Smoking is forbidden at all times during the flight.

Passenger: Ms Isabel Brebach
Depart: Nelspruit, Mpumalanga
Arrive: Cape Town
Seat: 17B
Boarding Time: 21:35

Flight: TAPO336
Booking Reference: DM0345
Flight Date: Thursday, Dec 14
E Class: Economy
Checked Baggage: 1 Bag (18 kg)

Passenger bags must not contain: Radioactive material / Any type of explosive material / Any object which presents a danger during air transport / Flammables, corrosives or gases

workbook
2-4

Ask your partner ...

1 ... where Isabel and Thabo begin their journey.
2 ... how much luggage Isabel takes.
3 ... what is forbidden on the plane.
4 ... what their flight number is.
5 ... when they have to board the plane.
6 ...

Where do they begin their journey?

They begin their journey at ...

LiF
13

5 Sightseeing in Cape Town

a) Read this page from Isabel's travel guide. Which is YOUR number one attraction? Rank the sights and activities mentioned here from 1 to 5.

CAPE TOWN

tip
You can learn more about Nelson Mandela on page 45.

How to ...
read

Robben Island

Robben Island is now a World Heritage Site, but was once the prison of Nelson Mandela and many other famous black freedom fighters. It provides fascinating views across the bay with Table Mountain in the background. A trip to the island gives you an idea of the apartheid era. Daily tours to the island include the ferry trip there and back, an island tour and a tour of the prison with a former political prisoner as your guide. The trip takes three and a half hours (this includes the 1/2 hour ferry trip each way). Ferries leave from the Clock Tower at the V&A Waterfront.

Two Oceans Aquarium, Waterfront

Located in the V&A Waterfront, the Two Oceans Aquarium is an exciting place for the whole family. It shows the incredible variety of marine life found in the Indian and the Atlantic Oceans. You can see over 3,000 sea animals including sharks, fish, turtles and penguins. One of the most spectacular exhibits in the Aquarium is the Predator Exhibit, a huge tank with a semi-tunnel where sharks swim above your head.
For more details visit www.aquarium.co.za

Whale Watching

About an hour and a half away from Cape Town is the seaside town of Hermanus. As a popular holiday destination, Hermanus offers the best land-based whale watching in the world. Starting in May, Southern Right Whales come to these warm waters to calve their young and to mate. The best time for whale watching is between August and November because at this time the bay is full of whales.

Shopping in Cape Town

Cape Town is a great shopping destination. From jewellery and traditional African art to designer labels and diamonds, Cape Town offers a shopping experience for everyone. Visit one of the trendy shopping malls or flea markets and streetside stalls for presents, souvenirs and a piece of Cape Town to take home.

Table Mountain & Cableway

The top of Table Mountain offers spectacular views of the city and the ocean. The cable car station on top of the mountain is located at 1,067 metres and the cable car makes sure that you have an easy trip and a good look in all directions. You can follow paths to different lookouts and enjoy a nice meal or a drink in the lovely restaurant. In summer, early evening is the greatest time to plan your trip as the sunsets are beautiful. Don't forget to take a jacket as it can often be cool on the mountain top.

LiF
7

b) Look at the travel guide again. What would/wouldn't YOU like to see and do if you had the chance to visit Cape Town?

If I had the chance to visit Cape Town, ➤ I would/ wouldn't ➤ like to see/watch visit go to ... ➤ ... ➤ because ➤ ...

c) Work with a partner and play 'True or false'. Take turns.

1 Hermanus is two hours away from Cape Town.
2 On Robben Island your tour guide will be a former
  political leader.
3 You should take a jacket when visiting Table Mountain.
4 If you walk through the semi-tunnel at the Aquarium,
  you can watch sharks swimming above your head.
5 Table Mountain can be seen from Robben Island.
6 You can get to the top of Table Mountain by ferry and cable car.
7 …

> Hermanus is two hours away from Cape Town. True or false?

> True.

> False. It's …

6 Describing things

a) Look at the texts from number 5 again. Find all the adjectives and write them down like this:

lucky – luckier – the luckiest   fascinating – more fascinating – the most fascinating

Compare your list with a partner's.

LiF
19

b) Choose the right form of an adjective from a) and complete the sentences.

1 The waters around Hermanus are   ???   than in other places.

2 The Predator Exhibit is   ???   than most other exhibits in the Two Oceans Aquarium.

3 The   ???   South African freedom fighter is Nelson Mandela.

4 Shopping malls can be as   ???   as flea markets.

5 Early evening in summer is the   ???   time to visit Table Mountain.

7 Phoning a friend

While in Cape Town Isabel phones her friend Kendra in the Kruger National Park.
a) Listen to the two girls and find out in what order Isabel visited the sights mentioned in number 5.

CD

b) Listen again and take notes to answer the questions.

• How does Isabel feel about Robben Island?
• Which sight is Isabel's favourite?
• Which sight interests her least?

How to …
listen

workbook
5

8 Choose an activity

• Create a flyer for one of Cape Town's attractions. You can look at number 5 for ideas or choose another attraction.

• Get together in groups of three. Act out a tour through Cape Town. One of you is the tour guide and points out sights. The other two are tourists and ask questions.

• Make a crossword puzzle or a multiple-choice quiz about Cape Town for your partner.

wordbank
travelling E

portfolio

9 Picture this

a) These photos from South Africa were taken during the last 50 years. What do they tell you about South Africa?

A

B

workbook
6
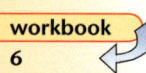

C

D

E

F

b) Work with a partner. Describe one of the photos and let your partner guess which one it is.

> In the photo there are … One of them is wearing …

> He/She looks sad/ …

> …

> In the foreground/ background you can see …

How to …
talk about pictures

c) If you could walk into the photos, what would you ask the people to find out more about their lives?

LiF
13

10 Listening in

a) Make a grid. Then look at the photos from number 9 again and listen to the CD. Match the sounds with the photos.

b) Listen again. What did you hear? Write down words or phrases that you understood.

sound	photo	words/phrases
1		

CD

How to …
listen

11 Nelson Mandela

a) Read this article about Nelson Mandela from an encyclopedia. What did he win the Nobel Peace Prize for?

Mandela, Nelson, first democratically elected president of South Africa (1994-99), spent most of his life fighting against apartheid, the political system in which non-whites were separated and discriminated against.
Having been born in 1918 into the royal family of the Thembu, he was a leading member of the African National Congress (ANC) – a political organization founded to fight for black rights – which has been the ruling party in South Africa since 1994. In 1964 he was sentenced to life imprisonment because of his work for the ANC and spent the next 26 years in prison. During this time his reputation as leader of the resistance movement against apartheid grew. Together with Frederik de Klerk, the president who officially ended apartheid, he won the Nobel Peace Prize in 1993 for the important role they played in ending apartheid and establishing democracy in South Africa.

Mandela always believed in a society where whites and non-whites could live together peacefully and he worked hard for racial equality while he was president. He is also actively involved in projects against AIDS in South Africa and is probably the most famous South African person.

How to …
read

workbook
7

b) What can you find out about Nelson Mandela's life? Make a timeline with dates and events.

 **PEOPLE & PLACES**

South Africa

In 1652 Jan van Riebeeck, a businessman from the Netherlands, founded Cape Town as a stop for Dutch ships on their way to India. When more and more Dutch settlers arrived, they began to take the natives' land to start their own farms and build a Dutch colony. During the 19th century these white settlers developed their own nationality as *Boers* or *Afrikaners*. When the Boers' National Party came into power in 1948, they established the apartheid system. This meant that black and white people were completely separated. Resistance to apartheid quickly grew all over the world. In the end it took the government until 1990 to take first steps towards ending discrimination. Nelson Mandela was freed and in 1994 he became president in the country's first democratic election. Today South Africa supports racial equality, but many blacks still don't feel equal. Unemployment rates and poverty among blacks remain much higher than among whites. There is still a lot of work to be done.

12 Gimme hope Jo'anna

CD

a) **Listen to Eddie Grant's song 'Gimme hope Jo'anna' from 1988. What do you think the song is about?**

b) **Read the lyrics of the song. Make a list of the things Jo'anna does to keep the apartheid system going.**

tip
Jo'anna = Johannesburg = South African government

Well Jo'anna she runs a country
She runs in Durban and in the Transvaal
She makes a few of her people happy, oh
She don't care about the rest at all
She's got a system they call apartheid
It keeps a brother ina subjection
But maybe pressure can make Jo'anna see
How everybody coulda live as one

How to ...
read

Chorus:
Gimme hope Jo'anna, Hope Jo'anna
Gimme hope Jo'anna
'Fore the morning come
Gimme hope Jo'anna, Hope Jo'anna
Hope before the morning come

workbook
8

I hear she makes all the golden money
To buy new weapons, any shape of guns
While every mother in a black Soweto fears
The killing of another son
Sneakin' across all the neighbours' borders
Now and again having little fun
She doesn't care if the fun and games she play
Is dang'rous to ev'ryone

Chorus

She's got supporters in high up places
Who turn their heads to the city sun
Jo'anna give them the fancy money
Oh to tempt anyone who'd come
She even knows how to swing opinion
In every magazine and the journals
For every bad move that this Jo'anna makes
They got a good explanation

Chorus

Even the preacher who works for Jesus
The Archbishop who's a peaceful man
Together say that the freedom fighters
Will overcome the very strong
I wanna know if you're blind Jo'anna
If you wanna hear the sound of drums
Can't you see that the tide is turning
Oh don't make me wait till the morning come

Chorus

c) **What will end apartheid, according to the singer?**

13 What apartheid meant

a) Read the texts and find out what apartheid meant to the interviewed people. What couldn't or weren't they allowed to do?

> He/She couldn't …

> He/She wasn't allowed to …

LiF
11

Phumzile Zwane, Eastern Cape

15 years ago black people weren't allowed to buy bread in the same shops as whites. We couldn't go to the same schools as they did. That's all different now, now we're the Rainbow Nation. But racism still exists at work and everywhere else. I hope that will change one day.

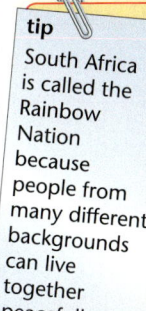

tip

South Africa is called the Rainbow Nation because people from many different backgrounds can live together peacefully.

Moloko Malakalaka, Gauteng

My dad and my granddad had to do jobs that white people didn't want to do. They didn't really have a choice and they got paid really badly. They weren't allowed to vote or travel. That's different now, I could go to school and I found a job that I like. You can't change people's behaviour by law though. Black and white people still live separate lives, most of the time. White people go to sports clubs that other white people go to and so on.

Jason Reddy, KwaZulu-Natal

Now I can work and live and go where I want to. We have black politicians, black stars, black people on TV. But there are still problems. It's hard to find work and accommodation for blacks. There is a lot of crime as well – the other day I saw a guy being mugged.

workbook
9

b) Read the comments again. What has changed since the abolition of apartheid? What problems still remain? Write two lists. Compare your lists with a partner's.

MORE
M6-M10
the people of the rainbow

14 Project: YOUR presentation of South Africa

Work in groups. Agree on an aspect of South Africa that you find interesting.

1 **PLAN IT** In your group think about:

- Where can you get information and pictures (books, films, the Internet, …)?
- Who is going to do what for your presentation?

2 **DO IT** Collect information and take notes. Then decide:

- What do you want to present?
- How do you want to present it?
- Who is going to present what?

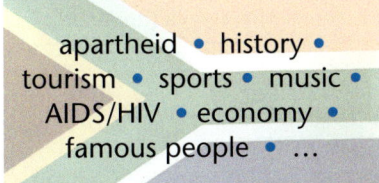

apartheid • history • tourism • sports • music • AIDS/HIV • economy • famous people • …

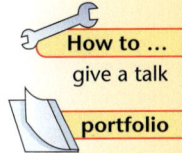
How to …
give a talk

3 **CHECK IT** Check your presentation:

- Are the photos, statistics, maps, … big enough for the class to see them?
- Are the texts correct?

portfolio

4 **PRESENT IT**

- Practise your presentation first, then present it to the class.

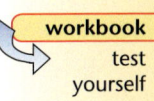
workbook
test yourself

M1 National parks

What do you know about national parks? Work in groups of four and make a placemat. Decide on the five most important facts and write them down in the middle of the placemat. Then talk about your ideas in class.

How to … work with others (5)

workbook M1

M2 The Kruger National Park

a) Listen to what tour guide Peter is telling a group of visitors about the Kruger National Park. Take notes on these points:

history • animals • other info

CD

How to … listen

b) Did you get all the information? Work with a partner and compare your notes.

M3 Planning a holiday

How to … help out in English

a) This is a brochure about different tours you can take in the Kruger National Park. Explain to someone who doesn't speak English which tours are offered.

tip 'Game' has two different meanings. What are they?

LUXURY TOUR
On our four-day guided luxury tour you will stay at Imbali Safari Lodge which is ideally located in the heart of the Kruger National Park. Twenty-four guests can look forward to five star luxury suites, each with its own private jacuzzi. Activities include game drives, guided walks and wellness treatments. Visitors are guaranteed an African safari experience of a lifetime.

BACK TO THE ROOTS
Shipandane Sleepover Hide, located about 3 km south of Mopani on the Tsendze River, is a unique place where guests can enjoy the beautiful nature around them. In this simple building a small group of people can experience the Kruger National Park nightlife first-hand. Large buffalo herds and many elephant bulls stay in the area just metres away from where you are sleeping. This is your chance to experience Africa in its truest form.

workbook M2-M3

FAMILY ADVENTURE
Khoka Moya not only welcomes children, but has even created a special programme for children, offering them the chance to enjoy the same activities as their parents. Children can go on walks around the camp with the rangers, learning about the wildlife, plants and the ecosystem of the Park. Children can also enjoy their African safari with drawing, reading and learning about the bush. There are even special children's menus so that mealtimes are fun, too.

b) Which tour would YOU choose? Why?

M4 An exciting trip

a) **Read this email from Darren, a teenager from Polokwane in South Africa, to his German e-pal Felix. What are the BIG 5?**

Subject: Re: My trip

Hi there,
How's your surfing going? Hopefully, you haven't been attacked by any sharks lately ...
Anyway, my holidays have been great! Although I was a little afraid that going on holiday with my parents would be horribly boring, it's fine actually.
We arrived here two days ago for our four-day tour of the Kruger National Park and spent the first night in a really cool lodge. For dinner we went to a restaurant that served traditional African food. It was soooooo good! Unfortunately, I ate so much Malva Pudding (a really sweet pudding which was brought to South Africa by the Dutch settlers) that I felt a little sick.
But I was better again yesterday morning which was good because we started our two-day game drive. We met at half past three in the morning with our tour guide Peter. There were 12 of us who piled into a kind of jeep. Peter told us that they can't guarantee that you will see a lot of animals on these tours. Sometimes the animals just don't come out of the bush and off-road driving is forbidden in the Kruger National Park. Nevertheless, we were lucky. The first animal we saw was an aardvark mother with her cub. Man, these animals look funny. They are nocturnal, which means they sleep by day and eat by night.
A little later we saw some giraffes. They were eating and moved very slowly. Moreover, we saw some elephants, a lonely lion, a rhino and a buffalo. If we had seen a leopard as well, we would have seen the so-called BIG 5 in one day.
A cheetah disappeared into the bush when it saw our car.
We spent the night in a campsite. There are, however, electrical fences round the camps to keep the animals out. Because this is an 'old style safari' we had to help with cooking dinner and wash up afterwards. The people in our group are OK and Peter is really nice. Today we started very early again and at first saw some smaller and less dangerous animals such as bushpigs, zebras and impalas.
Oh, and finally a warthog — we all had to laugh because it was so ugly!

How to ...
read

b) **Read the email again and finish the sentences.**

1 After Darren and his family had arrived, they spent ...
2 Unfortunately, Darren was feeling a little sick the first night because ...
3 Luckily, he was better again when they ...
4 Before they started the game drive, their tour guide ...
5 While they were driving through the park, Darren could watch ...
6 Finally, when they saw the warthog, the group ...

Aardvark

LiF
23

M5 Choose an activity

- **Would YOU like to spend your holidays at the Kruger National Park? Collect arguments for and against. Then write a text and read it to the class.**

workbook
M4

- **What do you know about aardvarks, bushpigs, impalas, cheetahs or warthogs? Search for information on one of these animals and make a poster or a PowerPoint presentation.**

How to ...
write your opinion

- **Create a brochure for a safari tour in the Kruger National Park. Think about:**

accommodation • transport • animals • dangers • ...

portfolio

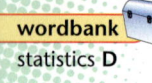
wordbank
statistics D

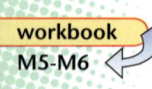
workbook
M5-M6

M6 The people of the rainbow

a) Look at the statistics. What do they tell you about modern South Africa?

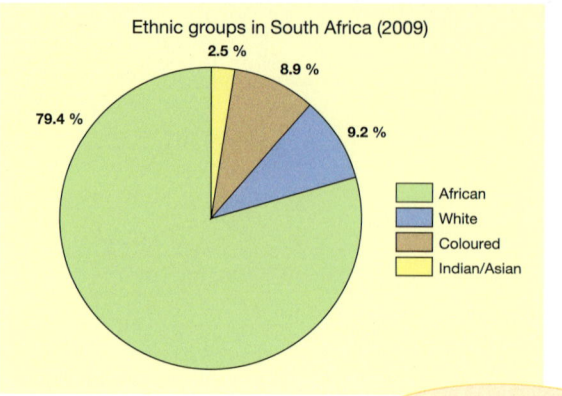

b) Talk about the statistics.

> Most South Africans are …

> Only about 5 per cent of South Africans are …

tip
Where is Durban? Look at the map at the front of your book.

M7 Durban – rainbow city?

a) Some teenagers from Durban were interviewed by a local radio station. Listen to the interviews. What kinds of area do the teenagers live in?

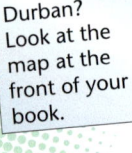
CD

How to …
listen

Sashi, Chatsworth

Jordan, Wentworth

Gemma, Hillcrest

Mnqobi, KwaMashu

b) First make a grid, then listen again and complete your grid.

name	background	likes	dislikes
Sashi	…	…	…

M8 What's life like?

LiF
13

How to …
write a letter

portfolio

Leeds in England is Durban's twin city. Mnqobi's school in Durban is linked to a school in Leeds. Imagine you are Mnqobi's exchange partner from Leeds. Write an email or a letter to him and ask him about his life, Durban and South Africa.

> Dear Mnqobi,
>
> How are you?
> We've been talking about South Africa at school this week. There are lots of things I'd like to ask you. First of all I'd like to know

CD

  **South Africa's angry youth**

a) **Listen to an example of South African music called 'kwaito'. What type of music do you think it is? Why do/don't you like it?**

b) **Form groups of three. Each of you reads one of the paragraphs about 'kwaito' until you get the main ideas.**

① Although there have been lots of changes for the better, not all South Africans are optimistic about their future. Almost half of the population is under the age of 21, which is why young people have got a strong voice. An important part of their culture is *kwaito*. It is a mixture of the 1990s music South African youth grew up with: South African disco music, hip hop, R&B, and a heavy dose of American and British house music. The lyrics are a mixture of local languages and street slang. But *kwaito* is not only music. It also means a unique style of dancing, dressing and performing.

How to ...
read

② The word *kwaito* comes from the Afrikaans word *kwaai*, which means "angry" in English. *Kwaito* deals with the township, knowing about it, understanding it and most importantly, being proud of these things. It has spread a spirit of optimism and self-confidence. This is especially interesting because the apartheid government originally created the township to keep cheap labour under control.

③ While black South Africans were celebrating their new social freedom, *kwaito* artists started questioning the problems they saw around them. They sang about the daily experiences and dreams of the first generation to come of age in the post-apartheid period. One of the famous *kwaito* stars is Esmile. "*Kwaito* is about the drug dealer in the ghetto who everyone is looking up to because he drives fine cars", he says. "It's about the single mother struggling to bring up three children. *Kwaito* is about ghetto life."

workbook
M7

c) **Close your textbook. Tell each other what you learned about 'kwaito' in your paragraph.**

d) **Now read the complete text. Then write a fact file about 'kwaito'. Find out about its origins, its themes, its style and its meaning for young South Africans.**

M10 Choose an activity

- **The term Rainbow Nation was first used by Archbishop Desmond Tutu. Find out more about Tutu and prepare a mini-presentation about his life.**

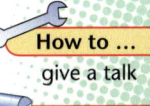

How to ...
give a talk

- **Find statistics about the population in Germany, the different ethnic groups and the age structure. Compare the information to what you learned about South Africa. Then report your findings to the class.**

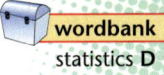

wordbank
statistics D

- **What sort of music do YOU listen to? Find out about its history and its characteristics. Present your results in class.**

portfolio

Check it out!

Did you get it all?

- Where does Isabel come from?
- Who is Baruti?
- Where can you see a famous former prison?
- What does 'Jo'anna' stand for?
- What is the ANC?
- When did Nelson Mandela become president of South Africa?
- Who did Nelson Mandela win the Nobel Peace Prize with?
- How can you reach the top of Table Mountain comfortably?
- Which animals can you watch in Hermanus?

Good to know ...

In South Africa people are often friendlier and warmer than in Western Europe. It is normal to hug and touch each other and they might even call you 'brother' or 'sister'.

Did you know that ...

... the entrance fee for the Kruger National Park in 1927 was one pound?

How much is it today?

... about half of the world's gold comes from South Africa?

... there are eleven official languages in South Africa?

Find four languages that are spoken in South Africa.

... the South African word 'lekker' means 'cool'?

... the South African version of a barbecue is called 'braai'?

... the world's largest diamond was found in South Africa in 1905?

... football, rugby and cricket are the most popular sports in South Africa?

What is special about a 'braai'?

What is the diamond's name?

CHANGES AND CHALLENGES

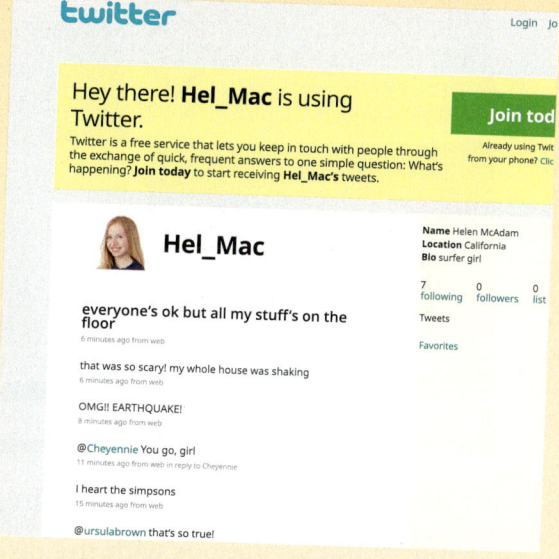

In this Theme …

- you will compare two articles reporting the same natural disaster.
- you will listen to a tornado warning.
- you will talk about different ways of communicating.
- you will have a class discussion about modern technology.
- you can learn about Hurricane Katrina.
- you will read about the advantages and dangers of gaming.

1 Natural disasters

a) Look at the pictures of natural disasters. Have you ever heard about or seen any of these disasters? If yes, where?

drought

flood

wildfire

volcanic eruption

tornado

earthquake

hurricane

workbook
1

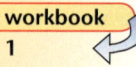

wordbank
environment **G**

b) Which other natural disasters can you think of?

c) Match the definitions with the disasters in a). Find your own definitions for the disasters which are not explained here.

A ... is a violent storm with heavy rain which begins at sea and becomes more powerful when it reaches land.

C ... happens when part of the earth's crust suddenly moves, sending out shock waves which cause the earth to shake.

B ... happens when lava or gases suddenly explode out from the earth's crust.

D ... is dangerous rotating air which usually develops on the land.

MORE
M1-M4
Hurricane
Katrina

2 The Oklahoma drama

a) Look at the picture in the article on page 55. What might have happened?

b) Work with a partner. Each of you reads one of the articles and collects the most important information.

Who? • What? • When? • Where?

Then use your notes to tell each other what happened.

4

A killer twister struck Oklahoma yesterday evening. At least 8 are dead and many more are injured.

Governor Brad Henry declared a state of emergency in Oklahoma, after a violent twister devastated large areas of the state. The storm has left a 25 mile-wide trail of destruction. Buildings were destroyed, trees uprooted and cars flattened.

The small town of Lone Grove was one of the worst hit by the twister.

"It blew right through the middle of town – I've never seen anything like it," said Luke Denton (42), who has lived in Lone Grove all his life. "It was a monster, it must've been half a mile wide, I was so scared!"

"We're just lucky to be alive," Mrs Denton (39) told us, standing in front of the debris where her house once stood. "We only just had time to get the dog and hurry to the basement." The couple's house was lifted off the ground and completely destroyed by the storm. "You work your whole life, and then in a few seconds everything's gone," said another shocked survivor, Rachel Taylor (63).

As the storm system moves east, there are fears that the Mid-South, already devastated by last month's ice storms, will once again be hit.

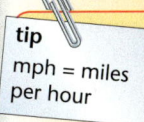

How to ...
read

tip
Twister is the American word for tornado.

A strong tornado hit Lone Grove, Oklahoma yesterday night, killing eight and seriously injuring fourteen. The half mile-wide tornado was classified as an EF-4 tornado, one of the strongest possible, and touched down in Carter County at about 7:30pm on Tuesday. According to the National Weather Service, the tornado reached wind speeds of about 175 mph and was on the ground for more than an hour.

This morning, the full extent of the damage in Lone Grove became clear. Mark Stephens, the City Administrator, estimated that 90 per cent of the town had been destroyed. "Not a single building is still standing," he told reporters earlier today. "This is one of the worst tornadoes to hit Oklahoma."

Eight people have been confirmed dead – seven from Lone Grove, and a truck driver from Jones, Oklahoma, who was driving through the area when the tornado struck. But rescue worker Robert Deaton fears that the death toll will rise, as the search for more victims goes on. A spokeswoman for Oklahoma Emergency Management announced that the National Guard has been sent to support rescue workers.

For the survivors, emergency shelters have been set up by the Red Cross. They are offering meals and beds to those without electricity or whose homes have been destroyed. Despite the destruction, survivors are trying to return to their daily lives. Governor Brad Henry looked to Lone Grove's future in a speech this morning: "I am confident that this community will be rebuilt soon."

tip
mph = miles per hour

c) Complete the sentences with the correct form of the verb – active or passive.

LiF
3, 9

1 The tornado (devastate) large parts of Oklahoma.
2 The small town of Lone Grove (hit) very badly.
3 Up to 90% of the town (destroy).
4 The storm (uproot) trees and (flatten) cars.
5 Unfortunately, eight people (kill).
6 About 14 people (injure).
7 Luke Denton's house (lift off) the ground.
8 He and his wife (spend) the whole night in the basement and (survive).

3 Different ways of reporting

a) Which of the headlines fits which article on page 55? Why?

TORNADO IN OKLAHOMA

DEADLY TWISTER DEVASTATES TOWN

workbook
2

b) Both of the articles describe the same event. What is the difference between the two? Think about:

information • language • layout

How to ...
work with
others (2)

c) Get together in buzz groups. Then choose a member of your group to present your results to the class.

4 A survival story

wordbank
environment G

a) Write a personal survival story to the Lone Grove Post. You can choose a person mentioned in one of the articles on page 55 or make up a new character. Your story should be interesting and logical. You can start like this:

How to ...
write

My name is … I'm … years old and I live in Lone Grove. I'm lucky to be alive. We were warned about the tornado on TV just before it happened. I was really scared …

b) Swap stories with a partner and give each other feedback on your texts.

portfolio

c) Form small groups and read the stories to each other. Which story do you like best? Why?

workbook
3-4

5 A tornado warning

CD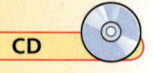

Look at the pictures and listen to the tornado warning. What should people do when a tornado is moving towards them? Write down the numbers of the correct pictures.

How to ...
listen

workbook
5

❶   ❷   ❸   ❹   ❺

6 Early warning systems

a) Look at the article on early warning systems and find the English verbs for:

vorhersagen • messen • sich verlassen auf • beobachten • unterscheiden

It is difficult to forecast tornadoes. They don't last very long and are also very complicated. Scientists don't really know how tornadoes form, but by using what they know about former ones, meteorologists can tell when they may form.

Every twelve hours meteorologists send up weather balloons, small ones and big ones. The balloons carry equipment to measure conditions such as atmospheric stability, temperature and humidity (the amount of water in the air). With the help of these measurements, meteorologists can tell if a tornado is likely to form.

By using a new kind of weather radar, a more reliable one than conventional radar, meteorologists can detect a tornado when it is forming – up to 20 minutes before it touches down. This gives meteorologists the time they need to issue a tornado warning. With conventional radar, they had to rely on reports by storm spotters. These are people who got special training to watch the development of weather events. Storm spotters observe storms and learn to distinguish between real tornadoes and false ones. They report their findings to the National Weather Service and to their local communities.

How to …
read

workbook
5

b) You have found this article on the Internet. A friend of yours is also interested in the information but doesn't understand much English. Try to answer his/her questions.

1 Wofür werden denn die Wetterballons benutzt?
2 Da ist von einem neuen Wetterradar die Rede. Was ist daran neu?
3 Hier steht 'storm spotters'. Das sind Menschen, richtig? Was machen die?

How to …
help out in
English

c) Find the sentences with *one* or *ones* in the article. What can you write instead of these words?

LiF
20

7 Project: YOUR poster of natural disasters

a) Work in groups. Decide on a natural disaster and find out:

- how it is defined
- where it takes place (areas)
- why it takes place (causes)
- extraordinary facts
- …

b) Write your texts and check them before you copy them onto your poster. Add pictures.

c) Hang up your posters in class. Present them to the others in a gallery walk.

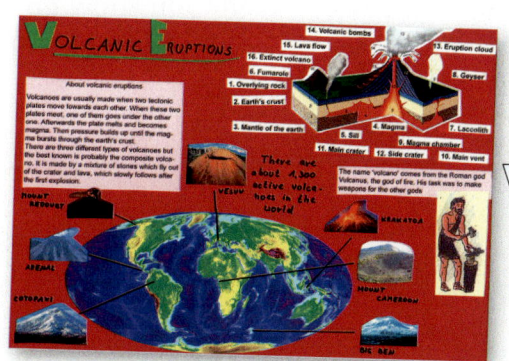

wordbank
environment G

How to …
work with
others (6)

portfolio

workbook
test
yourself

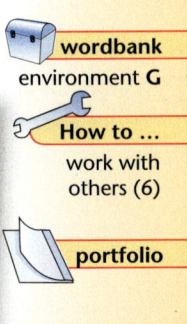

8 Keep in touch 🗣

People have always looked for ways to keep in touch with their friends and family, especially when something bad like a natural disaster happens.

a) Look at these pictures. They show ways of communicating throughout the last 300 years. Talk about what you can see.

A

B

C

D

> In picture B you can see a man writing a letter by hand.

> In picture C there is ...

E

F twitter

Login Jo

Hey there! **Hel_Mac** is using Twitter.

Twitter is a free service that lets you keep in touch with people through the exchange of quick, frequent answers to one simple question: What's happening? **Join today** to start receiving **Hel_Mac's** tweets.

Already using Twit
from your phone? Clic

Join tod

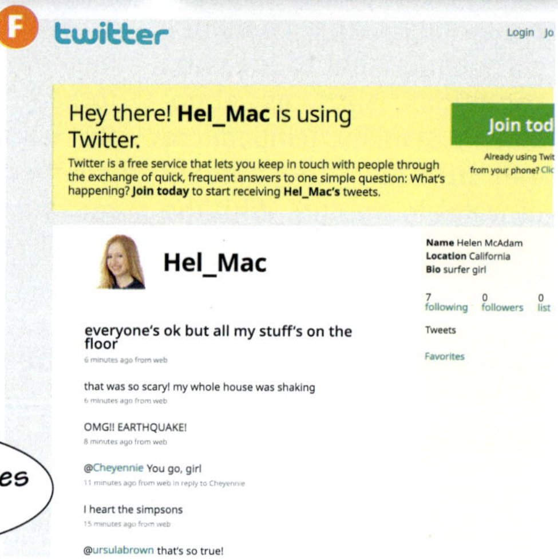

**workbook
6**

b) Now match the pictures with the years.

Hel_Mac

Name Helen McAdam
Location California
Bio surfer girl

| 7 | 0 | 0 |
| following | followers | list |

everyone's ok but all my stuff's on the floor
6 minutes ago from web

that was so scary! my whole house was shaking
6 minutes ago from web

OMG!! EARTHQUAKE!
8 minutes ago from web

@Cheyennie You go, girl
11 minutes ago from web in reply to Cheyennie

I heart the simpsons
15 minutes ago from web

@ursulabrown that's so true!

Tweets

Favorites

```
1760 • 2006 • 1915 •
1983 • 1992 • 2007
```

> I think picture A goes with the year ...

How to ...
work with others (2)

c) Think about other ways of communicating. Get together in buzz groups.

wordbank
technology **H**

d) What is YOUR favourite way to keep in touch?

9 Social networking 🗣

a) What do you know about social networking?

b) Have you or anyone you know got an account on a social networking site like SchülerVZ, Facebook, ICQ or MySpace? Work with a partner and tell him/her:

- where your account is
- how often you log on
- what you do when you're logged on
- what you like about it
- what you don't like about it

> My account is with ... I like it because ... I log on ...

> I have a Facebook account. I log on ... and I ...

LiF
12

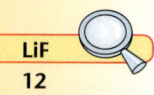

c) Report what your partner told you to the rest of the class.

> Martin said that he had an account on ... He told me he logged on ...

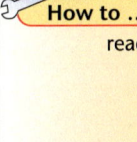

4

10 Meet Tessa Barinski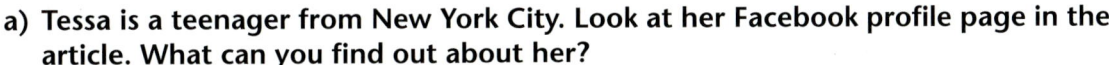

a) **Tessa is a teenager from New York City. Look at her Facebook profile page in the article. What can you find out about her?**

b) **Now read what Tessa wrote about Facebook.**

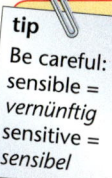
How to ...
read

Tessa Barinski, New York:

I discovered Facebook about two years ago. Some friends of mine signed up and told me about it, so I got my own account. Now all my friends are on Facebook and it has become our most favorite social network.

I really like Facebook. I can post pictures and videos more easily than anywhere else and get in touch with people I haven't spoken to for years. For example I met this guy I went to kindergarten with. And he's really cute now. :-)

I also love the status updates. You can see really quickly what your friends are doing or thinking. It's great how you can let people know that you like what they're doing or saying. I think Facebook is also a great way to support causes that interest you. I'm a member of lots of groups that are about reducing energy waste and saving the planet and protecting animals. So, there are lots more things than chatting and playing games on Facebook. But I do think that you have to be careful about the data you put on there.

I don't think you should put your home address on there and you shouldn't accept every friend request. You also have to be careful about the type of photos you put there. I mean I wouldn't want everyone at my school to see me in a bikini and I wouldn't want my dad to see a picture of me kissing my boyfriend. ;-) I've also heard sometimes employers check your profile page so it's best not to say anything bad about work. I heard of this one guy who lost his job after saying his boss was boring on Facebook. But I think as long as you're sensible and think about what you're doing, Facebook is just awesome! :-)

MORE
M5-M9
gaming

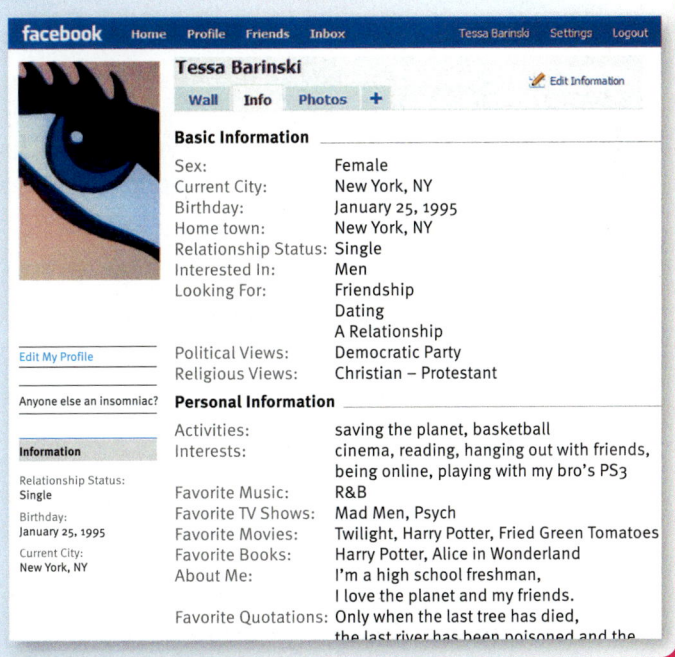

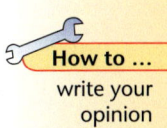
workbook
7-8

c) **Read the article again. What does Tessa like about Facebook? What advice does she give? Make two lists.**

d) **Look at the last sentence. Do you agree? Write a text and give reasons.**

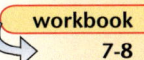
How to ...
write your opinion

11 Logged on

Look at number 10 again and complete the sentences with the words from the box.

1 On Facebook you can post pictures and videos **???** than anywhere else.
2 Tessa thinks Facebook works **???** than MySpace.
3 Some people use Facebook **???** than others.
4 Always check if you could behave even **???** on the Internet.
5 Try even **???** to protect your private data.

better • more carefully •
more easily • harder •
more frequently

LiF
22

workbook
9

12 Get the message

a) Listen to the radio interview with communications expert Dr Golda Weinstein. What does Dr Weinstein think about the Internet?

CD

b) Get together in groups and listen again. Take notes on what Dr Weinstein says about one of the following topics: Web 2.0 • Facebook • mobile phones

How to ...
give a talk

c) Give a one-minute talk about your group's topic. Use your notes from b).

13 Chatting with Dr Weinstein

a) After the radio interview Dr Weinstein answers listeners' questions in the chat. Read the chat.

How to ...
read

---

mom567: Do you really think the Internet is a safe place for teenagers?

Dr Weinstein: Well I think it depends on what they do online. It's true that teenagers and anyone should be very careful what kind of information they put out there. The Web can be a dangerous place, and there are people out there who want to take advantage of the anonymity it offers.

petey_box: What do you think the world would be like without the Internet?

Dr Weinstein: :-) Well you know the Internet has only really existed for about 20 years. If the Internet hadn't been invented, people would have found other ways to communicate. I'm sure libraries would be used more often if there was no Internet. I think there's a danger that people rely too much on modern technology and forget to use their brains sometimes.

carla: How did people manage to change the way we communicate? Can you give some examples?

Dr Weinstein: People have always looked for better ways to communicate with each other, especially since they have started to move all over the world. For example if the settlers in the US hadn't moved further and further west, the telegraph would not have been invented. If computers had been more powerful in the 1970s, the Internet would have been invented earlier. People want to keep in touch with friends and family, but they also want to learn more about the world and they want to do business with people at the other end of the world.

frodo_27: What do you think about privacy and data protection?

Dr Weinstein: People should be more aware of the need to protect their data. One of the dangers of modern technology is that your data can be found by almost anyone with a few hacking skills. You don't want the whole world to know your account or telephone number.

---

workbook
10–11

b) What are the dangers of modern technology? Take notes.

tip
You can use your notes for the discussion on page 61.

14 What would have been?

a) Look at this answer Dr Weinstein gave in the chat. Do you agree? Give reasons.

If the Internet hadn't been invented, people would have found other ways to communicate.

60

b) What could have been different? Look at the example in a) and complete the sentences.

If electricity hadn't existed in 1920, people …
If computers had been more powerful in the 1970s, the Internet …
If the telephone hadn't been invented in 1876, …

LiF
8

workbook
12

PEOPLE & PLACES

Samuel Morse

Samuel Morse (1791 – 1872) was an American painter and inventor. Although Morse worked as a painter throughout his life, today he is known for inventing the single wire telegraph.

In 1825 Morse was in Washington, working on a painting when he got a letter from his father in New Haven saying "Your wife is dead." Morse immediately went to New Haven but when he arrived his wife had already been buried. Moved by this tragic event in his private life, Morse decided to develop a means of fast long-distance communication.

For this he used electromagnetic power to send pulses of different lengths through a wire. At the other end of the wire the pulses were made visible in a pattern of dots and dashes.

In the following years the method and the code – later to be known as Morse Code – were developed further. In 1861 the first transcontinental telegraph line from Washington to Baltimore was built. For the first time in history people did not have to wait days or even weeks for news.

Today Morse Code is used in certain situations, for example when there is no Internet connection.

15 YOUR discussion: Modern technology

Choose one of the statements and have a class discussion:

a) What's YOUR opinion?
First do a quick survey in class.
Then get together in three groups:

- Group one agrees with the statement.
- Group two disagrees with the statement.
- Group three listens to the arguments and takes notes.

- Social networking sites make people lonely in real life.

- Mobile phones should be banned in school.

- The Internet is dangerous.

b) Prepare for the discussion:

- Collect arguments for or against the statement in your group.
- Group three thinks about the best way to take notes during the discussion and finds someone to lead the discussion.

c) Have a discussion in class:

- Present your arguments. Make sure group one and two take turns.

d) At the end of the discussion group three decides:
Which group had the best arguments?

How to …
discuss

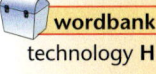

wordbank
technology H

workbook
test yourself

M1 Hurricane Katrina

New Orleans is the largest city in the state of Louisiana, USA. On August 29, 2005, New Orleans was hit by Hurricane Katrina. 80 per cent of the city was flooded with water, over 1,400 people died and hundreds of thousands lost their homes.

CD

How to ...
listen

a) **Listen to the interview with an expert on hurricanes. What type of hurricane was Katrina?**

b) **Listen again and match the sentence parts.**

LiF
15

1 Not only does New Orleans lie north of the Gulf of Mexico,	A than the city was flooded.
2 No sooner had parts of the levees been destroyed	B to really help the population.
3 Hardly had the poor found shelter in the Superdome	C but it is also surrounded by the Mississippi River and Lake Pontchartrain.
4 Only after several days did the American government manage	D how easily their city could be destroyed.
5 Only after the disaster did people realise	E when they had new problems to cope with.

workbook
M1-M2

c) **Now tell somebody who hasn't listened to the interview which piece of information you find the most surprising, shocking or interesting. Give reasons.**

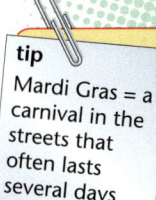

 **Hope and frustration**

After the hurricane many people have turned to poetry to express their feelings about the disaster.

a) Read the poem. What images or comparisons does the author use to describe her feelings?

ONLY THE ROOFTOPS

Only the rooftops   It's quiet   Thirst
Like islands   Very quiet   Dirt
Above the water   Except where people And fire
In rows   shout   Surrounded by water
Like the graves   At their frustrations So much water
In a graveyard   At their hope   Will Mardi Gras
                                        Ever return?

By Dawn Fox

tip
Mardi Gras = a carnival in the streets that often lasts several days

b) Why does the author only use short phrases or even single words in each line?

c) Read the poem to a partner. Try to express the atmosphere.

M3 Promises

The American government promised New Orleans and its citizens a lot of things.

Look at the example. Then write down the other promises into your exercise book.

Example: Citizens – help – to rebuild their ruined houses
   Citizens will be helped to rebuild their ruined houses.

1 The flood protection system – improve
2 Millions of dollars – spend – to build new homes
3 Roads, bridges and water systems – repair
4 Electric power – restore
5 Cheap building sites for new homes – give – to the poor
6 Health care – provide
7 Families who were separated during the evacuation – bring – together again
8 The streets of New Orleans – fill – with lovely homes and the sound of jazz music

M4 Choose an activity

- **Did the American government keep its promises? What is life like in New Orleans today? Search for information on the Internet. Then report your findings to the class.**

- **Work with a partner. Prepare an interview with a New Orleans city official about Hurricane Katrina. Think of ten questions you would like to ask about the hurricane. One of you takes the city official's role. Act out the interview in class.**

- **Write a poem about a natural disaster like 'Katrina'.**

LiF
10

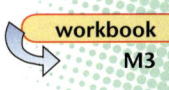
workbook
M3

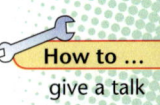
How to …
give a talk

How to …
talk

portfolio

4
MORE

M5 Games people play

a) **Read these ads for computer games. Which one do YOU find the most interesting? Why?**

ROCK CHICKS

You've always dreamed of being a star? Here's your chance to get to the top.
Be creative and form your own girl group! Find your unique outfit, make-up, hairstyle and the music you want to play.
Then jump on the stage and play as many gigs as you can. The more gigs you play, the more money you earn and the higher your popularity. You can also play with friends who have their own version of ROCK CHICKS.

CAR WARS

Fast cars, hot races, dangerous shoot-outs, cool music and brilliant graphics guarantee great game fun.
Two clans are fighting for power and land and the final battle is near. Lots of weapons are at your disposal: pistols, automatic guns, bazookas, rockets and fast cars. Just choose the side you want to join and go ahead.

WHEN IN ROME DO LIKE A ROMAN

Rome, 204 BC. Rome has been fighting against Carthage for the last fifteen years. Now the time has come to beat Hannibal once and for all. As the Roman emperor you have to organise the war. Raise enough money to build your army and save your city.

tip
BC = before Christ

workbook
M4-M5

How to …
read

b) **Find words in the texts that match these definitions:**

1 a live concert
2 the most powerful person in a state
3 when you can have something, it is …

4 a group of people who see themselves as a family
5 someone who is very famous
6 a fight between criminals who use guns

c) **Which games do YOU like to play? Talk to a partner.**

M6 Working together

a) **Listen to Ricardo from Italy, Tim from the Netherlands, Katja from Germany and Fergus from Scotland. Where are they?**

CD

b) **Listen again. What are the four planning to do? Put the actions in the right order.**

kill the humanoids

find the rings

collect gold

How to …
listen

M7 Lost to the real world?

a) **Read this article about computer games from an online magazine. What are the advantages and dangers of gaming? Take notes in a grid.**

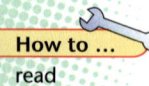
How to …
read

Lost to the real world?

More and more parents are worried about the amount of time their children spend in virtual worlds.

"Our son gets really aggressive when we try to make him stop gaming," one desperate mother writes in an Internet forum. "We don't know what to do anymore." Others complain about their children's grades getting worse, their losing interest in everything but the game they are playing and their mixing up of real and virtual world.

But is it really that bad? "Well, I wouldn't damn computer games completely," says Dr Golda Weinstein from New England College. "Apart from the possible costs there are also dangers and I ask every parent to look out for these dangers. The problem with MMORPGs especially is that there is no end and therefore no limit to those games. We do have cases in which players got so addicted to the game that their health and their social life were in danger. In Korea a young man actually died after playing non-stop for three days. I want parents to realise what is happening before it is too late. Another danger which one should be aware of are the many violent scenes and the fact that a number of children, especially boys, play games they should not be playing at their age.

On the other hand computer games can actually have positive aspects. There are lots of games where social interaction takes place and that's perfectly okay, as long as you remember that you have got a real life in the real world. There are also quite a lot of games in the e-learning sector. Some games teach you strategic thinking and train your ability to solve complex problems. But it is really important that parents know what their children are doing and take care that the kids do not spend too much time on the computer or play the wrong games."

b) Use your grid from a) and tell somebody who hasn't read the text about the advantages and dangers of gaming.

tip
MMORPG = Massively Multiplayer Online Role-Playing Game

workbook
M6

M8 Dr Weinstein's advice

a) Look at the article again and match the sentence parts. What word do you get?

1	Dr Weinstein advises parents	**A**	to play games which are very violent.
2	She asks parents	**R**	not to let their children spend too much time on the computer.
3	Parents should not allow their children	**L**	to keep an eye on their children before it is too late.
4	She wants parents	**E**	to look out for the dangerous effects that some games could have.

b) Do you agree with what Dr Weinstein says? Write a text. Give reasons and examples.

tip
You can also use your grid for the discussion on page 61.

LiF 14

workbook
M7

How to …
write your opinion

M9 YOUR survey: Computer habits

a) Look at the statistics. What do they tell you?

b) Work in groups. Do a class survey about YOUR computer habits and create a pie or a bar chart out of your findings.

c) Present your charts in class.

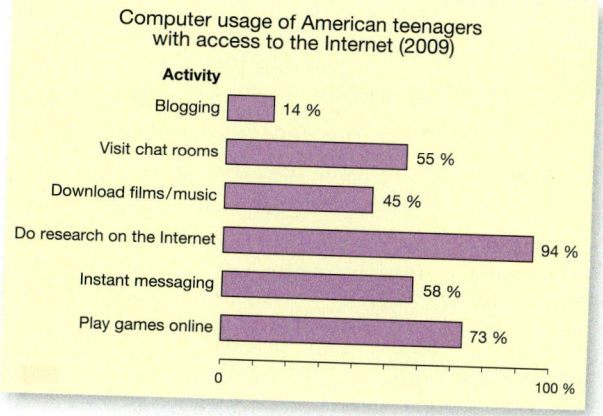

Computer usage of American teenagers with access to the Internet (2009)

Activity
- Blogging 14 %
- Visit chat rooms 55 %
- Download films/music 45 %
- Do research on the Internet 94 %
- Instant messaging 58 %
- Play games online 73 %

0 — 100 %

wordbank
statistics D

wordbank
technology H

portfolio

 Check it out!

Did you get it all?

tip
You can quiz your partner!

- Where is Lone Grove?
- What is the American word for tornado?
- Where inside your house should you go when a tornado is coming?
- What are weather balloons used for?
- When was Twitter invented?
- Where does Tessa Barinski come from?
- What is Golda Weinstein's job?
- What is MySpace?

Good to know ...

Peter Müller

Answering the phone works differently in different countries. In Germany it is polite to tell the caller your name when answering the phone. In English-speaking countries people often only say 'hello' or give their phone number.

Did you know that ...

... the number of text messages sent and received every day is larger than the world's population?

... more than 80% of homepages on the Web are in English?

Find out how many per cent are in German.

... the oldest still existing computer in the world is called CSIRAC?

... if MySpace was a country, it would be the 11th largest?

Where is it?

... wildfires move faster uphill than downhill?

... an average 21-year-old has spent 5,000 hours playing video games, has sent about 250,000 emails and text messages and has spent 10,000 hours talking on a mobile phone?

... 'tsunami' is a Japanese word, put together from 'tsu' (harbour) and 'nami' (wave)?

Find out how much time you spend on the Internet every week. Write a diary.

... there are more than 500 active volcanoes in the world?

EXAM PRACTICE SECTION

In this Theme ...

- you can practise different kinds of testing formats used in the final exam.
- you can work on testing formats from these competence areas: listening, reading, writing, mediation and speaking.
- you will find tips and explanations that will help you with your final exam.

In deiner Abschlussprüfung wird dir eine Auswahl verschiedener Aufgabenformate begegnen. Sie überprüfen deine Fähigkeiten in den Bereichen *Listening, Reading, Writing, Mediation* und *Speaking*. Theme 5 gibt dir die Möglichkeit, eine Vielfalt dieser Aufgabenformate auszuprobieren und dich mit ihnen vertraut zu machen. Dadurch gewinnst du mehr Sicherheit für deine Prüfung.

Um dich auf die Abschlussprüfung gut vorzubereiten, hast du in letzter Zeit schon viel geleistet. Deshalb musst du Theme 5 nicht chronologisch durcharbeiten. Du kannst ruhig zwischen verschiedenen Bereichen hin- und herwechseln. Vielleicht stellst du ja fest, dass du mit einzelnen Kompetenzen (z. B. *Listening*) oder mit bestimmten Aufgabenformaten (z. B. *multiple choice*) besondere Schwierigkeiten hast. Diese solltest du dann besonders intensiv üben. Es kann auch sinnvoll sein, Aufgaben zu wiederholen.

Jedem Aufgabenformat sind Tipps beigefügt, die dir bei der erfolgreichen Bearbeitung helfen sollen. Solltest du nach der Überprüfung deiner Lösungen feststellen, dass du mit einer Aufgabe größere Probleme hattest, empfiehlt es sich, diese Aufgabe mit zeitlichem Abstand noch einmal zu bearbeiten.

Viel Erfolg!

**Bitte nicht ins Buch schreiben!
Den nötigen Platz für deine Antworten findest du in Theme 5 deines Workbooks.**

5

LISTENING

 **L1 Short dialogues**

Bei dieser *multiple choice* Aufgabe wird eine Frage vorgegeben und du hörst einen kurzen Text (z.B. Dialog, Ansage, Monolog). Dann musst du eines von vier Bildern als richtige Antwort auswählen.

TIPP: Die drei falschen Antwortmöglichkeiten können Bildelemente enthalten, die zwar im Text erwähnt werden, aber nicht die richtige Antwort auf die Frage darstellen. Achte also darauf, dass <u>alle</u> Informationen stimmen.

You will hear two short dialogues. There is <u>one</u> question for each dialogue. Decide which picture is the right answer to the question.

CD

a) At what time does Amy start work?

 How to ...
listen

b) What is Pat going to buy?

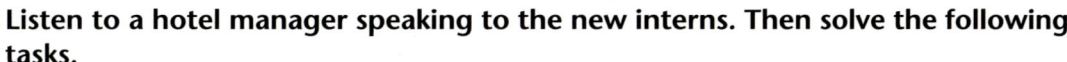 **L2 Welcoming the new interns**

Listen to a hotel manager speaking to the new interns. Then solve the following tasks.

CD

Bei dieser *gap filling* Aufgabe musst du gezielt Informationen aus dem Text heraushören und notieren.

TIPP: Lies vor dem Hören die Aufgabenstellung genau und stelle fest, welche Informationen (Zeitangaben, Ortsangaben usw.) benötigt werden. Du trägst hier nur Wörter bzw. Wortgruppen zusammen.

 How to ...
listen

a) Complete the notes with the missing information.

Length of work experience: ~~~~~~   Rooms for interns (where): ~~~~~~

Breakfast (when): ~~~~~~ (where): ~~~~~~

Working hours: from ~~~~~~ to ~~~~~~

Clothes to wear: ~~~~~~ , ~~~~~~ and ~~~~~~

5

Bei diesem Aufgabenformat musst du Sätze mit Informationen aus dem Hörtext vervollständigen.

TIPP: Beachte den Satzbau. Prüfe auch, ob die Ergänzungen aus mehreren Wörtern bestehen können.

b) Listen to the hotel manager again and finish the following sentences with the right information.

1 For breakfast you can have ⁓⁓⁓⁓⁓⁓⁓⁓⁓⁓⁓⁓⁓⁓ (2 things)

2 Interns are not allowed ⁓⁓⁓⁓⁓⁓⁓⁓⁓⁓⁓⁓ in the hotel.

3 At 10.30 there will be ⁓⁓⁓⁓⁓⁓⁓⁓⁓⁓

L3 The story of a teenage mum 👂

Bei dieser *multiple choice* Aufgabe gibt es bis zu vier Möglichkeiten, einen Satz zu beenden. Aber nur eine davon ist richtig.

TIPP: Lies dir (vor dem Hören) alle vier Antwortmöglichkeiten genau durch, damit du dich dann besser entscheiden kannst.

HINWEIS: Dieses Aufgabenformat kann dir auch bei *Reading* begegnen.

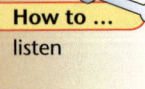
CD

a) Listen to Part I and underline the right ending of the sentence.

1 This radio programme is about

teenage pregnancies in Europe.
teenage pregnancies in Britain.
helping teenage mums to look after their babies.
teenage fathers.

How to ...
listen

2 The teenage pregnancy rate in Britain

is lower than in the Netherlands.
is the lowest rate in Western Europe.
is higher than in the Netherlands.
has risen by 27 per cent.

3 80 per cent of pregnant teenagers

had wanted to have a baby.
had used condoms.
hadn't planned to get pregnant.
don't talk to their parents about the pregnancy.

b) Listen to Part II and decide whether the following statements are true, false or not given. Tick (✔) the right box.

	true	false	not given
1 Katie and Martin weren't planning to have a baby.	☐	☐	☐
2 At first Katie didn't want to believe that she was pregnant.	☐	☐	☐
3 Martin's parents were quite happy about the 'baby news'.	☐	☐	☐
4 Katie couldn't pass her exams because she was pregnant.	☐	☐	☐
5 Emily was born a week after Katie had finished school.	☐	☐	☐
6 She lost contact with most of her friends after she'd had the baby.	☐	☐	☐
7 With Emily Katie can't go out to work and has to stay at home without a job.	☐	☐	☐
8 Katie and Martin are still together and feel happy as a family.	☐	☐	☐
9 They have had two more children now.	☐	☐	☐

READING

R1 **A sign**

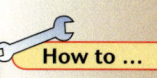

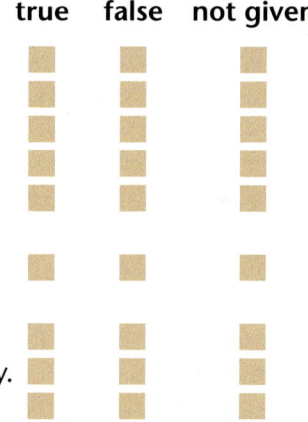

Wildlife Reserve
- Please don't enter after dark.
- No smoking and no alcoholic drinks allowed.
- Human food is not fit for animals. Use only the animal food sold in our wildlife shop.

Read the sign. Then underline the right statement.

You are not allowed to feed the animals.
You can't eat or drink in the park.
There are no shops in the park.
You shouldn't go into the reserve at night.

5

R2 Finding the right course

Bei dieser *matching* Aufgabe erhältst du Profile verschiedener Personen, für die du anhand von Beschreibungen passende Angebote (z. B. Urlaub, Beruf, Sportkurs usw.) auswählen sollst. Du hast immer mehr Beschreibungen als Profile zur Auswahl.

TIPP: Zuerst solltest du die Schlüsselinformationen in den Profilen markieren. Dann musst du für jedes Profil alle Auswahlmöglichkeiten einzeln durchgehen, bis du einen Text findest, auf den wirklich <u>alle</u> Schlüsselinformationen zutreffen. Beachte, dass du sehr oft Beschreibungen findest, die <u>nur Teile</u> der Schlüsselinformationen enthalten. Diese wurden in den Text eingearbeitet, um dich abzulenken.

How to …
read

Read Maria's and Peter's profiles. Then decide which English course is best for them.

Maria left school three years ago and hasn't spoken any English since then. Now she is in a job where she needs to get better at speaking English. In the summer she has a maximum of three weeks holiday. She wants to do an English course, but she also wants to relax because her work is hard and this is her only holiday. Maria doesn't really like living with other people.

Peter is a computer specialist. His spoken English is quite good but he has problems with writing. He is quite an active person so he would like to be in a place where things are happening and not in the countryside. He wants to learn as much English as possible and he is hoping to stay with a nice host family.

Do you need English for your job? Excellent English courses for professionals in the historical city of Edinburgh. Combine a Scottish experience with getting better at English. We offer English for special purposes, like business, management or information technology. Learn how to write emails and business letters. We offer a four-week intensive programme with six or eight lessons a day in small groups. You will live with our friendly host families or in good hotels.

Learn English in England If you need to improve your English, there is no better way. Come to the historical town of Winchester, stay with friendly host families and get your English going. Courses last one, two or four weeks with four to six hours a day. You will be taught in small groups by our qualified teachers. There are also many organised trips and activities in the afternoons and evenings, so you'll see as much as possible during your stay.

Have you forgotten your English? Take a 2- or 4-week refresher course on the sunny island of Malta and improve your English. Get better at basic grammar and conversation in small groups of not more than eight people. Our teachers are all native speakers and highly qualified. With four hours of English a day you will also have enough time to enjoy and explore the beautiful island of Malta. Accommodation in nice middle-class hotels is included in the course fees.

Maria: ～～～   Peter: ～～～

R3 'Little' big help

Read the text.

On January 12, 2010 the Caribbean island of Haiti, one of the poorest countries in the world, was hit by a catastrophic earthquake. The epicentre of the earthquake was Haiti's capital Port-au-Prince.
5 Millions of people lost their homes and belongings in the quake. Over two hundred thousand people died. The shocking pictures of death and destruction went all around the world. Everywhere people were trying to organise help. Specialists and doctors went
10 to help as volunteers, stars like Haitian-born Wyclef Jean, Madonna and Beyoncé performed in a concert and organised a phone-in where they answered phone calls to raise money.

But one little boy showed that you don't need to
15 be rich, a star or a specialist to help. Seven-year-old Charlie Simpson from Fulham, West London, saw a report about the earthquake and its victims on TV. "I just think it was quite sad when I saw the pictures on TV," he said. Charlie started crying and
20 then went to his mother Leonora. He wanted to do something and he worked out a plan: Together with his mum he created a sponsorship form and put it on the Internet: *"My name is Charlie Simpson, I want to do a Sponsored Bike Ride for Haiti because
25 there was a big earthquake and loads of people have lost their lives. I want to make some money to buy food, water and tents for everyone in Haiti."* Charlie was planning to do a 5-mile ride around South Park, Fulham – quite a distance for a seven-year-old.

With this idea Charlie had hoped to raise £500
30 for UNICEF. But especially after some newspapers started writing about the little boy, the reaction of the British people was amazing and exceeded all Charlie's hopes. Even with most people just giving small sums like £20 on his JustGiving page
35 (which can be found at www.justgiving.com/CharlieSimpson-HAITI), the boy has managed to raise over £150,000 for UNICEF/Haiti so far. His mum said: "What started off as a little cycle round the park with his dad has turned into something
40 a lot bigger than that and we can't believe it. I am extremely proud of our Charlie."

How to ...
read

Bei dieser *matching* Aufgabe musst du den einzelnen Textabschnitten vorgegebene Überschriften zuordnen. Dabei werden meist mehr Überschriften angeboten, als Textabschnitte vorhanden sind.

TIPP: Hier geht es um die Gesamtaussage eines Textabschnittes. Einzelinformationen treten eher in den Hintergrund.

---

a) Find the best headline for each paragraph. There is one more than you need.

A terrible disaster   Amazing results   A little boy's idea   Bicycle race

---

Bei diesem Aufgabenformat musst du vorgegebene Aussagen einem Textinhalt entsprechend in die richtige (zeitliche) Reihenfolge bringen.

TIPP: Konzentriere dich auf den Inhalt. Beachte, dass sich die sprachliche Gestaltung der vorgegebenen Aussagen von den Formulierungen im Text unterscheiden kann.

---

b) This is what Charlie's mum Leonora said to a newspaper afterwards. Put her statements in the right order.

☐ Soon the newspapers started writing about our project.

☐ We actually created the Internet form together, but it was Charlie's idea.

☐ Charlie came to me afterwards, he was still in tears and he wanted to help.

☐ We were watching these terrible pictures on the news that day.

☐ From that moment on we had more and more money coming in.

5

Bei dieser *multiple choice* Aufgabe zeigt du, dass du die Bedeutung eines Wortes erkennst, indem du ihm die entsprechende englische Umschreibung zuordnest.

TIPP: Versuche, das Wort im Text zu finden. Es ist wichtig, dass du dir den Gesamtzusammenhang klarmachst.

c) Which expression has the same meaning? Underline it.

1 to **raise** money

   to spend money
   to collect money
   to give money
   to lose money

2 … **exceeded** Charlie's hopes

   was more than he had hoped
   was not as good as he had hoped
   was exactly what he had hoped for
   was a terrible shock for him

Bei diesem Aufgabenformat musst du die benötigten Informationen aus einem Text herausschreiben, um Fragen gezielt zu beantworten.

TIPP: Beschränke dich nur auf die erforderlichen Informationen und schreibe nicht zu viel aus dem Text heraus. Oft genügen wenige Adjektive, Verben und/oder Substantive als Antwort.

d) Copy the words/phrases from the text that answer the following questions.

1 What did Charlie want to do in order to get money?
2 What did Charlie want to buy for the people of Haiti?
3 What was his reaction when he saw pictures from Haiti on TV?
4 How much money did he want to make originally?

Bei dieser *true/false* Aufgabe musst du feststellen, ob vorgegebene Aussagen zum Text richtig oder falsch sind bzw. ob der Text überhaupt Informationen über diese Aussagen enthält.

TIPP: Lies dir jede Aussage gründlich durch. Nur wenn der Sachverhalt einer Aussage überhaupt nicht im Text vorkommt, solltest du dich für *not given* entscheiden. Stütze dich bei deiner Entscheidung unter keinen Umständen darauf, was du allgemein schon über das Thema weißt!

HINWEIS: Dieses Aufgabenformat kann dir auch bei *Listening* begegnen. Manchmal enthält der Aufgabentyp nur die Kategorien *true* und *false*. Ab und zu wird in der dritten Spalte anstelle von *not given* auch *not in the text* verwendet.

e) Decide whether the following statements are true, false or not given. Tick (✔) the right box.

	true	false	not given
1 Some stars organised events to help the Haitian people.	■	■	■
2 With their concert the stars raised over one million dollars.	■	■	■
3 Most people supported Charlie's idea with quite big sums of money.	■	■	■
4 Charlie's mother was not surprised that people gave so much money.	■	■	■

5

 **R4 A blog** 👓

Read the blog.

---

traveller761

Hi guys out there. I'm eighteen, just finished school and my parents have helped me to find a job which starts in a month. But I'm not sure if I want to have that job right now. I'd love to go abroad for a year or two. I haven't been outside the country yet and I somehow don't feel ready for work. I have no money, my friends and parents think I'm crazy but I just can't stand the idea of going straight from school to work. On the other hand I'm a little scared: What will I do when I finish travelling? Will I find another job?

---

angel07

I think if you need a break, there's nothing wrong with taking time off to travel and starting a job later on. Being without money could be a problem. Working in youth hostels along the way doesn't exactly pay well. You should check out a work/tourism visa program. That way you could get a job as a waiter, farm helper or something in Australia or the UK and hopefully make enough money to travel.

sis5

Why don't you work first and travel later? If you're lucky enough to get a job in these times, you shouldn't throw this chance away. It will only get harder to find work the older you get. There's always time to travel later. Start your job now and get working!

suzi6

I had some time off after my first year at university and went to Africa for eight months. It was the best decision of my life. It cleared my head and because I did some volunteer work in the field I'm interested in, it gave me a better idea of what I wanted to do later in life. I now know what I'm studying for!

pink22

I don't know what you're talking about! You're only eighteen! I'm nineteen myself and I would never leave my family and friends behind just to travel. I would be too nervous. Count yourself lucky to have a job and earn some money. If I were you, I wouldn't think of travelling!

How to …
read

Bei dieser *matching* Aufgabe musst du zutreffende Aussagen zum Text anhand von Satzhälften zusammenbauen. Es gibt normalerweise mehr Satzenden als Satzanfänge.

TIPP: Beachte, dass der Satz sprachlich korrekt sein <u>und</u> dabei gleichzeitig inhaltlich auf den Text zutreffen muss.

HINWEIS: Dieses Aufgabenformat kann dir auch bei *Listening* begegnen.

---

a) What is traveller761's problem? Match the right sentence parts.
You have more sentence parts than you need.

1 Traveller761 wants to go abroad for some time
2 With the help of his parents he has found a job
3 He is worried about finding another job
4 Although he is eighteen years old,

A he has never been to another country.
B when he comes back from his travels.
C but he has just finished school.
D but hasn't got any money.
E which starts very soon.

1 ☐   2 ☐   3 ☐   4 ☐

5

Bei dieser *matching* Aufgabe musst du Aussagen aus einem Text den jeweiligen Personen zuordnen.

TIPP: Versuche, Grundhaltungen oder Einstellungen der Personen im Text zu verstehen, denn hier geht es nicht um Einzelinformationen.

HINWEIS: Dieses Aufgabenformat kann dir auch bei *Listening* begegnen.

b) Which blogger is saying what? Tick (✔) the right box.

	angel07	sis5	suzi6	pink22
1 This person thinks it wouldn't be easy for traveller761 to find a job when he is older.	■	■	■	■
2 This person gives practical tips on how to survive abroad.	■	■	■	■
3 This person wouldn't go abroad and thinks traveller761 is too young to do that.	■	■	■	■
4 This person thinks that you need some money to travel.	■	■	■	■
5 This person thinks traveller761 should work first and travel when he has earned enough money.	■	■	■	■
6 This person did some volunteer work abroad and found it very helpful.	■	■	■	■

Beim Aufgabenformat *answering questions* musst du Fragen beantworten, indem du passende Informationen aus einem Text herausarbeitest. Dabei musst du die Antwort selbst formulieren und an die Fragestellung anpassen.

TIPP: Lies die Fragen gründlich. Manchmal kannst du Formulierungen aus der Frage für deine Antwort umwandeln. Bedenke auch, aus welcher Sicht im Text berichtet/erzählt wird. Prüfe, ob du in deiner Antwort die gleiche Perspektive einnehmen musst.

c) Read what traveller761 wrote on his blog a few weeks later. Then answer the questions below with the help of the text.

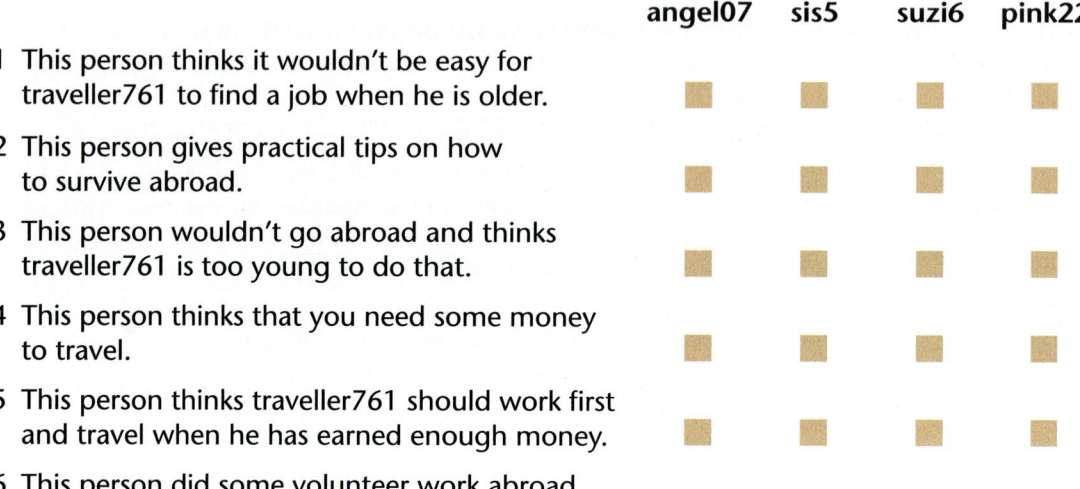

traveller761

Thank you all for your advice and information. It helped a lot when I couldn't decide whether I wanted to work or to travel and I've made up my mind now.

I actually started my new job a week ago. It's working as a cook in a restaurant – with training on the job and regular pay. I thought about what some of you'd said – times are hard and getting a job like this is too good a chance to miss. That's why I took the job in the end. I like the work, the money is not bad and I can save up for travelling later. I haven't quite given up my dream yet ... to be a cook on a big cruise ship or work in a restaurant on the other side of the world one day, perhaps ...

1 What are traveller761's reasons for taking the job?

2 What tells you that he has not given up his dream of travelling?

WRITING

 **A form** 🖉

Bei diesem Aufgabenformat musst du ein Formular/einen Fragebogen ausfüllen.

TIPP: Beachte, dass du keine vollständigen Sätze schreiben darfst/solltest.

You have travelled from Berlin to London to go on an English course.
When you arrive at Heathrow Airport, they have lost your luggage.
Now you have to fill in this form to get it back.
Give the information asked for. You don't need to write complete sentences.

How to ...
write

first name:	surname:
sex:	nationality:
home address (including country):	
age:	airport of departure:
final destination:	length of stay in Britain:
contact telephone number in Britain (mobile or landline):	
type of accommodation in Britain:	purpose of trip:
content of luggage (2 things):	description of luggage (2 details):
estimated value of luggage and contents (in €):	signature:

w2 A letter

Bei diesem Aufgabenformat musst du einen Brief verfassen.

TIPP: Falls ein Ausgangsbrief zugrunde liegt, nimm auf ihn Bezug. Achte darauf, dass du auf die gestellten Fragen eingehst. Vergiss nicht, deinen Brief angemessen zu eröffnen und zu beenden.

HINWEIS: Erkundige dich bei deiner Lehrerin/deinem Lehrer, wie viele Wörter du schreiben sollst.

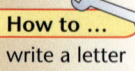
How to ...
write a letter

Read the following two letters. Then choose one of them and answer it.

3rd June 2010

Dear ...,

Sorry I haven't written to you for ages but I'm having real problems with my parents at the moment. They think I spend too much time online and don't work hard enough for school. So they only let me use the computer for half an hour a day. They have also banned me from using Facebook because they think it's too dangerous.

Do you have similar problems with your parents? Have you got any ideas what I could do? How can I explain to them how important Facebook and my computer are to me?

Please write back soon.

Yours,
Matthew

16th May 2010

Dear ...,

I'm having a bad time at the moment and I need help. I've got this new boyfriend. He is great. I think I really love him. But my parents hate him! They think he is bad for me, just because he isn't very good at school and plays in a band. They've also heard that he drinks a lot. That is not even true! My mother doesn't want me to go out with him. She told me that I am not allowed to see him anymore.

So what should I do? I can't really lie to my parents but I also don't want to stop seeing him. Any ideas? Have you ever had a problem like this? Please help me.

Lots of love,
Rachel

w3 An email

Bei diesem Aufgabenformat musst du eine E-Mail schreiben, in der du Informationen gibst oder erfragst.

TIPP: Schweife nicht ab. Achte auf den Empfänger deines Schreibens, damit du den richtigen Ton triffst.

HINWEIS: Erkundige dich bei deiner Lehrerin/deinem Lehrer, wie viele Wörter du schreiben sollst.

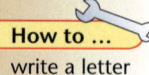
How to ...
write a letter

Three weeks ago you ordered a CD of your favourite band/singer online. You have paid for the CD but you still haven't received it. Write an email in which you

- explain your problem
- want to know why they haven't sent you the CD yet
- give them a final date for sending you the CD
- ask for your money back if they can't deliver

5

w4 A flyer or a poster

Bei diesem Aufgabenformat musst du den Text für ein Poster/einen Flyer/einen Aushang schreiben.

TIPP: Überprüfe, ob alle geforderten Informationen enthalten sind. Sie müssen klar und präzise formuliert sein.

HINWEIS: Für bestimmte Informationen (z.B. Orts- und Zeitangaben) sind manchmal vollständige Sätze nicht notwendig.

a) **You are on an exchange visit at an English school and have lost your mobile phone there. Write the text for a flyer/poster/notice that you can put on the information board.**

How to ...
write

On the flyer/poster/notice you should say

- what it is about
- where and when you think you lost the mobile
- what kind of mobile it is/what it looks like
- your contact details
- if there is any reward for the person who gets it back to you

Ask everybody to help you find it.

b) **As part of an English project you are organising a film evening about teenage relationships. Write a text for a poster for the event. Say**

- which film(s) you are going to show
- when and where it is going to be
- who can come
- what people should bring

w5 Creative writing

Bei diesem Aufgabenformat sollst du einen Text zu einem vorgegebenen Thema/einer vorgegebenen Situation verfassen.

TIPP: Finde zunächst heraus, welche Textsorte gefordert ist (*report, article, ...*). Überlege vor Beginn genau, wie du deinen Text aufbauen musst. Welche Argumente oder Beispiele möchtest du anführen?

HINWEIS: Bei manchen Textsorten kannst du eigene Ideen und deine Fantasie mit einbringen.
Erkundige dich bei deiner Lehrerin/deinem Lehrer, wie viele Wörter du schreiben sollst.

Choose <u>one</u> topic, mark it and write a text.

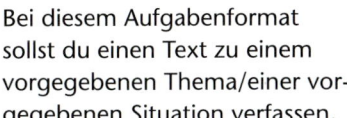
How to ...
write

1 The world of work – Write about a work experience or an after-school job that you have done. Talk about what you did, the things you learned and what you liked/didn't like about this experience.

2 The perfect wedding – How do you imagine 'The perfect wedding'? Write a personal article for the magazine 'Teenage Bride'.

3 Home attractions – Your home town wants to attract more foreign tourists. You were asked to help with the English website. Write a text for this website. Describe the attractions of your home town, things to do and other things that might interest foreign tourists (food, nightlife, etc.).

w6 **Discussing statements**

Bei diesem Aufgabenformat musst du deine Meinung zum vorgegebenen Thema schriftlich äußern.

TIPP: Begründe deine Position stets. Nutze dazu auch Beispiele aus deiner eigenen Erfahrung. Achte darauf, dass du nicht vom Thema abschweifst.

HINWEIS: Erkundige dich bei deiner Lehrerin/deinem Lehrer, wie viele Wörter du schreiben sollst. Dieses Aufgabenformat kann dir auch bei *Speaking* begegnen.

How to ...
write your opinion

Choose <u>one</u> of the following statements and write down your opinion. Give reasons for your opinion using examples where possible.

1 Parents shouldn't worry about social networking sites because these sites are an important part of teenage communication.

2 It is best for young people to take time out after school and travel to see the world.

3 There should be a compulsory volunteer or social year for every teenager after finishing school.

4 Life for teenagers today is much easier than it was thirty years ago.

5 In our modern world you can't survive without a computer and a mobile phone.

6 It is best to have children early in life because then you are fit and active enough for them.

MEDIATION

MD1 **Choosing a present**

How to ...
help out in English

Bei diesem Aufgabenformat musst du die wichtigsten Informationen aus einem deutschen Text ins Englische übertragen.

TIPP: Denke daran, dass du den Text nicht übersetzen sollst. Du musst also nicht jedes einzelne Wort ins Englische übertragen, sondern nur die Schlüsselinformationen. Sollte dir ein wichtiges Wort nicht einfallen, versuche, es zu umschreiben bzw. ein ähnliches Wort zu finden.

HINWEIS: Dieses Aufgabenformat kann dir in umgekehrter Form begegnen, d.h. du überträgst dann Informationen vom Englischen ins Deutsche.

Hi everybody out there,
I need a bit of help. It's my father's birthday soon and I would like to get him a nice surprise present. He has just bought a Wii box, so I think a game would be great. But it's my father! He doesn't like violent or aggressive games, he is more into sports, music and film. And, of course, it would be great if we could play together as a family. I don't know much about these games, so could you give me any tips?
Thanks for your help,
Annie

5

You have read Annie's message in a chat room and have found these two games. Choose <u>one</u> of them and write an answer to her in English. Tell her what kind of game it is and why you think it would be a good present for her father.

Family Party Winter Fun

bringt die ganze Familie an die Wii. Es bietet einen unterhaltsamen Mix aus verschiedenen traditionellen Wintersportarten und winterlichen Aktivitäten. Mit Sicherheit ist für jedes Familienmitglied etwas dabei. Bei über dreißig verschiedenen Minispielen wie Skifahren, Snowboarden, Hundeschlittenrennen, Schneeballschlachten, Eislaufen usw. kann keine Langeweile aufkommen. Family Party Winter Fun erlaubt das gleichzeitige Agieren mehrerer Spieler und ist für alle Altersgruppen geeignet.

The Beatles – Rock Band

ist ein Spiel, das sicherlich nicht nur für Beatles Fans viele unterhaltsame Stunden bietet. Schlüpft in die Rolle eines Mitgliedes der größten Band aller Zeiten, singt die berühmten Songs an bis zu drei Mikrofonen mit, spielt verschiedene Musikinstrumente wie Gitarren oder Schlagzeug. Unterschiedliche Schwierigkeitsgrade erlauben auch Anfängern große Erfolge. Entscheidet ihr euch für den Storymodus, erlebt ihr die Geschichte der Beatles von den Anfängen bis zu ihren größten Erfolgen mit. Ein Spiel mit tollen Features, liebevoll gemachten Animationen und großartigen Songs für alle Musikfans.

 **An advert**

Siehe MD1

You are in London with your parents. In a mobile phone shop you see this advert. Your parents are quite interested. Tell them what this advert is about and give them the most important information in German.

How to …
help out in English

No more high mobile phone bills when you are on holiday!

Get our prepaid global phone card now for just £9.99!

Call from anywhere in the world for just 10p a minute.

Buy today and get an extra £5 on your calling account for free.

For more information come into our shop and ask.

MD3 In a tourist information office

Bei diesem Aufgabenformat musst du Schlüsselinformationen in die jeweils andere Sprache übertragen. Dies kann mündlich oder schriftlich erfolgen.

TIPP: Auch hier geht es nur um die wichtigsten Informationen und nicht um die Übersetzung einzelner Wörter.

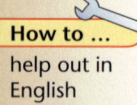

How to ...
help out in English

You are on holiday in Cape Town. In a tourist information office you notice an elderly German couple. They need some information and have problems with English. You offer to help them.
Put the most important information for them into English/German.

German couple: Wir würden gern zum Table Mountain und brauchen ein paar Informationen.

You: ~~~~~~

Tourist office clerk: There is the Table Mountain Aerial Cableway. This is the best way to get a good view. You can see the whole of Cape Town.

You: ~~~~~~

German couple: Was für eine Seilbahn ist denn das?

You: ~~~~~~

Tourist office clerk: These cable cars have huge windows and the floor rotates so that visitors get the full 360 degree view of the fantastic scenery.

You: ~~~~~~

German couple: Das hört sich toll an. Dauert die Fahrt denn lange?

You: ~~~~~~

Tourist office clerk: It takes less than ten minutes to the top of Table Mountain.

You: ~~~~~~

German couple: Hm. Das ist bestimmt teuer. Wie viel kostet denn die Fahrt mit der Seilbahn?

You: ~~~~~~

Tourist office clerk: The return ticket is 160 rand for adults and 80 rand for children. But if you go after 6pm, the tickets are half-price.

You: ~~~~~~

German couple: Das geht ja. Dann werden wir wohl heute Abend fahren. Vielen Dank für die Hilfe!

You (to the tourist office clerk): Thank you!

Tourist office clerk: Oh, by the way, tell them they should take a jacket. It might be hot down here but up there it can get cool.

You: ~~~~~~

German couple: Thank you!

SPEAKING

 **People**

Bei diesem Aufgabenformat sollst du Bilder beschreiben bzw. interpretieren.

TIPP: Bei deiner Beschreibung solltest du auf die Situation, die Atmosphäre und die abgebildeten Personen eingehen. Verwende die Verben im *present progressive (is/are playing, …)*, wenn du beschreibst, was Menschen auf den Bildern tun. Kennzeichne dabei sprachlich genau, ob du Tatsachen oder nur Vermutungen äußerst.

Choose <u>one</u> of the pictures and describe it. Then talk about it.

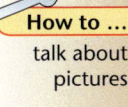

How to …
talk about
pictures

5

s2 Planning a holiday 👄

Bei diesem Aufgabenformat musst du dich gemeinsam mit einem Partner auf eine Auswahl einigen. Dabei ist es möglich, dass ihr euch über eine oder mehrere Sachen verständigen müsst.

TIPP: Du machst hier Vorschläge und begründest diese. Auf Vorschläge deines Partners gehst du ein, lehnst diese ab oder stimmst ihnen zu.

HINWEIS: Nutze so viele der vorgegebenen Hilfen wie möglich.

How to ...
discuss

You and a friend are planning to go on holiday.
Look at the pictures and discuss with a partner what you would like to take. In the end you have to decide on a maximum of <u>five</u> items.

Useful phrases:

What about ...?
What do you think of ...?
Let's take a ...
I think a ... would be a great idea because ...
Shouldn't we take a ...?
We mustn't forget to take a ...
In my opinion, we need a ...

Good idea, but ...
I'm not sure. I think it's better to take a ...
I agree with you ...
I don't think this is such a good idea.
I can see your point, but ...
I don't agree with you. We really don't need a ...
You're right. That's a brilliant idea.

S3 Film talk

Bei diesem Aufgabenformat sollst du gemeinsam mit einem Partner ein Gespräch nach Vorgaben führen.

TIPP: Höre deinem Partner genau zu und gehe auf seine Gesprächsbeiträge ein. Eure Fragen, Antworten und Reaktionen müssen zueinander passen. Achte darauf, dass du sprachlich genauso aktiv bist wie dein Partner.

Two friends are talking about a film. Act out their conversation.

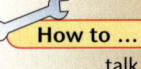

How to …
talk

Partner A	Partner B
1 Ask your partner what he/she did at the weekend.	2 Say that you watched a film on TV/at the cinema.
3 Ask what film it was.	4 Tell your partner which film it was.
5 Find out what the film was about.	6 Tell your partner more about it. Ask if he/she has seen/heard about it.
7 Answer your partner. Ask if he/she liked the film.	8 Answer honestly.
9 Find out why he/she liked/didn't like the film.	10 React to your partner's question. Suggest a cinema visit together.
11 React to your partner's suggestion.	12 See what your partner thinks and react.

S4 Looking for a youth hostel

Bei diesem Aufgabenformat sollst du in einem Gespräch mit einem Partner Informationen austauschen (geben bzw. erfragen).

TIPP: Lies dir deine Rollenkarte genau durch und beachte, dass du den dort verwendeten Wortschatz auch im Gespräch nutzen kannst.

Work in pairs. Look at the role cards and decide on a role. Act out the dialogue.

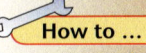

How to …
talk

Partner A	Partner B
You work in a tourist information office in Cape Town and have the following information:	You are in the tourist information office in Cape Town and need to find a youth hostel for tonight.
Cape Town Backpackers Youth Hostel 81 New Church Street double rooms, twin rooms and dorms (12 people) prices start at 100 rand/night free Internet access kitchen facilities friendly atmosphere close to sights, restaurants, shops maximum stay 14 nights	Find out: • the name of the hostel • the address of the hostel • what kind of rooms they have • about other facilities there • about prices • other things you need to know

LANGUAGE

In einigen Bundesländern werden in den Abschlussprüfungen auch deine Kompetenzen in den Bereichen Wortschatz und Grammatik getestet. Informiere dich rechtzeitig bei deiner Lehrerin/deinem Lehrer, ob solche Aufgaben Bestandteil der Prüfung in deinem Bundesland sind.

LG1 About 'Juno'

Bei diesem Aufgabenformat musst du Lücken in einem Text füllen. Für jede Lücke werden dir vier Möglichkeiten vorgeschlagen, von denen nur eine richtig ist. Diese Aufgabe prüft deine Wortschatz- und Grammatikkenntnisse.

TIPP: Um die richtige Wahl zu treffen, musst du viele verschiedene Dinge gleichzeitig prüfen, z.B. Wortart, Verbform, Schreibweise und Verben mit festen Präpositionen.

Read the text. Some words or expressions are missing. Mark them in the chart below.

'Juno' is a film about a teenage girl who (1) pregnant and knows she doesn't want to keep the baby. Juno's parents are shocked when she (2) them at first but then they support (3) daughter and her decision with a lot of warmth and understanding. She decides to give her baby up for adoption and starts looking (4) a nice family. She finds Vanessa and Mark, (5) seem to be a nice couple. During her pregnancy Juno begins to form a (6) friendship with Mark (7) they are both interested in horror films and punk music.

1	is getting	gets	was	get
2	speaks	talks	tells	says
3	there	her	they're	their
4	up	after	for	at
5	who	which	whose	they
6	near	close	nearly	best
7	because	when	then	although

LG2 Teenage pregnancy

Bei diesem Aufgabenformat musst du einen Satz sprachlich umformulieren, ohne dessen inhaltliche Aussage zu verändern.

TIPP: Oft kannst du den Satz umformulieren, indem du Gegenteile oder verwandte Wörter verwendest.

Read the sentences. Then complete the second sentence of each pair so that it means the same as the first.

1 The teenage pregnancy rate in Britain is higher than in any other country in Western Europe. – Britain has the ~~~~~~~~~~~~~~~~~~~~~~

2 For teenage mothers it is difficult to get a job. – Getting a job is not ~~~~~~~~~~~~~

3 You have to decide for yourself. – You should make ~~~~~~~~~~~~~~~~~~~

MOCK EXAM

Dieses Theme zeigt dir, wie deine Abschlussprüfung aussehen könnte. Die Inhalte der Texte und Aufgaben beziehen sich auf Themen, die dir aus den vorangegangenen Themes des Buches bekannt sind. Die Aufgabenformate dienen der Überprüfung deiner Kompetenzen in den Bereichen *Listening, Reading, Writing, Mediation* und *Speaking*. Solltest du in bestimmten Bereichen oder mit bestimmten Aufgabenformaten Schwierigkeiten haben, kannst du an den entsprechenden Beispielen in Theme 5 noch einmal üben.

Viel Erfolg!

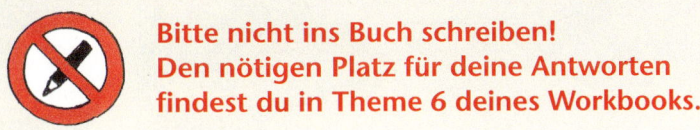

**Bitte nicht ins Buch schreiben!
Den nötigen Platz für deine Antworten
findest du in Theme 6 deines Workbooks.**

LISTENING

 **Short dialogues**

CD

You will hear four short dialogues. There is <u>one</u> question for each dialogue. Decide which picture is the right answer to the question.

a) At what time is their flight tomorrow?

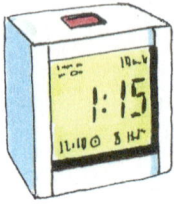         

■   ■   ■   ■

b) What is Katie doing in the summer holidays?

■   ■   ■   ■

c) What is Tom's job?

■   ■   ■   ■

d) How are they going to get to Paris?

■   ■   ■   ■

L2 Going on safari

You will hear a Kruger National Park tour guide talking about a safari the next day. Complete the notes with the missing information.

> **Kruger National Park Safari**
>
> Be at the meeting point at ～～～～～～～ . Each car will take ～～～～～～～ people.
>
> Take ～～～～～～～ for protection.
>
> You can get free ～～～～～～～ from the drivers.
>
> You might see animals like ～～～～～～～ and ～～～～～～～
>
> At the rest camp you can buy ～～～～～～～
>
> Don't forget your ～～～～～～～ . You will be back at ～～～～～～～

L3 A weather warning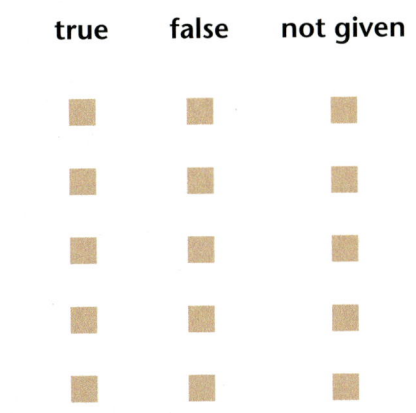

Listen to a weather warning. Then solve the following tasks.

a) Underline the right ending of the sentence.

1 This weather warning was broadcast
early in the morning.
around lunchtime.
in the evening.
in the afternoon.

2 The Bristol area and the West of England
had very windy weather and a lot of rain.
were flooded by a river.
have no transport because of a strike.
have problems because of a train accident.

b) Decide whether the following statements are true, false or not given. Tick (✔) the right box.

	true	false	not given
1 The weather in this area is changing and will get better in the next 12 hours.	☐	☐	☐
2 At the moment you can't go from Bristol to London by train.	☐	☐	☐
3 There are no flights from Bristol Airport at the moment.	☐	☐	☐
4 Many roads are under water so you should try not to drive.	☐	☐	☐
5 Most schools in the area will stay closed tomorrow.	☐	☐	☐

c) Listen again and complete the sentences with the right information.

1 School has finished early today and pupils should ～～～～～～～

2 You can get more weather information ～～～～～～～

L4 A radio interview on child labour

**You will hear a radio programme with an interview about child labour.
Listen carefully and underline the right ending of the sentence.**

1 Liam and Bernie are from
  the Netherlands.
  Ireland.
  Denmark.
  England.

2 Bernie got interested in the 'Stop Child Labour' campaign because
  she worked for UNICEF.
  her uncle talked to her about the problem.
  she did a web project at school.
  she saw a TV programme about it.

3 Liam was
  not really interested in the topic at first.
  told about child labour in his football team.
  trying to get Bernie interested in the problem.
  a UNICEF volunteer in Pakistan.

4 Liam's new football
  was really expensive.
  cost over €30.
  was a present from Bernie.
  was probably made by children in Pakistan.

5 As a normal consumer you
  don't have the power to end child labour.
  should try not to buy products made by children.
  should not buy any imported products.
  can't get enough information.

6 On the website of the campaign you can
  get free toys.
  buy fair trade chocolate.
  find out about typical child labour products.
  chat to others about the problem.

7 Liam says that teenagers should
  stop eating chocolate.
  inform other people about child labour.
  buy more expensive things.
  give money to children in poor countries.

8 Liam and Bernie think that
  all children should have the right and the time to go to school.
  it's wrong for children to have after-school jobs.
  more children in Western Europe should work after school.
  most children have problems with full-time education.

READING

 R1 **Signs and notices**

Look at the sign or notice in each task. Tick (✔) the statement that matches the correct meaning.

A Please switch off all mobile devices or gadgets before you enter the hospital rooms. They disturb our sensitive equipment and put lives in danger. Thank you!

Sensitive electronic gadgets don't work in there. ☐
It's dangerous to enter these rooms. ☐
You must turn off your mobile or MP3 player before you go in. ☐
You shouldn't disturb anybody in the hospital rooms. ☐

B Friday night's 7pm English conversation course is cancelled due to illness.
Please contact Michelle (017263516) for new date and time.
Call evenings only.

The English course won't take place on Friday night. ☐
You must call Michelle when you are ill and can't go. ☐
You can call Michelle at any time. ☐
The new time for the course is 7pm. ☐

C Sweaters from sweatshops? No, thank you!
Find out more about how to fight child labour worldwide. Get active and come to our information evening. Friday, 6pm, library.
Please register with Marc if you want to join as we only have 30 seats.

If you want to buy new sweaters, you should go there. ☐
This is an invitation for an information evening about the new library. ☐
If you want to go to this, you should tell Marc first. ☐
You should bring your own chair because they have only 30 seats. ☐

D For sale: Over 50 computer games in perfect condition. Almost new!
Mail me for list of titles and details. Prices start at $1.99 each. Get four for the price of three.
Mail to: winner@net.com

Somebody wants to buy computer games. ☐
If you buy four games, you can get them cheaper. ☐
If you want a list of the games, you must pay $1.99. ☐
This is an advert for a computer game evening. ☐

R2 Some crazy Facebook stories

Read the texts.

1 Colin Gunn, one of Britain's most dangerous gangsters, has been using Facebook to threaten his enemies from a high-security prison. From prison he was able to contact his over 560 'Facebook friends' freely whenever he wanted. Although serving a 35-year prison sentence, it is thought that he was still running a crime and drug empire from his cell with the help of Facebook. Gunn was allowed to open a Facebook account two months ago. The authorities have now closed it.

2 A family from Missouri was more than surprised when they found out that their picture ended up on a big poster advert for a supermarket in the Czech Republic. Mrs Smith had posted a photo, which showed her, her husband and her two children, on several social networking sites. Some weeks later a college friend of hers was driving through Prague and couldn't believe it when she saw the Smith family smiling from giant poster adverts of a supermarket. The store management said they had found the photo on the Web and thought it had been computer generated. They apologized to the Smiths and took the posters down.

3 Craig Lynch, 28, who escaped from Hollesley Bay Prison, Suffolk, in September, was arrested by the Metropolitan Police in Kent yesterday with the help of Facebook.
Lynch, who has to spend seven years in prison for burglary, had set up a fan page on the social networking site after his successful escape, where he was posting comments and reports about his life on the run. More than 40,000 people all around the world were following his escape before his profile on Facebook was closed down. In the end his comments and up-dates on the networking site helped the police to find and arrest him.

4 Emma B., a 35-year-old woman from Lancashire, England, was shocked to find out about the end of her marriage on Facebook. Her husband Neil had posted a message on the social networking site which read: "Neil has ended his marriage to Emma." The woman said she had had no idea that her six-year marriage was over. She only found out when her friend from Denmark, who had read the message on Facebook, phoned her and wanted to check if she was all right.

a) Match the texts with the headlines. Fill in the number of the text. There are more headlines than you need.

Headline	Number of text
Caught by Facebook	
A modern end to a relationship	
How to become an advert star without knowing	
Find the right partner through Facebook	
Organised crime with the help of Facebook	
Facebook helps to escape	

b) Decide whether the following statements are true, false or not given. Tick (✔) the right box.

	true	false	not given
1 Colin Gunn used his Facebook account for more than a year.	▢	▢	▢
2 Mrs Smith found out about their photo from a friend who saw it.	▢	▢	▢
3 You can still see the Smith's poster in Prague.	▢	▢	▢
4 Over 40,000 people helped the police to catch Craig Lynch.	▢	▢	▢
5 Craig Lynch got an extra six months in prison when he was caught.	▢	▢	▢
6 Emma B. was very surprised by her husband's message.	▢	▢	▢
7 Emma and Neil had been married for almost a year.	▢	▢	▢

 ## Harry Potter star enters world of fashion

Read the text.

"Rather than give cash to charities you can help people in poorer countries by buying the clothes they make," says 19-year-old Harry Potter star Emma Watson (Potter fans know her as Hermione), who's
5 helping to create a new fair trade clothing range.

Between studying English literature at an American university and filming the last Harry Potter film Emma Watson found the time to work as a designer for the ethical clothing brand People Tree. The aim was to
10 create fashion for teenagers – clothes that are cool but also produced in an ethical and environmentally friendly way. Emma not only helped to design the clothes, she and some of her friends also modelled for the new collection.

15 Emma Watson and People Tree have created a collection of clothes that is cool, clean and easy to wear. There are jersey T-shirts, dresses, skirts, and trousers for both men and women. Handmade products, recycled sweetie paper jewellery, banana
20 fibre beanies and scarves are also part of the collection.

Not only does the collection use 100% organic and fair trade cotton, but every single item is made by hand, using traditional techniques, by fair trade groups. Of course, the people who work for the 25 clothing range get paid fairly and need this money to keep their families alive. This way People Tree helps to create a chance for some of the most disadvantaged people in India, Bangladesh and Nepal. 30

Emma Watson says, "It's important to distinguish between fast fashion, which is made very quickly for a very small price, and fair trade fashion. So if you buy a T-shirt for £2, you just have to do the maths and work out how much the person who 35 made it is being paid." She hopes that more companies will follow People Tree's example and that more and more people will start thinking about environmental and humanitarian problems before they buy things. 40

a) Underline the right statement.

This text is about   Emma Watson making the last Harry Potter film.
a new ethical fashion collection designed by Emma Watson.
giving money to people in poor countries.
Emma Watson's life as a model.

b) Copy words or phrases from the text that tell you ...

1 what Emma does when she isn't working for People Tree.

2 what the clothes of the new People Tree collection are like.

3 what kind of clothes are part of the collection.

4 how the clothes are made.

c) Match the correct sentence parts. Be careful: There is one more ending than you need.

1 Emma thinks that buying things that people in poorer countries make

2 People Tree wanted to create clothes that are cool and trendy

3 Emma helped to design the clothes

4 The people who make the clothes

5 People should think about the environment and workers in other countries

A and modelled for the collection, too.

B get paid fairly for their work.

C can be better than giving money to them.

D and helps to create a chance for people in poorer countries.

E but also ethically made.

F before they buy clothes.

1 ☐   2 ☐   3 ☐   4 ☐   5 ☐

R4 South Africa's history through film

Read the text.

In 2009 Clint Eastwood, a famous American actor and director, decided to make a film based on Nelson Mandela's life before and during the Rugby World Cup in 1995, which took place in South Africa. The
5 film is autobiographical and stars Morgan Freeman as the South African president Nelson Mandela and Matt Damon as François Pienaar, the South African team captain.

Shortly after Mandela became president in 1994,
10 he went to a rugby match, in which South Africa's national rugby team, the Springboks, was playing. When blacks in the stadium started protesting against their home team, because almost all the players were white, Mandela realised once more
15 that it would take a lot of time and work before South Africa could find itself as a united nation after decades of apartheid. He gets together with the captain of South Africa's rugby team, François Pienaar, to help unite their country.

20 Both of them hope they can bring people together through the universal language of sport. Mandela believes that if he can get black and white South Africans to support the Springboks as their national rugby team in the World Cup, it would help the country to overcome its past and grow together. The 25 film shows how things slowly begin to change and how the Springboks in the end surprise everybody by making it to the final in the rugby championship. In the final they meet the 'All Blacks', New Zealand's team and probably one of the most famous rugby 30 teams in the world.

'Invictus' might sound strange as a title for a film like this, but the title is closely connected with Mandela's life. The word comes from Latin and means 'undefeated' or 'unconquered'. During his 35 years in prison on Robben Island, 'Invictus' by William Ernest Henley became Nelson Mandela's favourite poem. Its words gave him strength and helped him to "stand when all he wanted to do was lie down". 40

Tick (✔) the correct statement.

1 'Invictus' is a film about
    Nelson Mandela's life in prison.
    protests in South Africa.
    Nelson Mandela and the Rugby World Cup in 1995.
    how rugby became a popular sport in South Africa.

2 François Pienaar was
    an American actor and director.
    the president of South Africa before Nelson Mandela.
    the organizer of the Rugby World Cup in 1995.
    the captain of the South African rugby team.

3 The Springboks are a South African rugby team
    that didn't have many black players in 1994.
    that was only supported by black people.
    that was formed in 1994.
    without a team captain.

4 Mandela believed that
    a sport like rugby could help to bring black and white people together.
    he could never get black and white people to support the Springboks.
    South Africa could never be a united nation after decades of apartheid.
    the Springboks would win the World Cup.

5 In the end the Springboks
    won the final with only black players.
    played against the 'All Blacks' in the final.
    played well but didn't make it to the World Cup final.
    lost the rugby championship.

6 The title of the film 'Invictus'
    is the title of a poem that was very important to Mandela.
    comes from an old Afrikaans word.
    is a rugby word and has nothing to do with Mandela's life.
    is the name of the prison on Robben Island.

WRITING

 W1 Working as an au pair

You would like to work as an au pair in an English-speaking country. Fill in this form with your personal information:

Name: _____ Sex: _____

Nationality: _____ Country you would like to work in: _____

Date you would
like to start working: _____

What age range would you
like to au pair for? _____

What childcare experience have you had? _____

What would you be willing to do to help with the housework? _____

What are your hobbies? _____

6

A 'German evening'

You are on an exchange visit at an English school and want to organise a 'German evening' with films and/or music. Write the text for a poster/flyer for the evening in English.

Don't forget the following information:

- When is it (date and time)?
- Where is it (place)?
- What music and/or films are you going to play?
- Who can come?
- What should people bring?

w3 **Spending a year abroad**

You want to spend a year abroad after finishing school.

Choose <u>one</u> of the following adverts and write an email to apply for the job.

Don't forget to write why you would be a good candidate/why you would like to do the job, what experience you have and when you could start work.

We are looking for a German-speaking au pair.

We live in the English countryside, one hour's drive from London. Our children are four and seven years old. You should be responsible and tidy and have some experience with children. You will take the children to school, look after them in the afternoons and do a little housework like shopping or cooking. Free food and accommodation, an English course and pocket money are part of this offer.

Apply to Mr and Mrs Sheen
26 Church Street
Cambridge CB23 2SG
England

Help in busy youth hostel needed.

Are you able to speak English and one other European language? Can you work with a computer? Do you enjoy talking to people? Then you are perfect for us. Enjoy some time in Sydney, Australia and earn money at the same time. Applications to Glebe Village Backpackers, Fred Simmonds, 256 Glebe Point Road, Glebe NSW 2037, Australia or Fred@GlebeBackpackers.com

---

Are you good at working with your hands and don't mind a little dirt?

Do you like animals and are not afraid of them? Are you interested in working with nature and wildlife? Jersey Zoo on the Channel Island of Jersey (between France and England) needs helpers and animal carers. No experience necessary. We just need your enthusiasm. Write to Jersey Zoo, Ms Kathrin Boons, Les Augrés Manor, La Profonde Rue, Trinity, United Kingdom

---

MEDIATION

 **Notices**

You are at the school club with your English exchange partner. You find the following notices on the noticeboard.

A

Suche einmal wöchentlich Englisch-Nachhilfe.
Brauche vor allem Konversation.
Muttersprachler wäre toll.
Biete Gitarrenunterricht im Austausch
(Bezahlung leider nicht möglich).

Bitte meldet euch bei Sophie: 017634526

B

Zu viel Zeit im Netz?

Ein Freund von mir sitzt bis zu 10 Stunden täglich am Computer und kommt nicht von Jappy und Computerspielen los! Ich mache mir Sorgen und suche Leute, denen es auch so geht und die davon weg wollen. Vielleicht packen wir es gemeinsam!
Meldet euch bei Tommy: 015467324

C

Taschengeld zu knapp?

Suchen Samstagsaushilfe in freundlichem Blumenladen. Nur für Jugendliche 16+.
Bezahlung: 8€/Stunde.
Telefonische Bewerbungen abends unter:
09542678 (Frau Albrecht)

Tell your exchange partner in English what the notices are about.
Write down at least two details for each notice.

 Tips for staying healthy

Your family is planning a trip to South Africa. Your mum has found the following tips on the Internet and wants you to tell her in German what they are about.
Write down the five most important tips in German.

> **Planning a trip to South Africa? Here are some tips for staying healthy.**
>
> Before you travel, check with your doctor which medication (e.g. anti-malaria drugs) or vaccinations (e.g. tetanus) you need.
>
> Many diseases are caused by insect bites. So when you are there make sure
> - you have anti-insect spray and use it.
> - you wear long-sleeved shirts, long trousers and hats outdoors.
> - you stay indoors in the evening and at night.
> - you sleep in beds that are covered with nets or other insect protection if you are not in an air-conditioned room.
>
> Also don't touch or feed any animals and drink only bottled water. You should only eat food that is completely cooked.

SPEAKING

s1 A picture

Choose one of the following pictures and talk about it for at least one minute. Talk about

- the situation
- the atmosphere
- the people:
  – their relationship
  – how they might feel
  – what they might say
  – ...

A

B

C

s2 I couldn't live without it

Gadgets and electrical appliances play an important role in our modern lives. Look at the examples and discuss with a partner which **three** of these things you couldn't live without. Give reasons for your choice.

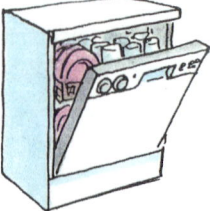
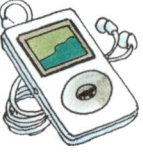

s3 Let's talk about it 👄

Work in pairs. Look at the role cards. Choose situation 1 or 2 and decide on a role. Act out the dialogue.

1 Inviting your boyfriend/girlfriend

Partner A	Partner B
• You have a new boyfriend/girlfriend. • You want to invite him/her home. • Your parents don't know him/her yet. • Tell your mother/father (Partner B) about it. • Ask them if you could invite him/her for dinner. (You start.)	• Your son/daughter (15) has been forgetting about school in the last weeks. • You think he/she might have a new girlfriend/boyfriend who is a bad influence. • You want to find out more. • You think your child is too young for relationships. • You believe this person is bad for him/her. (Partner A starts.)

2 Doing a volunteer programme

Partner A	Partner B
• Your best friend wants to do a volunteer programme in Africa after school. • You are worried about that and think he/she hasn't really thought about it. • Find out why he/she wants to go away. • Talk about possible dangers. (Partner B starts.)	• You are going to finish school soon and you need a break. • You want to see the world and experience new things. • That's why you've decided to do a volunteer programme in Africa for half a year. • Tell your best friend about it and explain your motivation. (You start.)

LANGUAGE

In einigen Bundesländern werden in den Abschlussprüfungen auch deine Kompetenzen in den Bereichen Wortschatz und Grammatik getestet. Hierzu findest du nun eine Aufgabe, wie sie dir dann in der Prüfung begegnen könnte. Informiere dich rechtzeitig bei deiner Lehrerin/deinem Lehrer, ob solche Aufgaben Bestandteil der Prüfung in deinem Bundesland sind.

LG1 What's your network?

Read the text and choose the correct word or expression for each space. Fill in the correct letter in each space.

Many teens today use social networking sites as their main form of communication. Facebook, MySpace and all the others give not only teenagers the chance of (1) ﹏﹏﹏ in touch. Social networking sites are definitely the virtual communities of the 21st century.

One of the most famous and popular communities is Facebook. It was founded (2) ﹏﹏﹏ the Harvard student Mark Zuckerberg in 2004 and in the beginning it was only there to help new Harvard students to get to know (3) ﹏﹏﹏ . Since then the number of registered Facebook users (4) ﹏﹏﹏ to over 30 million people worldwide. That makes Facebook one of the largest social networking sites (5) ﹏﹏﹏ it wasn't the first one. In 2002 Friendster started as the first networking site followed by MySpace in 2003.

Twitter was started in 2006. It is a very popular instant messaging system that lets a (6) ﹏﹏﹏ send short text messages to a list of followers. Twitter has (7) ﹏﹏﹏ users and was designed as a social network to keep friends and colleagues informed every day.
Twitter messages are (8) ﹏﹏﹏ 'tweets' and usually people can send or receive them via mobile phone or the Internet.

	A	B	C	D
1	keep	feeling	keeping	become
2	from	of	by	for
3	them	one another	themselves	yourself
4	grew	was growing	grows	has grown
5	but	and	because	so
6	people	person	somebody	individual
7	most	much	many	any
8	named	formed	known	called

TOOLBOX: HOW TO ... LISTEN

Höre genau hin! – So kannst du mehr verstehen

1 **Before you listen – Bevor du eine Höraufgabe bearbeitest**

- Sieh dir erst einmal die Bilder oder Überschriften an. Überlege: Um was für eine Art Hörtext könnte es sich handeln? Zum Beispiel um einen Bericht, eine Geschichte, ein (Telefon-)Gespräch, eine Radiosendung oder ein Interview.

- Bevor du den Text hörst, lies die Aufgabenstellung genau. Dann weißt du, worauf du beim Hören achten musst. Es gibt verschiedene Möglichkeiten, sich Notizen zu Hörtexten zu machen.

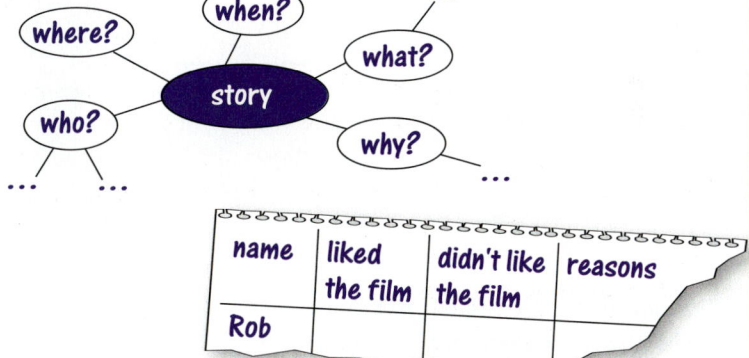

photo	words/ phrases
E	township ...

name	liked the film	didn't like the film	reasons
Rob			

2 **Now listen – Beim Hören**

- Beim ersten Hören musst du <u>nicht</u> unbedingt jedes Wort verstehen. Versuche herauszufinden, worum es in dem Text eigentlich geht:
  - → Was ist die Situation?
  - → Wer spricht mit wem?
  - → Worüber wird gesprochen?

  Die Hintergrundgeräusche und die Stimmen verraten oft viel, z. B.:
  - → Wo findet das Gespräch statt?
  - → Wie fühlt sich die Sprecherin oder der Sprecher (begeistert, aufgeregt, traurig, ...)?

- Beim zweiten Zuhören machst du dir Notizen – schreibe aber nur Stichworte auf. Benutze dabei ein Raster als Hilfe (siehe oben).

3 **Did you get it? – Hast du das Wesentliche verstanden?**

Vergleiche und vervollständige deine Notizen mit einer Partnerin oder einem Partner, bevor du sie in der Klasse vorträgst.

Tipp Tipp:

Practice makes perfect! – Nutze jede Gelegenheit, Englisch zu hören!
- Mit der Camden Market Schüler-CD kannst du zu Hause dein Hörverstehen trainieren.
- Höre dir englische Musik an und achte auf den Text – was kannst du schon verstehen?

TOOLBOX: *HOW TO … TALK ABOUT PICTURES*

Über Bilder sprechen

1 **Describing pictures – Bilder beschreiben**

Um zu beschreiben, was auf einem Bild (Gemälde, Foto, …) zu sehen ist, solltest du es dir genau ansehen. Denke dabei an die *wh*-Fragen: *Who? What? Where? When?*

at the top

in the background

on the left

on the right

in the foreground

in the middle

at the bottom

> The picture shows a couple getting married.
> In the foreground/background there is/are …
> On the left/right I can see …

> In the middle of the picture …
> At the top/bottom …
> In front of / Behind / Next to … there is/are …

Wenn du dich über die Kleidung und das Aussehen einer Person äußern möchtest:

> He/She is wearing …
> He/She is tall/small/ …
> He/She has long/short/dark/ … hair.

Beschreibe, was die abgebildeten Personen oder Tiere tun. Benutze dazu die Verlaufsform der Gegenwart (*present progressive*):

> The person/animal is eating …

2 **Interpreting pictures – Bilder interpretieren**

Auch die Interpretation des Abgebildeten spielt eine große Rolle. Welche Gefühle kannst du von den Gesichtern ablesen? Was verraten Kleidung und Körpersprache? In welcher Situation befinden sich die Personen? Welche Stimmung drückt das Bild aus?

Wenn du Vermutungen anstellen möchtest:

> The person looks (as if he/she is) happy/sad/
>   bored/lonely/ …
> He/she seems to be …   He/She might be …
> I think he/she is thinking/talking about …
> Maybe he/she …   He/She is probably …

Wenn du die Stimmung/Atmosphäre beschreiben möchtest:

> The colours in the picture are dark/light/
>   bright/warm/cold/ …
> The background colour is …
> I think the atmosphere of the picture is
>   positive/sad/ …

TOOLBOX: HOW TO … WATCH

Filme verstehen

1 Before you watch – Bevor du dir einen Film ansiehst

Überlege:
→ Was für eine Art von Film ist es?
→ Worum könnte es in dem Film gehen? Was erwartest du?

> documentary • drama • soap opera • animated film • cartoon • the news
> • sports programme • quiz show • reality show • action film • talk show
> • adventure story • talent show • romance/love story • comedy
> • horror film • science fiction

tip
Casting-Show heißt auf Englisch *talent show*.

2 Look closer – Sieh genau hin

Bei einem Film spielen Kamera-Einstellungen, Licht und natürlich die Schauspieler eine große Rolle. Die Bilder aus einem Film verraten daher viel über die Handlung. Sieh sie dir deshalb genau an:

→ Wer tut was?
→ Was verrät die Kleidung?
→ Welche Gefühle kannst du von den Gesichtern ablesen?
→ Was verrät die Körpersprache?
→ Welche Hinweise gibt dir die Umgebung?
→ Wie würdest du die Stimmung beschreiben?
→ Überlege, worum es in der Szene gehen könnte.

Tipp Tipp:
Practice makes perfect! – Trainiere dein Hörsehverstehen!
• Sieh dir doch mal einen Film, den du schon kennst, auf DVD an. Auf einer DVD kannst du fast immer den englischen Ton (mit oder ohne deutsche Untertitel) einschalten. Du kannst aber auch mit englischsprachigen Podcasts üben.

3 Useful phrases – Nützliche Redewendungen

Wenn du von einem Film erzählen möchtest:

> My favourite film is called …
> The film is about …
> It describes the life of …
> The film tells the story of …
> The story takes place in India/2007/…
> The part of … is played by …
> In some scenes the main character looks back on things that happened in the past.

So sagst du, was du an einem Film magst oder nicht magst:

> I think Ellen Page did a great job playing the role of …
> He/She is an excellent actor/actress.
> The best scene was when …
> I really enjoyed the film. It made me laugh.
> I liked the action scenes but I didn't like the soundtrack. Also, some scenes were very realistic/unrealistic, for example the happy ending.

TOOLBOX: HOW TO … TALK

Rollenspiele

Rollenspiele sind eine gute Methode, um dein Englisch zu trainieren.

1 **Before you do the role-play – Vor dem Rollenspiel**

- Denke dich in die Person hinein, die du spielen wirst. Überlege z. B., in was für einer Stimmung die Person ist.
- Mache dir Notizen mit Wörtern und Ausdrücken, die du benutzen möchtest.

2 **Now act out the scene – Spiele die Szene**

- Schlüpfe in die Rolle und benutze Mimik (Gesichtsausdruck) und Gestik (Bewegungen), um deine Rolle überzeugend zu spielen.
  Achte auch bei deinem Partner auf Mimik, Gestik und Tonfall, damit du angemessen reagieren kannst.
- Wenn dir ein Wort nicht einfällt, umschreibe es.
  Du kannst auch deine Hände zu Hilfe nehmen.
- Frage nach, wenn du etwas nicht verstanden hast.
- Versuche, immer deutlich zu sprechen.

Interviews

In einem Interview möchte man vom Interviewpartner etwas erfahren, das man selbst noch nicht weiß. Beachte folgende Punkte, wenn du ein Interview vorbereitest und durchführst:

1 **Prepare questions – Bereite Fragen vor**

- Überlege, was du erfahren möchtest und wie du deinen Interviewpartner ansprichst.
- Formuliere deine Fragen und notiere sie z. B. auf Karteikarten, dann kannst du sie leicht sortieren.
- Vermeide Ja/Nein-Fragen, denn schließlich möchtest du ja möglichst viel von deinem Gesprächspartner erfahren.

2 **Do the interview – Beim Interview**

Stelle dich höflich vor und sage, warum du das Interview machen möchtest:

> Hello, my name is … and I would like to ask you a few questions about …
> I would like to talk to you about … because … My first question is: …

Reagiere auf die Antworten, z. B.:

> That sounds interesting. Could you tell me more about that, please?
> Well, does that mean …?

Bedanke dich für das Interview:

> Thank you very much for talking to me. /
> Thank you for your time.
> I enjoyed the interview. I hope to see you again.

TOOLBOX: HOW TO … GIVE A TALK

Wenn du etwas vor der Klasse präsentierst

Sicherlich hast du schon häufiger etwas vor der Klasse präsentiert.
Hier findest du noch einmal wichtige Hinweise:

1 **Before you talk – Bevor du etwas präsentierst**

- Überlege dir eine gute Reihenfolge für das, was du vortragen möchtest.
- Fertige ein Poster oder eine Folie an, um deinen Vortrag anschaulich zu machen. Bilder und Schrift müssen so groß sein, dass jeder im Raum sie sehen und lesen kann. Du kannst aber auch eine PowerPoint Präsentation gestalten.
- Überlege dir kleine Aufgaben für deine Zuhörer, damit sie aufmerksam bleiben. Lass sie z. B. mitgebrachte Speisen oder Instrumente ausprobieren.
- Erstelle außerdem ein Arbeitsblatt für deine Klasse, z. B. einen Lückentext oder ein Quiz. Du kannst sie auch bitten, einen Feedback-Bogen zu deinem Vortrag auszufüllen. So erfährst du, was du demnächst noch besser machen kannst.
- Übe deinen Vortrag vor dem Spiegel, vor Freunden oder deiner Familie – oder nimm deinen Vortrag vorher zur Probe auf einem MP3-Player auf.

2 **Now talk – Bei deinem Vortrag**

Denke an die drei **T**s:

Touch: Zeige deinen Zuhörern auf einer Folie oder einem Plakat, worüber du gerade sprichst. So wird dein Vortrag für die Klasse interessanter.

Turn: Sieh deine Zuhörer an, wenn du sprichst. Halte immer Blickkontakt.

Talk: Sprich langsam und deutlich. Versuche, frei zu sprechen. Du kannst die wichtigsten Punkte von deinen Notizen oder deinem Poster ablesen.

3 **Useful phrases – Nützliche Redewendungen**

Diese Sätze kannst du in deinem Kurzvortrag verwenden:

Zu Beginn:
> Good morning. Today I'd like to talk about …
> Hello everybody. My talk is about …

Im Hauptteil:
> The picture shows …
> On my poster you can see …
> It's important …
> Another thing I would like to tell you about is …
> My first/second/next/last point is …

Zum Schluss:
> Finally, I'd like to say …
> Thank you for listening. Have you got any questions?

TOOLBOX: HOW TO ... DISCUSS

Wenn du etwas diskutierst

Diskussionen finden täglich über alle möglichen Themen statt. Oft sind solche Diskussionen spontan und ungeplant. Wenn es um ernsthaftere Themen geht, können dir die folgenden Hinweise nützlich sein.

1 Before you discuss – Bevor du diskutierst

- Sieh dir das Thema der Diskussion genau an.
  Wie stehst du zu dem Thema? Mache dir Gedanken über mögliche Argumente.
- Stichpunkte und *mindmaps* sind eine gute Hilfe, um nichts Wichtiges zu vergessen.
- Denke auch an Argumente, die gegen deine Meinung sprechen. Überlege dir Antworten auf diese Argumente.

2 While you discuss – Während du diskutierst

- Höre genau zu, was die anderen Diskussionsteilnehmer sagen. Stelle sicher, dass du ihre Argumente verstehst.
- Wenn du etwas nicht verstehst, frage höflich nach.
- Äußere deine Meinung. Bleibe dabei immer höflich und freundlich.

Tipp Tipp:
- Bestimmt einen Diskussionsleiter. Er/Sie sollte darauf achten, dass alle Gesprächsteilnehmer zu Wort kommen können, beim Thema bleiben und die vereinbarte Redezeit einhalten.
- Bildet eine neutrale Gruppe, die während der Diskussion Notizen macht und nachher Feedback gibt.

3 Useful phrases – Nützliche Redewendungen

Wenn du eine Meinung äußern möchtest:

> I think …
> I believe …
> In my opinion, …
> I would say …
> I'm sure …

Wenn du eine Meinung begründen möchtest:

> I think so because …
> Let me give you an example: …
> The reason is …
> Well, it's a fact that …

Wenn du jemandem zustimmen möchtest:

> Yes, that's true.
> I think you're right.
> I agree (with you).
> I think so, too.
> That's a good/important point.

Wenn du jemandem widersprechen möchtest:

> I know, but …
> Sorry, I don't agree with you.
> I don't think so.
> I don't think that's true.

Wenn du nachfragen möchtest:

> Could you say that again, please?
> I don't quite understand what you mean.
> Do you mean that …?
> Can you please explain what you mean?

TOOLBOX: *HOW TO … HELP OUT IN ENGLISH*

Tipps und Tricks für die Sprachmittlung

Dein Englisch ist jetzt schon so gut, dass du weiterhelfen kannst,
wenn jemand kein Deutsch oder Englisch versteht.
Der englische Begriff *mediation* bedeutet Sprachmittlung.

1 **Excuse me, …? – Kannst du helfen?**

Du musst nicht Wort für Wort übersetzen.
Es reicht, wenn du den Sinn einer Aussage
oder Information wiedergibst. Das kannst
du auch mit deinen eigenen Worten
machen.

> … of course I'm sometimes nervous when I sing in front of large crowds. But I really love to sing in Chicago!

> Sie sagt, dass sie manchmal aufgeregt ist vor vielen Leuten, aber sie singt gern in Chicago.

2 **In other words – Mit eigenen Worten**

Da du in solchen Situationen oft kein Wörterbuch zur Hand hast, kannst du wichtige
Wörter auch umschreiben.

> "KiBa"? "Apfelschorle"?! What does that mean?

> Also, KiBa ist ein Gemisch aus Kirsch- und Bananennektar. Und für Apfelschorle mischt man Apfelsaft mit Sprudel.

> "KiBa" is cherry and banana juice. And "Apfelschorle" is apple juice with mineral water.

3 **Keep it simple – Je einfacher, desto besser**

Bei der Sprachmittlung solltest du kurze Sätze benutzen. Das ist einfacher für dich und für
denjenigen, den du informieren willst.

> Man kann mit dem Auto die A61 Richtung Süchteln nehmen oder ab Viersen mit der Buslinie 83 und dann der Linie 67 fahren.

> How can you get there?

kletterwald niederrhein

Die Saison startet wieder am 04. April

Im Kletterwald gibt es diverse Hindernisparcours für alle
Altersgruppen und für verschiedene Schwierigkeitsstufen.
Hier ist für jeden etwas dabei.

Öffnungszeiten:
Mo–Mi: nur Gruppen
Do–Fr: 11–18 Uhr
Sa–So: 10–19 Uhr

Preise: 150 Minuten Nutzungsdauer
Kinder (bis 13 J.)   12,00 €
Erwachsene (ab 14 J.)   15,00 €
Familien (2 Erw./1 Ki.)   38,00 €

Informationen:
– Kinder unter sechs Jahren
  dürfen nicht klettern
– Hunde müssen an der Leine
  geführt werden
– bequeme Kleidung (z. B. Jeans)
  und festes Schuhwerk
  (keine Latschen oder Stiefel)
– Sicherheit durch TÜV-Prüfsiegel

Anfahrt:
Auto: A61 Richtung Süchteln
Bus: ab Viersen mit Linie 83,
dann weiter mit Linie 67

> You can get there by car. Or you can take the bus.

TOOLBOX: HOW TO … READ

Lesen leicht gemacht!

Beim Lesen von englischen Texten musst du nicht unbedingt jedes Wort verstehen. Wie viel du tatsächlich von einem Text verstehen solltest, hängt davon ab, was du mit ihm vorhast.

1 Skimming – Verschaffe dir einen Überblick

- Beim *skimming* möchtest du dir nur einen allgemeinen Überblick über den Inhalt des Textes verschaffen. Du streifst ganz leicht die Oberfläche, indem du dir zuerst die Überschrift und die den Text begleitenden Bilder und Bildunterschriften ansiehst. Sie geben dir schon einmal wichtige Hinweise.
- Beim anschließenden Lesen überfliegst du den Text schnell. Du musst nicht jedes Wort verstehen. Achte vielmehr auf die Wörter, die du schon kennst, und konzentriere dich auf die Hauptgedanken.
- Nach dem *skimming* kannst du in ein bis zwei Sätzen sagen, was das Thema des Textes ist.

2 Scanning – Auf der Suche nach bestimmten Informationen

- Beim *scanning* suchst du nach bestimmten Informationen. Dazu liest du den Text langsam mehrere Male und schreibst Schlüsselwörter (*keywords*) heraus zu den Fragen *Who? What? Where? When? Why?* Lies dann die Textstellen um die Schlüsselwörter herum noch einmal und ergänze deine Notizen.
- Wenn du eine Kopie des Textes vorliegen hast, kannst du die dir wichtig erscheinenden Textstellen markieren oder unterstreichen.
- Lass dich nicht durch unbekannte Wörter verunsichern. Versuche vielmehr, ihre Bedeutung aus dem Textzusammenhang zu erschließen. Oft kennst du auch ein deutsches Wort, das gleich oder ganz ähnlich aussieht (z. B. *series*). Oder dir sind einzelne Bestandteile eines englischen Wortes bekannt (z. B. *endangered*).

3 Reading for detail – Finde möglichst viele Einzelheiten

- Beim *reading for detail* liest du ganz genau, denn du möchtest so viele Einzelheiten zum Thema finden wie möglich. Am besten liest du den kompletten Text einmal zügig bis zum Ende und danach Absatz für Absatz mehrere Male.
- Versuche dabei, möglichst viele Einzelheiten zu verstehen und notiere gefundene Details.
- Da es hier um genaues Lesen und Verstehen geht, wirst du an manchen Stellen auch Wörter im Wörterbuch nachschlagen müssen.

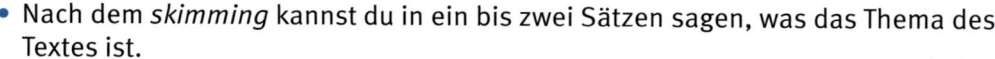

Tipp Tipp:
- In Camden Market begegnen dir unterschiedliche Leseverstehensaufgaben. Damit du zügig ans Ziel kommst, überlege dir gut, was gefragt ist: *skimming, scanning or reading for detail*?
- Je häufiger du englische Texte liest, desto besser wird dein Leseverstehen. Versuche, auch außerhalb der Schule englische Texte zu lesen, die Spaß machen!

TOOLBOX: HOW TO ... WRITE

Schreiben – Schritt für Schritt

1 **Make a draft! – Bevor du anfängst zu schreiben**

Überlege:

tip
Auf den Seiten 110-111 erfährst du, wie man auf Englisch einen Brief und eine Meinungs-äußerung schreiben kann.

- Welche Art von Text willst du schreiben? Zum Beispiel eine (Fantasie-)Geschichte, einen Sachtext, einen Text über dich, ein Gedicht, einen Brief oder eine E-Mail. Für jede Textsorte sind ganz bestimmte Dinge wichtig, z. B.:

  → Eine Geschichte, ein persönlicher Text und eine Meinungsäußerung bestehen aus Einleitung, Hauptteil und Schluss. Denke auch an eine Überschrift.
  → Zu einem Brief gehören Datum (*23rd March*), Anrede (*Dear Cheryl*) und Schluss (*Love, Emma*).
  → In eine E-Mail kannst du Emoticons wie :-) :-(;-) einsetzen.

- Sammle Ideen und Wörter zum Thema. Du kannst eine Liste schreiben, deine Ideen in einer *mindmap* sortieren oder dir Notizen zu *wh*-Fragen machen.

2 **Now write – Beim Schreiben**

Beachte folgende Regeln:

tip
Präge dir die Schritte ein:
1. Draft
2. Write
3. Check
4. Publish

- → Beginne nicht alle Sätze mit dem gleichen Wort.
- → Versuche, Wörter wie *really, normally, often, too, ...* zu benutzen.
- → Verbinde Sätze miteinander. Benutze dafür *and, then, because, but, that's why, ...*
- → Finde Adjektive, um Dinge oder Personen zu beschreiben, z. B. *great, fantastic, scary.* Im *G-E dictionary* ab Seite 224 kannst du Wörter nachschlagen. Auch die *wordbanks* ab Seite 114 liefern dir gutes Wortmaterial.

3 **Check it! – So kannst du Fehler aufspüren und verbessern**

- Hast du alles richtig geschrieben? Lies deinen Text noch einmal und schlage Wörter, bei denen du unsicher bist, im *dictionary* nach.

- Tauscht eure Texte untereinander aus und sprecht darüber,
  → was euch an dem Text gefällt,
  → was noch ergänzt werden könnte,
  → was verbessert werden sollte (siehe Punkt 2).

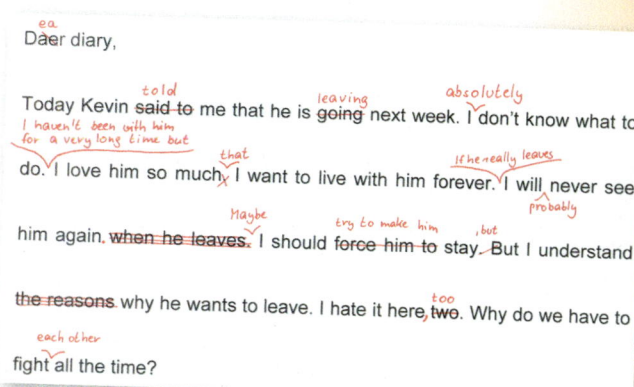

4 **Publish it! – Zeige deinen Text**

Wenn du deinen Text fertig hast, schreibe ihn ins Reine. Du kannst deinen Text präsentieren, indem du ihn z. B. vorliest, aufnimmst, aushängst oder in einem *class book* veröffentlichst. Danach heftest du deinen Text in deiner Portfolio-Mappe ab.

Einen Brief schreiben

 1 A personal letter – Ein persönlicher Brief

> Deine Adresse (ohne deinen Namen) gehört in die rechte obere Ecke.

So kannst du deinen Brief anfangen:
Dear …,
Hi …,

Fange die erste Zeile mit einem Großbuchstaben an.

So kannst du deinen Brief beenden:
Love,
Yours,
Best wishes,

Kranzallee 60
14055 Berlin
Germany

2nd March 2010

> Das Datum folgt unter der Adresse auf der rechten Seite.

Dear Bob,

Thanks a lot for your letter. It was great to hear about your school trip to France. Did you get a chance to go to Paris?

Yesterday I watched a programme about Africa on TV. I'd really like to go there one day to see Cape Town, Robben Island, Table Mountain and lots of other places. The animals there are also fascinating. Did you know that there is an animal called aardvark which looks really funny?

Hope to hear from you soon.

Love,
Ella

> Am Ende deines Briefes kannst du die andere Person bitten, dir zurückzuschreiben.

2 A formal letter – Ein formeller Brief

Schreibe den Namen und die Adresse der Organisation oder der Person auf die linke Seite.

Wenn du den Namen des Empfängers nicht kennst, schreibe Dear Sir or Madam. Kennst du den Namen, so beginne mit Dear Mr/Mrs …,

Sei immer höflich.

Hohenzollernstr. 54
66111 Saarbrücken
Germany

Stephen Roper
Home & Dry B&B
15 Kenilworth Rd
Stirling FK8 1JU

> In der Betreffzeile erklärst du, warum du den Brief schreibst. Fasse dich dabei kurz.

20th January 2010

Application for the position of reception staff

Dear Mr Roper,

I am writing to apply for the position of reception staff. As you will see from my CV, I have been working as a trainee in a large hotel for the last three years. My apprenticeship will be finished in September and I would like to work abroad then.

I am reliable and polite and I like communicating with people.

I am enclosing my CV and the names and addresses of two referees.

I look forward to hearing from you.

Yours sincerely,

Rebecca Mertens

> Beende den Brief mit Yours faithfully (= Mit freundlichen Grüßen/Hochachtungsvoll). Wenn du den Namen des Empfängers jedoch kennst, schreibst du Yours sincerely (= Mit freundlichen/herzlichen Grüßen).

Eine kurze Meinungsäußerung schreiben

In einer Meinungsäußerung nimmst du Stellung zu einem bestimmten Thema oder einem Problem, das in einem Text dargestellt ist. Dabei vergleichst du Vor- und Nachteile und begründest deine Meinung.

1 Before you write – Bevor du anfängst zu schreiben

- Notiere die Ideen, die dir zum Thema einfallen. Eine Tabelle mit *pros and cons* oder *examples and reasons* hilft, deine Ideen zu ordnen.
- Mache dir klar, welche Position oder Meinung du vertrittst. Entscheide dich: Bist du dafür? Bist du dagegen? Wenn du dir nicht sicher bist, zähle Beispiele dafür und dagegen auf und wäge sie mit Begründungen gegeneinander ab.

2 Now write – Beim Schreiben

> So kannst du anfangen:
> Formuliere einen Satz, der das Interesse der Leser weckt und das Thema einleitet.

> Drücke deine Meinung klar aus:
> I think …
> I believe …
> In my opinion, …
> I'm sure …
> Let me give you an
>   example: …

> Wäge deine Argumente gegeneinander ab:
> Some people say … but I think …
> I'm not so sure that …
> On the one hand …,
>   but on the other hand …
> Although …

About 950,000 people visit the Kruger National Park every year. Some people say that it is good to have so many visitors there, others say it is a bad thing. If you ask me, there are a lot of arguments for but also a lot of arguments against visiting Africa's most famous national park.
Firstly, I think it is a good thing that tourism creates jobs in a poor area. Secondly, the people living there realise that they have to protect the environment if they want to attract tourists. Thirdly, visitors learn that African wildlife is very special and has to be protected. So on the one hand it is a fact that visiting the Kruger Park is not only a unique experience, it is also good for the whole area.
But on the other hand most people go to South Africa by plane, which is not very 'green'. They use water, drive around in cars and produce rubbish. Some people say that these negative aspects are more important than the positive ones.
But all in all, I think that there are more important arguments for visiting the Kruger National Park: Tourists, people living there and wildlife – they all benefit from tourism to the Park.

> Bringe deine Ideen in eine gute Reihenfolge:
> Firstly, …
> Secondly, …
> Finally, …

> Begründe deine Meinung:
> I think so because …
> The reason is …
> It's a fact that …

> So kannst du enden:
> That's why I think …
> All in all, I would say …

3 Check it! – Überarbeite deinen Text

- Habe ich in der Einleitung verständlich ausgedrückt, worum es geht?
- Zeigt mein Text klar meine Entscheidung pro oder kontra bzw. mein Bemühen, Argumente gegeneinander abzuwägen?
- Habe ich Beispiele mit Begründungen genannt?
- Habe ich einen Schluss formuliert, der meine Meinung klar zum Ausdruck bringt?
- Stimmen Satzbau, Grammatik und Rechtschreibung?

TOOLBOX: HOW TO … WORK WITH OTHERS

Verschiedene Arbeitsformen

1 **Think – pair – share**

Um sich einem Thema zu nähern, kann man
in drei Schritten vorgehen:
1. *Think:* Sammle deine Gedanken und mache dir
   Notizen.
2. *Pair:* Tausche dich mit einem Partner/einer
   Partnerin aus. Ergänze neue Ideen in deiner Liste.
3. *Share:* Teilt dann eure Gedanken mit einem
   anderen Paar. Nun habt ihr schon Ideen und
   Meinungen von vier verschiedenen Leuten
   kennengelernt.

2 **Buzz groups**

Bei dieser Arbeitsform sprecht ihr alle mit leiser
Stimme, damit sich die verschiedenen Gruppen
nicht gegenseitig stören. *Buzz* heißt summen oder
brummen und beschreibt den Geräuschpegel, der
dabei im Raum entsteht.
In einer *buzz group* diskutieren drei bis fünf
Gruppenmitglieder. Ein Gruppenmitglied macht
Notizen. Jede Gruppe wählt anschließend einen
Sprecher/eine Sprecherin, der/die die Ergebnisse
vorträgt.

3 **Double circle**

Ihr bildet in der Klasse zwei einander
zugewandte Kreise. Diejenigen von euch, die
sich gegenüberstehen oder -sitzen, tauschen
sich zu einem vorher bestimmten Thema aus.
Danach dreht ihr euch in den beiden Kreisen in
entgegengesetzte Richtungen weiter und tauscht
euch mit einem neuen Partner/einer neuen
Partnerin über das Thema aus.

4 Give and take

Faltet ein Blatt Papier so, dass es aus sechs bis acht gleich großen Feldern besteht. Schreibt in zwei bis drei der Felder jeweils eine Idee oder Information. Dann befragt ihr eure Mitschüler/innen, um neue Ideen oder Informationen zu sammeln. Pro Mitschüler/in dürft ihr eine neue Idee/Information ‚geben' und eine neue Idee/Information ‚nehmen', um euer Blatt zu vervollständigen. Bildet dann kleine Gruppen und besprecht euer Material. Eure Ergebnisse könnt ihr abschließend in der Klasse vorstellen.

5 Placemat

Auf einer *placemat* (Tischvorlage, Platzdeckchen) sammeln vier Teilnehmer gleichzeitig Ideen. Jedes Gruppenmitglied macht auf einem Teil eines großen Bogens Papier Notizen. Anschließend wird die *placemat* so lange gedreht, bis jeder alle Beiträge gelesen hat.
In der Gruppe einigt ihr euch dann auf die wichtigsten Punkte und notiert sie in der Mitte des Blattes. Schließlich stellt ein Gruppenmitglied das Ergebnis in der Klasse vor.

6 Gallery walk

Wenn verschiedene Arbeitsgruppen Produkte (z. B. Poster) erstellt haben, führt ihr einen Rundgang in der Klasse durch.
Hängt die Poster an verschiedenen Stellen im Klassenzimmer auf. Findet euch dann in neuen Gruppen zusammen, sodass in jeder Gruppe ein Mitglied jeder Arbeitsgruppe vertreten ist. Die Gruppen gehen von Poster zu Poster, und der jeweilige Experte/die jeweilige Expertin erklärt sein/ihr Poster.

WORDBANK

A FEELINGS

be afraid of big dogs   be excited about a party   be nervous before a test
smile at somebody you like   cry because somebody hurt your feelings
feel sorry for someone   laugh about a joke   be worried about your marks
love your cat/dog   enjoy a good film   feel good about yourself
feel bad about something   miss a friend   be scared of spiders
be jealous of a classmate   be angry with your brother
feel embarrassed because …   hate cleaning your room
be ashamed of something you did   be sick of all the fighting   …

Positive feelings
brilliant • calm • comfortable •
excited • fantastic • free • glad •
good • grateful • great • happy •
optimistic • peaceful • proud •
safe • strong • surprised •
wonderful • …

Negative feelings
aggressive • angry • awful • bad • bored •
confused • depressed • desperate •
disappointed • embarrassed • exhausted •
frightened • guilty • helpless • homesick •
horrible • hurt • jealous • lonely • nervous •
sad • scared • shocked • stressed • terrible •
tired • unhappy • upset • worried • …

…
brilliant
great
good

Good to know …

And how was Disney World?

STOP It was all right.

Oh! Something went wrong. She did not like it.

And how was Disney World?

Absolutely fantastic! I loved it!

Oh good!

Try and be enthusiastic when expressing feelings. 'OK', 'all right', 'nice' and 'interesting' are not very positive.

Love
boyfriend
girlfriend
partner
be together
kiss
fall in love
marry – get married – marriage
wedding
pregnant – pregnancy
have a baby
start a family
…

(Best) friends
spend time with each other
make each other laugh
listen to each other
say sorry
share a secret
enjoy the same things
talk about problems
give advice to each other
get along with each other
miss each other
…

can
argue with each other
fight with each other
hurt each other's feelings
break a promise
be intolerant
be unfair
offend each other
…

Good to know …

I've got 300 friends on Facebook.

When people know each other, spend time with each other or chat on the Internet, they are 'friends'. This does not always mean that they are very good, close or even 'best friends'.

Good to know …

STOP He looks disgusting, like a monster, really scary. AND he is fat!

No, he's not disgusting. He's just very different and unusual. And of course, he's a big boy. I would not call him fat. He's only a bit on the large side. And he has beautiful hair!

People might hear you when you talk about them. So try not to say things that might hurt their feelings. Instead, choose a nice detail because there is always something nice to say.

WORDBANK

B GIVING ADVICE

Why do you think …?
Why don't you …?
You could …
I think it is/was a good idea to …
I'm not sure about …
I don't think it is/was such a good idea to …
If you ask me, I would …

If I were you, I would …
You might want to ask him/her if …
It's all right, but maybe you could try to …
That's a good idea, but maybe you
  could … instead.
I'm not sure. What about …?
That's OK. But how about …?

Girl: I told my mother that I did not want to go on holiday with her
  and she got really angry and I heard her crying.
Boy: She cried? Really? Did you say anything else?
Girl: I told her she was too old to have fun with.
Boy: Ahh.
Girl: But after all it is a fact that she is 45. It is not all my fault.
Boy: Of course, it isn't. Maybe it was the way you told her.
Girl: Yes, right, but what shall I do now? I wonder how she's
  feeling now. I'd love to ask her but I'm afraid to make
  things worse.
Boy: Why don't you tell her that you are sorry?
Girl: But I'm not sorry about not having to go hiking.
Boy: Sure. But maybe you could ask her to go somewhere else?
Girl: Hhm …
Boy: If I were you, I would tell her how I feel.
Girl: What shall I say?
Boy: How about telling her the truth, that you love her but that
  you would like to go camping instead?

Good to know …

In Germany you **STOP** must keep both hands on the table when eating.

Oh sorry.

How rude!

In the English-speaking world people feel that it is rude to tell others what to do and criticise them. So be careful with phrases like 'You must', 'You have to', 'It is wrong', 'You can't do this'.

C JOBS (1)

How to get a job

do work experience   write a CV   fill in an application form
write a letter of application   apply for a job   have a job interview
graduate from grade ...   do your A levels   do military/civilian service
find a position as a trainee   start training as a/an ...   start an apprenticeship
do vocational training   go to vocational school   do volunteer work
go to college   have qualifications   enclose names and addresses of referees   ...

... to have

an indoor/outdoor job.
a job where I can travel.
a job where I can earn a lot
  of money.
long holidays.
...

I would like
I wouldn't like

... to work

indoors/outdoors.
shifts.
regular hours.
full-time/part-time.
in my own country.
abroad.
in a(n) office/factory/bank/shop/
  at home/...
with my hands.
with people/children/...
in a team/on my own.
as a car mechanic/...
...

Skills you may need for work

be good with your hands   know how to ...   have experience in/with ...
have previous experience   be good at languages/maths/...
speak fluent English/French/...
be reliable/punctual/flexible/creative/polite/communicative/...
work well with others   ...

WORDBANK

C JOBS (2)

Jobs can be ...
badly paid • boring • creative •
dangerous • easy • exciting • fun •
great • hard • interesting • special •
terrible • unusual • well-paid • ...

Difficult situations at work

work in/under bad conditions   be forced to work   do dangerous work
get injured   do overtime   get fired   fire somebody
go on strike (for better wages)   work without pay   lose one's job
be out of work   get bullied   ...

Jobs	What these people do
builder	repair and build houses
butcher	produce and sell meat
car mechanic	repair cars
carpenter	make things from wood
check-in agent	check people's tickets at an airport
CPhT (certified pharmacy technician)	mix and sell medicine
electrician	repair or install electrical equipment
firefighter	put out fires
hair stylist/hairdresser	wash, cut, style and dye people's hair
joiner	make the wooden parts of buildings
office administrator	make phone calls and prepare/write letters
pilot	fly planes
plumber	repair water tanks, work with tools
police officer	keep people and the streets safe
programmer	create computer programmes
receptionist	welcome visitors in a hotel or an office, answer questions
security guard	protect buildings and shops
shop assistant	help customers and sell things
social worker	help people with their problems
taxi driver	drive customers
vet's assistant	look after (ill) animals
waiter/waitress	take orders and serve customers
welder	weld metal with heat and a hammer or a machine
...	...

WORDBANK

D STATISTICS

number   a/one billion   a/one million   a/one thousand   a/one hundred
per cent   total   a/one quarter   a/one third   two thirds   half
population   survey   pie chart   bar chart   ...

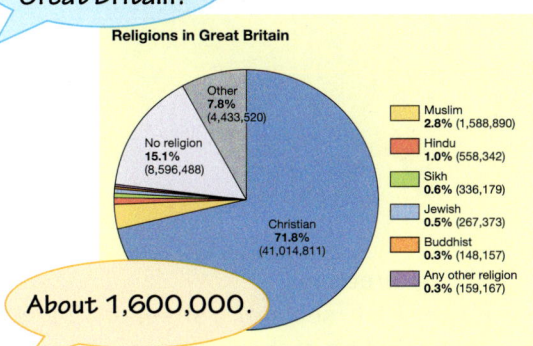

How many Muslims are there in Great Britain?

Religions in Great Britain

Other
7.8%
(4,433,520)

No religion
15.1%
(8,596,488)

Christian
71.8%
(41,014,811)

Muslim **2.8%** (1,588,890)
Hindu **1.0%** (558,342)
Sikh **0.6%** (336,179)
Jewish **0.5%** (267,373)
Buddhist **0.3%** (148,157)
Any other religion **0.3%** (159,167)

About 1,600,000.

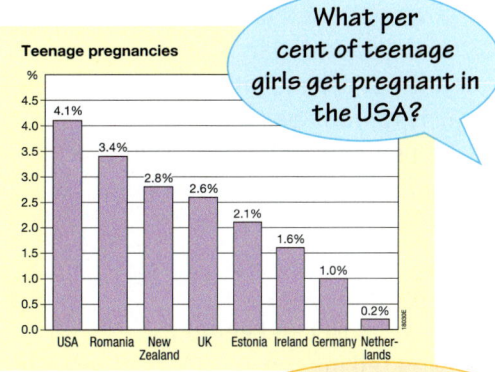

What per cent of teenage girls get pregnant in the USA?

Teenage pregnancies

%
4.5
4.0 — 4.1%
3.5 — 3.4%
3.0 — 2.8%
2.5 — 2.6%
2.0 — 2.1%
1.5 — 1.6%
1.0 — 1.0%
0.5
0.0 — 0.2%

USA   Romania   New Zealand   UK   Estonia   Ireland   Germany   Netherlands

It's around 4 per cent.

tip
You write
3.3%
You say:
three point three per cent

Talking about statistics
More than *x* per cent ...
Almost/About one third/*x* per cent work ...
Only *x* per cent ...   Most people ...
The statistics clearly show that ...
I was really shocked by the number of children working ...
x people said they ... That's almost one third of the class.
Fewer than *x* people ...
Less than half of the class ...

E TRAVELLING (1)

Getting around

travel by boat   take the train   change trains   go by ship/car
ride a bike   take a tour of a city   ride a motorbike
fly to London   take the underground   walk through the park
buy a ticket for the train   get on/off a bus   take the escalator/lift   ...

Things we do on holiday

visit friends/relatives   stay at a summer camp/youth hostel /hotel   go sightseeing
buy souvenirs   send postcards   go hiking/swimming/...   lie on the beach
speak a foreign language   meet new people   make a reservation   go shopping
visit an exhibition   take pictures of famous sights   enjoy the weather   sit in a coffee shop
have a barbecue   watch people   ask at the tourist information   ...

E TRAVELLING (2)

Talking about sights
On the left/right you can see …
In front of you there is/are …
… was built in …
… was opened in …
… was founded in …
… is the oldest/tallest/…
… is famous because …
You should really see/visit/…
It offers fascinating views of …
…

Asking for directions
Excuse me, how can I get to …?
Could you tell me the way to …, please?
Could you show it to me on the map, please?

Giving directions
It's the first /second/… street on the right/left.
Turn right/left at the next corner.
Just go across the street, it's on the left/right.
Go straight on.
It's opposite the theatre.

Good to know …

Excuse me, I'm in room 15. I'd like to know if there is a message for me.

Excuse me, have we met before?

No, I don't think so. Sorry!

I'm sorry, I'm a stranger here myself.

Excuse me, do you know the way to the museum?

Oh, I'm so sorry.

I'm sorry.

In English-speaking countries people are usually very polite, so make sure you say 'excuse me', 'please', 'thank you' and 'sorry' a lot.

Meeting people

Martin: Hi David, I want to introduce you to my new girlfriend. This is Karin. Karin, this is my friend David.

David: Hi Karin. Nice to meet you.

Karin: Hi David. Nice to meet you, too.

David: So where are you from, Karin?

Karin: I'm from Erfurt in Germany. How about you?

David: I'm from Scarborough. That's in North Yorkshire.

Chris: Hi Laura, how are you?

Laura: I'm fine, thank you. And you?

Chris: I'm OK, thanks.

Josipa: Bye, Mike

Mike: Goodbye, Josipa. Have a nice evening.

Josipa: Thanks, Mike. You, too. See you tomorrow.

At a youth hostel

Receptionist: Hi. What can I do for you?

Guest: Hello. I'm looking for a room for tonight.

Receptionist: We have private rooms and mixed dorms.

Guest: I'll take a private room, please. How much ist it?

Receptionist: It's 500 rand. Is that OK?

Guest: Yeah, that's fine. Is breakfast included?

Receptionist: It is. I just need your signature here, please. Your room is on the second floor. Have a good time.

Guest: Thanks a lot. See you later.

At a clothes shop

Yes, please. I'm looking for …
Well, … is my favourite colour.
I need …, please.
Yes, it's nice. I like it. Could I try it on?
Yes, it's perfect. I think I'll take it.
Where can I pay?

Can I help you?
Did you want a certain colour?
What size do you need?
What about this one?
The fitting rooms are on the left.
You can pay just over there.

WORDBANK

F FOOD

have tea · set the table · add some salt and pepper · bake a cake
cut the fruit · order takeaway food · make a salad · put something in the fridge
clean up the table/kitchen · wash the vegetables · use a fork and knife · feed the baby
eat in a cafeteria/canteen · go to a restaurant · lose/put on weight · start a diet · ...

Food can be ...
hot • cold • delicious • sweet •
traditional • disgusting • healthy •
unhealthy • fat-reduced •
hot and spicy • fresh • old • good •
bad • tasty • ...

Healthy eating
Vitamins keep your body healthy.
Carbohydrates give your body energy.
Try to eat less junk food.
People who are more active burn more
    calories.
Minerals in food are needed for good health.
Protein is found in milk, eggs, meat, fish and
    other food.
Try to eat many different kinds of food.

Keeping fit
Eat healthy food.
Drink lots of water.
Don't smoke.
Don't take drugs.
Stay away from alcohol.
Do sports.
Get enough sleep.
Feel good.

make	breakfast
have	lunch
cook	a meal
eat	dinner

Are you ready to order?
What would you like to eat?
Would you like anything to drink?
Anything else?
How's your meal?

Can I have the menu, please?
I'll have ..., please.
For dessert I'd like ..., please.
Could you bring the bill, please?

Good to know ...

In English-speaking countries
you should always wait to be
seated in restaurants.

WORDBANK

G ENVIRONMENT

Saving the environment

sort rubbish   turn off electrical appliances when they aren't needed
take a shower instead of a bath   use less water   use energy-saving light bulbs
use products that aren't dangerous for the environment   grow plants   recycle rubbish
repair things   reuse things   help to reduce pollution   pick up rubbish
use the bike or walk   reduce waste   save water/energy
raise money for a nature project   protect the forests
go on a sponsored walk   act green   ...

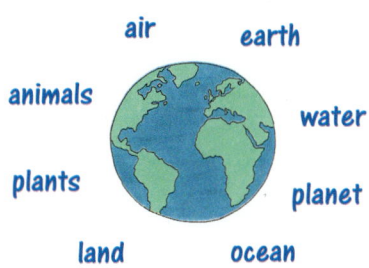

air   earth
animals
water
plants
planet
land   ocean

Let's start today to protect our environment!

Remember: Small things can make a big change!

reduce, reuse, recycle

Natural disasters

drought   flood   hurricane   earthquake   volcanic eruption
tornado (twister)   wildfire   blizzard   tsunami   ...

A natural disaster can ...
destroy an area
devastate buildings
lift things off the ground
uproot trees
flatten cars
injure people
kill people
...

After a natural disaster:
ask for help
send rescue workers
set up emergency shelters for the survivors
offer meals, beds, ...
donate money
repair roads
rebuild houses
...

Meteorologists
forecast natural disasters
use weather radar
detect a tornado/...
issue a warning
...

WORDBANK

H TECHNOLOGY

Electrical appliances

microwave   dishwasher   heating   washing machine   oven
fridge   light bulbs   stereo   television   mobile phone
alarm clock   radio   computer   MP3 player   ...

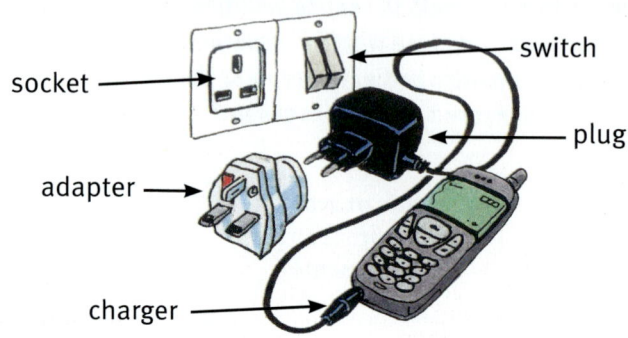

socket   switch   plug   adapter   charger

Things we do with technology

use a microwave   work on the computer   invent a machine
write a text message/text each other   talk on the phone/make a phone call
make a video   watch a DVD   take photos   send an email
log on/off ...   go online   surf the Internet   have an account on a social networking site
get/keep in touch with people   communicate with people
play computer games   ...

Staying safe online
Protect your private data.
Don't tell anyone your password.
Be careful about the things you put online.
Don't send a message when you are angry.
Be polite.

Useful phrases
My ... doesn't work.
I need help with my ...
Can you repair/fix it?
Do you know anyone who
    can repair it?

Good to know ...

The word 'SMS' or 'Handy' will not be understood in the same way as in Germany.
(Handy means 'handlich, praktisch' in German.)
Instead say that someone texted you on your mobile (British English) or cellphone
(American English).

WORDBANK

1 SPORTS

You play ...	You go ...	You do ...	You go/do ...
football	cycling	kickboxing	dancing
(ice) hockey	climbing	in-line skating	swimming
table tennis	skateboarding	aerobics	bungee jumping
(beach) volleyball	skiing	boxing	BMX biking
basketball	...	judo	...
handball		karate	
cricket		...	
...			

Sports can be ...
exciting • fun • great •
dangerous • fantastic •
extreme • interesting •
boring • expensive •
crazy • ...

People in sports
sportsperson • dancer •
runner • player •
teammate • team •
coach • referee •
team captain • fan •
goalkeeper • winner •
loser • ...

Playing sports

take part in a competition   score a goal   watch a game/match
train/practise once/twice/... times a week   have a match at the/every weekend
hit/catch the ball   beat the other team   have a break   cheer for/support your team
have the right equipment   build a ramp   try new tricks   play injured
become a professional   ...

Equipment

helmet   ball   goal   rope   shoulder/knee/elbow pads
skates   board   basket   (hockey/...) stick   trainers (BE)/sneakers (AE)
boat   paddle   raft   skis   sled   ...

You play/practise ...		
on ...	**at ...**	**in ...**
a playing field	a club	a park
a sports field	a sports centre	a gym
the street	a fitness centre	the garden
...	...	...

1 Into Exile

Read this extract from Joan Lingard's third book about Kevin and Sadie. They are now in London. What is their situation like?

"There!" she said, flipping Kevin's egg out on to the plate, and as she did so she thought of her mother standing in the kitchen at home [...] doing the very same thing [...].

"What are you thinking about?" asked Kevin, looking up at her.

"Me[1] ma," said Sadie [...].

"Aye[2]." Kevin sighed. "It'd be fine to see our families once in a while[3]."

Sadie was not so sure that she wanted to see hers. She had written to her mother after she and Kevin had been married [...] and her mother had written back to tell Sadie that she had broken her heart. [...] Kevin had written to his family too and his sister Brede had written back to say that she hoped they would be very happy together. But Brede was young, only seventeen, the same age as Sadie and also she knew Sadie and they liked one another. Kevin said he thought his mother would wish them well[4] but would be afraid for them[5], not knowing that in London nobody cared if you were a Catholic married to a Protestant. As far as they could see nobody cared here anyway. You could be writhing in agony[6] half the night and no one would even come to see if you were being murdered. At home in Belfast people cared too much in some ways. They could never let you be. Kevin said that his father certainly would not wish them well. He would take it as an insult to himself, his family, and his religion. Kevin had betrayed[7] them. [...]

They ate quickly, enjoying the hot tasty food, mopping[8] the egg from their plates with slices of bread taken from the packet that sat between them on the table. [...]

They had come to London without possessions[9], Sadie even without clothes, and so, being forced to buy the basic necessities[10], they had bought on credit and were paying back weekly. [...] But the weekly payments[11] had grown until now they were a sizeable[12] sum and Kevin said they must buy nothing more until these debts were cleared[13]. Sadie agreed. She did not mean to be extravagant. It was just that sometimes she saw things ...

Money was tight[14]. Sadie did not earn very much, travelling was expensive, and Kevin's work as a labourer[15] was casual[16] so that sometimes he had a week between jobs. He did not much like working as a labourer, and would have preferred a job where he could use the skill in his hands rather than[17] the strength[18].

Choose an activity

tip
You can write down the complete phone call first or use role cards with notes to help you.

- **Sadie has decided to phone her mother. Work with a partner and act out the dialogue.**

- **If you had to emigrate[19] and could only take a small suitcase, what would you want to take with you? Make a collage or draw the things you would pack.**

- **Imagine you are Kevin or Sadie. What do you miss most? Write a letter to Kevin's sister Brede and tell her about it.**

---

[1]me – *hier: meine*; [2]aye – *ja*; [3]once in a while – *hin und wieder*; [4]wish sb well – *jdm alles Gute/viel Glück wünschen*; [5]be afraid for sb – *um jdn Angst haben*; [6]writhe in agony – *sich vor Schmerzen winden*; [7]betray sb – *jdn verraten*; [8]mop – *(auf)wischen*; [9]possession – *Besitz*; [10]basic necessities – *Lebensnotwendige*; [11]payment – *hier: Zahlung*; [12]sizeable – *ziemlich groß, beträchtlich*; [13]clear – *begleichen*; [14]tight – *knapp*; [15]labourer – *(Hilfs)arbeiter/in*; [16]casual – *gelegentlich*; [17]rather than – *anstatt*; [18]strength – *Stärke, Kraft*; [19]emigrate – *auswandern, emigrieren*

2 love & betrayal[1] & hold the mayo[2]

In this book, Francine Pascal writes about 16-year-old Victoria Martin and her job as a waitress in a summer camp.

I'm packing to go away for the summer. I'm going to be a camper-waitress in a summer camp in the mountains in upstate New York. Being a camper-waitress means that you wait on tables[3] and get to be involved[4] in all the camp activities. The job is a snap[5]. All we have to do is set the tables and serve three meals a day. Each meal should take forty-five minutes and then freedom!!! And getting paid for it! I can hardly wait!
One week later …
The camp is divided[6] into two circles of houses, one for the boys and one for the girls. Both are fantastic. It looks more like a hotel than a camp.
"These are for the campers. Ours are further[7] back." Steffi goes round the back of the social hall. That's where they have all the dances. Terrific[8], we'll be close by the fun place.
I turn the corner of the building. There are two old shacks[9] in the middle of what looks like a garbage dump[10]. Could our bunk[11] be in the area behind these shacks? It must be. I hope it's far enough away from this mess.
"Victoria … here." A voice comes from inside the first shack. Then a head. Steffi's head. "What are you doing in there?" I ask. Then it hits[12] me. I just stare. It's the worst rathole[13] I've ever seen. Before anyone can unpack, the PA[14] starts screaming. "Attention[15] all waitresses. All waitresses to the flagpole[16]! Let's go, girls! Ten … nine … eight … seven … Move it, girls! … six …"

"Hurry, everybody!" Steffi shouts. I want to ask Steffi what's going on, but I'm running too hard to get out the words.
"Stand next to me with your hands at your sides," she says.
Just then all sound stops. It gets so quiet you could hear a pin[17] drop. A two-hundred pound monster lady introduces herself. "I'm Madame Katzoff, and this is Dr Davis. Let me read you a few of the rules that are going to make summer at the camp a joy[18] for everyone. Dr Davis and I think the best way to start any day is singing. Don't you agree, girls?"
"Yes." It sounds OK to me. "Good," Madame Katzoff says. "Then be here in front of the flagpole every morning … at six thirty. In your uniform. Each waitress will have two tables of twelve kids and three counsellors[19]." That's thirty!
"She will be responsible for seeing the tables are clean and set, the trays[20] are washed, the glasses shining[21] … There will be fifty-cent fines for lateness, talking, peanut butter on the tables or chairs, untidy uniforms, smoking, drinking, bikinis on the soccer field," and on and on she goes. I panic.
"I'll never remember all that," I whisper to Steffi.
Without moving her lips she says something that sounds like, "Everything's going to be all right," or "We'll never make it through the night."
I ask myself, "Could this be a horrible mistake or what?"

Choose an activity

- **Work in groups and act out the scene.**

- **If you applied for a summer job in a holiday camp, what would your CV look like?**

- **Create an advert for a job in a summer camp.**

---

[1]betrayal – *Verrat; Enttäuschung*; [2]mayo = mayonnaise; [3]wait on table(s) – *bedienen, als Kellner/in arbeiten*;
[4]be involved (in) – *beteiligt sein, engagiert sein*; [5]be a snap – *ein Kinderspiel sein*; [6]divide – *teilen, trennen*;
[7]further – *weiter*; [8]terrific – *großartig, super, toll*; [9]shack – *Hütte, Bretterbude*; [10]garbage dump – *Mülldeponie*;
[11]bunk – *Schlafstelle, Bett*; [12]hit sb – *hier: jdm aufgehen/auffallen*; [13]rathole – *Rattenloch*; [14]PA – *Lautsprecher*;
[15]attention – *Achtung*; [16]flagpole – *Fahnenstange, Fahnenmast*; [17]pin – *(Steck)nadel*; [18]joy – *Freude, Vergnügen*;
[19]counsellor – *Betreuer/in*; [20]tray – *Tablett*; [21]shine – *hier: glänzen*

3 My African dream

In the following article, Sarah, 18, from Canada describes her ideas about Africa. She would like to go there on a trip during her summer vacation. What would she like to do in Africa?

Most of my summers have been relaxing and, as you could well say, normal. I spend time with my friends, I go swimming, I ride my horse, and I have a summer job. I love my summers, but I wish that they were more fulfilling[1]. I want to use my summers to make a difference in someone's life. For that reason, my dream summer vacation would be to go on a trip to a country in Africa with an organization like UNICEF.

A beautiful and troubled[2] continent

Africa is the second largest continent on the planet, consisting[3] of 53 often unnoticed[4] countries. It is a beautiful continent with many incredible places to visit, such as Victoria Falls. Africa is also the land of giraffes, zebras, lions and other amazing[5] animals. But despite[6] the fact that it is a beautiful place to live, Africa is the world's poorest and most underdeveloped continent. The majority[7] of people who live in Africa are in need[8].

Many people suffer[9] from diseases, such as AIDS. There have also been many political problems in Africa. Hunger and limited[10] access[11] to safe drinking water is also a major[12] problem. Droughts[13] and floods[14] leave thousands of people hungry and without food. Safe drinking water is hard to get for many people, and so many Africans drink water that is contaminated[15] with parasites. Hunger and unclean drinking water leave many people sick.

If I went to Africa, I would go to places where people live in extreme poverty. I would live with and help these people. I would help build schools and houses for them, and I would teach children English.

A life-changing experience

I have watched videos of people going on trips to Africa and have seen the smiles on the faces of the people they visited. I have a friend who went to Africa a couple of years ago during his summer vacation. He said the experience was incredible, life-changing and fun.

I also want to undergo[16] a life-changing experience. I would love to travel and make a difference in people's lives. I know that, one day, I will get the chance to go on any vacation that I want, and I know that that place will be Africa.

Choose an activity

- **Imagine you are Sarah. Write her letter of application for a trip to Africa with UNICEF.**

- **Make a collage about Africa.**

- **Would you like to go on a trip like the one Sarah writes about? Say why/why not.**

[1]fulfilling – *erfüllend*; [2]troubled – *unruhig, in Schwierigkeiten*; [3]consist (of) – *bestehen (aus)*;
[4]unnoticed – *unbemerkt, unbeachtet*; [5]amazing – *toll, unglaublich*; [6]despite – *trotz*; [7]majority – *Mehrheit*;
[8]be in need – *Not leiden*; [9]suffer (from) – *leiden (an)*; [10]limited – *begrenzt, eingeschränkt*; [11]access – *Zugang*;
[12]major – *groß, schwerwiegend*; [13]drought – *Trockenheit, Dürre*; [14]flood – *Überschwemmung, Hochwasser*;
[15]contaminated – *verunreinigt, verseucht*; [16]undergo – *durchmachen, erleben*

4 TOP 8

**READING
IS
FUN**

Read about Madison McDonald, a teenager from Connecticut who makes a horrible discovery about her profile on *Friendverse* when she comes home from her holidays.

I blinked[1]. I didn't understand.

I just … didn't understand.

Had I somehow[2] logged in to the wrong profile?

I turned my computer off and waited a few seconds. I could feel sweat[3] beginning to form on my neck, and I had a feeling in my stomach like I'd swallowed a bowling ball. I restarted my computer, hoping that I'd somehow imagined[4] the profile that seemed to have my (misspelled[5]) name on it, and that turning my computer off and on – really the extent of my computer maintenance[6] skills – would fix[7] it.

I logged back onto Friendverse and groaned[8]. The profile was still there. And it appeared real, not a hallucination brought on by some rare[9] Ecuadorian brain fever[10].

But how could this be happening? I never would have written those things, and I knew how to spell my own last name.

Plus, I hadn't been online in two weeks. TWO!

I stared at the screen[11], my eyes burning. I hadn't been online … but someone had.

Someone who had been pretending[12] to be me.

But who would have done this?

I looked at the spelling mistakes, the terrible music choices, and my friends' angry comments. It had been someone who clearly was out to hurt me – and from the looks of it, someone who'd been pretty successful.

Maybe someone had meant it as a joke? But if that was the case, clearly nobody had gotten it. Which was actually bothering me a little bit. I mean, didn't my friends know me at all? Wouldn't they have known that I never would have listened to Yanni, let alone[13] buddied[14] him?

My eyes kept jumping back to Justin's comments about breaking up[15], my status as "Single", and the blog entry. But I didn't want to be single! I wanted to be not broken up with my boyfriend!

"Oh my God," I moaned[16], still trying to take in[17] the carnage[18] in front of me.

The profile picture was especially bad. I had never seen it before, but it must have been taken at Brian's last party – I recognized the overturned[19] couches that signaled a McMahon party in full swing[20]. My eyes were half-closed, and I was grinning[21] stupidly at the camera while simultaneously[22] looking like I was about to sneeze[23].

It was the WORST picture of myself that I'd ever seen.

Choose an activity

- **Imagine you are one of Madison's friends and find her changed profile. How do you react? Are you angry or confused? Write her an email and tell her what you think.**

- **Create a poster about dos and don'ts on the Internet.**

---

[1]blink – *blinzeln*; [2]somehow – *irgendwie*; [3]sweat – *Schweiß*; [4]imagine – *hier: sich einbilden*; [5]misspelled – *falsch geschrieben*; [6]maintenance – *Wartung*; [7]fix – *in Ordnung bringen, reparieren*; [8]groan – *(auf)stöhnen, ächzen*; [9]rare – *selten, rar*; [10]brain fever – *Hirnhautentzündung*; [11]screen – *hier: Bildschirm*; [12]pretend – *vorgeben, vortäuschen*; [13]let alone – *geschweige denn*; [14]buddy sb – *jdn in die Freundesliste aufnehmen*; [15]break up – *hier: sich trennen*; [16]moan – *stöhnen*; [17]take in – *hier: verarbeiten*; [18]carnage – *Blutbad, Gemetzel*; [19]overturn – *umkippen, umstürzen*; [20]in full swing – *in vollem Gange*; [21]grin – *grinsen*; [22]simultaneously – *gleichzeitig*; [23]sneeze – *niesen*

4 The Player

Computer games began, for me, in 1982. Which was precisely[2] the right moment. I was seven, we'd had a Sinclair Spectrum[3] for a month or two and into my life came The Hobbit text adventure game. My dad brought it home. "Look!" he said, "it comes with a copy of the book!"

The game was hard: sometimes fun, sometimes frustrating. Commands[4] had to be typed in using painfully[5] simple English. Go west. Look. Examine[6] Gandalf. We were simultaneously[7] amazed[8] by what the programme understood – and astounded[9] by what it didn't. Question Gandalf. No. Threaten Gandalf. No. Angrily demand[10] answers from Gandalf. No. In desperation, my dad typed: "Cut off Gandalf's ear." The game understood that. We were very impressed[11]. We had discovered computer-game violence. Gandalf killed us.

The Player

In the first of a new weekly column[1], Naomi Alderman suggests parents should stop worrying about their kids playing games too much – and join them instead.

by Naomi Alderman

We never got to the end of The Hobbit. Frankly[12], the book was a lot easier; and unlike a game you could skip[13] over the hard bits. But sitting in the living room with my dad, trying to solve a problem together, coming up with[14] ideas and making each other laugh makes it a time that I will never forget.

Sometimes, hearing that I've written for computer games, parents ask me despairingly[15] whether they ought[16] to worry that their child spends so much time playing. I always wonder why these parents don't just sit down and play alongside[17] their offspring[18]; or even ask their child to teach them how to play. Maybe they don't like admitting there are things they don't know. But if there's one thing that is guaranteed to make lasting memories[19], it is letting children be better than you at something. That and cutting off the ear of an imaginary wizard[20].

Choose an activity

- **Present your favourite computer game to the class.**
- **Design a cover for a computer game.**
- **What would you like to do with your family? Plan a weekend with different activities.**

---

[1]column – *Spalte, Kolumne (Zeitungsartikel)*; [2]precisely – *genau, exakt*; [3]Sinclair Spectrum – personal home computer that came onto the market in 1982; [4]command – *hier: Befehl, Kommando*; [5]painfully – *hier: schrecklich, furchtbar*; [6]examine – *untersuchen, prüfen, befragen*; [7]simultaneously – *gleichzeitig*; [8]amazed – *erstaunt, verblüfft*; [9]astounded – *verblüfft, bestürzt*; [10]demand – *verlangen, fordern*; [11]impressed – *beeindruckt*; [12]frankly – *ehrlich gesagt*; [13]skip – *überspringen*; [14]come up with sth – *sich etw einfallen lassen, etw entwickeln*; [15]despairingly – *verzweifelt, hoffnungslos*; [16]ought – *sollte, müsste*; [17]alongside – *parallel zu, daneben*; [18]offspring – *Sprössling, Nachkomme*; [19]memory – *Gedächtnis, hier: Erinnerung*; [20]wizard – *Zauberer*

LANGUAGE IN FOCUS

Im Grammatik-Teil *Language in Focus* (**LiF**) wird die englische Sprache ganz genau unter die Lupe genommen.

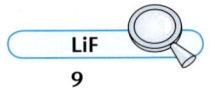

Immer, wenn du dieses Symbol vorn in deinem Buch siehst, kannst du hier nachsehen, welche Grammatikregeln es in der englischen Sprache gibt.

LiF

Um dir die Regeln besser einzuprägen, kannst du sie in deinen eigenen Worten und mit einigen Beispielsätzen oder Bildern notieren.

Im LiF-Teil findest du Erklärungen zu folgender Grammatik:

1	Die Gegenwart	*Present tense*
2	Die vollendete Gegenwart	*Present perfect*
3	Die Vergangenheit	*Past tense*
4	Die Vorvergangenheit	*Past perfect*
5	Die Zukunft	*Future tense*
6	Bedingungssätze (Typ I)	*Conditional clauses (type I)*
7	Bedingungssätze (Typ II)	*Conditional clauses (type II)*
8	Bedingungssätze (Typ III)	*Conditional clauses (type III)*
9	Das Passiv	*The passive*
10	Das Passiv in der Zukunft	*Future passive*
11	Modalverben und ihre Ersatzformen	*Modal verbs and their substitute forms*
12	Indirekte Rede	*Reported speech*
13	Wortstellung und Fragebildung	*Word order and questions*
14	Verb + Objekt mit Infinitiv	*Verb + object + infinitive with to*
15	Inversion bei einschränkenden und negativen Adverbien	*Inversion with restrictive and negative adverbs*
16	Relativsätze	*Relative clauses*
17	Partizipien zur Verkürzung von Adverbialsätzen	*Participles used to shorten adverbial clauses*
18	Die -ing-Form	*Gerund*
19	Adjektive	*Adjectives*
20	Stützwörter: ‚one/ones'	*Prop words: one/ones*
21	Adverbien der Art und Weise	*Adverbs of manner*
22	Steigerung von Adverbien	*Comparison of adverbs*
23	Satzadverbien	*Sentence adverbs*
24	Konjunktionen	*Conjunctions*
25	Emphatisches ‚do'	*Emphatic do*

LANGUAGE IN FOCUS

LiF

1 Die Gegenwart (Present tense)

a) Die einfache Gegenwart (Simple present)

- Das **simple present** benutzt du, wenn du über Gewohnheiten, Tatsachen und regelmäßig vorkommende Ereignisse sprichst.
  Signalwörter: always, often, sometimes, never, usually, every day/week/..., on Mondays/...

  Kevin usually **works** on Mondays.

- Die Verneinung bildest du mit **don't**, bei *he, she, it* mit **doesn't**:
  I **don't** eat tomatoes.   He **doesn't** like fish.   Birds **don't** like cats.

- Ja/Nein-Fragen:

Frage	bejahende Antwort	verneinende Antwort
Do you **live** here?	Yes, I **do**.	No, I **don't**.
Is James your boyfriend?	Yes, he **is**.	No, he **isn't**.

- Das **simple present** benutzt du auch, wenn du über einen festgelegten Zeitplan (zum Beispiel Fahrpläne von Zügen oder Bussen) sprichst, der in der Zukunft liegt.

  The safari **starts** at 6am.   The supermarket **closes** at ten.   The bus **leaves** at eight.

b) Die Verlaufsform der Gegenwart (Present progressive)

- Das **present progressive** beschreibt Ereignisse und Handlungen, die gerade stattfinden.
  Signalwörter: now, at the moment

- Das **present progressive** bildest du so:

  Form von **be** (*am/is/are*) + Verb + **ing**

  We **are eating** at the moment.   They **are enjoying** their meal.

- Die Verneinung bildest du mit **not**:
  The sun **isn't shining**.   They **aren't talking**.

- Ja/Nein-Fragen:

Frage	bejahende Antwort	verneinende Antwort
Is Bob **cleaning** the kitchen?	Yes, he **is**.	No, he **isn't**.

- Fragen mit **Fragewort**:
  What is Thabo **doing** at the moment?   **Why are** you **leaving**?
  Where are you **going**?   **When is** Sadie **coming** home?

c) Die Gegenwart mit Zukunftsbedeutung (Present tense with future meaning)

- Das **present progressive** benutzt du auch, wenn du über mit anderen vereinbarte Pläne oder Verabredungen sprichst, die in der Zukunft liegen.

  I**'m going** to Durban on Friday.   What **are** you **doing** next Sunday?

2 Die vollendete Gegenwart (Present perfect)

a) Die vollendete Gegenwart (Present perfect)

- Du benutzt das **present perfect**, um über Handlungen oder Ereignisse zu sprechen, die schon beendet sind, aber noch in die Gegenwart hineinwirken. Auch für Handlungen oder Ereignisse, die in der Vergangenheit begonnen haben und bis in die Gegenwart andauern, verwendest du das **present perfect**.
  Signalwörter: ever, never, yet, already, just

- Das **present perfect** bildest du so: **Form von have** (*have/has*) **+ Partizip** (*past participle*)

  My friend Brian **has done** kickboxing for some time (and is still doing it).
  Ethel **has worked** as a receptionist for many years (and is still working in that job).

- Regelmäßige Verben bilden das Partizip mit **-ed**.
  walk ➔ walk**ed**   play ➔ play**ed**

- Unregelmäßige Verben haben auch ein unregelmäßiges Partizip:

infinitive	simple past	past participle
go	went	**gone**

Who hasn't done their homework for today?

tip
You can find the irregular verbs on pages 253-254.

- Bei der Verneinung steht **not** hinter **have/has**:

  Ben **hasn't tried** free climbing before.
  We **haven't had** lunch yet.

- Ja/Nein-Fragen:

Frage	bejahende Antwort	verneinende Antwort
Have you ever **been** to Cape Town?	Yes, I **have**.	No, I **haven't**.
Has Kevin **spoken** to his parents yet?	Yes, he **has**.	No, he **hasn't**.

- Fragen mit Fragewort:
  Where have you **been** the whole day?   **Why haven't** you **tidied** up your room yet?

b) Die Verlaufsform der vollendeten Gegenwart (Present perfect progressive)

- Du benutzt das **present perfect progressive**, um über Handlungen oder Ereignisse zu sprechen, die in der Vergangenheit begonnen haben und bis in die Gegenwart andauern. Dabei ist die Handlung oder das Ereignis selbst wichtiger als der Zeitpunkt, zu dem sie stattgefunden haben.

- Das **present perfect progressive** bildest du so:

  Form von **have** (*have/has*) + been + **-ing**-Form des jeweiligen Verbs

She **has been crying** for hours now.

Melinda **has been talking** to her grandfather for hours now (and is still talking to him).
They **have been learning** English for three years (and are still learning it).

LANGUAGE IN FOCUS

c) Die vollendete Gegenwart mit ‚since' und ‚for' (Present perfect with since and for)

- **Since** und **for** werden häufig mit dem **present perfect** benutzt. Sprichst du von einem genauen Zeit<u>punkt</u>, an dem eine Handlung oder ein Ereignis begonnen hat, benutzt du **since**, z.B. **since** 1986, **since** April, **since** Monday, **since** then.

  Kate has wanted to become a hairdresser **since** she was about five.

I've known my sister *since* 1993.

I've known my sister *for* 16 years.

- Wenn du hingegen einen Zeit<u>raum</u> (Monate, Jahre, Tage usw.) angibst, benutzt du das **present perfect** mit **for**, z.B. **for** six months, **for** a long time.

  Aaron has been writing applications **for** three hours now.

3 Die Vergangenheit (Past tense)

a) Die einfache Vergangenheit (Simple past)

- Für Ereignisse und Handlungen, die in der Vergangenheit liegen und abgeschlossen sind, verwendest du das **simple past**.
  Signalwörter: yesterday, last week, two days/years/… ago

  Mike **went** to Australia last winter.   When I **was** little, I **started** collecting model aeroplanes.

- Das **simple past** von regelmäßigen Verben bildest du, indem du **-ed** an den Infinitiv anhängst. Bei unregelmäßigen Verben ist das **simple past** die zweite Form in der Liste auf den Seiten 253 und 254.

- regelmäßige Verben   unregelmäßige Verben
  visit → visit**ed**   go → **went**
  look → look**ed**   leave → **left**

- Die Verneinung bildest du bei den meisten Verben mit **didn't**, bei **was/were** mit **not**:

  I **didn't like** my work experience.
  We **weren't** very happy to see them.

  Yesterday the children **stayed** at home because the weather **was** bad.

- Ja/Nein-Fragen:

Frage	bejahende Antwort	verneinende Antwort
Did you **go** to the cinema last night?	Yes, I **did**.	No, I **didn't**.
Was it a good film?	Yes, it **was**.	No, it **wasn't**.

- Fragen mit Fragewort:
  Where did you **go** yesterday?   **Why didn't** you **ask** me to come to the party?

b) Die Verlaufsform der Vergangenheit (Past progressive)

- Das **past progressive** drückt aus, dass eine Handlung in der Vergangenheit über einen längeren Zeitraum im Gange war. Setzt eine zweite Handlung plötzlich ein, steht diese im *simple past*.
  Signalwörter: while, when

- Das **past progressive** bildest du so:

> **was/were + -ing**-Form des Verbs

When I **was walking** to school yesterday, I saw a car accident.

- Das **past progressive** benutzt du auch für gleichzeitig ablaufende Handlungen.

The crowd **was cheering** loudly while the teams **were playing** the match.

While the woman **was taking** a picture, a man stole her bag.

- Ja/Nein-Fragen:

Frage	bejahende Antwort	verneinende Antwort
Were you **watching** the match?	Yes, I **was**.	No, I **wasn't**.

- Fragen mit Fragewort: **What were** you **doing** yesterday at four o'clock?

4 Die Vorvergangenheit (Past perfect)

- Wenn eine Handlung vor einer anderen Handlung in der Vergangenheit stattgefunden hat, drückst du das mit dem **past perfect** aus. Die zweite Handlung steht im *simple past*. Beide Handlungen sind abgeschlossen.

- Das **past perfect** bildest du so:

> **had + Partizip** *(past participle)*

After Darren and his family **had booked** the safari, they were looking forward to the holidays.

After Marylin **had hit** herself, her finger hurt for a month.

1. Handlung	2. Handlung
After Kevin and Sadie **had left** Ireland,	they could live together.
After Juno **had done** three pregnancy tests,	she talked to Paulie.

5 | Die Zukunft (Future tense)

a) Die Zukunft mit ‚will' (Will future)

- Wenn du über die Zukunft sprechen willst, benutzt du das **will future**. Mit dieser Zeitform kannst du auch Vermutungen ausdrücken und Vorhersagen oder Versprechen machen. **Signalwörter: tomorrow, next week/month, in two years, probably, maybe, perhaps.** Auch folgende Verben können Signalwörter sein: **think, hope, promise**.

> On Wednesday there will be some dark clouds but there won't be any rain.

- Das **will future** bildest du so: **will + Infinitiv** des Verbs

  Michael thinks he **will have** a good job one day.
  The friends **will meet** after school today.

- Verneinung: Du benutzt **will not** oder die Kurzform **won't**, um Sätze zu verneinen.

  I promise I **will not** be late.
  I hope I **won't** make any mistakes in the test.

- Ja/Nein-Fragen:

Frage	**bejahende Antwort**	**verneinende Antwort**
Will you be here tomorrow?	Yes, I **will**.	No, I **won't**.

- Fragen mit Fragewort:
  When **will** Sally be back?

b) Die Zukunft mit ‚going to' (Going to future)

- Du verwendest **going to**, wenn du sagen willst, was jemand für die Zukunft plant oder vorhat.

- Die Zukunft mit **going to** bildest du so: Form von **be** (*am/is/are*) + **going to** + Infinitiv

  I'm really tired. I'm **going to** go to bed soon.

- Bei einer Verneinung von **going to** steht **not** immer hinter (*am/is/are*).

  They **aren't going to** fly to San Francisco.

Aiman is very hungry. He is **going to** buy a hamburger.

- Ja/Nein-Fragen:

Frage	**bejahende Antwort**	**verneinende Antwort**
Are you **going to** call your mother tonight?	Yes, I **am**.	No, I'm **not**.

- Fragen mit Fragewort:
  Where are you **going to go** on holiday?

- **Will future** oder **going to future**?

  > **will future:** Vermutungen, Versprechen, Vorhersagen, spontane Entschlüsse
  > **going to future:** Pläne, Vorhaben, feste Absichten

6 Bedingungssätze, Typ I (Conditional clauses, type I)

- Du benutzt den Bedingungssatz Typ I, um eine <u>realistische</u> Bedingung (etwas, das eintreten kann, soll oder wird) zu beschreiben. Der Hauptsatz drückt aus, was passiert, wenn die Bedingung erfüllt ist.

- Im *if*-Satz steht das **simple present**, im Hauptsatz das **will future**.

if-clause (Bedingung)	Hauptsatz (Folge)
If the weather **is** nice,	we**'ll go** on a bike ride.
If you **miss** the bus,	you **won't be** on time for school.

- Statt des **will future** kann auch **can/can't** im Hauptsatz stehen.

  If you **do** your homework now, you **can** watch TV later.

- Bedingungssätze können entweder mit dem *if*-Satz oder mit dem Hauptsatz beginnen. Wenn sie mit dem *if*-Satz beginnen, werden beide Teilsätze mit einem Komma voneinander getrennt. Steht der Hauptsatz vorne, wird kein Komma gesetzt.

  If it rains, I**'ll** stay in bed all day.
  I**'ll** stay in bed all day **if** it rains.

7 Bedingungssätze, Typ II (Conditional clauses, type II)

- Mit dem Bedingungssatz Typ II drückst du aus, was unter einer nur <u>gedachten</u> Bedingung passieren würde oder könnte. Dabei geht es um Ereignisse, die <u>unwahrscheinlich</u> oder <u>unmöglich</u> sind.

- Bei dieser Art von Bedingungssätzen steht der *if*-Satz im **simple past**. Im Hauptsatz steht **would** oder **could** vor dem Infinitiv.

  If I **had** a lot of money, I **would visit** New York.

- **Aufgepasst!** Bei *if*-Sätzen heißt es normalerweise „I were", aber du kannst auch „I was" sagen. Beide Formen sind hier richtig.

  If I **were** rich, I **could** buy a fast car.
  If I **was** a millionaire, I **would** buy lots of cars.

LANGUAGE IN FOCUS

8 Bedingungssätze, Typ III (Conditional clauses, type III)

- Mit dem Bedingungssatz Typ III drückst du aus, was in der Vergangenheit <u>hätte</u> passieren <u>können</u>, aber nicht passiert ist.

- Bei dieser Art von Bedingungssätzen steht der *if*-Satz im **past perfect**. Im Hauptsatz steht **would** oder **could + have + Partizip** *(past participle)*.

  If I **had won** the race, I **would have got** a prize.
  If she **had called** him, he **could have helped** her.

If I **hadn't missed** the last basket, we **would have won** the game.

9 Das Passiv (The passive)

- Wenn mit einer Person, einem Tier oder einer Sache etwas getan wird, kannst du das durch das **Passiv** ausdrücken. Man benutzt es dann, wenn nicht wichtig oder nicht klar ist, *wer* handelt oder gehandelt hat.

  He took this picture in India. → This picture **was taken** in India.

- Das Passiv in der Gegenwart bildest du so: Form von **be** *(am/is/are)* + **past participle**

  Today letters **are written** on the computer.

  I often read those diaries on the Internet. They **are called** 'blogs'.

- Das Passiv in der Vergangenheit bildest du so: Form von **be** *(was/were)* + **past participle**

  My computer **was made** in China.   Slaves **were brought** from Africa to America.

- Wenn du trotzdem in einem Passiv-Satz die handelnde Person oder die Ursache für etwas nennen willst, kannst du sie mit **by** an den Satz anhängen.

  The house was destroyed **by** <u>fire</u>.
  The apartheid regime was overcome **by** <u>the people</u>.

10 Das Passiv in der Zukunft (Future passive)

- Das Passiv in der Zukunft bildest du so: Form von **be** *(will be)* + **past participle**

  New Orleans **will be rebuilt.**

  Houses **will be repaired.**

11 Modalverben und ihre Ersatzformen (Modal verbs and their substitute forms)

- Die Modalverben geben an, ob etwas erlaubt oder notwendig ist. Die meisten Modalverben haben nur eine Form für die *present tenses*. Im *present perfect*, *simple past* und im *will future* musst du deshalb Ersatzformen (**substitute forms**) verwenden.

simple present	substitute	simple past	present perfect	future
can	be able to	was able to; could	have been able to	will be able to
can't	not be able to	was not able to; couldn't	haven't been able to	won't be able to
must	have to	had to	have had to	will have to
mustn't	not be allowed to	wasn't allowed to	haven't been allowed to	won't be allowed to
needn't	don't have to	didn't have to	–	won't have to

a) Fähigkeit: can/can't – be able to/not be able to

- Mit **can** und **be able to** kannst du sagen, was jemand kann. Im *simple past* kannst du auch **could** benutzen.

  She **is able to** sit and stand but she **can't** walk.
  She **can** speak English and Spanish fluently.
  Sadie **could** work for Mr Blake after she had lost her job.

You won't be able to ride that bike anymore.

- **Could** benutzt du auch für höfliche Bitten und Aufforderungen:

  Could someone open the window, please?

b) Erlaubnis: can/can't – must not – be allowed to/not be allowed to

- **Can/can't, must not** und **be allowed to/not be allowed to** benutzt du, wenn du
  - um etwas bittest,
  - um Erlaubnis fragst oder
  - jemandem etwas erlaubst oder verbietest.

You mustn't eat in class.

  You **can** swim in the pool but you **are not allowed** to swim in the lake.
  In the UK motorists **mustn't** drive on the right.

- **Aufgepasst!** **Must not** oder die Kurzform **mustn't** klingt wie im Deutschen „muss nicht", heißt aber „etwas nicht dürfen"!

LANGUAGE IN FOCUS

c) Notwendigkeit: must/have to – needn't/don't have to

- **Must** klingt wie das deutsche Wort „müssen" und heißt auch *müssen*. In der Regel kannst du **must** auch durch **have to/has to** ersetzen.

  Claire **must** tidy up her room.   oder   Claire **has to** tidy up her room.

- Wenn du sagen willst, was jemand nicht tun muss, benutzt du **don't/ doesn't have to**.

  You **don't have to** finish your meal.

- **Must** hat keine eigene Vergangenheitsform. Daher wird die **simple past-Form** von **have to** (= *had to*) benutzt.

  Before there were emails, people **had to** write letters.

Before there were lights, people **had to** use candles.

- Wenn du sagen willst, dass jemand etwas nicht zu tun braucht, benutzt du **need not** oder die Kurzform **needn't**. **Needn't** hat die gleiche Bedeutung wie **don't have to**, ist aber etwas förmlicher.

  You **needn't** do your homework now.

d) Empfehlung: should/shouldn't

- Mit **should** drückst du aus, dass etwas deiner Ansicht nach passieren sollte:

  You **should** leave now if you want to catch the bus.

- Mit **should** kannst du auch die Meinung einer anderen Person erfragen.

e) Modalverben mit Passivformen (Modal verbs with passive forms)

- Du kannst Modalverben und ihre Ersatzformen wie *can*, *should*, *need*, *have to* usw. in Kombination mit dem Passiv verwenden. Damit drückst du aus, dass eine Handlung ausgeführt bzw. nicht ausgeführt werden soll, muss, kann usw.

  A lot of the animals in Africa **have to be protected**.

  Lots of famous people **can be seen** in Hollywood.

  Plastic bottles **shouldn't be left** after a picnic.

  Animals **mustn't be fed** by tourists.

12 Indirekte Rede (Reported speech)

- Wenn du berichten willst, was jemand gesagt hat, benutzt du die Form der **indirekten Rede**. Die **indirekte Rede** besteht aus einem übergeordneten Satz (*reporting clause*) und der wiedergegebenen Aussage (*reported clause*).

direct speech	reported speech	
	reporting clause	reported clause
Melinda: "I want to train as a car mechanic." →	Melinda **says (that)**	**she wants** to train as a car mechanic.

- Beide Satzteile können durch ein *that* verbunden werden, man kann es aber auch weglassen.

- Wenn du etwas berichten willst, das du gerade gehört hast und das jetzt noch stimmt oder allgemeingültig ist, benutzt du im Begleitsatz und in der wiedergegebenen Aussage die Zeitformen der Gegenwart.

- Peter: "Wild animals **have to be protected.**" → Peter **thinks** (that) wild animals **have to be protected.**

- Im Allgemeinen stehen die Verben im Begleitsatz und in der wiedergegebenen Rede in der Vergangenheit. Die Zeitform der wiedergegebenen Rede rückt dann sozusagen eine Stufe weiter in die Vergangenheit als die direkte Rede. Aus dieser Tabelle kannst du ablesen, wie sich die Zeiten verändern.

direct speech	reported speech
present	→ past
past	→ past perfect
present perfect	→ past perfect
will	→ would
can	→ could
should	→ should

> Yesterday he said he loved me. Today he told me he had met someone else.

- Juno: "I'm pregnant." → Juno told Paulie (that) she **was** pregnant.

- Paulie: "It **was** an accident." → Paulie said (that) it **had been** an accident.

- Juno: "I'll give up the baby for adoption." → Juno said (that) she **would give** up the baby for adoption.

- Meistens musst du Teile der indirekten Rede anpassen oder ergänzen, damit dein Gesprächspartner versteht, was du meinst. Das betrifft zum Beispiel die Pronomen und die Verbform, aber auch Angaben zu Zeit und Ort.

- Mrs Denton: "**We** only just had time to get the dog and hurry to the basement when the tornado struck **yesterday.**" → Mrs Denton told the reporter (that) **she and her husband** had only had time to get the dog and hurry to the basement when the tornado had struck **the day before.**

LANGUAGE IN FOCUS

- Wenn du eine Frage wiedergeben möchtest, die jemand anders gestellt hat, benutzt du **if** oder **whether**. Auch bei Fragen musst du darauf achten, dass die Zeitformen sich ändern:

  Erkhan: "Do you **go** to your Facebook account every day?" ➔ Erkhan asked **if** I **went** to my Facebook account every day.

- Wenn die Frage mit einem Fragewort eingeleitet wird, übernimmst du einfach das Fragewort:

  Sally: "**How often** were you logged on last week?" ➔ Sally asked **how often** Demir had been logged on the week before.

13 Wortstellung und Fragebildung (Word order and questions)

a) Aussagesätze

- Der Bauplan für englische Aussagesätze sieht so aus:

(Vorfeld)	Subjekt	Häufigkeits-adverb	Prädikat	Objekt	andere Ergänzungen
Last week	Ethan		was		ill.
	Amy	usually	eats	two apples	for lunch.

- Orts- und Zeitangaben stehen in der Regel am Ende eines Satzes. Dabei steht immer „Ort" vor „Zeit". Um eine Zeitangabe besonders zu betonen, kannst du sie an den Satzanfang stellen.

- Häufigkeitsadverbien (*always*, *usually*, *sometimes*, *never*) stehen meistens zwischen Subjekt und Prädikat. Aufgepasst bei *be* und *can*:

  Susan is **sometimes** late for school.
  You can **always** call me.

tip
Remember: Like nine before ten, it's 'where' before 'when'.

b) Fragen

- Ja/Nein-Fragen bildet man so:

Hilfsverb	Subjekt	Prädikat	andere Ergänzungen
Is	Brian	talking	on the phone?
Does	Phoebe	know	the answer?

- Fragen mit Fragewort folgen demselben Bauplan, aber sie beginnen mit dem Fragewort:

Fragewort	Hilfsverb	Subjekt	Prädikat	andere Ergänzungen
Why	is	the train	not going	faster?
Where	do	you	do	your homework?
How long	will	the trip	take?	

LANGUAGE IN FOCUS

LiF

14 Verb + Objekt mit Infinitiv (Verb + object + infinitive with to)

- Nach bestimmten Verben, die eine Erlaubnis, einen Wunsch oder einen Willen ausdrücken **(ask, allow, tell, want/would like)**, kannst du den **Infinitiv mit to** verwenden. **To** steht in diesen Fällen nach dem Objekt.

Dr Weinstein	**wants**	parents	**to** take care of their children.
Kevin	**didn't ask**	Sadie	**to** come to England with him.
I	**wouldn't like**	you	**to** go there.

15 Inversion bei einschränkenden und negativen Adverbien (Inversion with restrictive and negative adverbs)

- Im Englischen steht das Subjekt in Haupt- und auch in Nebensätzen normalerweise immer vor dem Verb. In manchen Fällen steht aber das Verb vor dem Subjekt. Dies nennt man **Inversion**.

- Insbesondere nach negativen oder einschränkenden Adverbien wie *not only ... but also, no sooner ... than, hardly, only after, not until* wird im Englischen häufig die Reihenfolge von Verb und Subjekt getauscht.

| New Orleans <u>lies</u> north of the Gulf of Mexico and is surrounded by the Mississippi River and Lake Pontchartrain. | → | **Not only does** New Orleans <u>lie</u> north of the Gulf of Mexico, **but** it is **also** surrounded by the Mississippi River and Lake Pontchartrain. |
| She <u>did not know</u> that this day would change her life. | → | **Hardly did** she <u>know</u> that this day would change her life. |

16 Relativsätze (Relative clauses)

a) Relativpronomen (Relative pronouns)

- Um eine Person oder eine Sache genauer zu beschreiben, verwendest du Relativsätze. Ein Relativsatz beginnt meist mit einem Relativpronomen: **who, which, that.**

- **Who** steht für Personen, **which** für Tiere und Dinge und **that** für Tiere, Dinge oder Personen.

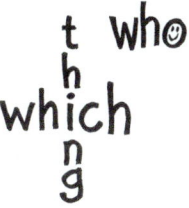

A doctor is someone **who** works in a hospital.
I've got a video game **which/that** is really good.
I saw a band **that/which** played great music.

b)   Relativsätze ohne Pronomen (Contact clauses)

- Das Relativpronomen *(who, which, that)* kann im Englischen weggelassen werden, wenn es das Objekt des Relativsatzes ist.
  Wenn dem Relativpronomen ein <u>Verb</u> folgt, muss das Relativpronomen bleiben. Folgt ein <u>Substantiv</u>, kannst du das Relativpronomen weglassen. Im Deutschen ist dies nicht möglich.

  The people **who** <u>live</u> in Liverpool are called Liverpudlians.
  The town **(which)** <u>Jacky</u> went to a year ago is London.

c)   Partizipien zur Verkürzung von Relativsätzen (Participles used to shorten relative clauses)

- Im Englischen gibt es zwei Partizipien: das *present participle*, das auf *-ing* endet, und das *past participle* (= 3. Verbform), das bei regelmäßigen Verben auf *-ed* endet. Diese Partizipformen kannst du benutzen, um einen Relativsatz zu verkürzen.

People **who leave** their car during a trip in the bush are very stupid.	→ People **leaving** their car during a trip in the bush are very stupid.
Some of the emails **that were written** by the secretary did not arrive.	→ Some of the emails **written** by the secretary did not arrive.

17 Partizipien zur Verkürzung von Adverbialsätzen (Participles used to shorten adverbial clauses)

- Neben dem *present* und dem *past participle* gibt es im Englischen auch noch das **perfect participle**.

- Das **perfect participle** bildest du so: **having + past participle**

- Um Adverbialsätze zu verkürzen, kannst du das **perfect participle** verwenden.

After **he had seen** Juliet for the first time, Romeo couldn't sleep anymore.	→ **Having seen** Juliet for the first time, Romeo couldn't sleep anymore.
Because **he spent** his money on the car, Jack has nothing left for petrol.	→ **Having spent** his money on the car, Jack has nothing left for petrol.

18 Die -ing-Form (Gerund)

a)   Die -ing-Form als Nomen

- Du verwendest die **-ing-Form**, wenn du über Tätigkeiten, Gewohnheiten und Hobbys sprichst. Im Englischen machst du dazu aus dem Verb ein Nomen, indem du ein **-ing** an das Verb hängst:

  Walking keeps you fit.   **Travelling** is a lot of fun.

b) Die -ing-Form nach bestimmten Verben

- Oft folgt die **-ing-Form** nach bestimmten Verben.
  Dazu gehören **like, love, enjoy, hate, start, stop, prefer**.

  Bella **likes watching** TV.

  Olivia **loves going** on holiday.

  I **hate putting on** costumes.

c) Die -ing-Form nach bestimmten Ausdrücken

- Du verwendest die **-ing-Form** nach Ausdrücken wie **good at, bad at, interested in, afraid of, look forward to, fond of** und **terrible at**.

  Nicola is **good at doing** gymnastics.   He is **fond of eating** big pizzas.

19 Adjektive (Adjectives)

- Du benutzt Adjektive, um Personen, Tiere oder Sachen zu beschreiben. Willst du Personen oder Sachen vergleichen, steigerst du die Adjektive. Die Steigerungsformen heißen **comparative** (Komparativ) und **superlative** (Superlativ).

a) Steigerung von Adjektiven mit *-er* und *-est*

- Einsilbige Adjektive (z. B. *cheap, old, young*) werden durch das Anhängen von **-er** und **-est** gesteigert.

Grundform (Positiv)	Komparativ	Superlativ
cheap	cheap**er**	(the) cheap**est**
old	old**er**	(the) old**est**
young	young**er**	(the) young**est**

- Diese Regel gilt auch für zweisilbige Adjektive, die auf **-y** enden (z. B. *pretty, trendy, easy*), allerdings wird dabei aus dem **-y** ein **-i**.

pretty	pret**tier**	(the) prett**iest**
trendy	trend**ier**	(the) trend**iest**
easy	eas**ier**	(the) eas**iest**

- Aufgepasst! Bei manchen Adjektiven ändert sich die Schreibweise:

nice	nic**er**	(the) nic**est**
hot	hot**ter**	(the) hot**test**
big	big**ger**	(the) big**gest**

- Einige Adjektive haben unregelmäßige Steigerungsformen. Diese Formen musst du wie Vokabeln lernen.

good	**better**	(the) **best**
bad	**worse**	(the) **worst**

LANGUAGE IN FOCUS

LiF

b) Steigerung von Adjektiven mit *more* und *most*

- Mehrsilbige Adjektive werden mit **more** und **most** gesteigert. Du stellst **more** und **most** vor das Adjektiv. Das Adjektiv bleibt dabei unverändert.

| interesting | **more** interesting | (the) **most** interesting |
| beautiful | **more** beautiful | (the) **most** beautiful |

c) Vergleiche mit Adjektiven

- Willst du ungleiche Dinge miteinander vergleichen, benutzt du den Komparativ mit **than**.

  The black jacket is more expensive **than** the white T-shirt.

- Sind die Eigenschaften von zwei Dingen oder Personen gleich, benutzt du **as … as** mit der Grundform des Adjektivs.

  The grey T-shirt is **as** expensive **as** the white T-shirt.

20 Stützwörter: ‚one/ones' (Prop words: one/ones)

- Du benutzt **one/ones**, um ein Substantiv nicht zu wiederholen.

  Emma has got three **exercise books**, a blue **one** and two red **ones**.
  Our teacher said we should bring a **calculator**, but I haven't got **one**.
  Do you need a **pencil**? – No thanks, I've got **one**.

- **Aufgepasst!** Im Deutschen kannst du das Substantiv einfach weglassen, wenn du es nicht wiederholen möchtest. Im Englischen ist das nicht möglich. Du musst **one** (für ein Wort im Singular) oder **ones** (für ein Wort im Plural) benutzen.

  Which **shoes** should I take? The **black ones** or the **brown ones**?

- Auch nach *the, that, this, which, these, those* kann **one/ones** ein Substantiv ersetzen.

  Which film would you like to see? **The one** with Daniel Craig
      or **the one** with Robert Pattinson?
  I've got some CDs here. **Which ones** do we need for the party?
  I don't usually like history books, but **this one** is really good.

  Which one do you like better? The green one or the blue one?

21 Adverbien der Art und Weise (Adverbs of manner)

- Wenn du beschreiben willst, wie jemand etwas tut oder wie etwas geschieht, benutzt du ein Adverb der Art und Weise. Adverbien der Art und Weise bildest du, indem du an das Adjektiv die Endung **-ly** anhängst.

He is a bad singer.	→	He sings **badly**.
Susan is a slow walker.	→	She walks **slowly**.
Dawn is quiet.	→	She talks **quietly**.

LANGUAGE IN FOCUS

- Bei manchen Adjektiven ändert sich die Schreibweise, wenn **-ly** angehängt wird:

happy	happ**ily**
easy	eas**ily**
angry	angr**ily**
beautiful	beautiful**ly**
careful	careful**ly**
terrible	terri**bly**

She can skate **beautifully**.

- Einige Adverbien haben Sonderformen. Diese Formen musst du wie Vokabeln lernen.

fast	**fast**
hard	**hard**
good	**well**

- Adverbien der Art und Weise stehen in Sätzen ohne Objekt nach dem Verb. In Sätzen mit Objekt folgen sie dem Objekt.

Subjekt	Verb	Objekt	Adverb
A lion	runs		fast.
Bob	plays	the guitar	well.

22 Steigerung von Adverbien (Comparison of adverbs)

- Adverbien werden unterschiedlich gesteigert. Endet das Adverb auf **-ly,** steigerst du es mit **more** und **most**.

Grundform	Komparativ	Superlativ
happily	**more** happily	(the) **most** happily
carefully	**more** carefully	(the) **most** carefully

- Adverbien, die die gleiche Form wie das Adjektiv haben, werden mit **-er** und **-est** gesteigert.

Grundform	Komparativ	Superlativ
fast	fast**er**	(the) fast**est**
friendly	friendl**ier**	(the) friendl**iest**

- Einige Adverbien haben unregelmäßige Steigerungsformen. Diese musst du wie Vokabeln lernen.

Grundform	Komparativ	Superlativ
well	**better**	(the) **best**
badly	**worse**	(the) **worst**
little	**less**	(the) **least**

23 Satzadverbien (Sentence adverbs)

- Beziehen Adverbien wie **luckily, before, while, finally, after, however, moreover, unfortunately** sich nicht nur auf ein einzelnes Verb, sondern auf einen gesamten Satz, sind es so genannte **Satzadverbien**.

  Unfortunately, Darren was feeling a little sick.

  Jessica learns a lot at the restaurant. **Moreover,** she meets very interesting people.

  I would like to go to the cinema tonight. **However,** I have to do my homework first.

  Luckily, she reached the car **before** the tiger could get her.

24 Konjunktionen (Conjunctions)

- Du benutzt eine **Konjunktion,** um Sätze oder Satzglieder zu verbinden. Mit Konjunktionen wie **and, but, so, or** verbindest du Hauptsätze.

Hauptsatz	Konjunktion	Hauptsatz
Sadie said she had to think about it	but	she couldn't promise not to see Kevin again.
Mira works twelve hours a day	so	she can earn money for her family.

- Mit Konjunktionen wie **because, although, if, when** und **while** verbindest du einen Hauptsatz mit einem Nebensatz.

Hauptsatz	Konjunktion	Nebensatz
Melinda wants to train as a car mechanic	although	her mother is against it.
Jessica likes her job	because	she meets very interesting people.

25 Emphatisches ‚do' (Emphatic do)

- Das emphatische *do* benutzt du, um einer Aussage besonderen Nachdruck zu verleihen. Wenn du betonen möchtest, dass etwas *wirklich* wahr ist oder *wirklich* stattgefunden hat, kannst du **do, does** oder **did** + Infinitiv zur Betonung verwenden.

  I **did** do my homework.   Your shirt **does** look silly.   I **do** like you.

- **Aufgepasst!** Du kannst das *emphatic do* nicht mit *be* verwenden.

GRAMMATICAL TERMS

German	LiF	English	Example
Adjektiv	19	adjective [ˈædʒɪktɪv]	nice, tall, big
als Substantiv		as noun [æz ˈnaʊn]	the British, the young
Adverb	21	adverb [ˈædvɜːb]	
der Art und Weise		of manner [əv ˈmænə]	angrily, quickly, badly
Häufigkeitsadverb		of frequency [əv ˌfriːkwənsi]	sometimes, often, never
der Zeit		of time [əv ˈtaɪm]	this morning, early
Artikel		article [ˈɑːtɪkl]	
bestimmter		definite [ˈdefnət]	the
unbestimmter		indefinite [ɪnˈdefnət]	a, an
Aussagesatz	13	statement [ˈsteɪtmənt]	Her name is Cheryl.
Bedingungssatz, Typ I	6	conditional clause, type I [kənˌdɪʃnəl ˈklɔːz]	If it's cold outside, I'll wear a jacket.
Bedingungssatz, Typ II	7	conditional clause, type II	If it were cold outside, I would wear a jacket.
Bedingungssatz, Typ III	8	conditional clause, type III	If it had been cold outside, I would have worn a jacket.
Bestätigungsfrage		question tag [ˈkwestʃn ˌtæg]	That's Katie's wallet, isn't it?
Einzahl (Singular)		singular [ˈsɪŋjʊlə]	house, school, brother
Ersatzform	11	substitute form [ˈsʌbstɪˌtjuːt ˌfɔːm]	have to, be able to, be allowed to
Frage	13	question [ˈkwestʃn]	How old are you?
Fragewort		question word [ˈkwestʃn ˌwɜːd]	who, when, what, whose
Futur (Zukunft)	5	future tense [ˌfjuːtʃə ˈtens]	
einfache Gegenwart mit Futurbedeutung		simple present with future meaning	The movie starts at 8pm.
Futur mit *going to*		going to future [ˈgəʊɪŋ tʊ ˌfjuːtʃə]	She is going to buy a CD.
Futur mit *will*		will future [ˈwɪl ˌfjuːtʃə]	She will be a pop star.
Gegenwart	1	present tense [ˌpreznt ˈtens]	
einfache Gegenwart		simple present [ˌsɪmpl ˈpreznt]	He plays tennis on Mondays. He doesn't play soccer.
Verlaufsform der Gegenwart		present progressive [ˌpreznt prəʊˈgresɪv]	It is raining. It isn't snowing.
Vollendete Gegenwart	2	present perfect [ˌpreznt ˈpɜːfɪkt]	We have been to Perth before.
Verlaufsform der vollendeten Gegenwart		present perfect progressive [ˌpreznt ˌpɜːfɪkt prəʊˈgresɪv]	I have been living here since my birth.
Genitiv		genitive [ˈdʒenətɪv]	Brian's photo, the title of the story
Imperativ (Befehlsform)		imperative [ɪmˈperətɪv]	Go and wash your hands.
indirekte Rede	12	reported speech [rɪˌpɔːtɪd ˈspiːtʃ]	I read a lot. ➔ She says (that) she reads a lot.
Infinitiv (Grundform)		infinitive [ɪnˈfɪnɪtɪv]	be, sit, listen
***-ing*-Form (Gerundium)**	18	gerund [ˈdʒerənd]	I like <u>going</u> to parties.
Konjunktion	24	conjunction [kənˈdʒʌŋkʃn]	and, or, because, when, until
Kurzantwort		short answer [ˌʃɔːt ˈɑːnsə]	Yes, I do. / No, we haven't.
Kurzform		short form [ˈʃɔːt ˌfɔːm]	I'm, they've got, it's
Langform		long form [ˈlɒŋ ˌfɔːm]	I am, they have got, it is

GRAMMATICAL TERMS

	LiF		
Mehrzahl (Plural)		plural ['plʊərəl]	houses, schools, brothers
unregelmäßig		irregular [ɪ'regjʊlə]	child – children, tooth – teeth
Mengenangabe		quantifier ['kwɒntɪˌfaɪə]	some juice, much money
Modalverb	11	modal verb [ˌməʊdl 'vɜːb]	can, must, should
Objekt	14	object ['ɒbdʒekt]	We've got a <u>cat</u>. I like <u>music</u>.
Partizip Perfekt	17	past participle [ˌpɑːst 'pɑːtɪsɪpl]	eaten, gone, started
Passiv	9	passive ['pæsɪv]	My watch was made in China.
Präposition		preposition [ˌprepə'zɪʃn]	in, into, next to, on, over
Pronomen (Fürwort)		pronoun ['prəʊnaʊn]	
Personalpronomen		personal pronoun [ˌpɜːsnəl 'prəʊnaʊn]	I, you, he/she/it, we, you, they
Possessivbegleiter		possessive determiner [pəˌzesɪv dɪ'tɜːmɪnə]	my, your, his/her/its, our, your, their
Possessivpronomen		possessive pronoun [pəˌzesɪv 'prəʊnaʊn]	mine, yours, his/hers, ours, yours, theirs
Reflexivpronomen		reflexive pronoun [rɪˌfleksɪv 'prəʊnaʊn]	myself, yourself, himself/herself/itself, ourselves, yourselves, themselves
Relativpronomen	16	relative pronoun [ˌrelətɪv 'prəʊnaʊn]	who, which, that
Relativsatz	16	relative clause [ˌrelətɪv 'klɔːz]	That's the man <u>who helped me</u>.
ohne Relativpronomen		contact clause ['kɒntækt ˌklɔːz]	The town <u>(that) Oliver is going to</u> is called London.
Satz		sentence ['sentəns]	
bejaht/positiv		positive ['pɒzətɪv]	She's from the US.
verneint/negativ		negative ['negətɪv]	We haven't got a car.
Steigerung von Adjektiven	19	comparison [kəm'pærɪsn]	
Grundform		positive ['pɒzətɪv]	tall, important
Komparativ		comparative [kəm'pærətɪv]	taller, more important
Superlativ		superlative [sʊ'pɜːlətɪv]	(the) tallest, (the) most important
Stützwort: *one/ones*	20	prop word: one/ones ['prɒp ˌwɜːd: wʌn/wʌnz]	Which one do you like best?
Subjekt	13	subject ['sʌbdʒekt]	<u>We</u>'ve got a cat.
Substantiv (Hauptwort)		noun [naʊn]	market, Adam, brother
zählbares		countable ['kaʊntəbl]	bottle – bottles, tooth – teeth
unzählbares		uncountable [ʌn'kaʊntəbl]	butter, water, sand
Verb		verb [vɜːb]	
regelmäßig		regular ['regjʊlə]	play, clean, like
unregelmäßig		irregular [ɪ'regjʊlə]	come, do, eat
Vergangenheit	3	past tense [ˌpɑːst 'tens]	
einfache Vergangenheit		simple past [ˌsɪmpl 'pɑːst]	We played games at the party.
Verlaufsform der Vergangenheit		past progressive [ˌpɑːst prəʊ'gresɪv]	Yesterday at 6pm Andy was cooking dinner.
Vorvergangenheit	4	past perfect [ˌpɑːst 'pɜːfɪkt]	He didn't bring his homework because the dog <u>had eaten</u> it.
Verneinung		negation [nɪ'geɪʃn]	No, I don't like it.
Wortstellung	13	word order ['wɜːdˌˌɔːdə]	subject – verb – object

WORDS

Alphabetische Wortlisten

In der alphabetischen Wortliste findest du den Lernwortschatz aus Camden Market 1–5 sowie alle Wörter aus diesem Buch (*Themes* 1–6). Wenn du also ein Wort noch nicht kennst oder dich nicht mehr an seine deutsche Bedeutung erinnerst, kannst du es im *English-German dictionary* ab **Seite 182** nachschlagen.

Wenn du für eine Aufgabe ein englisches Wort brauchst, kannst du es im *German-English dictionary* ab **Seite 224** nachschlagen.

Die Wortlisten nach *Themes*

Hier sind alle neuen Wörter der *Themes* 1–4 in der Reihenfolge angegeben, in der sie vorne im Buch vorkommen. Wörter mit einem ° brauchst du dir nicht zu merken.

Hier siehst du, wie du die Wortlisten ab **Seite 153** benutzen kannst:

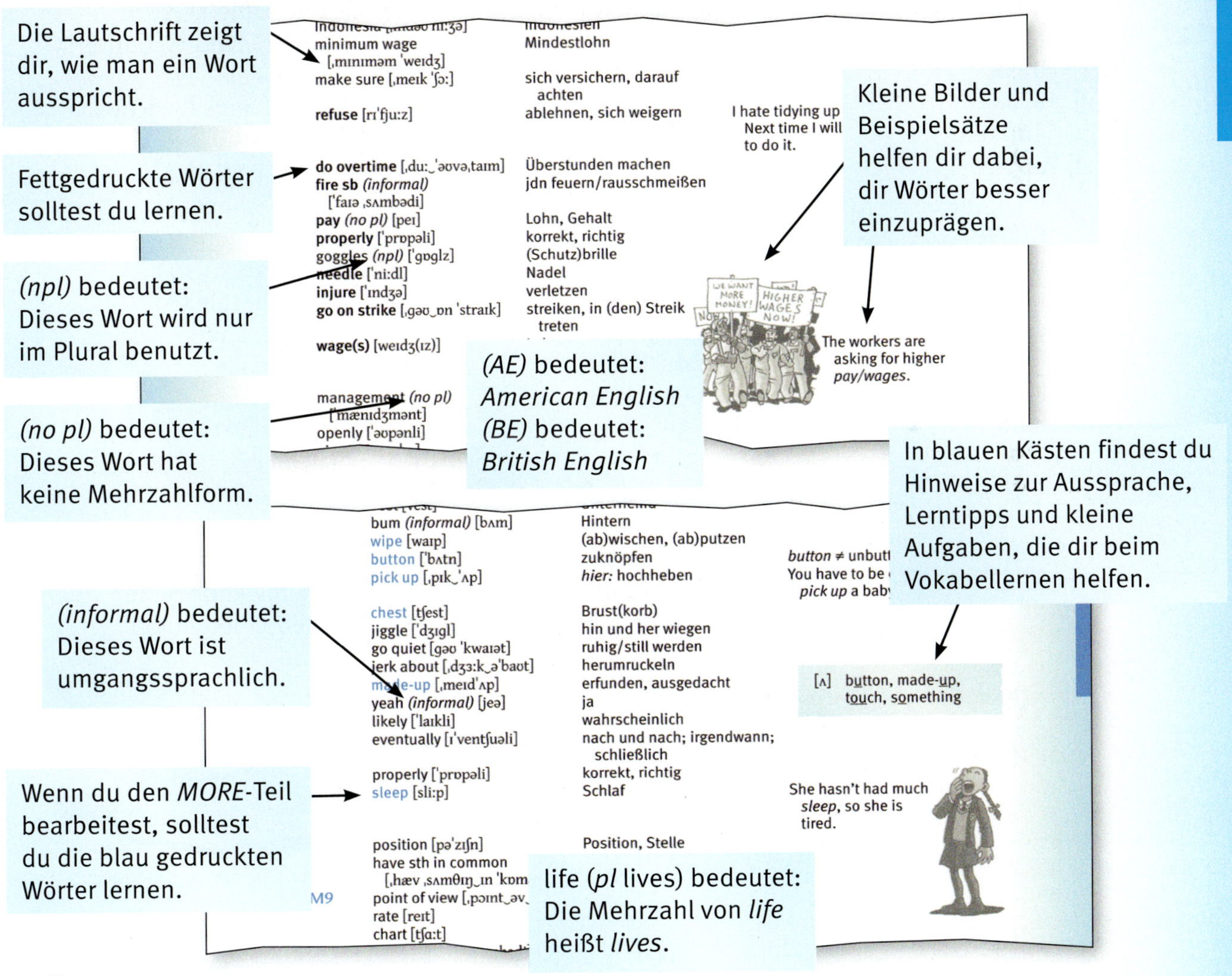

Die Lautschrift zeigt dir, wie man ein Wort ausspricht.

Fettgedruckte Wörter solltest du lernen.

(npl) bedeutet: Dieses Wort wird nur im Plural benutzt.

(no pl) bedeutet: Dieses Wort hat keine Mehrzahlform.

(informal) bedeutet: Dieses Wort ist umgangssprachlich.

Wenn du den *MORE*-Teil bearbeitest, solltest du die blau gedruckten Wörter lernen.

Indonesia [ˌɪndəʊˈniːʒə]	Indonesien
minimum wage [ˌmɪnɪməm ˈweɪdʒ]	Mindestlohn
make sure [ˌmeɪk ˈʃɔː]	sich versichern, darauf achten
refuse [rɪˈfjuːz]	ablehnen, sich weigern
do overtime [ˌduːˈˌəʊvəˌtaɪm]	Überstunden machen
fire sb *(informal)* [ˈfaɪə ˌsʌmbədi]	jdn feuern/rausschmeißen
pay *(no pl)* [peɪ]	Lohn, Gehalt
properly [ˈprɒpəli]	korrekt, richtig
goggles *(npl)* [ˈɡɒɡlz]	(Schutz)brille
needle [ˈniːdl]	Nadel
injure [ˈɪndʒə]	verletzen
go on strike [ˌɡəʊ ɒn ˈstraɪk]	streiken, in (den) Streik treten
wage(s) [weɪdʒ(ɪz)]	
management *(no pl)* [ˈmænɪdʒmənt]	
openly [ˈəʊpənli]	

I hate tidying up Next time I will to do it.

Kleine Bilder und Beispielsätze helfen dir dabei, dir Wörter besser einzuprägen.

The workers are asking for higher *pay/wages*.

(AE) bedeutet: *American English*
(BE) bedeutet: *British English*

In blauen Kästen findest du Hinweise zur Aussprache, Lerntipps und kleine Aufgaben, die dir beim Vokabellernen helfen.

bum *(informal)* [bʌm]	Hintern
wipe [waɪp]	(ab)wischen, (ab)putzen
button [ˈbʌtn]	zuknöpfen
pick up [ˌpɪkˈˌʌp]	*hier:* hochheben
chest [tʃest]	Brust(korb)
jiggle [ˈdʒɪɡl]	hin und her wiegen
go quiet [ɡəʊ ˈkwaɪət]	ruhig/still werden
jerk about [ˌdʒɜːk əˈbaʊt]	herumruckeln
made-up [ˌmeɪdˈʌp]	erfunden, ausgedacht
yeah *(informal)* [jeə]	ja
likely [ˈlaɪkli]	wahrscheinlich
eventually [ɪˈventʃuəli]	nach und nach; irgendwann; schließlich
properly [ˈprɒpəli]	korrekt, richtig
sleep [sliːp]	Schlaf
position [pəˈzɪʃn]	Position, Stelle
have sth in common [ˌhæv ˌsʌmθɪn ɪn ˈkɒm	
point of view [ˌpɔɪnt əv	
rate [reɪt]	
chart [tʃɑːt]	

M9

button ≠ unbutt
You have to be *pick up* a baby

[ʌ] button, made-up, touch, something

She hasn't had much *sleep*, so she is tired.

life (*pl* lives) bedeutet: Die Mehrzahl von *life* heißt *lives*.

Names

Auf den **Seiten 249–251** findest du alle Namen aus den *Themes* mit Lautschrift.

Irregular verbs

Alle unregelmäßigen Verben, die in den *Themes* vorkommen, findest du auf den **Seiten 253–254**.

151

WORDS

English sounds

Im Englischen spricht man Wörter oft anders aus, als man sie schreibt. Das ist aber kein Problem. Denn die Aussprache der Wörter ist in jedem Wörterbuch angegeben. So kann man auch neue Wörter richtig aussprechen, ohne sie vorher gehört zu haben.
Dazu nimmt man die sogenannte Lautschrift zu Hilfe. Das ist eine Schrift, deren Symbole jeden Laut genau bezeichnen. Die Lautschrift wird in jedem Wörterbuch benutzt.

Hier findest du eine Liste mit den Symbolen dieser Lautschrift zusammen mit Beispielwörtern, in denen der entsprechende Laut vorkommt.

Vokale

[ɑ:] arm
[ʌ] but
[e] desk
[ə] a, an
[ɜ:] girl, bird
[æ] apple
[ɪ] in, it
[i] every
[i:] easy, eat
[ɒ] orange, sorry
[ɔ:] all, call
[ʊ] look
[u] February
[u:] food

Doppellaute

[aɪ] eye, buy
[aʊ] our
[eə] there
[eɪ] take, they
[ɪə] here
[ɔɪ] boy
[əʊ] go, gold
[ʊə] you're

Konsonanten

[b] bag, club
[d] duck, card
[f] fish, laugh
[g] get, dog
[h] hot
[k] can, duck
[l] lot, small
[m] more, mum
[n] now, sun
[ŋ] song, long

[p] present, top
[r] red, right
[s] sister, class (scharfes s)
[t] time, cat
[z] nose, dogs (weiches s)
[dʒ] orange
[ʃ] sure, English
[tʃ] child, cheese
[ð] these, mother (weicher Laut)
[θ] mouth, think (harter Laut)
[v] very, have
[w] what, word

['] Betonungszeichen für die folgende Silbe (Hauptbetonung)
[ˌ] Betonungszeichen für die folgende Silbe (Nebenbetonung)

The English alphabet

[eɪ] a	[bi:] b	[si:] c	[di:] d	[i:] e	[ef] f	[dʒi:] g
[eɪtʃ] h	[aɪ] i	[dʒeɪ] j	[keɪ] k	[el] l	[em] m	[en] n
[əʊ] o	[pi:] p	[kju:] q	[ɑ:] r	[es] s	[ti:] t	[ju:] u
[vi:] v	['dʌblju:] w	[eks] x	[waɪ] y	[zed] z		

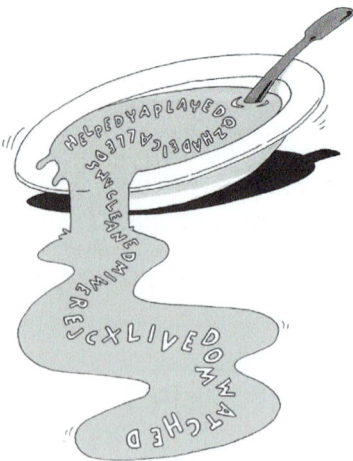

Theme 1 – Growing up

I	couple ['kʌpl]	Paar
	arranged marriage [əˌreɪndʒd 'mærɪdʒ]	arrangierte Hochzeit
	love marriage ['lʌv ˌmærɪdʒ]	Liebesheirat
1	graduation [ˌgrædʒu'eɪʃn]	Schulabschluss, Studienabschluss
	brainstorm ['breɪnˌstɔːm]	ein Brainstorming machen
2	barricade [ˌbærɪ'keɪd]	Barrikade
	deal with ['diːl wɪð]	handeln von; sich befassen mit
	character ['kærɪktə]	Charakter; Figur
	Catholic ['kæθlɪk]	Katholik/in; katholisch
	unskilled worker [ˌʌnˌskɪld 'wɜːkə]	Hilfsarbeiter
	brothers and sisters [ˌbrʌðəz‿ænd 'sɪstəz]	Geschwister
	Northern Ireland [ˌnɔːðn‿'aɪələnd]	Nordirland
	Protestant ['prɒtɪstənt]	Protestant/in; protestantisch
	up [ʌp]	(nach) oben; hinauf
	tirade [taɪ'reɪd]	Tirade *(Redeschwall)*
	roar [rɔː]	brüllen
	roof [ruːf]	Dach
	go on (seventeen) [ˌgəʊ‿ˌɒn ˌsevn'tiːn]	(schon) fast (siebzehn) sein
	get sb to do sth [ˌget ˌsʌmbədi tə 'duː ˌsʌmθɪŋ]	jdn dazu bringen, etw zu tun
	make to do sth [ˌmeɪk tə 'duː ˌsʌmθɪŋ]	Anstalten machen, etw zu tun
	let sb be [ˌlet ˌsʌmbədi 'biː]	jdn in Ruhe lassen
	headstrong ['hedˌstrɒŋ]	eigensinnig, eigenwillig
	turn sb against sb [ˌtɜːn ˌsʌmbədi‿ə'genst ˌsʌmbədi]	jdn gegen jdn aufbringen
3	seaside ['siːˌsaɪd]	Küste
	hey there ['heɪ ðeə]	he, hallo
	burn down [ˌbɜːn 'daʊn]	abbrennen, niederbrennen
	Prod *(informal)* [prɒd]	Protestant/in
	out [aʊt]	aus
	wearily ['wɪərəli]	müde; lustlos
	seize sb (by the shoulder) [ˌsiːz‿ˌsʌmbədi baɪ ðə 'ʃəʊldə]	jdn (an der Schulter) packen
	spin (a)round [ˌspɪn (ə)'raʊnd]	(um)drehen
	face to face [ˌfeɪs tə 'feɪs]	einander gegenüber, Auge in Auge
	do good [duː 'gʊd]	nützen, bringen
	be sick of sth [biː 'sɪk‿əv ˌsʌmθɪŋ]	etw satt haben, von etw genug haben

Nur zehn Minuten
Übe die Vokabeln immer nur fünf bis zehn Minuten, aber dafür regelmäßig! Das ist viel wirkungsvoller als eine ganze Stunde oder nur zweimal im Monat. Probiere dabei die Vokabeltipps auf den nächsten Seiten aus.

Brothers and sisters have the same parents.

roof

sb = somebody
sth = something

The firefighter rescues him from the building before it *burns down*.

He *spun around* quickly after hearing a loud noise.

I am *sick of* reading this book. It is so boring.

take oneself off [ˌteɪk wʌnˌselfˈɒf]	sich davonmachen	
depend on sth [dɪˈpendˌɒn ˌsʌmθɪŋ]	von etw abhängen	
shove [ʃʌv]	schieben, schubsen	
off [ɒf]	weg von	
blonde [blɒnd]	blond	
by the name of [ˌbaɪ ðə ˈneɪmˌəv]	namens	
so what? *(informal)* [ˌsəʊ ˈwɒt]	na und?	
mind one's own business *(informal)* [ˌmaɪnd wʌnzˌˌəʊn ˈbɪznəs]	sich um seinen (eigenen) Kram/seine (eigenen) Angelegenheiten kümmern	
fierce [fɪəs]	heftig, scharf	
business *(no pl)* [ˈbɪznəs]	Angelegenheit, Sache	
lean [liːn]	lehnen	

Schwierige Wörter
Wenn du merkst, dass du bei der Schreibweise einiger englischer Wörter Schwierigkeiten hast, kannst du Folgendes tun: Schreibe das Wort auf ein großes Blatt und markiere die Stelle, die dir Probleme macht. Hänge das Blatt in deinem Zimmer auf. Du wirst merken, dass du das Wort bald richtig schreiben kannst!

He *leaned* forward to look out of the window.

4

following [ˈfɒləʊɪŋ]	folgende(r, s)	
link [lɪŋk]	verbinden	
conjunction [kənˈdʒʌŋkʃn]	Konjunktion	
beat up [ˌbiːtˌˈʌp]	verprügeln, zusammenschlagen	

If you *beat* someone *up*, you hurt them badly by kicking or hitting them.

traitor [ˈtreɪtə]	Verräter	
° century [ˈsentʃəri]	Jahrhundert	
° famine [ˈfæmɪn]	Hungersnot	
° starve [stɑːv]	(ver)hungern	
° resistance *(no pl)* [rɪˈzɪstns]	Widerstand	
° the English [ðiˌˈɪŋglɪʃ]	die Engländer	
° the Irish [ðiˌˈaɪərɪʃ]	die Iren	
° independence [ˌɪndɪˈpendəns]	Unabhängigkeit	
° southern [ˈsʌðən]	südlich, Süd-	
° Republic of Ireland [rɪˌpʌblɪkˌəvˌˈaɪələnd]	Republik Irland	
° majority [məˈdʒɒrəti]	Mehrheit	
° Nationalist [ˈnæʃnəlɪst]	Nationalist *(Anhänger der Republik Irland)*	
° Unionist [ˈjuːnjənɪst]	Unionist *(Anhänger der Union)*	
° from ... onwards [frəm ˈɒnwədz]	von ... an	
° violent [ˈvaɪələnt]	brutal, gewalttätig	
° see [siː]	*hier:* (mit)erleben	
° so-called [ˈsəʊkɔːld]	so genannt	
° the Troubles [ðə ˈtrʌblz]	*Zeit der Unruhen in Nordirland*	
° paramilitary [ˌpærəˈmɪlɪtri]	paramilitärisch	
° carry out [ˌkæriˌˈaʊt]	durchführen, verüben	
° bombing [ˈbɒmɪŋ]	Bombenanschlag	
° attack [əˈtæk]	Angriff	
° innocent [ˈɪnəsnt]	unschuldig; unbeteiligt	

PP

Spell check
Buchstabiere ein Wort für einen Partner. Wechselt euch ab und kontrolliert anschließend gegenseitig, ob alles richtig geschrieben ist. Für jedes richtige Wort gibt es einen Punkt. Wer ist der *spelling king* oder die *spelling queen*?

I have decided to become a vegetarian. *From* now *onwards* I'm not going to eat meat.

Eleven people were injured in the *bombing* last week.

° hold peace talks [ˌhəʊld ˈpiːs tɔːks]	Friedensverhandlungen führen	
° peaceful [ˈpiːsfl]	friedlich	
° conflict [ˈkɒnflɪkt]	Konflikt	
° mistrust *(no pl)* [mɪsˈtrʌst]	Misstrauen, Argwohn	There is *mistrust* between Catholics and Protestants in Ireland.

° violence [ˈvaɪələns]	Gewalt, Gewalttätigkeit	
5 elderly [ˈeldəli]	ältere(r, s)	
recognize [ˈrekəgnaɪz]	(wieder)erkennen	
former [ˈfɔːmə]	ehemalige(r, s), frühere(r, s)	A *former* friend is not a friend anymore.
at someone's place [ət ˈsʌmwʌnz ˌpleɪs]	bei jdm zu Hause	Let's meet *at my place* tomorrow.
housekeeper [ˈhaʊsˌkiːpə]	Haushälter/in	
anonymous [əˈnɒnɪməs]	anonym	We don't know who wrote the letter. It is *anonymous*.

6 bomb [bɒm]	Bombe	
funeral [ˈfjuːnrəl]	Beerdigung, Begräbnis	
tighten [ˈtaɪtn]	verstärken	
hold [həʊld]	Griff	
not ... any longer [ˌnɒt ˌeni ˈlɒŋgə]	nicht länger	I'm so excited, I ca*n't* wait *any longer*.
pause [pɔːz]	innehalten	
continue [kənˈtɪnjuː]	fortfahren	
case [keɪs]	Fall	
run away [rʌn ə ˈweɪ]	weglaufen	
anyway [ˈeniˌweɪ]	sowieso, jedenfalls	
swallow [ˈswɒləʊ]	schlucken	You shouldn't *swallow* chewing gum.

7 harbour [ˈhɑːbə]	Hafen	
beside [bɪˈsaɪd]	neben	
shed [ʃed]	*hier:* Regendach, Wartehäuschen	
yard [jɑːd]	Yard (= 0,91 Meter)	
reach [riːtʃ]	greifen; *hier:* erreichen	He was the first to *reach* the finish line.

see sb off [ˌsiː ˌsʌmbədi ˈɒf]	jdn verabschieden	
amazement *(no pl)* [əˈmeɪzmənt]	Erstaunen, Verwunderung	
anxious [ˈæŋkʃəs]	besorgt	
mind [maɪnd]	etw dagegen haben	
suitcase [ˈsuːtˌkeɪs]	Koffer	Have you packed my pink shirt in the *suitcase*?

lift up [ˌlɪft ˈʌp]	(hoch)heben	
whirl (a)round [ˈwɜːl (ə)ˌraʊnd]	herumwirbeln	
breathless [ˈbreθləs]	atemlos, außer Atem	
laughter *(no pl)* [ˈlɑːftə]	Lachen, Gelächter	I heard *laughter*, so I knew they were having fun.

news *(no pl)* [njuːz]	Neuigkeit; Nachrichten	

WORDS THEME 1

	in (months) [ɪn ˈmʌnθs]	seit (Monaten)
	luggage *(no pl)* [ˈlʌgɪdʒ]	Gepäck

luggage = bags and suitcases that you take on a trip

	hold out [ˌhəʊldˈaʊt]	hinhalten
	across [əˈkrɒs]	*hier:* durch
8	entry [ˈentri]	*hier:* Eintrag
	farewell [ˌfeəˈwel]	Abschied(s)-
9	blues [bluːz]	Blues *(schwermütiges Lied der Afroamerikaner)*

Can you sort these words into alphabetical order?
luggage, roof, breathless, roar, blonde, traitor, lean, burn down, anonymous, recognize

	still [stɪl]	Standfoto
	atmosphere [ˈætməsˌfɪə]	Atmosphäre, Stimmung
	(in the) foreground [ˈfɔːˌgraʊnd]	(im) Vordergrund
	(in the) background [ˈbækˌgraʊnd]	(im) Hintergrund
	dearest [ˈdɪərəst]	Liebste/r, Liebling
10	review [rɪˈvjuː]	Kritik, Rezension
	teenage [ˈtiːneɪdʒ]	jugendlich; *hier:* Teenager-
	after all [ˌɑːftəˈrɔːl]	schließlich
	make an appointment [ˌmeɪkˌənˌəˈpɔɪntmənt]	einen Termin ausmachen/ vereinbaren

If you want to speak to a doctor, you usually have to *make an appointment.*

	abortion [əˈbɔːʃn]	Abtreibung, Schwangerschaftsabbruch
	give up for adoption [ˌgɪvˌʌp fərˌəˈdɒpʃn]	zur Adoption freigeben

If parents can't care for their children, they can *give them up for adoption.*

	shock [ʃɒk]	Schock
	understanding [ˌʌndəˈstændɪŋ]	verständnisvoll

It is good to have friends who are *understanding.*

	decision [dɪˈsɪʒn]	Entscheidung, Entschluss
	support [səˈpɔːt]	(unter)stützen
	pregnancy [ˈpregnənsi]	Schwangerschaft
	be okay with sth [bɪˌəʊˈkeɪ wɪð ˌsʌmθɪŋ]	mit etw einverstanden sein
	whatever [wɒtˈevə]	was (auch immer)
	adopt [əˈdɒpt]	adoptieren
	couple [ˈkʌpl]	Paar

She couldn't get pregnant, so she *adopted* a baby. They are such a cute *couple.*

	unrealistic [ˌʌnrɪəˈlɪstɪk]	unrealistisch
	tolerant [ˈtɒlərənt]	tolerant
	calm [kɑːm]	ruhig, gelassen
	handle [ˈhændl]	mit etw umgehen; bewältigen, regeln
	matter [ˈmætə]	Angelegenheit, Sache
	emotional [ɪˈməʊʃnəl]	emotional

She's really *emotional.* She cries all the time.

	chaos *(no pl)* [ˈkeɪɒs]	Chaos, Durcheinander
	face [feɪs]	etw ausgesetzt sein, mit etw konfrontiert sein
	most of all [ˌməʊstˌəvˈɔːl]	am meisten; *hier:* vor allem
	damn [dæm]	verurteilen, verdammen

WORDS   *Theme 1*

	clear [klɪə]	klar, eindeutig	
	state [steɪt]	aussprechen	
	in the first place [ɪn ðə ˈfɜːst ˌpleɪs]	zunächst (einmal), an erster Stelle	
	cast [kɑːst]	*hier:* Besetzung, Ensemble	The *cast* of a film or play are the actors.
	script [skrɪpt]	Drehbuch, Skript	
	enjoyable [ɪnˈdʒɔɪəbl]	unterhaltsam	
12	reviewer [rɪˈvjuːə]	Rezensent/in, Kritiker/in	
13	screen [skriːn]	Leinwand	At the cinema you watch a film on a big *screen*.
14	helpline [ˈhelpˌlaɪn]	telefonischer Beratungsdienst; Notruf	
	decision-making process [dɪˌsɪʒnˌmeɪkɪŋ ˈprəʊses]	Entscheidungsprozess	
	involve [ɪnˈvɒlv]	beinhalten; betreffen	
	toll-free [ˌtəʊlˈfriː]	gebührenfrei	
	option [ˈɒpʃn]	Wahl, Möglichkeit, Option	When you leave school, you have lots of *options*: you can travel, find a job or go to college.
	put sb in touch with sb [ˌpʊt ˌsʌmbədiˌɪn ˈtʌtʃ wɪð ˌsʌmbədi]	jdm helfen, mit jdm Kontakt aufzunehmen	
	assist [əˈsɪst]	helfen, unterstützen	
	parenting *(no pl)* [ˈpeərəntɪŋ]	Verhalten als Eltern, Kindererziehung	
	require sb to do sth [rɪˌkwaɪə ˌsʌmbədi tə ˈduː ˌsʌmθɪŋ]	von jdm verlangen, etw zu tun	
	child support [ˈtʃaɪld səˌpɔːt]	Unterhalt, Alimente	
	adoption [əˈdɒpʃn]	Adoption	
	adoptive [əˈdɒptɪv]	Adoptiv-	
	keep in touch with sb [ˌkiːpˌɪn ˈtʌtʃ wɪð ˌsʌmbədi]	mit jdm in Kontakt bleiben	

Find the nouns to these words:
laugh – ???
decide – ???
pregnant – ???
adopt – ???

Although I have left school, I *keep in touch with* my old friends by email.

M1	**wedding** [ˈwedɪŋ]	Hochzeit	
	take pictures [ˌteɪk ˈpɪktʃəz]	Bilder machen, fotografieren	
M2	throughout [θruːˈaʊt]	während, im Laufe	
	everlasting [ˌevəˈlɑːstɪŋ]	immerwährend, ewig	
	fancy [ˈfænsi]	ausgefallen, aufwändig	
	married [ˈmærid]	verheiratet	*married* ≠ divorced
	tell sb to do sth [ˌtel ˌsʌmbədi tə ˈduː ˌsʌmθɪŋ]	jdm etw vorschreiben/ befehlen	
	have sb around [ˌhæv ˌsʌmbədiˌəˈraʊnd]	jdn in der Nähe haben	
M3	**view** [vjuː]	*hier:* Ansicht, Meinung	They have different *views* on the subject.
	radio station [ˈreɪdɪəʊ ˌsteɪʃn]	Radiosender	
	listener [ˈlɪsnə]	(Zu)hörer/in	
	leave out [ˌliːvˌˈaʊt]	auslassen, weglassen	
	relative pronoun [ˌrelətɪv ˈprəʊnaʊn]	Relativpronomen	

WORDS THEME 1

157

	raise [reɪz]	großziehen, aufziehen	It is hard work *raising* children.
	marriage ['mærɪdʒ]	Heirat	
	ruin ['ruːɪn]	ruinieren, zerstören	
M4	arranged marriage [əˌreɪndʒd 'mærɪdʒ]	arrangierte Hochzeit	
	common ['kɒmən]	üblich, normal	Marriage is not as *common* as fifty years ago.
	love marriage ['lʌv ˌmærɪdʒ]	Liebesheirat	
	girlfriend ['gɜːlˌfrend]	Freundin *(eines Jungen)*	
	extract ['ekstrækt]	Auszug	
	deal [diːl]	*hier:* Angelegenheit, Sache	
	threaten to do sth [ˌθretn tə 'duː ˌsʌmθɪŋ]	damit drohen, etw zu tun	He *threatened to* kill me.

	keep sb happy [ˌkiːp ˌsʌmbədi 'hæpi]	jdn bei Laune halten	
	in old age [ɪn ˌəʊld 'eɪdʒ]	im (hohen) Alter	
	distant ['dɪstənt]	entfernt, fern	
	down [daʊn]	unten	
	shame [ʃeɪm]	Schande; Scham	
	slap [slæp]	schlagen	She was so angry with him that she *slapped* him.
	thigh [θaɪ]	(Ober)schenkel	
	squeeze [skwiːz]	drücken	
	reassure [ˌriːə'ʃʊə]	beruhigen	
	while *(no pl)* [waɪl]	Weile	
	set [set]	festgefahren	
	selfish ['selfɪʃ]	egoistisch, selbstsüchtig	
	end up [ˌend 'ʌp]	enden	He *ended up* in prison after stealing a car.
	provided [prə'vaɪdɪd]	sofern, vorausgesetzt	
	cast sb aside [ˌkɑːst ˌsʌmbədi ə'saɪd]	jdn fallenlassen	
	kiss sb on the lips [ˌkɪs ˌsʌmbədi ɒn ðə 'lɪps]	jdn auf den Mund küssen	
	hug [hʌg]	Umarmung	
	conversation [ˌkɒnvə'seɪʃn]	Gespräch, Unterhaltung	
M6	out of date [ˌaʊt əv 'deɪt]	überholt, nicht mehr aktuell, nicht mehr zeitgemäß	We only watch DVDs. Videos are *out of date*.
M8	sleepless ['sliːpləs]	schlaflos	
	shit *(informal)* [ʃɪt]	Kacke, Scheiße	
	(it's) your turn [ɪts jɔː 'tɜːn]	du bist dran	
	awake [ə'weɪk]	wach	
	as though [əz 'ðəʊ]	als ob	
	all over again [ˌɔːl ˌəʊvər ə'gen]	noch einmal (ganz von vorn)	

Now *it's your turn!*

weird *(informal)* [wɪəd]	merkwürdig, seltsam, komisch	
wind [wɪnd]	ein Bäuerchen machen	
nappy ['næpi]	Windel	
change [tʃeɪndʒ]	*hier:* wickeln	
put on sth [ˌpʊt 'ɒn ˌsʌmθɪŋ]	etw einschalten/anmachen	
bedside light ['bedsaɪd laɪt]	Nachttischlampe	
greasy ['griːsi]	fettig	

take seriously [teɪk ˈsɪərɪəsli] — ernst nehmen

He *takes* his training very *seriously*.

cot [kɒt] — Kinderbett
bend down [ˌbendˌˈdaʊn] — sich herunterbeugen
changing table ['tʃeɪndʒɪŋ ˌteɪbl] — Wickeltisch
unbutton [ʌnˈbʌtn] — aufknöpfen
sleep suit ['sliːp ˌsuːt] — (Baby-)Schlafanzug
vest [vest] — Unterhemd
bum (informal) [bʌm] — Hintern
wipe [waɪp] — (ab)wischen, (ab)putzen
button ['bʌtn] — zuknöpfen
pick up [ˌpɪkˌˈʌp] — hier: hochheben

button ≠ unbutton
You have to be careful when you *pick up* a baby.

chest [tʃest] — Brust(korb)
jiggle ['dʒɪgl] — hin und her wiegen
go quiet [gəʊ ˈkwaɪət] — ruhig/still werden
jerk about [ˌdʒɜːkˌəˈbaʊt] — herumruckeln
made-up [ˌmeɪdˈʌp] — erfunden, ausgedacht
yeah (informal) [jeə] — ja
likely ['laɪkli] — wahrscheinlich
eventually [ɪˈventʃuəli] — nach und nach; irgendwann; schließlich

[ʌ]   b**u**tton, made-**u**p, t**ou**ch, s**o**mething

properly ['prɒpəli] — korrekt, richtig
sleep [sliːp] — Schlaf

She hasn't had much *sleep*, so she is tired.

position [pəˈzɪʃn] — Position, Stelle
have sth in common [ˌhæv ˌsʌmθɪŋ ɪn ˈkɒmən] — etwas gemein haben

M9   point of view [ˌpɔɪntˌəvˌˈvjuː] — Standpunkt, Gesichtspunkt
rate [reɪt] — Rate, Quote
chart [tʃɑːt] — Diagramm, Schaubild, Grafik
CIO   quiz sb ['kwɪzˌsʌmbədi] — jdn befragen/prüfen
be set somewhere [biː ˌset ˈsʌmweə] — irgendwo spielen/ stattfinden

The film *is set* in New York.

go abroad [ˌgəʊˌəˈbrɔːd] — ins Ausland gehen/reisen
culture ['kʌltʃə] — Kultur
avoid [əˈvɔɪd] — (ver)meiden, ausweichen
topic ['tɒpɪk] — Thema
° Gaelic ['geɪlɪk] — Gälisch; gälisch
° Eire ['eərə] — Eire, Irland
° wedding ring ['wedɪŋ rɪŋ] — Ehering, Trauring

People who are married usually wear a *wedding ring*.

° wedding costume ['wedɪŋ ˌkɒstjuːm] — Hochzeitskleidung
° newborn baby [ˌnjuːˌbɔːn 'beɪbi] — Neugeborene/s
° breastfeed ['brestˌfiːd] — stillen
° musical instrument [ˌmjuːzɪklˌˈɪnstrʊmənt] — Musikinstrument
° harp [hɑːp] — Harfe

The *harp* is Ireland's *national* symbol.

° national ['næʃnəl] — national; National-
° billion ['bɪljən] — Milliarde

WORDS *Theme 2*

Theme 2 – Making it on your own

I	make it ['meɪk‿ɪt]	es schaffen
	(letter of) application [ˌæplɪ'keɪʃn]	Bewerbung(sschreiben)
	abroad [ə'brɔːd]	im Ausland
1	start [stɑːt]	Anfang, Beginn
	° bell [bel]	Klingel, Glocke
	° ring [rɪŋ]	klingeln, läuten
	° go by [ˌgəʊ 'baɪ]	vergehen; vorbeigehen
	° at last [ət 'lɑːst]	endlich, schließlich
	° whoever [huː'evə]	wer (auch immer)
	° hope [həʊp]	Hoffnung
	° turn into sth [ˌtɜːn‿ˌɪntə sʌmθɪŋ]	zu etw werden
	° fear [fɪə]	Angst, Furcht; Sorge
	° face sth ['feɪs‿ˌsʌmθɪŋ]	etw ausgesetzt sein, mit etw konfrontiert sein
	° go to plan [ˌgəʊ tə 'plæn]	nach Plan verlaufen
	double circle [ˌdʌbl 'sɜːkl]	Doppelkreis
2	realistic [ˌrɪə'lɪstɪk]	realistisch
3	exchange [ɪks'tʃeɪndʒ]	Austausch
	future ['fjuːtʃə]	zukünftig, später
	electronics *(npl)* [ˌelek'trɒnɪks]	Elektronik
	programmer ['prəʊˌgræmə]	Programmierer/in
	plumber ['plʌmə]	Klempner/in, Sanitärinstallateur/in
	office ['ɒfɪs]	Büro
	chemical ['kemɪkl]	Chemikalie
	(letter of) application [ˌæplɪ'keɪʃn]	Bewerbung(sschreiben)
	position [pə'zɪʃn]	Position, Stelle
	trainee [ˌtreɪ'niː]	Auszubildende/r; Praktikant/in
	firm [fɜːm]	Firma, Unternehmen
	however [haʊ'evə]	aber, jedoch
	job interview ['dʒɒb‿ˌɪntəvjuː]	Bewerbungsgespräch, Vorstellungsgespräch
	hairdresser ['heəˌdresə]	Friseur/Friseuse
	hairdressing salon ['heəˌdresɪŋ ˌsælɒn]	Friseur(geschäft)
	allergic [ə'lɜːdʒɪk]	allergisch
	dye [daɪ]	Färbemittel
	allergy ['ælədʒi]	Allergie
	apply (for/to) [ə'plaɪ]	sich bewerben (um/für)
	hairdressing course ['heəˌdresɪŋ ˌkɔːs]	Ausbildung zum Friseur/zur Friseuse
	beauty therapy ['bjuːti ˌθerəpi]	Kosmetik
	not either [nɒt‿'aɪðə]	auch nicht
	aeroplane ['eərəˌpleɪn]	Flugzeug
	fascinate ['fæsɪneɪt]	faszinieren
	hardly ['hɑːdli]	kaum
	do well [du: 'wel]	gut abschneiden
	that [ðæt]	*hier:* so

How many jobs do you know in English? Make a list.

Zirkeltraining
Manchmal muss man den Kreislauf erst in Schwung bringen, damit man wieder konzentriert lernen kann. Für das Zirkeltraining schreibst du schwierige Wörter oder Formulierungen auf Zettel und verteilst diese dann in deinem Zimmer oder in der Wohnung. Dann gehst du an alle Stationen und formulierst Sätze mit den Wörtern auf den Zetteln. Kniebeugen nicht vergessen!

My dad works in an *office*.

I have found a position as a *trainee*. I start next month.

hairdresser

I'm going to *apply* for a job.

The carpet is so heavy, he can *hardly* carry it.

GCSE (= General Certificate of Secondary Education) [ˌdʒiː siː ˌes ˈiː] — britische Schulabschlussprüfung

exam (= examination) [ɪgˈzæm] — Prüfung

He found the maths *exam* really hard.

sixth form *(BE)* [ˈsɪksθ fɔːm] — die letzten zwei Schuljahre für Schüler zwischen 16 und 18

practical [ˈpræktɪkl] — praktisch

Mechanics need to be *practical*. They are always working with their hands.

rather [ˈrɑːðə] — *hier:* lieber

airfield [ˈeəˌfiːld] — Flugplatz

sb cannot wait to do sth [ˌsʌmbədi ˌkænɒt ˈweɪt tə duː ˌsʌmθɪŋ] — jmd kann es kaum erwarten, etw zu tun

[iː] airf**ie**ld, train**ee**, l**ea**n, r**ea**ch, s**e**cret

down *(informal)* [daʊn] — niedergeschlagen, down

for ages *(informal)* [fər ˈeɪdʒɪz] — ewig, seit Ewigkeiten

repair [rɪˈpeə] — Reparatur

you lot *(informal)* [ju ˈlɒt] — ihr

depressed [dɪˈprest] — deprimiert

depressed = very unhappy/sad

job counsellor [ˈdʒɒb ˌkaʊnslə] — Berufsberater/in

5 **butcher** [ˈbʊtʃə] — Metzger/in, Fleischer/in

You can buy meat at the *butcher's*.

carpenter [ˈkɑːpɪntə] — Zimmerer/Zimmerin

office administrator [ˌɒfɪs ədˈmɪnɪˌstreɪtə] — Bürokaufmann/Bürokauffrau

CPhT (= certified pharmacy technician) [ˌsiː piː ˌeɪtʃ ˈtiː] — PTA (= pharmazeutisch-technische/r Assistent/in)

taxi [ˈtæksi] — Taxi

welder [ˈweldə] — Schweißer/in

order [ˈɔːdə] — *hier:* Bestellung

The waiter is writing down the *order*.

type [taɪp] — Maschine schreiben, tippen

portable [ˈpɔːtəbl] — tragbar

produce [prəˈdjuːs] — herstellen, erzeugen, produzieren

typewriter [ˈtaɪpˌraɪtə] — Schreibmaschine

mix [mɪks] — (ver)mischen, anrühren

If you *mix* yellow and blue, you make green.

(at the) chemist's [ˈkemɪsts] — (in der) Drogerie; (in der) Apotheke

route [ruːt] — Route, Strecke, Verlauf

navigation system [ˌnævɪˈgeɪʃn ˌsɪstəm] — Navigationssystem

weld [weld] — schweißen

heat *(no pl)* [hiːt] — Wärme; Hitze

The cat is enjoying the *heat* from the fire.

hammer [ˈhæmə] — Hammer

6 working life [ˈwɜːkɪŋ laɪf] — Arbeitsleben

acrostic [əˈkrɒstɪk] — *Gedichtform, bei der bestimmte Buchstaben aus jeder Zeile untereinander ein Wort ergeben*

7 **child labour** [ˈtʃaɪld ˌleɪbə] — Kinderarbeit

chores [tʃɔːz] — (Haushalts)pflichten

WORDS THEME 2

	have sth in common [hæv ˌsʌmθɪŋ‿ɪn ˈkɒmən]	etwas gemein haben
	one another [ˌwʌn‿əˈnʌðə]	einander
	caption [ˈkæpʃn]	Bildunterschrift; Titel
8	statistics *(npl)* [stəˈtɪstɪks]	Statistik
	estimate [ˈestɪmeɪt]	(ein)schätzen, annehmen
	worldwide [ˌwɜːldˈwaɪd]	weltweit

Child labour should be illegal *worldwide*.

	forced labour [ˌfɔːst ˈleɪbə]	Zwangsarbeit
	trafficked [ˈtræfɪkt]	verschleppt
	war [wɔː]	Krieg
	warlike [ˈwɔːˌlaɪk]	kriegerisch
	prostitution *(no pl)* [ˌprɒstɪˈtjuːʃn]	Prostitution
	pornography *(no pl)* [pɔːˈnɒɡrəfi]	Pornografie
	total [ˈtəʊtl]	Gesamtsumme
9	schooling *(no pl)* [ˈskuːlɪŋ]	Schulbildung; Ausbildung
	journalist [ˈdʒɜːnəlɪst]	Journalist/in
	sew [səʊ]	nähen
10	**conditions** *(npl)* [kənˈdɪʃnz]	Bedingungen, Verhältnisse

> **What are the opposites of these words?**
> peace – ???
> cold – ???
> very happy – ???
> past – ???

sew – sewed – sewn
The *conditions* in the factory were terrible.

	developing country [dɪˈveləpɪŋ ˌkʌntri]	Entwicklungsland
	Indonesia [ˌɪndəʊˈniːʒə]	Indonesien
	minimum wage [ˌmɪnɪməm ˈweɪdʒ]	Mindestlohn
	make sure [ˌmeɪk ˈʃɔː]	sich versichern, darauf achten
	refuse [rɪˈfjuːz]	ablehnen, sich weigern

I hate tidying up my room. Next time I will *refuse* to do it.

	do overtime [ˌduː‿ˈəʊvəˌtaɪm]	Überstunden machen
	fire sb *(informal)* [ˈfaɪə ˌsʌmbədi]	jdn feuern/rausschmeißen
	pay *(no pl)* [peɪ]	Lohn, Gehalt
	properly [ˈprɒpəli]	korrekt, richtig
	goggles *(npl)* [ˈɡɒɡlz]	(Schutz)brille
	needle [ˈniːdl]	Nadel
	injure [ˈɪndʒə]	verletzen
	go on strike [ˌɡəʊ‿ɒn ˈstraɪk]	streiken, in (den) Streik treten
	wage(s) [weɪdʒ(ɪz)]	Lohn

The workers are asking for higher *wages*.

	management *(no pl)* [ˈmænɪdʒmənt]	Management, (Unternehmens)leitung
	openly [ˈəʊpənli]	offen; öffentlich
	give in [ˌɡɪv‿ˈɪn]	nachgeben
	secretly [ˈsiːkrətli]	heimlich, im Stillen
	strike [straɪk]	Streik
	desperately [ˈdesprətli]	verzweifelt; dringend

The man was so depressed; he *desperately* needed to talk to a friend.

	apart from [əˈpɑːt frəm]	abgesehen von
	soldier [ˈsəʊldʒə]	Soldat/in
	prostitute [ˈprɒstɪˌtjuːt]	Prostituierte/r

	domestic servant [də,mestɪk 'sɜ:vnt]	Hausangestellte/r
	complete [kəm'pli:t]	vervollständigen
	adverb ['ædvɜ:b]	Adverb
	owner ['əʊnə]	Besitzer/in, Eigentümer/in
	worker [wɜ:kə]	Arbeiter/in, Angestellte/r
PP	° the United Nations Organization [ðə ju:,naɪtɪd 'neɪʃnz‿,ɔ:gənaɪ,zeɪʃn]	die Vereinten Nationen
	° found [faʊnd]	gründen
	° aim [eɪm]	Ziel, Absicht
	° secure [sɪ'kjʊə]	sichern, garantieren
	° peace [pi:s]	Frieden
	° human rights *(npl)* [,hju:mən 'raɪts]	Menschenrechte
	° publish ['pʌblɪʃ]	veröffentlichen
	° convention [kən'venʃn]	Konvention, Abkommen
	° state sth [steɪt]	*hier:* etw nennen, etw angeben
	° basic ['beɪsɪk]	grundlegend, wesentlich; Grund-
	° survival [sə'vaɪvl]	Überleben
	° development [dɪ'veləpmənt]	Entwicklung; Wachstum
	° protection [prə'tekʃn]	Schutz
	° cultural ['kʌltʃrəl]	kulturell
	° social ['səʊʃl]	gesellschaftlich, sozial
	° Europe ['jʊərəp]	Europa
	° the Second World War [ðə ,sekənd ,wɜ:ld 'wɔ:]	der Zweite Weltkrieg
	° Nobel Peace Prize [nəʊ,bel 'pi:s ,praɪz]	Friedensnobelpreis
	° medical ['medɪkl]	medizinisch, ärztlich
	° financial [faɪ'nænʃl]	finanziell
	° educational [,edjʊ'keɪʃnəl]	Bildungs-, pädagogisch
11	industry ['ɪndəstri]	Branche, Gewerbe
	protest ['prəʊtest]	Protest(kundgebung)
	label ['leɪbl]	Etikett, Label; Marke
	production *(no pl)* [prə'dʌkʃn]	Produktion, Herstellung
	finding ['faɪndɪŋ]	Entdeckung; Ergebnis
M2	**international** [,ɪntə'næʃnəl]	international
	youth [ju:θ]	Jugend; Jugendliche/r; Jugend-
	apprenticeship [ə'prentɪʃɪp]	Ausbildung, Lehre
	conference ['kɒnfrəns]	Konferenz, Tagung
	service ['sɜ:vɪs]	Service; Bedienung; Dienst
	cruise ship ['kru:z ʃɪp]	Kreuzfahrtschiff
	vocational school [vəʊ'keɪʃnəl sku:l]	Berufsschule
	whenever [wen'evə]	immer wenn, wann (auch) immer
	joiner ['dʒɔɪnə]	Tischler/in, Schreiner/in
	craftsman/craftswoman ['krɑ:ftsmən/'krɑ:fts,wʊmən]	gelernte/r Handwerker/in
	home town ['həʊm taʊn]	Heimatstadt

This man is the dog's *owner*.
He owns the dog.

Konditionstraining
Schreibe einen kleinen Text mit den Wörtern, die du lernen willst. Die Liste hängst du in deinem Zimmer auf – möglichst weit weg von deinem Schreibtisch.
Gehe zu dem Blatt und merke dir einen Teil des Textes. Setze dich wieder an deinen Schreibtisch und notiere, was du behalten hast.
Das wiederholst du, bis du den gesamten Text geschrieben hast. Um zu sehen, ob du alles richtig geschrieben hast, gehst du wieder los …

If you want to be a mechanic, you have to go to *vocational school*.
Whenever I hear that song, I think of you.

	colleague [ˈkɒliːg]	Kollege/Kollegin, Mitarbeiter/in	The people you work with are your work *colleagues*.
	surf the Internet [ˌsɜːf ðiˈɪntənet]	im Internet surfen	How often do you *surf the Internet?*
	Scandinavia [ˌskændɪˈneɪviə]	Skandinavien	
	match [mætʃ]	passen zu	
	train for a job [ˌtreɪn fərˌə ˈdʒɒb]	eine Ausbildung machen	
M5	building firm [ˈbɪldɪŋ fɜːm]	Bauunternehmen, Baufirma	
	in town [ɪn ˈtaʊn]	in der Stadt	I know the best shops *in town*.
	Copenhagen [ˌkəʊpənˈheɪgən]	Kopenhagen	
	poor man *(informal)* [ˌpɔː ˈmæn]	der Arme	
M6	horizon [həˈraɪzn]	Horizont	I can see the sun on the *horizon.*
	embark onto new horizons [ɪmˌbɑːkˌˌɒntə njuː həˈraɪzənz]	zu neuen Horizonten aufbrechen	
	currently [ˈkʌrəntli]	zur Zeit, momentan	
	recruit sb [rɪˈkruːt ˌsʌmbədi]	jdn einstellen	
	command *(no pl)* [kəˈmɑːnd]	Beherrschung	
	previous experience [ˌpriːviəsˌɪkˈspɪəriəns]	Vorkenntnisse	Although I had no *previous experience* of working in a hotel, I got the job.
	candidate [ˈkændɪdeɪt]	Bewerber/in, Kandidat/in	
	motivated [ˈməʊtɪˌveɪtɪd]	motiviert	They were *motivated* students. They went to the library every day.
	dedicated [ˈdedɪˌkeɪtɪd]	engagiert	
	career change [kəˈrɪə tʃeɪndʒ]	berufliche Umorientierung/ Abwechslung	
	cruise [kruːz]	Kreuzfahrt	
	staff *(no pl)* [stɑːf]	Mitarbeiter, Personal, Belegschaft	All the people who work for a company are the *staff*.
	the Caribbean Sea [ðə ˌkærɪˌbiən ˈsiː]	das Karibische Meer, die Karibik	
	the Mediterranean Sea [ðə ˌmedɪtəˌreɪniən ˈsiː]	das Mittelmeer	
	fluent [ˈfluːənt]	fließend	She lived in England for two years, so she can speak *fluent* English.
	required [rɪˈkwaɪəd]	erforderlich	
	further [ˈfɜːðə]	zusätzlich, noch mehr	
	contact sb [ˈkɒntækt ˌsʌmbədi]	jdn kontaktieren, sich mit jdm in Verbindung setzen	If you have any questions, you can *contact me*.
	certified [ˈsɜːtɪfaɪd]	(staatlich) geprüft	
	Sweden [ˈswiːdn]	Schweden	
	necessary [ˈnesəsri]	nötig, notwendig, erforderlich	
	absolutely [ˈæbsəluːtli]	absolut, völlig	The football player looked *absolutely* exhausted.
	industry [ˈɪndəstri]	Branche, Gewerbe; *hier:* Industrie	
	support *(no pl)* [səˈpɔːt]	Unterstützung	
	reception *(no pl)* [rɪˈsepʃn]	Empfang, Rezeption	
	run [rʌn]	*hier:* etw leiten/betreiben/ führen	

	B&B (= bed and breakfast) [ˌbiˌən ˈbiː]	Frühstückspension	
M7	enclose [ɪnˈkləʊz]	beilegen, beifügen	If you send your CV and other documents with a letter, you *enclose* them.
	include [ɪnˈkluːd]	beinhalten, einschließen	
	referee [ˌrefəˈriː]	*hier:* Referenz	
	yours sincerely [ˌjɔːzˌsɪnˈsɪəli]	mit freundlichen/herzlichen Grüßen	
	edit [ˈedɪt]	bearbeiten, redigieren	
M8	phrase book [ˈfreɪz bʊk]	Sprachführer	
M10	from rags to riches [frəm ˌrægz tə ˈrɪtʃɪz]	vom Tellerwäscher zum Millionär	
	slum [slʌm]	Slum, Elendsviertel	
	portrait [ˈpɔːtrɪt]	Porträt, Darstellung	
M11	on location [ˌɒn ləʊˈkeɪʃn]	vor Ort, Außenaufnahmen	
	production assistant [prəˈdʌkʃnˌəˌsɪstnt]	Produktionsassistent/in	
	film [fɪlm]	filmen, drehen	Some of the Harry Potter films were *filmed* in Oxford.
	process [ˈprəʊses]	Prozess, Vorgang	
	settle on sb [ˈsetlˌɒn ˌsʌmbədi]	sich für jdn entscheiden, sich auf jdn einigen	
	amazing *(informal)* [əˈmeɪzɪŋ]	toll, unglaublich	
	studio [ˈstjuːdiəʊ]	Studio	
	set up [ˌsetˌˈʌp]	aufbauen, einrichten	
	dust *(no pl)* [dʌst]	Staub	Nobody has cleaned the room for years. There is thick *dust* everywhere.
	actually [ˈæktʃuəli]	*hier:* wirklich, tatsächlich	
	stress [stres]	betonen, hervorheben	
M12	director [dəˈrektə]	Regisseur/in	
M13	research *(no pl)* [rɪˈsɜːtʃ]	Forschung, Erforschung, Recherche	
	interest sb [ˈɪntrəst]	jdn interessieren, bei jdm Interesse wecken	
CIO	yo *(informal)* [jəʊ]	hi	
	What's up? *(informal)* [wɒtsˌˈʌp]	Wie geht's?; Was geht?	
	English-speaking [ˈɪŋglɪʃˌspiːkɪŋ]	englischsprachig	
	right from the start [ˌraɪt frəm ðə ˈstaːt]	von vornherein, von Beginn/ Anfang an	
	formal [ˈfɔːml]	formal; formell	
	common [ˈkɒmən]	üblich, normal	
	address sb [əˈdres]	jdn anreden	
	° known [nəʊn]	bekannt	
	° graduate [ˈgrædʒuət]	Schulabgänger/in; Absolvent/in	
	° coal mine [ˈkəʊl maɪn]	Kohlengrube, Kohlenzeche	
	° pass [paːs]	verabschieden *(Gesetz)*	
	° cruise ship [ˈkruːz ʃɪp]	Kreuzfahrtschiff	
	° one in six [ˌwʌnˌɪn ˈsɪks]	eine(r,s) von sechs	
	° Hindi [ˈhɪndi]	Hindi *(Amtssprache in Indien)*	
	° subtitle [ˈsʌbˌtaɪtl]	Untertitel	

Mache sie zu deinen Wörtern!
Am besten kannst du dir Wörter merken, die du selbst verwendet hast. Darum: Schreibe ein Gedicht oder eine verrückte Geschichte mit folgenden Wörtern aus dem *Theme: cruise ship, colleague, horizon, fluent, necessary.*

Australia is an *English-speaking* country.

Kim's game
Schreibe zehn Vokabeln auf ein Blatt Papier. Sieh dir die Wörter drei Minuten lang an. Dann drehst du das Blatt um. Versuche nun, alle Wörter auswendig auf die Rückseite zu schreiben. Wie viele hast du dir gemerkt?

Theme 3 – South Africa – the Rainbow Nation

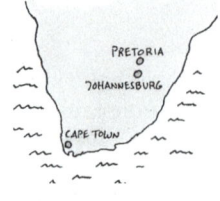

I	South Africa [saʊθˌˈæfrɪkə]	Südafrika
	rainbow [ˈreɪnˌbəʊ]	Regenbogen
	nation [ˈneɪʃn]	Nation, Land
	Cape Town [ˈkeɪptaʊn]	Kapstadt
	attraction [əˈtrækʃn]	Attraktion; Anziehung(skraft)
	present [ˈpreznt]	Gegenwart
	give a presentation [ˌgɪvˌə ˌpreznˈteɪʃn]	eine Präsentation halten
	South African [saʊθˌˈæfrɪkən]	Südafrikaner/in; südafrikanisch

1	**South Africa** [saʊθˌˈæfrɪkə]	Südafrika	
2	volunteer [ˌvɒlənˈtɪə]	freiwillig, ehrenamtlich	
	animal carer [ˈænɪml ˌkeərə]	Tierpfleger/in	
	colleague [ˈkɒliːg]	Kollege/Kollegin; Mitarbeiter/in	
	home country [ˌhəʊm ˈkʌntri]	Heimatland	I am English. England is my *home country*.
	overcome [ˌəʊvəˈkʌm]	überwinden, bewältigen	
	fear [fɪə]	Angst, Furcht; Sorge	He has a *fear* of spiders.
	animal care *(no pl)* [ˈænɪml ˌkeə]	Tierpflege	
	come true [ˌkʌm ˈtruː]	wahr werden	If you work hard, your dreams will *come true*.

	take a tour [ˌteɪkˌə ˈtʊə]	eine Tour/Führung machen	
	mammal [ˈmæml]	Säugetier	
	in general [ɪn ˈdʒenrəl]	im Allgemeinen, generell	
	contrast [ˈkɒntrɑːst]	Gegensatz, Kontrast	
	violence [ˈvaɪələns]	Gewalt, Gewalttätigkeit	
	the other day [ðiˌˈʌðə ˈdeɪ]	neulich, vor einigen Tagen	I met Sam *the other day*.
	economy [ɪˈkɒnəmi]	Wirtschaft	
	African [ˈæfrɪkən]	Afrikaner/in; afrikanisch	
	continent [ˈkɒntɪnənt]	Kontinent, Erdteil	
	surprise [səˈpraɪz]	überraschen	

She is going to *surprise* him.

	South African [saʊθˌˈæfrɪkən]	Südafrikaner/in; südafrikanisch	
	poverty [ˈpɒvəti]	Armut	
	discriminate against sb [dɪˈskrɪmɪneɪtˌəˌgenst ˌsʌmbədi]	jdn diskriminieren/ benachteiligen	Everyone is equal, you must not *discriminate against* anyone.

	township [ˈtaʊnʃɪp]	Township *(von Schwarzen bewohnte, abseits der Stadt gelegene Siedlung)*	
	idea [aɪˈdɪə]	*hier:* Vorstellung, Eindruck	
	guide [gaɪd]	Führer/in	
	in the beginning [ɪn ðə bɪˈgɪnɪŋ]	am Anfang, zu Beginn	

3	**text** [tekst]	SMS verschicken	My friends *text* me every day.
	brilliant *(informal)* [ˈbrɪljənt]	*hier:* toll, hervorragend	
	flight [flaɪt]	Flug	

offer [ˈɒfə]	Angebot	I made him an *offer* to buy his bike.
get (a week) off [ˌget (ə ˌwiːk) ˈɒf]	(eine Woche) freibekommen	
be out [ˌbi‿ˈaʊt]	nicht zu Hause sein	
say sth out loud [ˌseɪ ˌsʌmθɪŋ‿aʊt ˈlaʊd]	etw laut sagen	
conversation [ˌkɒnvəˈseɪʃn]	Gespräch, Unterhaltung	
read out [ˌriːd‿ˈaʊt]	(laut) vorlesen	
boarding pass [ˈbɔːdɪŋ pɑːs]	Bordkarte	
check in [ˌtʃek‿ˈɪn]	einchecken	You need your passport to *check in*.
passenger [ˈpæsɪndʒə]	Passsagier/in, Fluggast; Fahrgast	
Ms [məz]	Frau *(Anrede für verheiratete und unverheiratete Frauen)*	
depart [dɪˈpɑːt]	abfliegen, starten	
booking reference [ˈbʊkɪŋ ˌrefrəns]	Buchungsnummer	
seat [siːt]	(Sitz)platz	Could I have the *seat* next to the window, please?

economy class [ɪˈkɒnəmi klɑːs]	*zweite Klasse im Flugverkehr*	
boarding time [ˈbɔːdɪŋ taɪm]	Einsteigezeit	
baggage [ˈbægɪdʒ]	Gepäck	
non-smoking [ˌnɒnˈsməʊkɪŋ]	Nichtraucher-	
forbidden [fəˈbɪdn]	verboten, nicht zulässig	It is *forbidden* to smoke inside.
at all times [ət‿ˌɔːl ˈtaɪmz]	stets, jederzeit	
contain [kənˈteɪn]	enthalten	
radioactive [ˌreɪdiəʊˈæktɪv]	radioaktiv	
explosive [ɪkˈspləʊsɪv]	explosiv	
object [ˈɒbdʒekt]	Objekt, Gegenstand, Sache	
present [prɪˈzent]	*hier:* darstellen	
flammable [ˈflæməbl]	leicht entflammbarer/ entzündlicher Stoff	
corrosive [kəˈrəʊsɪv]	korrodierender Stoff	
gas [gæs]	Gas	
journey [ˈdʒɜːni]	Reise	
board (a plane) [bɔːd]	(ein Flugzeug) besteigen	In five minutes we can *board* the plane.

> [ɒ] <u>o</u>ffer, c<u>o</u>ntrast, p<u>o</u>verty
> [ɔː] <u>o</u>rder, w<u>a</u>r, supp<u>o</u>rt
> [əʊ] h<u>o</u>me, s<u>o</u>ldier, expl<u>o</u>sive

travel guide [ˈtrævl gaɪd]	Reiseführer	
rank [ræŋk]	einstufen; anordnen	
mention [ˈmenʃn]	erwähnen	
World Heritage Site [ˌwɜːld ˈherɪtɪdʒ ˌsaɪt]	Weltkulturerbe, Weltkulturdenkmal	
fighter [ˈfaɪtə]	Kämpfer/in	This man does not like to lose, he is a *fighter*.
provide [prəˈvaɪd]	bieten, geben, sorgen für	
fascinating [ˈfæsɪneɪtɪŋ]	faszinierend	
bay [beɪ]	Bucht	

Table Mountain ['teɪbl ˌmaʊntɪn]	Tafelberg	
apartheid *(no pl)* [ə'paːtˌheɪt]	Apartheid, Rassentrennung	
era ['ɪərə]	Ära, Epoche	
daily ['deɪli]	täglich	*daily* = every day
include [ɪn'kluːd]	beinhalten, einschließen	
political [pə'lɪtɪkl]	politisch	
whale [weɪl]	Wal	
seaside ['siːˌsaɪd]	Küste	I want to go to the *seaside*.
destination [ˌdestɪ'neɪʃn]	(Reise)ziel	
land-based ['lændbeɪst]	vom Land aus	
Southern Right Whale [ˌsʌðən ˌraɪt 'weɪl]	Südlicher Glattwal	
water ['wɔːtə]	*hier:* Gewässer	
calve [kɑːv]	kalben	
young [jʌŋ]	Junge(s)	
mate [meɪt]	sich paaren	
jewellery *(no pl)* ['dʒuːəlri]	Schmuck	She loves *jewellery*.
diamond ['daɪəmənd]	Diamant	
shopping mall ['ʃɒpɪŋ mɔːl]	Einkaufszentrum	
flea market ['fliː ˌmaːkɪt]	Flohmarkt, Trödelmarkt	
streetside ['striːtsaɪd]	an der Straße gelegen	
aquarium [ə'kweəriəm]	Aquarium	
be located [bi: ləʊ'keɪtɪd]	sich befinden, liegen, gelegen sein	
marine [mə'riːn]	Meeres-, See-	
the Indian Ocean [ðiˌɪndiənˈəʊʃn]	der Indische Ozean	What's the name of the world's largest ocean?
the Atlantic Ocean [ðiˌətˌlæntɪkˈəʊʃn]	der Atlantische Ozean	
including [ɪn'kluːdɪŋ]	einschließlich	
turtle ['tɜːtl]	Meeresschildkröte	
spectacular [spek'tækjʊlə]	fantastisch, sensationell	
exhibit [ɪg'zɪbɪt]	Ausstellungsstück	
predator ['predətə]	Raubtier	
tank [tæŋk]	(Wasser)becken	We collect rainwater in a *tank* so that we can water the flowers.
semi-tunnel ['semiˌtʌnl]	Halbtunnel	
cableway ['keɪblweɪ]	Seilbahn	
direction [dɪ'rekʃn]	Richtung	Which *direction* is the town centre?
cable car ['keɪbl kɑː]	Seilbahn(kabine)	
lookout ['lʊkaʊt]	Aussichtspunkt	
as [əz]	*hier:* weil, da	
sunset ['sʌnˌset]	Sonnenuntergang	
cool [kuːl]	kalt, kühl; cool	
leader ['liːdə]	Leiter/in, Führer/in	

7	**interest sb** ['ɪntrəst ˌsʌmbədi]	jdn interessieren, bei jdm Interesse wecken	Football has always *interested* him.
	least [liːst]	am wenigsten	*least* ≠ most
8	create [kri'eɪt]	erschaffen; gestalten	
	point out sth [ˌpɔɪntˈaʊt ˌsʌmθɪŋ]	auf etw hinweisen/zeigen	

	crossword puzzle ['krɒswɜːd ˌpʌzl]	Kreuzworträtsel	
9	picture sth ['pɪktʃə ˌsʌmθɪŋ]	sich etw vorstellen	
10	listen in [ˌlɪsn̩ˈɪn]	mithören; Radio hören	
11	encyclopedia [ɪnˌsaɪkləˈpiːdiə]	Lexikon, Enzyklopädie	
	Nobel Peace Prize [nəʊˌbel ˈpiːs praɪz]	Friedensnobelpreis	
	democratic [ˌdeməˈkrætɪk]	demokratisch	Germany is a *democratic* country.
	elect [ɪˈlekt]	wählen	The country has *elected* a new president.
	system ['sɪstəm]	System	
	non-white [ˌnɒn ˈwaɪt]	Farbige/r	
	separate ['sepəreɪt]	trennen	During apartheid black and white people were *separated*.
	royal ['rɔɪəl]	königlich	
	leading ['liːdɪŋ]	führend	
	found [faʊnd]	gründen	The organization was *founded* in 1903.
	ruling ['ruːlɪŋ]	herrschend, regierend	
	party ['pɑːti]	*hier:* Partei	
	sentence sb to sth ['sentəns ˌsʌmbədi tə ˌsʌmθɪŋ]	jdn zu etw verurteilen	The judge *sentenced* the criminal *to* six years in prison.
	life imprisonment *(no pl)* [ˌlaɪf ɪmˈprɪznmənt]	lebenslängliche Freiheitsstrafe	
	reputation *(no pl)* [ˌrepjʊˈteɪʃn]	Ruf, Ansehen	
	resistance *(no pl)* [rɪˈzɪstns]	Widerstand	
	movement ['muːvmənt]	Bewegung	
	establish [ɪˈstæblɪʃ]	einführen, aufbauen	
	democracy [dɪˈmɒkrəsi]	Demokratie	Mandela helped to *establish democracy* in South Africa.
	society [səˈsaɪəti]	Gesellschaft	*Society* is always changing.
	peaceful ['piːsfl]	friedlich	*peaceful* ≠ violent
	racial ['reɪʃl]	rassisch, Rassen-	
	equality [ɪˈkwɒləti]	Gleichberechtigung; Gleichheit	
	be involved (in) [bɪ ɪnˈvɒlvd (ɪn)]	beteiligt sein, engagiert sein	
	timeline ['taɪmˌlaɪn]	Zeitstrahl	
PP	° businessman ['bɪznəsmæn]	Geschäftsmann, Unternehmer	
	° the Netherlands [ðə ˈneðlənz]	die Niederlande	
	° stop [stɒp]	(Zwischen)halt; Anlegestelle	
	° Dutch [dʌtʃ]	Niederländer/in; niederländisch	
	° native ['neɪtɪv]	Eingeborene/r, Einheimische/r	
	° colony ['kɒləni]	Kolonie	
	° nationality [ˌnæʃəˈnæləti]	Nationalität; Staatsangehörigkeit	
	° Boer [bɔː]	Bure/Burin	

Verknüpfungen herstellen
Bei Wörtern, die überhaupt nicht in deinen Kopf wollen, kannst du:
- dir das Wort bildlich vorstellen,
- ein kleines Bild dazu zeichnen,
- an ein Ereignis denken, das du selbst erlebt hast,
- einen Satz, in dem das Wort vorkommt, auswendig lernen,
- dir eine Eselsbrücke (z. B. einen Reim) ausdenken.

° Afrikaner [ˌæfrɪˈkɑːnə]	Afrika(a)nder/in *(Bezeichnung für in Südafrika geborene Weiße)*
° come into power [ˌkʌm ˌɪntə ˈpaʊə]	an die Macht kommen
° completely [kəmˈpliːtli]	völlig, ganz
° take [teɪk]	*hier:* brauchen
° take a first step [ˌteɪk ə ˌfɜːst ˈstep]	einen ersten Schritt machen/unternehmen
° discrimination *(no pl)* [dɪˌskrɪmɪˈneɪʃn]	Diskriminierung, Benachteiligung
° free sb [ˈfriː ˌsʌmbədi]	jdn freilassen
° equal [ˈiːkwəl]	gleich; *hier:* gleichberechtigt
° unemployment rate [ˌʌnɪmˈplɔɪmənt reɪt]	Arbeitslosenrate, Arbeitslosenzahl
° remain [rɪˈmeɪn]	bleiben, anhalten
hope [həʊp]	Hoffnung
keep sth going [ˌkiːp ˌsʌmθɪŋ ˈɡəʊɪŋ]	etw in Gang halten
° run [rʌn]	*hier:* regieren
° not at all [ˌnɒt ət ˈɔːl]	überhaupt nicht
° subjection *(no pl)* [səbˈdʒekʃn]	Unterwerfung; Abhängigkeit
° pressure [ˈpreʃə]	Druck
° as one [æz ˈwʌn]	(einmütig) zusammen
° chorus [ˈkɔːrəs]	Refrain
° golden [ˈɡəʊldn]	golden
° weapon [ˈwepən]	Waffe
° shape [ʃeɪp]	Form; Art
° gun [ɡʌn]	(Schuss)waffe
° killing [ˈkɪlɪŋ]	Tötung, Mord
° sneak [sniːk]	schleichen
° now and again [ˌnaʊ ənd əˈɡen]	ab und zu
° supporter [səˈpɔːtə]	Anhänger/in, Unterstützer/in
° fancy [ˈfænsi]	*hier:* extrem viel
° tempt sb [ˈtempt ˌsʌmbədi]	jdn in Versuchung führen; jdn locken
° swing opinions [ˌswɪŋ əˈpɪnjənz]	Meinungen manipulieren
° journal [ˈdʒɜːnl]	Zeitschrift, Zeitung
° move [muːv]	Bewegung; Schritt
° explanation [ˌekspləˈneɪʃn]	Erklärung
° preacher [ˈpriːtʃə]	Geistliche/r, Pfarrer/in
° archbishop [ɑːtʃˈbɪʃəp]	Erzbischof
° blind [blaɪnd]	blind
° drum [drʌm]	Trommel
° tide [taɪd]	Gezeiten; *hier:* (öffentliche) Meinung
° turn [tɜːn]	*hier:* umschlagen
according to [əˈkɔːdɪŋ tʊ]	laut, nach, gemäß

12

Sing a song!
Weißt du eigentlich genau, was du singst, wenn du deinen englischen Lieblingssong vor dich hin trällerst? Übersetze ihn doch einfach mal. Anschließend kannst du singend Vokabeln üben!

Gimme hope Jo'anna
gimme = give me
she don't care = she doesn't care
I wanna know = I want to know
Can you find more examples of informal language used in the song?

Partner quiz
Zu zweit macht das Vokabellernen viel mehr Spaß! Bilde einen Rätselsatz, in dem du ein englisches Wort umschreibst. Kann deine Partnerin/dein Partner das Wort erraten?

A very large animal that lives in the sea.

A whale?

13	**rainbow** [ˈreɪnˌbəʊ]	Regenbogen	 When it is sunny and rainy, there is a *rainbow* in the sky.
	racism *(no pl)* [ˈreɪˌsɪzm]	Rassismus	
	everywhere else [ˌevriˌweərˌˈels]	überall sonst	
	politician [ˌpɒləˈtɪʃn]	Politiker/in	
	accommodation *(no pl)* [əˌkɒməˈdeɪʃn]	Unterkunft	
	mug sb [ˈmʌg ˌsʌmbədi]	jdn überfallen und ausrauben	
	though [ðəʊ]	trotzdem, dennoch	
	separate [ˈseprət]	getrennt, separat	Keep the dog and the cat *separate*.
	and so on [ænd ˌsəʊˌˈɒn]	und so weiter	
	abolition *(no pl)* [ˌæbəˈlɪʃn]	Abschaffung	
	remain [rɪˈmeɪn]	bleiben, anhalten	
14	aspect [ˈæspekt]	Aspekt, Gesichtspunkt	
	tourism *(no pl)* [ˈtʊərɪzm]	Tourismus	
M1	placemat [ˈpleɪsˌmæt]	Set, Platzdeckchen	
M3	luxury [ˈlʌkʃəri]	Luxus	It is a *luxury* to be able to go on holiday.
	(four-)day [(ˈfɔː)deɪ]	(vier)tägig	
	guided [ˈgaɪdɪd]	geführt	
	be located [bi: ləʊˈkeɪtɪd]	sich befinden, liegen, gelegen sein	The shop is *located* at the end of the road.
	lodge [lɒdʒ]	Lodge, Hütte	
	suite [swiːt]	Suite, Apartment, Wohnung	
	jacuzzi [dʒəˈkuːzi]	Jacuzzi, Whirlpool	
	game *(no pl)* [geɪm]	Wild	*game* = wild animals that people hunt
	drive [draɪv]	Fahrt	
	treatment [ˈtriːtmənt]	Behandlung	
	guarantee [ˌgærənˈtiː]	garantieren	
	of a lifetime [əvˌə ˈlaɪfˌtaɪm]	des Lebens	
	root [ruːt]	Wurzel	
	experience [ɪkˈspɪəriəns]	erleben, erfahren	
	nightlife *(no pl)* [ˈnaɪtˌlaɪf]	Nachtleben	
	first-hand [ˌfɜːstˈhænd]	aus erster Hand	I got it *first-hand* from Tina that she's pregnant.
	buffalo [ˈbʌfələʊ]	Büffel	
	herd [hɜːd]	Herde, Rudel	
	bull [bʊl]	Bulle, Stier	
	welcome [ˈwelkəm]	willkommen heißen, begrüßen	He *welcomed* the actress. 
	ecosystem [ˈiːkəʊˌsɪstəm]	Ökosystem	
	bush *(no pl)* [bʊʃ]	*hier:* Wildnis	
	mealtime [ˈmiːltaɪm]	Essenszeit	
M4	e-pal [ˈiːpæl]	E-Mail-Freund/in	
	hopefully [ˈhəʊpfli]	hoffentlich	
	lately [ˈleɪtli]	kürzlich, in letzter Zeit	*Lately* I've been so tired, I think I need more sleep.

WORDS THEME 3

Dutch [dʌtʃ]	Niederländer/in; niederländisch	
sb feels sick [ˌsʌmbədi fiːlz ˈsɪk]	jdm ist schlecht/übel	
pile into (the car) [ˌpaɪl ˈɪntʊ]	sich in (das Auto) zwängen	
off-road [ˌɒfˈrəʊd]	im Gelände	
nevertheless [ˌnevəðəˈles]	trotzdem, dennoch	My head was hurting but *nevertheless* I went to work.
aardvark [ˈɑːdˌvɑːk]	Erdferkel	
cub [kʌb]	Junge(s)	
nocturnal [nɒkˈtɜːnl]	nachtaktiv; nächtlich	
giraffe [dʒəˈrɑːf]	Giraffe	
moreover [mɔːrˈəʊvə]	darüber hinaus, zudem, ferner	It was cold and *moreover* the bus was late.
rhino (= rhinocerus) [ˈraɪnəʊ, raɪˈnɒsrəs]	Nashorn, Rhinozeros	
leopard [ˈlepəd]	Leopard/in	
as well [æz ˌwel]	auch	*as well* = too
so-called [ˌsəʊˈkɔːld]	so genannt	
cheetah [ˈtʃiːtə]	Gepard	
electrical [ɪˈlektrɪkl]	elektrisch, Elektro-	
fence [fens]	Zaun	There is a *fence* around the garden to stop the dog running away.
keep out [ˌkiːpˈaʊt]	nicht hereinlassen	
old style [ˌəʊld ˈstaɪl]	im alten Stil	
bushpig [ˈbʊʃpɪg]	Buschschwein	
zebra [ˈzebrə]	Zebra	
impala [ɪmˈpɑːlə]	Impala, Schwarzfersenantilope	
warthog [ˈwɔːtˌhɒg]	Warzenschwein	
luckily [ˈlʌkɪli]	glücklicherweise	*Luckily*, I had my mobile phone with me when my car broke down.

M6	ethnic [ˈeθnɪk]	ethnisch, Volks-	
	Coloured [ˈkʌləd]	Farbige/r	
	coloured [ˈkʌləd]	farbig; gemischtrassig	
	structure [ˈstrʌktʃə]	Gefüge, Struktur	
M8	twin city [ˌtwɪn ˈsɪti]	Partnerstadt	
	exchange [ɪksˈtʃeɪndʒ]	(Aus)tausch-	
M9	for the better [fə ðə ˈbetə]	zum Besseren, zum Guten	
	mixture [ˈmɪkstʃə]	Mischung	
	heavy [ˈhevi]	*hier:* stark	There was *heavy* traffic on the way to work today.
	dose [dəʊs]	Dosis, Menge	
	house music [ˈhaʊs ˌmjuːzɪk]	*Musikstil*	
	bold [bəʊld]	kräftig; mutig; gewagt; frech	
	style [staɪl]	Stil	They have a very unique *style*.
	Afrikaans *(no pl)* [ˌæfrɪˈkɑːns]	Afrikaans *(eine der elf Amtssprachen in Südafrika)*	

deal with ['di:l wɪð]   handeln von; sich befassen mit

spread [spred]   verbreiten, ausbreiten

spirit *(no pl)* ['spɪrɪt]   *hier:* Stimmung, Geist

optimism *(no pl)* ['ɒptɪ,mɪzəm]   Optimismus

self-confidence *(no pl)* [self'kɒnfɪdns]   Selbstvertrauen

Simon has had more *self-confidence* since he started playing in a band.

originally [əˈrɪdʒnəli]   ursprünglich

labour *(no pl)* ['leɪbə]   Arbeitskräfte

control [kənˈtrəʊl]   Kontrolle

 He did not have *control* of the dog.

social ['səʊʃl]   gesellschaftlich, sozial

question sth ['kwestʃn ˌsʌmθɪŋ]   etw in Frage stellen, etw hinterfragen

come of age [ˌkʌm_əv 'eɪdʒ]   volljährig werden

Many people have a big party when they *come of age.*

post- [pəʊst]   nach-/Nach-, post-/Post-

period ['pɪəriəd]   Periode, Zeitraum

fine [faɪn]   *hier:* toll, edel

single mother [ˌsɪŋgl 'mʌðə]   allein erziehende Mutter

struggle ['strʌgl]   sich abmühen

bring up sb [ˌbrɪŋ_'ʌp ˌsʌmbədi]   jdn großziehen, jdn aufziehen

bring up a child = raise a child

textbook ['tekst,bʊk]   Lehrbuch

complete [kəmˈpli:t]   vollständig, komplett

origin ['ɒrɪdʒɪn]   Ursprung, Herkunft

theme [θi:m]   Thema; Lektion, Kapitel

M10   term [tɜːm]   Ausdruck

archbishop [ɑːtʃˈbɪʃəp]   Erzbischof

characteristic [ˌkærɪktəˈrɪstɪk]   (charakteristisches) Merkmal

What are the adjectives to these nouns?
democracy – ???
equality – ???
peace – ???
violence – ???
poverty – ???

CIO   warm [wɔːm]   *hier:* warmherzig, herzlich

Western Europe [ˌwestən 'jʊərəp]   Westeuropa

hug [hʌg]   umarmen

° entrance fee ['entrəns ˌfiː]   Eintritt(sgeld)

° gold *(no pl)* [gəʊld]   Gold

° version ['vɜːʃn]   Version

° barbecue ['bɑːbɪˌkjuː]   Grillparty; Grill

Theme 4 – Changes and challenges

I	challenge ['tʃælɪndʒ]	Herausforderung
	natural disaster [ˌnætʃrəl dɪˈzɑːstə]	Naturkatastrophe
	tornado(*pl* -es) [tɔːˈneɪdəʊ, tɔːˈneɪdəʊz]	Tornado
	warning ['wɔːnɪŋ]	Warnung
	communicate [kəˈmjuːnɪkeɪt]	sich verständigen, kommunizieren
	technology [tekˈnɒlədʒi]	Technik, Technologie
	hurricane ['hʌrɪkən]	Orkan, Hurrikan
	advantage [ədˈvɑːntɪdʒ]	Vorteil
	gaming *(no pl)* ['geɪmɪŋ]	Spielen (am Computer)
1	**natural disaster** [ˌnætʃrəl dɪˈzɑːstə]	Naturkatastrophe
	disaster [dɪˈzɑːstə]	Katastrophe, Unglück
	drought [draʊt]	Trockenheit, Dürre(periode)

Plants can't grow and lots of animals die when there is a *drought*.

	flood [flʌd]	Überschwemmung, Hochwasser
	hurricane ['hʌrɪkən]	Orkan, Hurrikan
	volcanic eruption [vɒlˌkænɪkˌɪˈrʌpʃn]	Vulkanausbruch
	tornado (*pl* -es) [tɔːˈneɪdəʊ, tɔːˈneɪdəʊz]	Tornado
	definition [ˌdefəˈnɪʃn]	Definition, Erklärung
	violent ['vaɪələnt]	brutal, gewalttätig; *hier:* heftig
	heavy ['hevi]	*hier:* stark

volcanic eruption

The rain is really *heavy* today.

	powerful ['paʊəfl]	mächtig; *hier:* stark, heftig
	lava *(no pl)* ['lɑːvə]	Lava
	explode [ɪkˈspləʊd]	explodieren

A volcano can *explode* at any time.

	crust [krʌst]	(Erd)kruste
	send out sth [ˌsendˌaʊt sʌmθɪŋ]	*hier:* etw aussenden, etw abgeben
	shock wave ['ʃɒk weɪv]	Stoßwelle, Druckwelle
	cause sth ['kɔːzˌsʌmθɪŋ]	etw verursachen, etw veranlassen
	shake [ʃeɪk]	*hier:* beben

It felt like the whole world *shook*.

	rotating [rəʊˈtaɪtɪŋ]	rotierend
2	drama ['drɑːmə]	*hier:* Drama, Tragödie
	killer ['kɪlə]	mörderisch
	twister *(informal)* ['twɪstə]	Tornado
	strike [straɪk]	angreifen, treffen, zuschlagen
	governor ['gʌvənə]	Gouverneur
	declare [dɪˈkleə]	erklären, verkünden
	state of emergency [ˌsteɪtˌəvˌɪˈmɜːdʒnsi]	Ausnahmezustand

strike – struck – struck

devastate [ˈdevəˌsteɪt]	vernichten, (völlig) zerstören, verwüsten	The building was *devastated* by the storm.

wide [waɪd]	breit	
trail [treɪl]	Weg, Pfad	
destruction *(no pl)* [dɪˈstrʌkʃn]	Zerstörung	destroy – *destruction*
uproot [ʌpˈruːt]	entwurzeln	The storm *uprooted* lots of trees.
flatten [ˈflætn]	zerdrücken, dem Erdboden gleich machen	
hit [hɪt]	*hier:* treffen, erschüttern	
blow [bləʊ]	wehen, blasen	*blow* – blew – blown
right [raɪt]	*hier:* genau, direkt	
middle [ˈmɪdl]	Mitte	
be alive [ˌbi_əˈlaɪv]	leben, am Leben sein	*alive* ≠ dead
debris *(no pl)* [ˈdebriː]	Trümmer, Schutt	
basement [ˈbeɪsmənt]	Keller, Untergeschoss	
completely [kəmˈpliːtli]	völlig, ganz	My heart is *completely* broken.

survivor [səˈvaɪvə]	Überlebende/r	
the Mid-South [ðə ˌmɪd ˈsaʊθ]	der Mittlere Süden	
seriously [ˈsɪəriəsli]	ernst(lich), schwer	
classify [ˈklæsɪfaɪ]	klassifizieren	
touch down [ˌtʌtʃ ˈdaʊn]	aufsetzen, landen, niedergehen	
speed [spiːd]	Geschwindigkeit, Tempo	Sports cars can go at really high *speeds*.
extent *(no pl)* [ɪkˈstent]	Ausmaß, Umfang	
damage [ˈdæmɪdʒ]	Schaden	The firefighter went into the house to look at the *damage*.
city administrator [ˌsɪtiˌədˈmɪnɪˌstreɪtə]	*hier:* Bürgermeister	
estimate [ˈestɪmeɪt]	(ein)schätzen, annehmen	
single [ˈsɪŋgl]	einzelne(r, s)	
confirm [kənˈfɜːm]	bestätigen	
truck [trʌk]	Last(kraft)wagen, Laster	
rescue worker [ˈreskjuː ˌwɜːkə]	Rettungskraft	After a natural disaster *rescue workers* try to find people who are hurt.
death toll [ˈdeθ təʊl]	Zahl der Todesopfer	
rise [raɪz]	(auf)steigen	
search [sɜːtʃ]	Suche	
victim [ˈvɪktɪm]	Opfer	They took the *victim* to hospital.
spokesman/spokeswoman [ˈspəʊksmən, ˈspəʊksˌwʊmən]	Sprecher/in	
announce [əˈnaʊns]	bekannt geben, verkünden	
the National Guard [ðə ˌnæʃnəl ˈgɑːd]	die Nationalgarde (USA)	
emergency shelter [ɪˈmɜːdʒnsi ˌʃeltə]	Notunterkunft	
set up [ˌset ˈʌp]	aufbauen, einrichten	
the Red Cross [ðə ˌred ˈkrɒs]	das Rote Kreuz	

electricity [ɪˌlekˈtrɪsəti] Elektrizität, Strom *electricity*
home [həʊm] *hier:* Haus; Wohnung
despite [dɪˈspaɪt] trotz
speech [spiːtʃ] Rede
confident [ˈkɒnfɪdnt] zuversichtlich
rebuild [ˌriːˈbɪld] wieder aufbauen After the tornado had destroyed the church, it was *rebuilt*.

verb [vɜːb] Verb
passive [ˈpæsɪv] passiv
up to [ʌp tʊ] bis zu The football player trains *up to* four hours every day.

3 reporting *(no pl)* [rɪˈpɔːtɪŋ] Berichterstattung
deadly [ˈdedli] tödlich
buzz group [ˈbʌz gruːp] *Form der Gruppenarbeit*
4 survival [səˈvaɪvl] Überleben Lone Grove Post is the name of a newspaper.
logical [ˈlɒdʒɪkl] logisch
warn [wɔːn] warnen
5 **warning** [ˈwɔːnɪŋ] Warnung
6 early warning system Frühwarnsystem
  [ˌɜːli ˈwɔːnɪŋ ˌsɪstəm]
forecast [ˈfɔːkɑːst] vorhersagen
last [lɑːst] halten; (an)dauern; (aus)reichen The match *lasts* 90 minutes.

complicated [ˈkɒmplɪˌkeɪtɪd] kompliziert
meteorologist Meteorologe/Meteorologin
  [ˌmiːtiəˈrɒlədʒɪst]
balloon [bəˈluːn] Ballon *balloon*
measure [ˈmeʒə] messen A ruler is used to *measure* how long something is.

atmospheric [ˌætməsˈferɪk] atmosphärisch
stability *(no pl)* [stəˈbɪləti] Stabilität; Gleichgewicht
temperature [ˈtemprɪtʃə] Temperatur
humidity *(no pl)* [hjuːˈmɪdəti] (Luft)feuchtigkeit
measurement [ˈmeʒəmənt] Messung
likely [ˈlaɪkli] wahrscheinlich
radar [ˈreɪdɑː] Radar
conventional [kənˈvenʃnəl] herkömmlich, konventionell
detect [dɪˈtekt] entdecken, orten, bemerken He tried to *detect* as much as possible by asking lots of questions.

issue [ˈɪʃuː] *hier:* veröffentlichen, aussprechen
rely on [rɪˈlaɪ ‿ɒn] sich verlassen auf A good friend is someone you can *rely on*.

spotter [ˈspɒtə] *Person, die Extremwetterlagen aufspürt und meldet*

development [dɪˈveləpmənt] Entwicklung; Wachstum develop – *development*
observe [əbˈzɜːv] beobachten
distinguish [dɪˈstɪŋgwɪʃ] unterscheiden
7 define [dɪˈfaɪn] definieren
extraordinary [ɪkˈstrɔːdnri] außerordentlich, ungewöhnlich

8	**communicate** [kəˈmjuːnɪkeɪt]	sich verständigen, kommunizieren	We *communicate* by telephone every day.
	throughout [θruːˈaʊt]	während, im Laufe	
9	**social networking** [ˌsəʊʃl ˈnetˌwɜːkɪŋ]	soziales Netzwerken	
	site *(informal)* [saɪt]	Website	
	log on [ˌlɒɡ ˈɒn]	sich einloggen, sich anmelden	Before you can use the computer, you have to *log on*.
10	profile [ˈprəʊfaɪl]	Profil	
	discover [dɪˈskʌvə]	entdecken, herausfinden	The man *discovered* a really old pot.
	sign up [ˌsaɪn ˈʌp]	sich anmelden	
	social network [ˌsəʊʃl ˈnetˌwɜːk]	soziales Netzwerk	
	post sth [ˈpəʊst ˌsʌmθɪŋ]	*hier:* etw ins Internet stellen	
	get in touch with sb [ˌɡet ɪn ˈtʌtʃ wɪð ˌsʌmbədi]	mit jdm in Kontakt treten	He *got in touch with* a friend he had not seen for a long time.
	status update [ˈsteɪtəs ˌʌpˌdeɪt]	Aktualisierung des Status	
	waste [weɪst]	Verschwendung	
	chatting [tʃætɪŋ]	Chatten	
	data *(pl)* [ˈdeɪtə]	Daten, (persönliche) Angaben	
	friend request [ˈfrend rɪˌkwest]	Freundschaftsanfrage	
	kiss [kɪs]	küssen	
	employer [ɪmˈplɔɪə]	Arbeitgeber/in	
	sensible [ˈsensəbl]	vernünftig	
	awesome *(informal)* [ˈɔːsm]	super, spitze	
	basic [ˈbeɪsɪk]	grundlegend, wesentlich; Grund-	
	sex [seks]	Geschlecht	
	current [ˈkʌrənt]	jetzig, gegenwärtig, aktuell	
	relationship [rɪˈleɪʃnʃɪp]	Beziehung	
	dating [deɪtɪŋ]	*hier:* Verabredungen	
	religious [rəˈlɪdʒəs]	religiöse(r, s), Religions-	
	view [vjuː]	*hier:* Ansicht, Meinung	
	Christian [ˈkrɪstʃən]	Christ/in; christlich	
	interest [ˈɪntrəst]	Interesse	
	bro *(informal)* [brəʊ]	Bruder	
	freshman *(AE)* [ˈfreʃmən]	Studienanfänger/in	
	quotation [kwəʊˈteɪʃn]	Zitat	
	sensitive [ˈsensətɪv]	sensibel	
11	even [ˈiːvn]	*hier:* noch	
	frequent [ˈfriːkwənt]	häufig, regelmäßig	The buses are very *frequent* from London Victoria Bus Station.
12	expert [ˈekspɜːt]	Experte/Expertin	
	give a talk [ˌɡɪv ə ˈtɔːk]	einen Vortrag halten	
13	listener [ˈlɪsnə]	(Zu)hörer/in	
	take advantage of sth [ˌteɪk ədˈvɑːntɪdʒ əv ˌsʌmθɪŋ]	etw (aus)nutzen	They *took advantage* of the special offer and ate lots of cake.

favorite *(AE)* = favourite *(BE)*

False friends – nicht verwechseln!
Im Englischen gibt es viele Wörter, die deutschen Wörtern zwar sehr ähnlich sehen, aber eine ganz andere Bedeutung haben. Man nennt sie deshalb *false friends* (falsche Freunde).
Für diese Wörter kannst du dir ein Merkblatt „Vorsicht Falle" anlegen.
sensible = vernünftig (NICHT: sensibel)
roof = Dach (NICHT: Ruf)
spin = drehen (NICHT: spinnen)
also = auch (NICHT: also)
chef = Koch (NICHT: Chef)
capital = Hauptstadt (NICHT: Kapital)
floor = Boden; Stockwerk (NICHT: Flur)

TODAY:
Special offer!
3 pieces
of cake
for the price of
2 pieces!

WORDS THEME 4

	anonymity *(no pl)* [ˌænəˈnɪməti]	Anonymität
	technology [tekˈnɒlədʒi]	Technik, Technologie
	brain [breɪn]	Gehirn; Verstand
	further [ˈfɜːðə]	weiter
	telegraph *(no pl)* [ˈtelɪˌɡrɑːf]	Telegraf
	powerful [ˈpaʊəfl]	mächtig; *hier:* leistungsfähig
	do business [ˌduː ˈbɪznəs]	Geschäfte machen, Handel treiben
	privacy *(no pl)* [ˈprɪvəsi]	Privatsphäre
	data protection *(no pl)* [ˌdeɪtə prəˈtekʃn]	Datenschutz
	be aware of sth [bi_əˈweər_əv ˌsʌmθɪŋ]	sich einer Sache bewusst sein
	need *(no pl)* [niːd]	Notwendigkeit
	hacking skills [ˈhækɪŋ ˌskɪlz]	Hacker-Fähigkeiten
PP	° inventor [ɪnˈventə]	Erfinder/in
	° single wire telegraph [ˌsɪŋɡl ˌwaɪə ˈtelɪˌɡrɑːf]	Eindrahttelegraf, Schreibtelegraf
	° bury [ˈberi]	begraben
	° moved [muːvd]	bewegt, angetrieben
	° tragic [ˈtrædʒɪk]	tragisch
	° means *(pl)* [miːnz]	Mittel, Möglichkeit
	° long-distance [ˌlɒŋ ˈdɪstəns]	Fern-, Langstrecken-
	° electromagnetic [ɪˌlektrəʊmæɡˈnetɪk]	elektromagnetisch
	° power [ˈpaʊə]	*hier:* Kraft
	° pulse [pʌls]	(Im)puls
	° length [leŋθ]	Länge, Dauer
	° wire [ˈwaɪə]	Draht; Leitung, Kabel
	° visible [ˈvɪzəbl]	sichtbar
	° pattern [ˈpætən]	Muster
	° dot [dɒt]	Punkt
	° dash [dæʃ]	Strich
	° method [ˈmeθəd]	Methode, Verfahren, System
	° Morse Code *(no pl)* [ˌmɔːs ˈkəʊd]	Morsezeichen, Morsealphabet
	° further [ˈfɜːðə]	zusätzlich, noch mehr, weiter
	° transcontinental [ˌtrænzkɒntɪˈnentl]	transkontinental
	° line [laɪn]	*hier:* Leitung, Verbindung
	° certain [ˈsɜːtn]	sicher; gewisse(r, s), bestimmte(r, s)
	° connection [kəˈnekʃn]	Verbindung, Anschluss
M1	flood [flʌd]	überschwemmen, (über)fluten
	hundreds of thousands *(pl)* [ˌhʌndrədz_əv ˈθaʊzndz]	Hunderttausende
	Gulf of Mexico [ˌɡʌlf_əv ˈmeksɪkəʊ]	Golf von Mexiko

brain

Vielseitige Verben
Im Englischen kann ein Verb ganz verschiedene Bedeutungen haben – je nachdem, mit welchen Wörtern es kombiniert wird. Zum Beispiel kann *get* wie folgt übersetzt werden:
get ready – fertig werden
get a present – ein Geschenk bekommen
get sb a burger – jdm einen Burger bringen
get along with sb – sich mit jdm verstehen
get in touch with sb – mit jdm in Kontakt treten
get into debt – Schulden machen

Reimwörter
Damit du dir besser merken kannst, wie bestimmte Wörter ausgesprochen werden, suche Reimwörter für sie. Dir wird auffallen, dass die Reimwörter nicht immer dieselbe Schreibweise haben.
Hier ein Beispiel:
blow – *toe* – *sew*

Two months ago our village was *flooded.*

	not only ... but also [ˌnɒtˌˌəʊnli ˌbʌtˌˈɔːlsəʊ]	nicht nur ... sondern auch	*Not only* does he play guitar, *but* he is *also* good-looking.

	no sooner ... than [ˌnəʊ ˈsuːnə ðæn]	gerade, kaum ... als, da
	levee [ˈlevi]	Damm
	the poor *(pl)* [ðə pɔː]	die Armen
	shelter [ˈʃeltə]	Schutz, Zuflucht
	surrounded (by) [səˈraʊndɪd]	umgeben (von)
	cope with sth [ˈkəʊp wɪð ˌsʌmθɪŋ]	etw bewältigen, mit etw fertig werden
	shocking [ˈʃɒkɪŋ]	schockierend
M2	frustration [frʌˈstreɪʃn]	Niedergeschlagenheit; Frustration
	turn to sth [ˈtɜːn tʊ ˌsʌmθɪŋ]	sich etw zuwenden
	poetry *(no pl)* [ˈpəʊɪtri]	Lyrik, Dichtung
	image [ˈɪmɪdʒ]	*hier:* Bild, Metapher
	comparison [kəmˈpærɪsn]	Vergleich
	° rooftop [ˈruːfˌtɒp]	(Haus)dach
	° row [rəʊ]	Reihe
	° grave [greɪv]	Grab
	° except [ɪkˈsept]	außer, bis auf
	° thirst [θɜːst]	Durst
	° dirt [dɜːt]	Schmutz, Dreck
M3	**protection** [prəˈtekʃn]	Schutz
	electric power [ɪˌlektrɪk ˈpaʊə]	elektrischer Strom
	restore [rɪˈstɔː]	wiederherstellen

the poor ≠ the rich

She couldn't *cope with* it all and so she started crying.

[z] di**s**aster, ob**s**erve, victim**s**
[s] compari**s**on, **s**earch, ba**s**ement**s**

protect – *protection*

The man is *restoring* the old furniture to make it look good again.

	building site [ˈbɪldɪŋ saɪt]	Baugelände, Baugrundstück
	health care [ˈhelθ keə]	Gesundheitsfürsorge, Gesundheitsversorgung
	provide [prəˈvaɪd]	zur Verfügung stellen, sorgen für

He *provided* her with lots of food and drink to take on the picnic.

	evacuation [ɪˌvækjuˈeɪʃn]	Evakuierung
M4	city official [ˌsɪti əˈfɪʃl]	Angestellte/r der Stadt
M5	chick *(informal)* [tʃɪk]	Mädchen
	outfit [ˈaʊtfɪt]	Kleidung, Outfit
	hairstyle [ˈheəˌstaɪl]	Frisur
	gig *(informal)* [gɪg]	Auftritt, Konzert, Gig
	popularity *(no pl)* [ˈpɒpjʊˈlærəti]	Beliebtheit, Popularität
	version [ˈvɜːʃn]	Version
	hot [hɒt]	*hier:* toll
	shoot-out [ˈʃuːtˌaʊt]	Schießerei
	graphics *(pl)* [ˈgræfɪks]	Grafik(en), grafische Darstellung(en)
	clan [klæn]	Clan, Sippe, Stamm, Familie

Den richtigen Ton treffen
Im gesprochenen Englisch gibt es viele umgangssprachliche Wörter und Ausdrücke. Ihre Verwendung hängt sehr von der Situation und der Herkunft des Sprechers ab. Wenn du nicht weißt, ob ein Ausdruck angemessen ist, benutze ihn lieber nicht. Verwende stattdessen Wörter, die dir vertraut sind.

WORDS THEME 4

WORDS THEME 4

power ['paʊə]	Macht; Einfluss	
final ['faɪnl]	letzte(r, s); endgültig	
battle ['bætl]	Kampf, Schlacht	*battle* = fight
weapon ['wepən]	Waffe	
be at sb's disposal [ˌbi‿ət ˌsʌmbədiz dɪˈspəʊzl]	jdm zur Verfügung stehen	Three dictionaries *are at my disposal*. I can use them at any time.
pistol ['pɪstl]	Pistole	
automatic gun [ˌɔːtəˌmætɪk‿'gʌn]	Selbstladegewehr	
rocket ['rɒkɪt]	(Marsch)flugkörper, Rakete(ngeschoss)	

Can you sort these words into alphabetical order?
shake, wide, speed, victim, uproot, rebuild, forecast, discover, further, sensitive

go ahead [ˌgəʊ‿ə'hed]	loslegen	
Rome [rəʊm]	Rom	
Roman ['rəʊmən]	Römer/in; römisch	
BC (= before Christ) [bɪˌfɔː 'kraɪst]	vor Christus	
Carthage ['kɑːθɪdʒ]	Karthago	
once and for all [ˌwʌns‿ənd fər‿'ɔːl]	endgültig, ein für alle Mal	
emperor ['emprə]	Kaiser/in; Imperator	
gun [gʌn]	(Schuss)waffe	

The soldier is carrying a *gun*.

M6 the Netherlands [ðə 'neðlənz]	die Niederlande	
ring [rɪŋ]	Ring	
humanoid ['hjuːmənɔɪd]	menschenartiges Wesen, Humanoid	
M7 gold (no pl) [gəʊld]	Gold	
advantage [əd'vɑːntɪdʒ]	Vorteil	*advantage* ≠ disadvantage
virtual ['vɜːtʃʊəl]	virtuell	
forum ['fɔːrəm]	Forum	
complain [kəm'pleɪn]	klagen, sich beklagen	Don't *complain* all the time!
but [bʌt]	*hier:* außer	
mix up sb/sth [ˌmɪks‿'ʌp ˌsʌmbədi/ˌsʌmθɪŋ]	jdn/etw verwechseln	
cost [kɒst]	Kosten, Preis	
parent ['peərənt]	Elternteil, Erziehungsberechtigte/r	
look out (for sth) [ˌlʊk‿'aʊt (fə ˌsʌmθɪŋ)]	(nach etw) Ausschau halten; auf etw aufpassen	A policeman *looks out* for trouble.
MMORPG (= Massively Multiplayer Online Role-Playing Game) [ˌem‿em‿əʊ‿ɑː‿ˌpiː‿'dʒiː]	*Rollenspiel im Internet mit extrem vielen Spielern*	

limit ['lɪmɪt]	Grenze, Limit	
case [keɪs]	Fall	
addicted (to) [ə'dɪktɪd]	abhängig (von), süchtig (nach)	I love chocolate. I'm *addicted* to it.
non-stop [ˌnɒn 'stɒp]	nonstop, ununterbrochen	
positive ['pɒzətɪv]	positiv	*positive* ≠ negative
interaction [ˌɪntər'ækʃn]	Interaktion	
perfectly ['pɜːfɪktli]	vollkommen	

	e-learning ['iː ˌlɜːnɪŋ]	E-Learning, elektronisches Lernen
	sector ['sektə]	Bereich, Sektor
	strategic thinking [strəˌtiːdʒɪk 'θɪŋkɪŋ]	strategisches Denken
	complex ['kɒmpleks]	komplex, kompliziert, vielschichtig
M8	**advise** [əd'vaɪz]	(be)raten

Our teacher *advises* us to work hard.

	keep an eye on sb [ˌkiːp ən ˈaɪ ɒn ˌsʌmbədi]	ein (wachsames) Auge auf jdn haben, jdn im Auge behalten
	effect [ɪ'fekt]	(Aus)wirkung, Konsequenz, Einfluss

Adding salt to the soup had a bad *effect*.

M9	**habit** ['hæbɪt]	Gewohnheit
	pie chart ['paɪ tʃɑːt]	Tortendiagramm
	bar chart ['bɑː ˌtʃɑːt]	Säulendiagramm, Balkendiagramm
	usage ['juːsɪdʒ]	*hier:* Benutzung, Gebrauch
	access ['ækses]	Zugang
	blogging *(no pl)* [blɒgɪŋ]	Blogging, Bloggen
	download [ˌdaʊn'ləʊd]	herunterladen, downloaden
	do research [duː rɪ'sɜːtʃ]	recherchieren
	instant messaging [ˌɪnstənt 'mesɪdʒɪŋ]	Instant Messaging *(sofortige Nachrichtenübermittlung)*
CIO	answer the phone [ˌɑːnsə ðə 'fəʊn]	ans Telefon gehen, einen Anruf entgegennehmen
	° receive [rɪ'siːv]	empfangen, erhalten
	° uphill [ˌʌp'hɪl]	bergauf (führend)
	° downhill [ˌdaʊn'hɪl]	bergab (führend)
	° average ['ævrɪdʒ]	durchschnittlich
	° volcano *(pl* -oes *or* -os) [vɒl'keɪnəʊ, vɒl'keɪnəʊz]	Vulkan
	° Japanese [ˌdʒæpə'niːz]	Japaner/in; Japanisch; japanisch
	° wave [weɪv]	Welle

Wortbedeutungen erschließen
Bevor du zum Wörterbuch greifst, um die Bedeutung eines englischen Wortes nachzuschlagen, solltest du dir das Wort genau ansehen. Vielleicht ist es ein Wort, das aus zwei Einzelwörtern besteht. Die Bedeutung kannst du erschließen, wenn dir ein Bestandteil schon bekannt ist, z. B.:
emergency shelter
flea market
child labour

Die Vokabeln aus den *Themes* 5 und 6 findest du im *English-German dictionary* ab **Seite 182.**

WORDS THEME 4

A

a [ə, eɪ] pro

do one's A levels [du: wʌnz‿'eɪ ˌlevlz] das Abitur machen V/5/2

a/an [ə, ən] ein(e)

aardvark ['ɑːd,vɑːk] Erdferkel VI/3/M5

ability [ə'bɪləti] Fähigkeit; Talent V/3/4

be able to do [bi‿ˌeɪbl tə 'du:] tun können

abolition *(no pl)* [ˌæbə'lɪʃn] Abschaffung VI/3/13

Aboriginal [ˌæbə'rɪdʒnl] ... der Aboriginals V/1/10

Aborigine [ˌæbə'rɪdʒəni] australische/r Ureinwohner/in, Aborigine V/1/I

abortion [ə'bɔːʃn] Abtreibung, Schwangerschaftsabbruch VI/1/10

about [ə'baʊt] über; wegen; ungefähr

be about [ˌbi‿ə'baʊt] handeln von

above [ə'bʌv] über

abroad [ə'brɔːd] im Ausland V/5/M1

absolutely ['æbsəluːtli] absolut, völlig VI/2/M6

accent ['æksnt] Akzent

accept [ək'sept] annehmen; akzeptieren V/3/10

access ['ækses] Zugang VI/5/S4

accident ['æksɪdnt] Unfall

by accident [baɪ‿'æksɪdnt] aus Versehen; zufällig

accommodation *(no pl)* [əˌkɒmə'deɪʃn] Unterkunft VI/3/13

according to [ə'kɔːdɪŋ tʊ] laut, nach, gemäß VI/3/12

account [ə'kaʊnt] Konto V/5/13

across [ə'krɒs] über

across [ə'krɒs] durch VI/1/7

acrostic [ə'krɒstɪk] *Gedichtform, bei der bestimmte Buchstaben aus jeder Zeile untereinander ein Wort ergeben* VI/2/6

act [ækt] handeln, sich verhalten V/6/2

act out [ækt‿'aʊt] nachspielen

action ['ækʃn] Handlung; Aktion

active ['æktɪv] aktiv V/3/1

activity [æk'tɪvəti] Aktivität

actor/actress ['æktə/'æktrəs] Schauspieler/in

actually ['æktʃuəli] eigentlich

actually ['æktʃuəli] wirklich, tatsächlich VI/5/R3

add [æd] hinzufügen

addicted (to) [ə'dɪktɪd] abhängig (von), süchtig (nach) VI/4/M7

address [ə'dres] Adresse

address sb [ə'dres] jdn anreden VI/2/CIO

adjective ['ædʒɪktɪv] Adjektiv

admit sth [əd'mɪt] etw zugeben, etw eingestehen V/2/M5

adopt [ə'dɒpt] adoptieren VI/1/10

adoption [ə'dɒpʃn] Adoption VI/1/14

give up for adoption [ˌgɪv‿ˌʌp fər‿ə'dɒpʃn] zur Adoption freigeben VI/1/10

adoptive [ə'dɒptɪv] Adoptiv- VI/1/14

adult ['ædʌlt] Erwachsene/r

advantage [əd'vɑːntɪdʒ] Vorteil VI/4/M7

take advantage of sth [ˌteɪk‿əd'vɑːntɪdʒ‿əv ˌsʌmθɪŋ] etw (aus)nutzen VI/4/13

adventure [əd'ventʃə] Abenteuer, Erlebnis

adverb ['ædvɜːb] Adverb VI/2/10

advert (= advertisement) ['ædvɜːt, əd'vɜːtɪsmənt] Anzeige, Inserat; Werbung

advice *(no pl)* [əd'vaɪs] Rat

advise [əd'vaɪz] (be)raten VI/4/M8

aerial ['eərɪəl] Luft-, aus der Luft VI/5/MD3

aeroplane ['eərə,pleɪn] Flugzeug VI/2/3

afford [ə'fɔːd] sich leisten V/5/13

be afraid (of) [ˌbi‿ə'freɪd] Angst haben/sich fürchten (vor)

Africa ['æfrɪkə] Afrika

African ['æfrɪkən] Afrikaner/in; afrikanisch VI/3/2

African American [ˌæfrɪkən‿ə'merɪkən] Afroamerikaner/in; afroamerikanisch

Afrikaans *(no pl)* [ˌæfrɪ'kɑːns] Afrikaans *(eine der elf Amtssprachen in Südafrika)* VI/6/R4

° **Afrikaner** [ˌæfrɪ'kɑːnə] Afrika(a)nder/in *(Bezeichnung für in Südafrika geborene Weiße)* VI/3/PP

after ['ɑːftə] nach; nachdem

after all [ˌɑːftə‿'ɔːl] schließlich VI/1/10

afternoon [ˌɑːftə'nuːn] Nachmittag

in the afternoon [ˌɪn ðiː‿ˌɑːftə'nuːn] am Nachmittag, nachmittags

this afternoon [ðɪs‿ˌɑːftə'nuːn] heute Nachmittag

afterwards ['ɑːftəwədz] danach, anschließend; später V/5/2

again [ə'gen] wieder, noch einmal, noch mal

all over again [ˌɔːl‿ˌəʊvər‿ə'gen] noch einmal (ganz von vorn) VI/1/M8

against [ə'genst] gegen

age [eɪdʒ] Alter

come of age [ˌkʌm‿əv 'eɪdʒ] volljährig werden VI/3/M9

in old age [ɪn‿ˌəʊld‿'eɪdʒ] im (hohen) Alter VI/1/M4

for ages *(informal)* [fər‿'eɪdʒɪz] ewig, seit Ewigkeiten VI/2/3

aggressive [ə'gresɪv] aggressiv; energisch V/1/10

(two days) ago [ə'gəʊ] vor (zwei Tagen)

agree on [ə'griː‿ɒn] einer Meinung sein über; sich einigen auf

agree (with) [ə'griː] zustimmen

go ahead [ˌgəʊ‿ə'hed] loslegen VI/4/M5

aim [eɪm] Ziel, Absicht VI/6/R3

air [eə] Luft

air-conditioned ['eə kən,dɪʃnd] klimatisiert, mit Klimaanlage VI/6/MD2

airfield ['eə,fiːld] Flugplatz VI/2/3

airport ['eə,pɔːt] Flughafen V/5/M1

alarm clock [ə'lɑːm ,klɒk] Wecker

album ['ælbəm] (Musik)album V/3/M8

alcohol ['ælkə,hɒl] Alkohol

alcoholic [ælkə'hɒlɪk] alkoholisch, alkoholhaltig VI/5/R1

be alive [,bi ə'laɪv] leben, am Leben sein VI/4/2

all [ɔːl] alle(s); ganz, völlig

all day [,ɔːl 'deɪ] den ganzen Tag V/4/9

all in all [,ɔːl ɪn 'ɔːl] alles in allem V/2/2

all over ['ɔːl ,əʊvə] überall in/auf

all over again [,ɔːl ,əʊvər ə'gen] noch einmal (ganz von vorn) VI/1/M8

all right [,ɔːl 'raɪt] in Ordnung VI/6/R2

all the time [,ɔːl ðə 'taɪm] dauernd, ständig

allergic [ə'lɜːdʒɪk] allergisch VI/2/3

allergy ['ælədʒi] Allergie VI/2/3

be allowed to do sth [bi ə,laʊd tə 'duː sʌmθɪŋ] etw tun dürfen

almost ['ɔːlməʊst] fast, beinahe

alone [ə'ləʊn] allein

leave sb alone [,liːv sʌmbədi ə'ləʊn] jdn in Ruhe lassen V/2/2

along [ə'lɒŋ] entlang

along the way [ə,lɒŋ ðə 'weɪ] unterwegs, auf dem Weg VI/5/R4

aloud [ə'laʊd] laut

alphabet ['ælfə,bet] Alphabet

already [ɔːl'redi] schon

also ['ɔːlsəʊ] auch

alternative [ɔːl'tɜːnətɪv] Alternative V/5/M11

although [ɔːl'ðəʊ] obwohl, obgleich

always ['ɔːlweɪz] immer

am (= ante meridiem) [,eɪ 'em, ,ænti mə'rɪdiəm] morgens, vormittags *(nur hinter Uhrzeit zwischen Mitternacht und 12 Uhr mittags)*

amazement *(no pl)* [ə'meɪzmənt] Erstaunen, Verwunderung VI/1/7

amazing *(informal)* [ə'meɪzɪŋ] toll, unglaublich VI/5/R3

American [ə'merɪkən] Amerikaner/in; amerikanisch

Amish ['ɑːmɪʃ] amisch

the Amish [ði 'ɑːmɪʃ] die Amischen

among [ə'mʌŋ] unter

amount [ə'maʊnt] Menge V/5/15

and [ænd] und

and so on [ænd ,səʊ 'ɒn] und so weiter VI/3/13

angel ['eɪndʒl] Engel VI/5/R4

angry ['æŋgri] verärgert; zornig; wütend

animal ['ænɪml] Tier

animal care *(no pl)* ['ænɪml ,keə] Tierpflege VI/3/2

animal carer ['ænɪml ,keərə] Tierpfleger/in VI/3/2

animated film [,ænɪmeɪtɪd 'fɪlm] (Zeichen)trickfilm, Animationsfilm V/6/8

announce [ə'naʊns] bekannt geben, verkünden VI/4/2

annoy [ə'nɔɪ] ärgern, nerven V/4/M3

anonymity *(no pl)* [,ænə'nɪməti] Anonymität VI/4/13

anonymous [ə'nɒnɪməs] anonym VI/1/5

anorexia *(no pl)* [,ænə'reksiə] Magersucht, Anorexie V/4/9

anorexic [,ænə'reksɪk] magersüchtig V/4/9

another [ə'nʌðə] noch ein(e, r, s); ein zweiter/zweites, eine zweite; ein anderer/anderes, eine andere

answer ['ɑːnsə] (be)antworten; Antwort

answer the phone [,ɑːnsə ðə 'fəʊn] ans Telefon gehen, einen Anruf entgegennehmen VI/4/CIO

anti-malaria drug [,ænti mə'leəriə ,drʌg] *Medikament gegen Malaria* VI/6/MD2

anxious ['æŋkʃəs] besorgt VI/1/7

any ['eni] irgendein(e); jede(r, s)

not ... any longer [,nɒt eni 'lɒŋgə] nicht länger VI/1/6

not anymore [nɒt eni'mɔː] nicht mehr

anyone ['eni,wʌn] jede/r, jemand

anything ['eni,θɪŋ] alles; etwas

Anything else? [,eniθɪŋ 'els] Darf es noch etwas sein?

anyway ['eni,weɪ] sowieso, jedenfalls; trotzdem

anyway ['eni,weɪ] sowieso, jedenfalls VI/1/6

anywhere ['eni,weə] überall; irgendwo VI/5/MD2

apart from [ə'pɑːt frəm] abgesehen von VI/2/10

apartheid *(no pl)* [ə'pɑːt,heɪt] Apartheid, Rassentrennung VI/3/5

apartment *(AE)* = flat *(BE)* [ə'pɑːtmənt] Wohnung; Apartment

apologize [ə'pɒlədʒaɪz] sich entschuldigen

apology [ə'pɒlədʒi] Entschuldigung V/2/M5

appear [ə'pɪə] erscheinen V/2/M5

appetite ['æpɪtaɪt] Appetit V/4/M3

apple ['æpl] Apfel

apple pie ['æpl ,paɪ] gedeckter Apfelkuchen

(letter of) application [,æplɪ'keɪʃn] Bewerbung(sschreiben) VI/2/3

application form [,æplɪ'keɪʃn fɔːm] Bewerbungsformular V/5/M2

apply (for/to) [ə'plaɪ] sich bewerben (um/für) VI/2/3

make an appointment [,meɪk ən ə'pɔɪntmənt] einen Termin ausmachen/ vereinbaren VI/1/10

apprenticeship [ə'prentɪʃɪp] Ausbildung, Lehre VI/2/M2

April ['eɪprəl] April

aquarium [ə'kweəriəm] Aquarium VI/3/5

archbishop [ɑːtʃˈbɪʃəp] Erzbischof VI/3/M10

Are you all right? [ɑː ˌjʊˌɔːl ˈraɪt] Ist alles in Ordnung?

area [ˈeəriə] Gebiet, Region

argue [ˈɑːgju] sich streiten

argue [ˈɑːgju] argumentieren V/5/M11

argument [ˈɑːgjʊmənt] Argument V/2/8

arm [ɑːm] Arm

armchair [ˈɑːmˌtʃeə] Sessel, Lehnstuhl

army [ˈɑːmi] Armee, Heer V/6/8

around [əˈraʊnd] um; in

arranged marriage [əˌreɪndʒd ˈmærɪdʒ] arrangierte Hochzeit VI/1/M4

arrest sb [əˈrest ˌsʌmbədi] jdn verhaften V/3/5

arrival [əˈraɪvl] Ankunft V/6/8

arrive [əˈraɪv] ankommen

art [ɑːt] Kunst

article [ˈɑːtɪkl] Artikel

artist [ˈɑːtɪst] Künstler/in

as [əz] als

as [əz] weil, da VI/3/5

as ... as ... [əz əz] (genau)so ... wie ...

° **as one** [æz ˈwʌn] (einmütig) zusammen VI/3/12

as soon as [əzˌˈsuːnˌəz] sobald

as though [əz ˈðəʊ] als ob VI/1/M8

as well [æz ˌwel] auch VI/3/M4

be ashamed [ˌbiˌəˈʃeɪmd] sich schämen

Asia [ˈeɪʃə] Asien V/1/2

Asian [ˈeɪʒn] Asiat/in; asiatisch

ask [ɑːsk] fragen; bitten

ask questions [ɑːskˌˈkwestʃnz] Fragen stellen

ask sb out [ˌɑːsk sʌmbədiˌˈaʊt] sich mit jdm verabreden

be asleep [ˌbiˌəˈsliːp] schlafen

fall asleep [ˌfɔːlˌəˈsliːp] einschlafen

aspect [ˈæspekt] Aspekt, Gesichtspunkt VI/3/14

assist [əˈsɪst] helfen, unterstützen VI/1/14

astronaut [ˈæstrəˌnɔːt] Astronaut/in

at [æt] auf, an, in, bei; um

at all times [ətˌˈɔːl ˈtaɪmz] stets, jederzeit VI/3/4

at first [ət ˈfɜːst] anfangs, zuerst

° **at last** [ət ˈlɑːst] endlich, schließlich VI/2/1

at least [ət ˈliːst] mindestens, wenigstens

athlete [ˈæθliːt] Athlet/in

the Atlantic Ocean [ðiˌətˌlæntɪkˌˈəʊʃn] der Atlantische Ozean VI/3/5

atmosphere [ˈætməsˌfɪə] Atmosphäre, Stimmung VI/1/9

atmosphere [ˈætməsˌfɪə] Erdatmosphäre V/6/M1

atmospheric [ˌætməsˈferɪk] atmosphärisch VI/4/6

attack [əˈtæk] angreifen V/3/M2; Angriff V/2/M1

attract [əˈtrækt] anziehen VI/5/W5

attraction [əˈtrækʃn] Attraktion; Anziehung(skraft)

au-pair [ˌəʊ ˈpeə] als Au-pair arbeiten VI/6/W1

audition [ɔːˈdɪʃn] Vorsprechen; Vorsingen; Vortanzen; Vorspielen

August [ˈɔːgəst] August

aunt [ɑːnt] Tante

Australia [ɒˈstreɪliə] Australien V/1/I

Australian [ɒˈstreɪliən] Australier/in; australisch

author [ˈɔːθə] Schriftsteller/in; Verfasser/in, Autor/in

authority [ɔːˈθɒrəti] Amtsgewalt; Behörde V/1/M6

autobiographical [ˌɔːtəʊbaɪəˈgræfɪkl] autobiografisch VI/6/R4

autograph [ˈɔːtəˌgrɑːf] Autogramm

automatic gun [ˌɔːtəˌmætɪkˌˈgʌn] Selbstladegewehr VI/4/M5

° **average** [ˈævrɪdʒ] durchschnittlich VI/4/CIO

avoid [əˈvɔɪd] (ver)meiden, ausweichen VI/1/CIO

awake [əˈweɪk] wach VI/1/M8

award [əˈwɔːd] Auszeichnung, Preis V/3/M8

be aware of sth [biˈəˈweərˌəv ˌsʌmθɪŋ] sich einer Sache bewusst sein

away [əˈweɪ] weg

awesome *(informal)* [ˈɔːsm] super, spitze VI/4/10

awful [ˈɔːfl] furchtbar, schrecklich V/4/9

B

B&B (= bed and breakfast) [ˌbiˈən ˈbiː] Frühstückspension VI/2/M6

back [bæk] Rücken; Rückseite; zurück

at the back of [ət ðə ˈbækˌəv] hinten in

backache [ˈbækeɪk] Rückenschmerzen

background [ˈbækˌgraʊnd] Herkunft, Verhältnisse; Hintergrund V/2/M2

(in the) background [ˈbækˌgraʊnd] (im) Hintergrund VI/1/9

backpacker [ˈbækˌpækə] Rucksackreisende/r VI/5/S4

bacon [ˈbeɪkən] (Schinken)speck

bad [bæd] schlecht; schlimm

use bad language [juːz bæd ˈlæŋgwɪdʒ] Schimpfwörter benutzen

bag [bæg] Tasche

baggage [ˈbægɪdʒ] Gepäck VI/3/4

bake [beɪk] backen

baker [ˈbeɪkə] Bäcker/in

ball [bɔːl] Ball

balloon [bəˈluːn] Ballon VI/4/6

ballpoint [ˈbɔːlˌpɔɪnt] Kugelschreiber

ban sb from doing sth [ˌbæn ˌsʌmbədi frəm ˈduːɪŋ ˌsʌmθɪŋ] jdm verbieten, etw zu tun VI/5/W2

ban sth [ˈbæn ˌsʌmθɪŋ] etw verbieten V/4/5

banana [bəˈnɑːnə] Banane

bandage [ˈbændɪdʒ] Verband

bottle bank ['bɒtl bæŋk]
Altglascontainer V/6/M4

can bank ['kæn bæŋk]
Dosencontainer V/6/M4

paper bank ['peɪpə bæŋk]
Altpapiercontainer V/6/M4

plastic bottle bank
['plæstɪk ˌbɒtl bæŋk]
Plastikflaschencontainer
V/6/M4

bar chart ['bɑː ˌtʃɑːt]
Säulendiagramm,
Balkendiagramm VI/4/M9

° barbecue ['bɑːbɪˌkjuː] Grillparty;
Grill VI/3/CIO

have a barbecue [ˌhæv‿ə
'bɑːbɪˌkjuː] grillen, eine
Grillparty feiern V/1/5

bark [bɑːk] bellen

barricade [ˌbærɪˈkeɪd] Barrikade
VI/1/2

be based on sth [ˌbi: 'beɪst‿ɒn
ˌsʌmθɪŋ] auf etw basieren/
beruhen VI/6/R4

basement ['beɪsmənt] Keller,
Untergeschoss VI/4/2

basic ['beɪsɪk] grundlegend,
wesentlich; Grund- VI/4/10

basket ['bɑːskɪt] Korb

bath [bɑːθ] (Bade)wanne;
Bad(ezimmer)

take a bath [teɪk‿ə 'bɑːθ] baden
V/6/4

bathroom ['bɑːθˌruːm]
Bad(ezimmer)

bathroom *(AE)* here: toilet *(BE)*
['bɑːθˌruːm] Toilette

battery ['bætri] Batterie V/6/M5

battle ['bætl] Kampf, Schlacht
VI/4/M5

bay [beɪ] Bucht VI/3/5

BC (= before Christ) [biˌfɔː 'kraɪst]
vor Christus VI/4/M5

be [biː] sein

be into sth [ˌbiˌˈɪntʊ ˌsʌmθɪŋ] an
etw interessiert sein, auf etw
stehen VI/5/MD1

be okay with sth [biˌˌəʊˈkeɪ wɪð
ˌsʌmθɪŋ] mit etw einverstanden
sein VI/1/10

be out [ˌbiˈaʊt] nicht zu Hause
sein VI/3/3

be sick of sth [biː 'sɪk‿əv ˌsʌmθɪŋ]
etw satt haben, von etw genug
haben VI/1/3

beach [biːtʃ] Strand

bean [biːn] Bohne

beanie ['biːni] Beanie-Mütze
VI/6/R3

bear [beə] Bär

beat [biːt] schlagen; besiegen

beat up [ˌbiːt‿ˈʌp] verprügeln,
zusammenschlagen VI/1/4

beautiful ['bjuːtəfl] schön

beauty therapy ['bjuːti ˌθerəpi]
Kosmetik VI/2/3

because [bɪˈkɒz] weil

because of [bɪˈkɒz‿əv] wegen

become [bɪˈkʌm] werden

bed [bed] Bett

bedroom ['bedruːm]
Schlafzimmer

bedside light ['bedsaɪd laɪt]
Nachttischlampe VI/1/M8

beer [bɪə] Bier V/2/M5

before [bɪˈfɔː] bevor; vor; zuvor,
vorher

beg [beg] betteln V/5/M11

beggar ['begə] Bettler/in
V/5/M11

begin [bɪˈgɪn] anfangen,
beginnen

beginning [bɪˈgɪnɪŋ] Anfang

in the beginning [ɪn ðə bɪˈgɪnɪŋ]
am Anfang, zu Beginn VI/3/2

behave [bɪˈheɪv] sich verhalten,
sich benehmen V/5/3

behavior *(no pl) (AE)* =
behaviour *(BE)* [bɪˈheɪvjə]
Verhalten, Benehmen V/2/M5

behaviour *(no pl)* [bɪˈheɪvjə]
Verhalten, Benehmen V/6/4

behind [bɪˈhaɪnd] hinter;
dahinter

believe (in) [bɪˈliːv] glauben (an)

° bell [bel] Klingel, Glocke VI/2/1

belongings *(pl)* [bɪˈlɒŋɪŋz] Hab
und Gut, Habseligkeiten
VI/5/R3

below [bɪˈləʊ] unten

bench [bentʃ] Bank

bend [bend] (sich) biegen

bend down [ˌbendˈdaʊn] sich
herunterbeugen VI/1/M8

bend over [bend 'əʊvə] sich
vorbeugen

beside [bɪˈsaɪd] neben VI/1/7

best [best] am meisten/liebsten/
besten; beste(r, s)

best wishes [ˌbest 'wɪʃɪz] viele/
beste Grüße

bet [bet] wetten

for the better [fə ðə 'betə] zum
Besseren, zum Guten VI/3/M9

between [bɪˈtwiːn] zwischen

bicycle ['baɪsɪkl] Fahrrad

big [bɪg] groß

bike [baɪk] (Fahr)rad

bill [bɪl] Rechnung

° billion ['bɪljən] Milliarde VI/1/CIO

bin [bɪn] Mülleimer, Mülltonne

compost bin ['kɒmpɒst bɪn]
Komposttonne V/6/M4

biology [baɪˈɒlədʒi] Biologie

bird [bɜːd] Vogel

birth [bɜːθ] Geburt

birthday ['bɜːθdeɪ] Geburtstag

biscuit ['bɪskɪt] Keks

bit [bɪt] Stück, Stückchen V/3/5

a bit [ə 'bɪt] ein bisschen

bite [baɪt] beißen

bite [baɪt] Biss; Stich VI/6/MD2

black [blæk] schwarz

blackboard ['blækˌbɔːd] Tafel

° blind [blaɪnd] blind VI/3/12

block [blɒk] blockieren,
verstellen; den Weg versperren

blogging *(no pl)* [blɒgɪŋ]
Blogging, Bloggen VI/4/M9

blonde [blɒnd] blond VI/1/3

blow [bləʊ] wehen, blasen
VI/4/2

blue [bluː] blau

blues [bluːz] Blues
*(schwermütiges Lied der
Afroamerikaner)* VI/1/9

board [bɔːd] Brett

board (a plane) [bɔːd] (ein
Flugzeug) besteigen VI/3/4

boarding pass ['bɔːdɪŋ pɑːs]
Bordkarte VI/3/4

boarding school ['bɔːdɪŋ ˌskuːl]
Internat V/1/5

boarding time ['bɔːdɪŋ taɪm]
Einsteigezeit VI/3/4

boat [bəʊt] Boot

body ['bɒdi] Körper
° Boer [bɔ:] Bure/Burin VI/3/PP
boiled [bɔɪld] gekocht V/4/9
bold [bəʊld] kräftig; mutig; gewagt; frech VI/3/M9
bomb [bɒm] Bombe VI/1/5
° bombing ['bɒmɪŋ] Bombenanschlag VI/1/PP
bone [bəʊn] Knochen V/3/5
book [bʊk] Buch; buchen V/1/6
booking reference ['bʊkɪŋ ˌrefrəns] Buchungsnummer VI/3/4
boot [bu:t] Stiefel
border ['bɔ:də] Grenze
be bored [bi 'bɔ:d] sich langweilen
boring ['bɔ:rɪŋ] langweilig
born [bɔ:n] geboren
borrow ['bɒrəʊ] leihen
boss [bɒs] Chef V/4/5
both [bəʊθ] beide
bother sb ['bɒðə ˌsʌmbədi] jdn stören; jdn belästigen V/3/6
bottle ['bɒtl] Flasche
bottle bank ['bɒtl bæŋk] Altglascontainer V/6/M4
bottled ['bɒtld] in Flaschen abgefüllt VI/6/MD2
bottom ['bɒtəm] Boden; Unterseite; unteres Ende
bowl [bəʊl] Schüssel
box office ['bɒks ˌɒfɪs] Kasse (im Kino, Theater)
boy [bɔɪ] Junge
boyfriend ['bɔɪˌfrend] Freund (eines Mädchens)
brain [breɪn] Gehirn; Verstand VI/4/13
brainstorm ['breɪnˌstɔ:m] ein Brainstorming machen VI/1/1
branch [brɑ:ntʃ] Zweig; Ast
brand [brænd] Marke VI/6/R3
brave [breɪv] mutig, unerschrocken
bread [bred] Brot
break [breɪk] (zer)brechen; verstoßen, übertreten, ignorieren; Pause
break down [ˌbreɪk 'daʊn] kaputtgehen, zusammenbrechen V/6/8

breakfast ['brekfəst] Frühstück
° breastfeed ['brestˌfi:d] stillen VI/1/CIO
breathless ['breθləs] atemlos, außer Atem VI/1/7
bride [braɪd] Braut VI/5/W5
bridge [brɪdʒ] Brücke
bright [braɪt] hell
brilliant (informal) ['brɪljənt] toll, hervorragend VI/3/3
bring [brɪŋ] (mit)bringen
bring up sb [ˌbrɪŋ 'ʌp ˌsʌmbədi] jdn großziehen, jdn aufziehen VI/3/M9
Britain ['brɪtn] Großbritannien
British ['brɪtɪʃ] britische(r, s)
the British (pl) [ðə 'brɪtɪʃ] die Briten
bro (informal) [brəʊ] Bruder VI/4/10
broadcast ['brɔ:dˌkɑ:st] senden, ausstrahlen VI/6/L3
brochure ['brəʊʃə] Broschüre
broken ['brəʊkən] zerbrochen, kaputt
brother ['brʌðə] Bruder
brothers and sisters [ˌbrʌðəz ænd 'sɪstəz] Geschwister VI/1/2
brown [braʊn] braun
bruised [bru:zd] geprellt
brush [brʌʃ] (ab)bürsten; putzen
buffalo ['bʌfələʊ] Büffel VI/3/M3
build [bɪld] bauen
builder ['bɪldə] Bauarbeiter/in V/5/2
building ['bɪldɪŋ] Gebäude, Bau
building firm ['bɪldɪŋ fɜ:m] Bauunternehmen, Baufirma VI/2/M5
building site ['bɪldɪŋ saɪt] Baugelände, Baugrundstück VI/4/M3
bull [bʊl] Bulle, Stier VI/3/M3
bully ['bʊli] Tyrann, Rüpel, Rabauke; tyrannisieren, drangsalieren
bullying ['bʊliɪŋ] Mobbing
bum (informal) [bʌm] Hintern VI/1/M8
burglary ['bɜ:gləri] Einbruch, Einbruchdiebstahl VI/6/R2

burn [bɜ:n] (ver)brennen
burn down [ˌbɜ:n 'daʊn] abbrennen, niederbrennen VI/1/3
° bury ['beri] begraben VI/4/PP
bus [bʌs] Bus
bus stop ['bʌs ˌstɒp] Bushaltestelle
bush [bʊʃ] Busch
bush (no pl) [bʊʃ] Wildnis VI/3/M3
bushpig ['bʊʃpɪg] Buschschwein VI/3/M5
business ['bɪznəs] Handel, Gewerbe VI/5/R2
business (no pl) ['bɪznəs] Angelegenheit, Sache VI/1/3
do business [ˌdu: 'bɪznəs] Geschäfte machen, Handel treiben VI/4/13
mind one's own business (informal) [ˌmaɪnd wʌnzˌˌəʊn 'bɪznəs] sich um seinen (eigenen) Kram/seine (eigenen) Angelegenheiten kümmern VI/1/3
° businessman ['bɪznəsmæn] Geschäftsmann, Unternehmer VI/3/PP
busker ['bʌskə] Straßenmusikant/in
busy ['bɪzi] beschäftigt; arbeitsreich
but [bʌt] aber
but [bʌt] außer VI/4/M7
butcher ['bʊtʃə] Metzger/in, Fleischer/in VI/2/5
butter ['bʌtə] Butter
button ['bʌtn] zuknöpfen VI/1/M8
buy [baɪ] kaufen
buyer ['baɪə] Käufer/in
buzz group ['bʌz gru:p] Form der Gruppenarbeit VI/4/3
by [baɪ] bei, in der Nähe; mit, durch; (spätestens) bis; von
by accident [baɪˌˈæksɪdnt] aus Versehen; zufällig
by the name of [ˌbaɪ ðə 'neɪmˌəv] namens VI/1/3
by the way [baɪ ðə 'weɪ] übrigens V/1/5

Bye! *(informal)* [baɪ] Tschüss!
Bye-bye! *(informal)* [bəˈbaɪ]
  Tschüss!

C

cable car [ˈkeɪbl kɑː]
  Seilbahn(kabine) VI/3/5
cableway [ˈkeɪblweɪ] Seilbahn
  VI/3/5
cafeteria [ˌkæfəˈtɪərɪə] Cafeteria
cake [keɪk] Kuchen
calendar [ˈkælɪndə] Kalender
call [kɔːl] (Telefon)anruf;
  anrufen; nennen
call sb names [ˌkɔːl sʌmbədi
  ˈneɪmz] jdn beschimpfen
called [kɔːld] genannt
caller [ˈkɔːlə] Anrufer/in
calling account [ˈkɔːlɪŋˌəˌkaʊnt]
  Prepaid-Guthaben VI/5/MD2
calm [kɑːm] ruhig, gelassen
  VI/1/10
calorie [ˈkæləri] Kalorie V/4/3
calve [kɑːv] kalben VI/3/5
camera [ˈkæmrə] Kamera,
  Fotoapparat
cameraman/-woman
  [ˈkæmrəˌmæn, ˈkæmrəˌwʊmən]
  Kameramann/-frau
campaign [kæmˈpeɪn]
  Kampagne, Aktion V/4/5
campsite [ˈkæmpˌsaɪt]
  Campingplatz, Zeltplatz
can [kæn] können; Dose V/6/4
can bank [ˈkæn bæŋk]
  Dosencontainer V/6/M4
Canada [ˈkænədə] Kanada
  V/3/5
cancel [ˈkænsl] absagen VI/6/R1
cancer [ˈkænsə] Krebs *(Krankheit)*
  V/1/M3
candidate [ˈkændɪdeɪt]
  Bewerber/in, Kandidat/in
  VI/2/M6
candle [ˈkændl] Kerze
canteen [kænˈtiːn] Kantine;
  Mensa V/4/5
cap [kæp] Mütze, Kappe
Cape Town [ˈkeɪptaʊn] Kapstadt
  VI/3/1
capital [ˈkæpɪtl] Hauptstadt
captain [ˈkæptɪn] Kapitän/in

caption [ˈkæpʃn] Bildunterschrift;
  Titel VI/2/7
car [kɑː] Auto
car boot sale [ˌkɑː ˈbuːt ˌseɪl]
  *Verkauf persönlicher
  Gegenstände aus dem
  Kofferraum auf einem
  Parkplatz*
carbohydrate [ˌkɑːbəʊˈhaɪdreɪt]
  Kohle(n)hydrat V/4/3
card [kɑːd] Pappe, Karton; Karte
cardboard *(no pl)* [ˈkɑːdˌbɔːd]
  Pappe, (Papp)karton V/6/M2
sb does not care [ˌsʌmbədi dʌz
  nɒt ˈkeə] jdm ist es gleich/egal
care for sb/sth [ˈkeə fə ˌsʌmbədi/
  ˌsʌmθɪŋ] sich um jdn/etw
  kümmern V/3/4
take care of [teɪkˈkeərˌəv] sich
  kümmern um, versorgen
career [kəˈrɪə] Beruf; Karriere
career change [kəˈrɪə tʃeɪndʒ]
  berufliche Umorientierung/
  Abwechslung VI/2/M6
careful [ˈkeəfl] vorsichtig;
  sorgfältig, gründlich
Caribbean [ˌkærɪˈbiːən] karibisch
the Caribbean [ðə ˌkærɪˈbiːən] die
  Karibik, die Karibischen Inseln
the Caribbean Sea [ðə ˌkærɪˌbiːən
  ˈsiː] das Karibische Meer, die
  Karibik VI/2/M6
carnival [ˈkɑːnɪvl] Volksfest;
  Karneval
carpenter [ˈkɑːpɪntə] Zimmerer/
  Zimmerin VI/2/5
carpet [ˈkɑːpɪt] Teppich
carrot [ˈkærət] Möhre, Karotte,
  Mohrrübe
carry [ˈkæri] tragen
° **carry out** [ˌkæriˈaʊt]
  durchführen, verüben VI/1/PP
Carthage [ˈkɑːθɪdʒ] Karthago
  VI/4/M5
cartoon [kɑːˈtuːn]
  Zeichentrickfilm
case [keɪs] Fall VI/4/M7
cash machine [ˈkæʃ məˌʃiːn]
  Geldautomat
cash *(no pl)* [kæʃ] Bargeld
cast [kɑːst] Besetzung, Ensemble
  VI/1/10

cast sb aside [ˌkɑːst
  ˌsʌmbədiˌəˈsaɪd] jdn
  fallenlassen VI/1/M4
castle [ˈkɑːsl] Burg; Schloss
cat [kæt] Katze
catastrophic [ˌkætəˈstrɒfɪk]
  katastrophal VI/5/R3
catch [kætʃ] fangen; kriegen
catch [kætʃ] festnehmen V/2/M5
caterer [ˈkeɪtərə] Lieferant/in
  für Speisen und Getränke;
  Partyservice
Catholic [ˈkæθlɪk] Katholik/in;
  katholisch VI/1/2
cause [kɔːz] Grund, Ursache;
  Sache
cause sth [ˈkɔːzˌsʌmθɪŋ] etw
  verursachen, etw veranlassen
  VI/4/1
causeway [ˈkɔːzweɪ] Damm
celebrate [ˈseləˌbreɪt] feiern
celebration [ˌseləˈbreɪʃn] Feier
cell [sel] Zelle VI/6/R2
cellar [ˈselə] Keller V/4/M7
cent [sent] Cent, Centmünze
  (amerikanische Währung)
centre [ˈsentə] Zentrum, Center
  V/5/4
century [ˈsentʃəri] Jahrhundert
cereal [ˈsɪərɪəl] Getreide(sorte);
  Frühstückszerealien V/4/1
certain [ˈsɜːtn] sicher;
  gewisse(r, s), bestimmte(r, s)
certified [ˈsɜːtɪfaɪd] (staatlich)
  geprüft VI/2/M6
chain [tʃeɪn] Kette
chair [tʃeə] Stuhl
chalk *(no pl)* [tʃɔːk] Kreide
challenge [ˈtʃælɪndʒ]
  Herausforderung V/3/M2
championship [ˈtʃæmpiənʃɪp]
  Meisterschaft
chance [tʃɑːns] Möglichkeit;
  Chance
change [tʃeɪndʒ] (sich)
  (ver)ändern; (Ver)änderung;
  Wechselgeld; wechseln V/5/8
change [tʃeɪndʒ] wickeln
  VI/1/M8
changing table [ˈtʃeɪndʒɪŋ ˌteɪbl]
  Wickeltisch VI/1/M8
channel [ˈtʃænl] Kanal, Programm

DICTIONARY *English–German*

DICTIONARY ENGLISH–GERMAN

chaos *(no pl)* [ˈkeɪɒs] Chaos,
Durcheinander VI/1/10
character [ˈkærɪktə] Charakter;
Figur VI/1/2
characteristic [ˌkærɪktəˈrɪstɪk]
(charakteristisches) Merkmal
VI/3/M10
charity [ˈtʃærəti]
Wohltätigkeitsveranstaltung;
wohltätige Zwecke
charming [ˈtʃɑːmɪŋ] bezaubernd,
reizend
chart [tʃɑːt] Diagramm,
Schaubild, Grafik VI/5/LG1
chat [tʃæt] chatten, sich
unterhalten VI/6/L4
chat-up line *(informal)* [ˈtʃætʌp
ˌlaɪn] Anmache
chatting [tʃætɪŋ] Chatten VI/4/10
cheap [tʃiːp] billig, preiswert
check [tʃek] überprüfen,
kontrollieren
check in [ˌtʃekˈɪn] einchecken
VI/3/4
check out sth [ˌtʃekˈaʊt ˌsʌmθɪŋ]
sich etw ansehen VI/5/R4
cheek [tʃiːk] Wange, Backe
cheer [tʃɪə] jubeln; anfeuern
cheer up [tʃɪərˈʌp] vergnügt(er)
werden; aufmuntern
Cheer up! [tʃɪərˈʌp] Lass (doch)
den Kopf nicht hängen!, Kopf
hoch!
cheerleading [ˈtʃɪəˌliːdɪŋ]
Cheerleaden
cheese [tʃiːz] Käse
cheetah [ˈtʃiːtə] Gepard VI/3/M5
chef [ʃef] Koch/Köchin V/4/5
chemical [ˈkemɪkl] Chemikalie
VI/2/3
(at the) chemist's [ˈkemɪsts]
(in der) Drogerie; (in der)
Apotheke VI/2/5
cherry [ˈtʃeri] Kirsche
chess [tʃes] Schach(spiel)
chest [tʃest] Brust(korb) VI/1/M8
chest of drawers [ˌtʃestəv ˈdrɔːz]
Kommode
chewing gum *(no pl)* [ˈtʃuːɪŋ
ˌgʌm] Kaugummi
chick *(informal)* [tʃɪk] Mädchen
VI/4/M5

chicken [ˈtʃɪkɪn] Huhn
chickenpox [ˈtʃɪkɪnˌpɒks]
Windpocken
chief [tʃiːf] Führer/in; Oberhaupt;
Häuptling
child labour [ˈtʃaɪld ˌleɪbə]
Kinderarbeit VI/2/7
child *(pl* **children)** [tʃaɪld,
ˈtʃɪldrən] Kind
child support [ˈtʃaɪld səˌpɔːt]
Unterhalt, Alimente VI/1/14
childcare *(no pl)* [ˈtʃaɪldˌkeə]
Kinderbetreuung, Kinderpflege
VI/6/W1
chimpanzee [ˌtʃɪmpænˈziː]
Schimpanse
China [ˈtʃaɪnə] China
Chinese [ˌtʃaɪˈniːz] Chinese/
Chinesin; chinesisch
chips *(pl)* [tʃɪps] Pommes frites
chocolate [ˈtʃɒklət] Schokolade
choice [tʃɔɪs] Wahl
choose [tʃuːz] auswählen
chores [tʃɔːz]
(Haushalts)pflichten VI/2/7
° **chorus** [ˈkɔːrəs] Refrain
VI/3/12
Christian [ˈkrɪstʃən] Christ/in;
christlich VI/4/10
Christmas [ˈkrɪsməs]
Weihnachten
church [tʃɜːtʃ] Kirche
cinema [ˈsɪnəmə] Kino
circle [ˈsɜːkl] Kreis
citizen [ˈsɪtɪzn] (Staats)bürger/in
city [ˈsɪti] (Groß)stadt
city administrator
[ˌsɪtiədˈmɪnɪˌstreɪtə]
Bürgermeister VI/4/2
city official [ˌsɪtiəˈfɪʃl]
Angestellte/r der Stadt
VI/4/M4
do civilian service [duː səˌvɪliən
ˈsɜːvɪs] Zivildienst leisten
V/5/2
clan [klæn] Clan, Sippe, Stamm,
Familie VI/4/M5
class [klɑːs] (Schul)klasse;
Unterricht
(class) schedule *(AE)* =
timetable *(BE)* [ˈklɑːsˌskedʒəl]
Stundenplan

classify [ˈklæsɪfaɪ] klassifizieren
VI/4/2
classmate [ˈklɑːsˌmeɪt]
Klassenkamerad/in,
Mitschüler/in
classroom [ˈklɑːsˌruːm]
Klassenzimmer
clean [kliːn] sauber; sauber
machen, reinigen, putzen
clean up [kliːnˈʌp] sauber
machen, reinigen
clear [klɪə] klar, eindeutig
VI/1/10
clear one's head [ˌklɪə wʌnz ˈhed]
einen klaren Kopf bekommen
VI/5/R4
clerk [klɑːk] (Büro)angestellte/r
VI/5/MD3
clever [ˈklevə] klug, gescheit,
schlau
click [klɪk] (an)klicken, drücken
V/2/9
climb [klaɪm] (hinauf)steigen;
(hinauf)klettern
clock [klɒk] Uhr
(eight) o'clock [əˈklɒk] (acht)
Uhr
close [kləʊs] nah(e)
close [kləʊz] schließen,
zumachen
close [kləʊs] eng VI/5/LG1
close down [ˌkləʊz ˈdaʊn]
schließen, stilllegen VI/6/R2
closed [kləʊzd] geschlossen, zu
VI/6/L3
closely [ˈkləʊsli] eng VI/6/R4
clothes *(npl)* [kləʊðz] Kleider,
Bekleidung
clothing *(no pl)* [ˈkləʊðɪŋ]
Kleidung
cloud [klaʊd] Wolke
cloudy [ˈklaʊdi] bewölkt,
bedeckt
club [klʌb] Klub, Verein
coach [kəʊtʃ] Trainer
° **coal mine** [ˈkəʊl maɪn]
Kohlengrube, Kohlenzeche
VI/2/CIO
coast [kəʊst] Küste
coffee [ˈkɒfi] Kaffee
coffin [ˈkɒfɪn] Sarg V/4/M7
coin [kɔɪn] Münze, Geldstück

cold [kəʊld] kalt; Erkältung, Schnupfen

cold [kəʊld] Kälte

colleague [ˈkɒliːɡ] Kollege/ Kollegin, Mitarbeiter/in VI/2/M2

colleague [ˈkɒliːɡ] Kollege/ Kollegin, Mitarbeiter/in VI/3/2

collect [kəˈlekt] sammeln

collect [kəˈlekt] abholen

collection [kəˈlekʃn] (Mode)kollektion VI/6/R3

college [ˈkɒlɪdʒ] Bildungseinrichtung; Universität, Hochschule

colony [ˈkɒləni] Kolonie V/1/M1

colour [ˈkʌlə] Farbe

coloured [ˈkʌləd] farbig; gemischtrassig VI/3/M6

Coloured [ˈkʌləd] Farbige/r VI/3/M6

colourful [ˈkʌləfl] farbenfroh, farbenprächtig

comb [kəʊm] Kamm

combine [kəmˈbaɪn] verbinden, kombinieren VI/5/R2

come [kʌm] kommen

come for [ˈkʌm fə] (ab)holen, kommen wegen

come in [kʌm ˈɪn] hereinkommen

° come into power [ˌkʌm ɪntə ˈpaʊə] an die Macht kommen VI/3/PP

come of age [ˌkʌm əv ˈeɪdʒ] volljährig werden VI/3/M9

Come on! [kʌm ˈɒn] Komm(t) jetzt!, Mach(t) schon!

come out [kʌm ˈaʊt] herauskommen

come over [ˌkʌm ˈəʊvə] (her)überkommen

come to sb's mind [kʌm tə ˌsʌmbədiz ˈmaɪnd] jdm einfallen

come true [ˌkʌm ˈtruː] wahr werden VI/3/2

comedy [ˈkɒmədi] Komödie

comfortable [ˈkʌmftəbl] bequem

command (no pl) [kəˈmɑːnd] Beherrschung VI/2/M6

comment [ˈkɒment] Kommentar, Bemerkung

commercial [kəˈmɜːʃl] Werbespot; Fernseh-/ Radiowerbung

commit [kəˈmɪt] begehen (Verbrechen) V/2/5

common [ˈkɒmən] üblich, normal VI/1/M4

have sth in common [hæv ˌsʌmθɪŋ ɪn ˈkɒmən] etwas gemein haben VI/2/7

communicate [kəˈmjuːnɪkeɪt] sich verständigen, kommunizieren VI/4/8

communication [kəˌmjuːnɪˈkeɪʃn] Kommunikation V/5/4

communicative [kəˈmjuːnɪkətɪv] mitteilsam, gesprächig V/5/3

community [kəˈmjuːnəti] Gemeinde; Gemeinschaft

company [ˈkʌmpni] Firma; Gesellschaft

compare [kəmˈpeə] vergleichen

comparison [kəmˈpærɪsn] Vergleich VI/4/M2

compete (for) [kəmˈpiːt] wetteifern (um), kämpfen (um)

competence [ˈkɒmpɪtəns] Fähigkeit, Kompetenz VI/5/I

competition [ˌkɒmpəˈtɪʃn] Wettbewerb

complain [kəmˈpleɪn] klagen, sich beklagen VI/4/M7

complete [kəmˈpliːt] vervollständigen

complete [kəmˈpliːt] vollständig, komplett VI/5/W1

completely [kəmˈpliːtli] völlig, ganz VI/4/2

complex [ˈkɒmpleks] komplex, kompliziert, vielschichtig VI/4/M7

complicated [ˈkɒmplɪˌkeɪtɪd] kompliziert VI/4/6

compost bin [ˈkɒmpɒst bɪn] Komposttonne V/6/M4

compulsory [kəmˈpʌlsəri] verpflichtend, obligatorisch, Pflicht- VI/5/W6

be concerned (about) [ˌbiː kənˈsɜːnd] sich Sorgen machen (um)

concert [ˈkɒnsət] Konzert

condition [kənˈdɪʃn] Zustand VI/6/R1

conditions (npl) [kənˈdɪʃnz] Bedingungen, Verhältnisse VI/2/10

condom [ˈkɒndɒm] Kondom VI/5/L3

conference [ˈkɒnfrəns] Konferenz, Tagung VI/2/M2

confident [ˈkɒnfɪdnt] zuversichtlich VI/4/2

confirm [kənˈfɜːm] bestätigen VI/4/2

° conflict [ˈkɒnflɪkt] Konflikt VI/1/PP

confused [kənˈfjuːzd] verwirrt, durcheinander

congratulations (npl) [kənˌɡrætʃʊˈleɪʃnz] Glückwunsch, Glückwünsche

conjunction [kənˈdʒʌŋkʃn] Konjunktion VI/1/4

connect [kəˈnekt] verbinden V/5/8

° connection [kəˈnekʃn] Verbindung, Anschluss VI/4/PP

consequence [ˈkɒnsɪkwəns] Folge, Konsequenz V/6/M1

constant [ˈkɒnstənt] dauernd, ständig V/1/M1

consumer [kənˈsjuːmə] Verbraucher/in, Konsument/in VI/6/L4

contact [ˈkɒntækt] Kontakt V/3/M5

contact sb [ˈkɒntækt ˌsʌmbədi] jdn kontaktieren, sich mit jdm in Verbindung setzen VI/2/M6

contain [kənˈteɪn] enthalten VI/3/4

content [ˈkɒntent] Inhalt VI/5/W1

contest [ˈkɒntest] Wettbewerb

context [ˈkɒntekst] Kontext, Zusammenhang

continent [ˈkɒntɪnənt] Kontinent, Erdteil VI/3/2

continue [kənˈtɪnjuː] fortfahren VI/1/6

contrast [ˈkɒntrɑːst] Gegensatz, Kontrast VI/3/2

control [kən'trəʊl] Kontrolle VI/3/M9

° convention [kən'venʃn] Konvention, Abkommen VI/2/PP

conventional [kən'venʃnəl] herkömmlich, konventionell VI/4/6

conversation [ˌkɒnvə'seɪʃn] Gespräch, Unterhaltung VI/3/3

cook [kʊk] Koch/Köchin; kochen

cool [kuːl] kalt, kühl; cool VI/3/5

cope with sth ['kəʊp wɪð ˌsʌmθɪŋ] etw bewältigen, mit etw fertig werden VI/4/M1

Copenhagen [ˌkəʊpən'heɪgən] Kopenhagen VI/2/M5

copy ['kɒpi] abschreiben; kopieren

coral ['kɒrəl] Koralle V/1/M1

coral reef [ˌkɒrəl 'riːf] Korallenriff V/1/2

corn [kɔːn] Getreide, Korn

corner ['kɔːnə] Ecke

correct [kə'rekt] korrigieren; richtig, korrekt

corrosive [kə'rəʊsɪv] korrodierender Stoff VI/3/4

cost [kɒst] kosten

cost [kɒst] Kosten, Preis VI/4/M7

costume ['kɒstjuːm] Tracht, Kostüm

cot [kɒt] Kinderbett VI/1/M8

cotton ['kɒtn] Baumwolle VI/6/R3

count [kaʊnt] zählen

count oneself lucky [ˌkaʊnt wʌnˌself 'lʌki] sich glücklich schätzen VI/5/R4

country ['kʌntri] Land

in the countryside [ɪn ðə 'kʌntriˌsaɪd] auf dem Land VI/5/R2

couple ['kʌpl] Paar VI/1/10

course [kɔːs] Kurs

of course [əv 'kɔːs] natürlich

court [kɔːt] Gericht V/2/M5

cousin ['kʌzn] Cousin/e

covered ['kʌvəd] bedeckt, überzogen, überdacht VI/6/MD2

cow [kaʊ] Kuh

coward ['kaʊəd] Feigling

CPhT (= certified pharmacy technician) [ˌsiː piːˌeɪtʃ 'tiː] PTA (= pharmazeutisch-technische/r Assistent/in) VI/2/5

craftsman/craftswoman ['krɑːftsmən/'krɑːftsˌwʊmən] gelernte/r Handwerker/in VI/2/M2

crazy ['kreɪzi] verrückt

cream [kriːm] Sahne

cream cheese [ˌkriːm 'tʃiːz] Frischkäse V/4/1

create [kri'eɪt] erschaffen; gestalten V/6/M2

creative [kri'eɪtɪv] kreativ V/5/3

credit card ['kredɪt ˌkɑːd] Kreditkarte

crime [kraɪm] Verbrechen V/2/5

criminal ['krɪmɪnl] Kriminelle/r V/2/M5

crisps (npl) [krɪsps] Chips

crocodile ['krɒkədaɪl] Krokodil

cross [krɒs] durchqueren; überqueren

crossword puzzle ['krɒswɜːd ˌpʌzl] Kreuzworträtsel VI/3/8

crowd [kraʊd] (Menschen)menge, Zuschauermenge

crown [kraʊn] Krone

cruel ['kruːəl] grausam V/1/12

cruise [kruːz] Kreuzfahrt VI/2/M6

cruise ship ['kruːz ʃɪp] Kreuzfahrtschiff VI/2/M2

crust [krʌst] (Erd)kruste VI/4/1

cry [kraɪ] Weinen; Schrei; Ruf; weinen; schreien

cub [kʌb] Junge(s) VI/3/M4

cucumber ['kjuːˌkʌmbə] (Salat)gurke

° cultural ['kʌltʃrəl] kulturell VI/2/PP

culture ['kʌltʃə] Kultur V/2/M2

cup [kʌp] Tasse

cupboard ['kʌbəd] Schrank

curious ['kjʊəriəs] neugierig

current ['kʌrənt] jetzig, gegenwärtig, aktuell VI/4/10

currently ['kʌrəntli] zur Zeit, momentan VI/2/M6

curry ['kʌri] Curry(gericht)

curtain ['kɜːtn] Vorhang

cushion ['kʊʃn] Kissen

custom ['kʌstəm] Brauch, Sitte

customer ['kʌstəmə] Kunde/Kundin

cut [kʌt] schneiden; mähen

cut down [kʌt 'daʊn] umhauen, fällen

cute [kjuːt] süß, niedlich

CV (= curriculum vitae) [ˌsiː 'viː (= kəˌrɪkjʊləm 'viːtaɪ)] Lebenslauf V/5/4

cycle ['saɪkl] Rad fahren

cycling ['saɪklɪŋ] Radfahren, Radeln

cyclist ['saɪklɪst] Radfahrer/in V/3/M2

the Czech Republic [ðə ˌtʃek ri'pʌblɪk] die Tschechische Republik, Tschechien VI/6/R2

D

dad (informal) [dæd] Papa, Vati

daily ['deɪli] täglich VI/3/5

dairy food ['deəri fuːd] Milchprodukt V/4/4

damage ['dæmɪdʒ] Schaden VI/4/2

damage ['dæmɪdʒ] (be)schädigen V/6/M6

damn [dæm] verurteilen, verdammen VI/1/10

dance [dɑːns] Tanz; tanzen

dancer ['dɑːnsə] Tänzer/in

dancing ['dɑːnsɪŋ] Tanzen

danger ['deɪndʒə] (Lebens)gefahr

dangerous ['deɪndʒərəs] gefährlich

dare [deə] wagen, sich trauen V/4/M6

dark [dɑːk] dunkel

dark [dɑːk] Dunkelheit VI/5/R1

° dash [dæʃ] Strich VI/4/PP

data (pl) ['deɪtə] Daten, (persönliche) Angaben VI/4/10

data protection (no pl) [ˌdeɪtə prə'tekʃn] Datenschutz VI/4/13

date [deɪt] Datum; Termin

date [deɪt] Verabredung; Rendezvous

out of date [ˌaʊt‿əv ˈdeɪt] überholt, nicht mehr aktuell, nicht mehr zeitgemäß VI/1/M6

date of birth [ˈdeɪt‿əv ˌbɜ:θ] Geburtsdatum

date sb *(informal)* [ˈdeɪt ˌsʌmbədi] mit jdm gehen; sich mit jdm verabreden

dating [deɪtɪŋ] Verabredungen VI/4/10

daughter [ˈdɔ:tə] Tochter

day [deɪ] Tag

the other day [ði‿ˌʌðə ˈdeɪ] neulich, vor einigen Tagen VI/3/2

dead [ded] tot V/4/9

deadly [ˈdedli] tödlich VI/4/3

deal [di:l] Angelegenheit, Sache VI/1/M4

deal with [ˈdi:l wɪð] handeln von; sich befassen mit VI/3/M9

dear [dɪə] liebe(r) *(Anrede)*

dearest [ˈdɪərəst] Liebste/r, Liebling VI/1/9

death [deθ] Tod V/3/10

death toll [ˈdeθ təʊl] Zahl der Todesopfer VI/4/2

debris *(no pl)* [ˈdebri:] Trümmer, Schutt VI/4/2

get into debt [ˌget‿ɪntə ˈdet] Schulden machen, sich verschulden V/5/13

decade [ˈdekeɪd] Jahrzehnt, Dekade VI/6/R4

December [dɪˈsembə] Dezember

decide [dɪˈsaɪd] sich entscheiden; beschließen

decision [dɪˈsɪʒn] Entscheidung, Entschluss VI/1/10

decision-making process [dɪˌsɪʒnˌmeɪkɪŋ ˈprəʊses] Entscheidungsprozess VI/1/14

declare [dɪˈkleə] erklären, verkünden VI/4/2

decorate [ˈdekəreɪt] schmücken

dedicated [ˈdedɪˌkeɪtɪd] engagiert VI/2/M6

deep [di:p] tief

defend [dɪˈfend] verteidigen

define [dɪˈfaɪn] definieren VI/4/7

definitely [ˈdefnətli] eindeutig, definitiv V/3/M8

definition [ˌdefəˈnɪʃn] Definition, Erklärung V/3/M2

degree [dɪˈgri:] Grad VI/5/MD3

delicious [dɪˈlɪʃəs] köstlich, lecker

deliver [dɪˈlɪvə] liefern VI/5/W3

democracy [dɪˈmɒkrəsi] Demokratie VI/3/11

democratic [ˌdeməˈkrætɪk] demokratisch VI/3/11

Denmark [ˈdenmɑ:k] Dänemark VI/6/L4

depart [dɪˈpɑ:t] abfahren

depart [dɪˈpɑ:t] abfliegen, starten VI/3/4

department store [dɪˈpɑ:tmənt ˌstɔ:] Kaufhaus

departure [dɪˈpɑ:tʃə] Abreise; Abflug VI/5/W1

depend on sth [dɪˈpend‿ɒn ˌsʌmθɪŋ] von etw abhängen VI/1/3

depressed [dɪˈprest] deprimiert VI/2/3

deputy head [ˈdepjʊti ˌhed] Konrektor

describe [dɪˈskraɪb] beschreiben

description [dɪˈskrɪpʃn] Beschreibung

desert [ˈdezət] Wüste

design [dɪˈzaɪn] entwerfen

desk [desk] Schreibtisch

desperate [ˈdesprət] verzweifelt V/4/M6

desperately [ˈdesprətli] verzweifelt; dringend VI/2/10

despite [dɪˈspaɪt] trotz VI/4/2

dessert [dɪˈzɜ:t] Nachtisch, Dessert

destination [ˌdestɪˈneɪʃn] (Reise)ziel VI/3/5

destroy [dɪˈstrɔɪ] zerstören

destruction *(no pl)* [dɪˈstrʌkʃn] Zerstörung VI/4/2

detail [ˈdi:teɪl] Detail, Einzelheit

detect [dɪˈtekt] entdecken, orten, bemerken VI/4/6

detective [dɪˈtektɪv] (Privat)detektiv/in

devastate [ˈdevəˌsteɪt] vernichten, (völlig) zerstören, verwüsten VI/4/2

develop [dɪˈveləp] (sich) entwickeln V/3/4

developing country [dɪˈveləpɪŋ ˌkʌntri] Entwicklungsland VI/2/10

development [dɪˈveləpmənt] Entwicklung; Wachstum VI/4/6

device [dɪˈvaɪs] Gerät, Apparat VI/6/R1

dialogue [ˈdaɪəlɒg] Gespräch, Dialog

diamond [ˈdaɪəmənd] Diamant VI/3/5

diary [ˈdaɪəri] Tagebuch

dictionary [ˈdɪkʃənri] Wörterbuch

die [daɪ] sterben

diet [ˈdaɪət] Nahrung, Ernährung; Diät V/4/6

difference [ˈdɪfrəns] Unterschied

different [ˈdɪfrənt] anders, andere(r, s); verschieden

difficult [ˈdɪfɪklt] schwierig, schwer

difficulty [ˈdɪfɪklti] Schwierigkeit, Problem V/3/M2

dingo *(pl -es)* [ˈdɪŋgəʊ, ˈdɪŋgəʊz] Dingo, australischer Windhund V/1/5

dining room [ˈdaɪnɪŋ ˌru:m] Esszimmer

dinner [ˈdɪnə] Abendessen; Mittagessen

dinosaur [ˈdaɪnəˌsɔ:] Dinosaurier

direct [dɪˈrekt] direkt V/2/10

direction [dɪˈrekʃn] Richtung VI/3/5

give directions [ˌgɪv dɪˈrekʃnz] den Weg beschreiben

director [dəˈrektə] Regisseur/in VI/6/R4

dirt [dɜ:t] Schmutz, Dreck VI/6/W3

dirty [ˈdɜ:ti] dreckig, schmutzig

disabled [dɪsˈeɪbld] behindert

disadvantaged [ˌdɪsədˈvɑ:ntɪdʒd] benachteiligt VI/6/R3

disagree [ˌdɪsəˈgri:] nicht übereinstimmen; nicht einverstanden sein

DICTIONARY *English–German*

disappear [ˌdɪsəˈpɪə] verschwinden

disappointed [ˌdɪsəˈpɔɪntɪd] enttäuscht

disaster [dɪˈzɑːstə] Katastrophe, Unglück VI/4/1

discover [dɪˈskʌvə] entdecken, herausfinden VI/4/10

discriminate against sb [dɪˈskrɪmɪneɪt ˌəˌgenst ˌsʌmbədi] jdn diskriminieren/ benachteiligen VI/3/2

° **discrimination** *(no pl)* [dɪˌskrɪmɪˈneɪʃn] Diskriminierung, Benachteiligung VI/3/PP

discuss [dɪˈskʌs] besprechen

discuss [dɪˈskʌs] diskutieren VI/4/15

discussion [dɪˈskʌʃn] Diskussion, Erörterung V/2/8

disease [dɪˈziːz] Krankheit

disgusting [dɪsˈgʌstɪŋ] widerlich

dish *(pl -es)* [dɪʃ] Schale; Gericht

dishwasher [ˈdɪʃˌwɒʃə] Geschirrspülmaschine V/6/1

dislikes *(pl)* [dɪsˈlaɪks] Abneigungen

be at sb's disposal [ˌbiˌət ˌsʌmbədiz dɪˈspəʊzl] jdm zur Verfügung stehen VI/4/M5

distance [ˈdɪstəns] Entfernung; Strecke VI/5/R3

distant [ˈdɪstənt] entfernt, fern VI/1/M4

distinguish [dɪˈstɪŋgwɪʃ] unterscheiden VI/4/6

disturb [dɪˈstɜːb] stören, durcheinanderbringen V/1/M1

divorced [dɪˈvɔːst] geschieden

do [duː] machen, tun

do business [ˌduː ˈbɪznəs] Geschäfte machen, Handel treiben VI/4/13

do civilian service [duː səˌvɪliən ˈsɜːvɪs] Zivildienst leisten V/5/2

do good [duː ˈgʊd] nützen, bringen VI/1/3

do military service [duː ˌmɪlɪtri ˈsɜːvɪs] Wehrdienst leisten V/5/2

do one's A levels [duː wʌnzˌˈeɪ ˌlevlz] das Abitur machen V/5/2

do overtime [ˌduːˌˈəʊvəˌtaɪm] Überstunden machen VI/2/10

do research [duː rɪˈsɜːtʃ] recherchieren VI/4/M9

tell sb to do sth [ˌtel ˌsʌmbədi tə ˈduː ˌsʌmθɪŋ] jdm etw vorschreiben/befehlen VI/1/M2

do the maths [ˌduː ðə ˈmæθs] (aus)rechnen VI/6/R3

do vocational training [duː vəʊˌkeɪʃnəl ˈtreɪnɪŋ] eine Berufsausbildung machen V/5/2

do volunteer work [duː ˈvɒləntɪə ˌwɜːk] Freiwilligenarbeit leisten VI/5/R4

do well [duː ˈwel] gut abschneiden VI/2/3

doctor [ˈdɒktə] Arzt/Ärztin

documentary [ˌdɒkjʊˈmentri] Dokumentation, Dokumentarfilm

dog [dɒg] Hund

doll [dɒl] Puppe

dolphin [ˈdɒlfɪn] Delphin

domestic servant [dəˌmestɪk ˈsɜːvnt] Hausangestellte/r VI/2/10

donate [dəʊˈneɪt] spenden V/6/5

door [dɔː] Tür

doorbell [ˈdɔːbel] Türklingel, Türglocke

dorm (= dormitory) [dɔːm, ˈdɔːmɪtri] Schlafsaal VI/5/S4

dos and don'ts [ˌduːzˌ ənd ˈdəʊnts] was man tun und was man nicht tun sollte

dose [dəʊs] Dosis, Menge VI/3/M9

° **dot** [dɒt] Punkt VI/4/PP

double circle [ˌdʌbl ˈsɜːkl] Doppelkreis VI/2/1

double room [ˈdʌbl ˌruːm] Doppelzimmer V/1/6

down [daʊn] hinunter, hinab

down [daʊn] unten VI/1/M4

down *(informal)* [daʊn] niedergeschlagen, down VI/2/3

° **downhill** [ˌdaʊnˈhɪl] bergab (führend) VI/4/CIO

download [ˌdaʊnˈləʊd] herunterladen, downloaden VI/4/M9

dragon [ˈdrægən] Drache

drama [ˈdrɑːmə] Drama, Tragödie VI/4/2

drama *(no pl)* [ˈdrɑːmə] Schauspielerei; Theater

draw [drɔː] zeichnen

dream [driːm] Traum

dream [driːm] träumen V/4/M2

dress [dres] Kleid; sich kleiden; sich anziehen V/2/2

dress up [ˌdresˌˈʌp] sich herausputzen; sich verkleiden

drink [drɪŋk] Getränk; Drink; trinken

drive [draɪv] fahren

drive [draɪv] Fahrt VI/3/M4

driver [ˈdraɪvə] Fahrer/in

drop [drɒp] fallen lassen

drought [draʊt] Trockenheit, Dürre(periode) VI/4/1

drug [drʌg] Medikament; Droge

° **drum** [drʌm] Trommel VI/3/12

dry [draɪ] trocken

duck [dʌk] Ente

due to sth [ˌdjuː tʊ ˈsʌmθɪŋ] wegen/aufgrund einer Sache VI/6/R1

dumpling [ˈdʌmplɪŋ] Knödel, Kloß

during [ˈdjʊərɪŋ] während

dust *(no pl)* [dʌst] Staub VI/2/M11

Dutch [dʌtʃ] Niederländer/in; niederländisch VI/3/M4

dye [daɪ] färben V/3/M8

dye [daɪ] Färbemittel VI/2/3

E

e-learning [ˈiː ˌlɜːnɪŋ] E-Learning, elektronisches Lernen VI/4/M7

e-pal [ˈiːpæl] E-Mail-Freund/in VI/3/M4

each [iːtʃ] jede(r, s)

each other [iːtʃˌˈʌðə] einander

ear [ɪə] Ohr

early [ˈɜːli] früh

early warning system
[ˌɜːli ˈwɔːnɪŋ ˌsɪstəm]
Frühwarnsystem VI/4/6

earn [ɜːn] verdienen

earring [ˈɪərɪŋ] Ohrring

earth [ɜːθ] die Erde

earthquake [ˈɜːθˌkweɪk]
Erdbeben

east [iːst] östlich, Ost-; Osten
V/1/7

Easter [ˈiːstə] Ostern, Osterfest

eastern [ˈiːstən] östlich, Ost-
V/1/7

easy [ˈiːzi] einfach; leicht

easy [ˈiːzi] angenehm, bequem
VI/6/R3

eat [iːt] essen

eating habits *(npl)* [ˈiːtɪŋ ˈhæbɪts]
Essgewohnheiten

economy [ɪˈkɒnəmi] Wirtschaft
VI/3/2

economy class [ɪˈkɒnəmi klɑːs]
zweite Klasse im Flugverkehr
VI/3/4

ecosystem [ˈiːkəʊˌsɪstəm]
Ökosystem VI/3/M3

edit [ˈedɪt] bearbeiten,
redigieren VI/2/M7

education [ˌedjʊˈkeɪʃn]
(Aus)bildung

° **educational** [ˌedjʊˈkeɪʃnəl]
Bildungs-, pädagogisch
VI/2/PP

effect [ɪˈfekt] (Aus)wirkung,
Konsequenz, Einfluss VI/4/M8

egg [eg] Ei

° **Eire** [ˈeərə] Eire, Irland VI/1/CIO

not either [nɒtˌˈaɪðə] auch nicht
VI/2/3

either ... or ... [ˌaɪðə ... ˈɔː]
entweder ... oder ... V/5/M2

elbow [ˈelbəʊ] Ellbogen

elderly [ˈeldəli] ältere(r, s)
VI/1/5

elect [ɪˈlekt] wählen VI/3/11

election [ɪˈlekʃn] Wahl V/2/5

elective *(AE)* [ɪˈlektɪv] Wahlfach,
Wahlkurs

electric power [ɪˌlektrɪk ˈpaʊə]
elektrischer Strom VI/4/M3

electrical [ɪˈlektrɪkl] elektrisch,
Elektro- VI/3/M4

electrical appliance
[ɪˌlektrɪklˌəˈplaɪəns]
Elektrogerät V/6/1

electrician [ɪˌlekˈtrɪʃn] Elektri-
ker/in V/5/2

electricity [ɪˌlekˈtrɪsəti]
Elektrizität, Strom VI/4/2

° **electromagnetic**
[ɪˌlektrəʊmægˈnetɪk]
elektromagnetisch VI/4/PP

electronic [ˌelekˈtrɒnɪk]
elektronisch VI/6/R1

electronics *(npl)* [ˌelekˈtrɒnɪks]
Elektronik VI/2/3

elegant [ˈelɪgənt] elegant
V/3/M8

elephant [ˈelɪfənt] Elefant

Anything else? [ˌeniθɪŋˈels] Darf
es noch etwas sein?

embark onto new horizons
[ɪmˌbɑːkˌɒntə njuː həˈraɪzənz]
zu neuen Horizonten
aufbrechen VI/2/M6

embarrassed [ɪmˈbærəst]
verlegen, peinlich berührt

embarrassing [ɪmˈbærəsɪŋ]
peinlich

emergency [ɪˈmɜːdʒnsi] Notfall
V/1/5

emergency shelter [ɪˈmɜːdʒnsi
ʃeltə] Notunterkunft VI/4/2

emotional [ɪˈməʊʃnəl] emotional
VI/1/10

emperor [ˈemprə] Kaiser/in;
Imperator VI/4/M5

empire [ˈempaɪə] Imperium,
Reich VI/6/R2

employer [ɪmˈplɔɪə] Arbeitge-
ber/in VI/4/10

empty [ˈempti] leer

enclose [ɪnˈkləʊz] beilegen,
beifügen VI/2/M7

encyclopedia [ɪnˌsaɪkləˈpiːdiə]
Lexikon, Enzyklopädie VI/3/11

end [end] (be)enden; Ende

in the end [ˌɪn ðiˈend] letzten
Endes; schließlich

end up [ˌendˌˈʌp] enden VI/1/M4

ending [ˈendɪŋ] Ende, Schluss

enemy [ˈenəmi] Feind/in VI/6/R2

energy [ˈenədʒi] Energie, Kraft
V/3/5

energy-saving [ˈenədʒi ˌseɪvɪŋ]
energiesparend V/6/3

engine [ˈendʒɪn] Motor,
Maschine V/5/8

England [ˈɪŋglənd] England

English [ˈɪŋglɪʃ] englisch

in English [ˌɪnˌˈɪŋglɪʃ] auf
Englisch

° the English [ðiˌˈɪŋglɪʃ] die
Engländer VI/1/PP

English-speaking [ˈɪŋglɪʃˌspiːkɪŋ]
englischsprachig VI/2/CIO

enjoy [ɪnˈdʒɔɪ] genießen

Enjoy your meal! [ɪnˌdʒɔɪ jə ˈmiːl]
Guten Appetit!

enjoyable [ɪnˈdʒɔɪəbl]
unterhaltsam VI/1/10

enough [ɪˈnʌf] genügend,
ausreichend, genug

enter [ˈentə] betreten V/2/7

enthusiasm [ɪnˈθjuːziˌæzəm]
Enthusiasmus, Begeisterung
VI/6/W3

° **entrance fee** [ˈentrəns ˌfiː]
Eintritt(sgeld) VI/3/CIO

entry [ˈentri] Eintrag VI/1/8

entry form [ˈentri ˌfɔːm]
Anmeldeformular

envelope [ˈenvələʊp]
Briefumschlag, Kuvert

environment [ɪnˈvaɪrənmənt]
Umgebung; Umwelt

environmental [ɪnˌvaɪrənˈmentl]
Umwelt- VI/6/R3

environmentally friendly
[ɪnˌvaɪrənˌmentli ˈfrendli]
umweltfreundlich VI/6/R3

epicentre [ˈepiˌsentə] Epizentrum
VI/5/R3

episode [ˈepɪsəʊd] Episode, Folge

equal [ˈiːkwəl] gleich;
gleichberechtigt

equality [ɪˈkwɒləti]
Gleichberechtigung; Gleichheit
VI/3/11

equipment [ɪˈkwɪpmənt]
Ausrüstung, Ausstattung

era [ˈɪərə] Ära, Epoche VI/3/5

escalator [ˈeskəˌleɪtə] Rolltreppe

escape [ɪˈskeɪp] (ent)fliehen;
entkommen

escape [ɪˈskeɪp] Flucht VI/6/R2

especially [ɪˈspeʃli] besonders
establish [ɪˈstæblɪʃ] einführen, aufbauen VI/3/11
estimate [ˈestɪmeɪt] (ein)schätzen, annehmen VI/2/8
ethical [ˈeθɪkl] ethisch (korrekt) VI/6/R3
ethnic [ˈeθnɪk] ethnisch, Volks- VI/3/M10
Europe [ˈjʊərəp] Europa V/4/M5
European [ˌjʊərəˈpiːən] Europäer/in; europäisch
evacuation [ɪˌvækjuˈeɪʃn] Evakuierung VI/4/M3
even [ˈiːvn] selbst; sogar
even [ˈiːvn] noch VI/4/11
evening [ˈiːvnɪŋ] Abend
in the evening [ˌɪn ðiː ˈiːvnɪŋ] am Abend, abends
eventually [ɪˈventʃuəli] nach und nach; irgendwann; schließlich VI/1/M8
ever [ˈevə] jemals
everlasting [ˌevəˈlɑːstɪŋ] immerwährend, ewig VI/1/M2
every [ˈevri] jede(r, s)
everybody [ˈevriˌbɒdi] jede(r); alle
everyday [ˈevrideɪ] alltäglich
everyone [ˈevriwʌn] jede(r); alle
everything [ˈevriˌθɪŋ] alles
everywhere [ˈevriˌweə] überall
everywhere else [ˌevriˌweərˈels] überall sonst VI/3/13
exactly [ɪgˈzæktli] genau
exam (= examination) [ɪgˈzæm] Prüfung VI/2/3
example [ɪgˈzɑːmpl] Beispiel
for example [ˌfɔːr ɪgˈzɑːmpl] zum Beispiel
exceed [ɪkˈsiːd] übertreffen, übersteigen VI/5/R3
excellent [ˈeksələnt] ausgezeichnet, hervorragend V/5/4
° **except** [ɪkˈsept] außer, bis auf VI/4/M2
exchange [ɪksˈtʃeɪndʒ] Austausch VI/2/3; (Aus)tausch- VI/5/W4

excited [ɪkˈsaɪtɪd] aufgeregt
exciting [ɪkˈsaɪtɪŋ] aufregend; spannend
excuse [ɪkˈskjuːs] Entschuldigung, Grund
Excuse me! [ɪkˈskjuːz ˌmi] Entschuldigen Sie bitte!, Entschuldigung!
exercise [ˈeksəsaɪz] Übung
exercise [ˈeksəsaɪz] trainieren; bewegen V/5/M1
exercise book [ˈeksəsaɪz ˌbʊk] Heft
exhausted [ɪgˈzɔːstɪd] erschöpft
exhibit [ɪgˈzɪbɪt] Ausstellungsstück VI/3/5
exhibition [ˌeksɪˈbɪʃn] Ausstellung
exist [ɪgˈzɪst] existieren, vorkommen V/5/13
exit [ˈeksɪt] Ausgang
expect [ɪkˈspekt] erwarten
expedition [ˌekspəˈdɪʃn] Expedition, (Forschungs)reise V/3/4
expensive [ɪkˈspensɪv] teuer
experience [ɪkˈspɪəriəns] Erfahrung V/3/4
experience [ɪkˈspɪəriəns] erleben, erfahren VI/3/M3
expert [ˈekspɜːt] Experte/ Expertin VI/4/12
explain [ɪkˈspleɪn] erklären
explanation [ˌekspləˈneɪʃn] Erklärung VI/5/I
explode [ɪkˈspləʊd] explodieren VI/4/1
explore [ɪkˈsplɔː] erkunden, entdecken VI/5/R2
explorer [ɪkˈsplɔːrə] Forscher/in, Entdecker/in
explosive [ɪkˈspləʊsɪv] explosiv VI/3/4
express [ɪkˈspres] ausdrücken V/2/10
expression [ɪkˈspreʃn] Ausdruck VI/5/R3
extent *(no pl)* [ɪkˈstent] Ausmaß, Umfang VI/4/2
extra [ˈekstrə] zusätzlich
extra [ˈekstrə] besonders V/4/M2

extract [ˈekstrækt] Auszug VI/1/M7
extraordinary [ɪkˈstrɔːdnri] außerordentlich, ungewöhnlich VI/4/7
extreme [ɪkˈstriːm] extrem V/3/4
extremely [ɪkˈstriːmli] äußerst, höchst VI/5/R3
eye [aɪ] Auge
keep an eye on sb [ˌkiːp ən ˈaɪ ɒn ˌsʌmbədi] ein (wachsames) Auge auf jdn haben, jdn im Auge behalten VI/4/M8

F

face [feɪs] Gesicht
face [feɪs] etw ausgesetzt sein, mit etw konfrontiert sein VI/1/10
face to face [ˌfeɪs tə ˈfeɪs] einander gegenüber, Auge in Auge VI/1/3
facility [fəˈsɪləti] Einrichtung, Anlage VI/5/S4
fact [fækt] Tatsache, Fakt V/1/2
fact file [ˈfækt ˌfaɪl] Steckbrief
factory [ˈfæktri] Fabrik; Werk
faint [feɪnt] ohnmächtig werden
fair trade [ˌfeə ˈtreɪd] fairer Handel, Fair Trade VI/6/L4
fairly [ˈfeəli] fair, gerecht VI/6/R3
fall [fɔːl] fallen; stürzen
fall *(AE)* = autumn *(BE)* [fɔːl] Herbst
fall asleep [ˌfɔːl əˈsliːp] einschlafen
fall in love (with) [ˌfɔːl ɪn ˈlʌv] sich verlieben (in) V/6/8
fall off [ˈfɔːl ɒf] herunterfallen
false [fɔːls] falsch
family [ˈfæmli] Familie
° **famine** [ˈfæmɪn] Hungersnot VI/1/PP
famous [ˈfeɪməs] berühmt
fancy *(informal)* [ˈfænsi] wollen, mögen
fancy [ˈfænsi] ausgefallen, aufwändig VI/1/M2; extrem viel VI/3/12
fancy dress [ˌfænsi ˈdres] Verkleidung, Kostüm

fantastic *(informal)* [fæn'tæstɪk] fantastisch
fantasy ['fæntəsi] Fantasie
far [fɑː] von weit her; weit
farewell [ˌfeə'wel] Abschied(s)- VI/1/8
farm [fɑːm] Bauernhof
farm (land) [fɑːm] (Land) bebauen
farmer ['fɑːmə] Bauer/Bäuerin, Farmer/in
fascinate ['fæsɪneɪt] faszinieren VI/2/3
fascinating ['fæsɪneɪtɪŋ] faszinierend VI/3/5
fashion ['fæʃn] Mode VI/6/R3
fast [fɑːst] schnell
fat [fæt] dick, fett; Fett V/4/4
fat-reduced [ˌfætrɪ'djuːst] fettreduziert V/4/3
father ['fɑːðə] Vater
fault [fɔːlt] Schuld; Fehler V/2/2
favourite ['feɪvrət] Liebling; Favorit/in; Lieblings-
fear [fɪə] fürchten, befürchten V/3/10; Angst, Furcht; Sorge VI/3/2
feather ['feðə] Feder
February ['februəri] Februar
fee [fiː] Gebühr VI/5/R2
feed [fiːd] zu essen geben, füttern
feeding time ['fiːdɪŋ ˌtaɪm] Fütterungszeit
feel [fiːl] (sich) fühlen
feel sorry for sb [ˌfiːl 'sɒri fə sʌmbədi] Mitleid mit jdm haben V/2/2
feeling ['fiːlɪŋ] Gefühl
female ['fiːmeɪl] weiblich
fence [fens] Zaun VI/3/M4
ferry ['feri] Fähre
few [fjuː] einige; wenige
a few [ə 'fjuː] einige
fibre ['faɪbə] Faser VI/6/R3
field [fiːld] Wiese, Weide, Feld
field [fiːld] Bereich, Gebiet VI/5/R4
fierce [fɪəs] heftig, scharf VI/1/3
fifth [fɪfθ] Fünftel V/1/4
fight [faɪt] kämpfen, streiten; Kampf, Streit V/6/8

fighter ['faɪtə] Kämpfer/in VI/3/5
figure out [ˌfɪgər ʲ'aʊt] herausfinden; ausrechnen; verstehen
fill [fɪl] füllen V/6/M6
fill in [fɪl ʲ'ɪn] ausfüllen; einsetzen
fill out [fɪl ʲ'aʊt] ausfüllen
film [fɪlm] Film
film [fɪlm] filmen, drehen VI/2/M11
film studio ['fɪlm ˌstjuːdiəʊ] Filmstudio
final ['faɪnl] letzte(r, s); endgültig VI/4/M5
final ['faɪnl] Endspiel, Finale VI/6/R4
final exam [ˌfaɪnl ɪg'zæm] Abschlussprüfung VI/5/I
finally ['faɪnli] schließlich, endlich
° financial [faɪ'nænʃl] finanziell VI/2/PP
find [faɪnd] finden
find out [faɪnd ʲ'aʊt] herausfinden
finding ['faɪndɪŋ] Entdeckung; Ergebnis VI/2/11
fine [faɪn] in Ordnung, gut; Geldstrafe, Bußgeld V/3/5
fine [faɪn] toll, edel VI/3/M9
finger ['fɪŋgə] Finger
finish ['fɪnɪʃ] beenden, aufhören; austrinken V/6/4
finish ['fɪnɪʃ] Ziel
finished ['fɪnɪʃt] fertig, beendet V/3/M2
fire ['faɪə] Feuer
be on fire [ˌbi ɒn 'faɪə] brennen, in Flammen stehen
fire sb *(informal)* ['faɪə ˌsʌmbədi] jdn feuern/rausschmeißen VI/2/10
firefighter ['faɪəˌfaɪtə] Feuerwehrmann/-frau
firework ['faɪəˌwɜːk] Feuerwerk
firm [fɜːm] Firma, Unternehmen VI/2/3
first [fɜːst] erste(r, s); zuerst; als Erstes
at first [ət 'fɜːst] anfangs, zuerst

first language [ˌfɜːst 'læŋgwɪdʒ] Muttersprache
first name ['fɜːst ˌneɪm] Vorname
in the first place [ɪn ðə 'fɜːst ˌpleɪs] zunächst (einmal), an erster Stelle VI/1/10
first-hand [ˌfɜːst'hænd] aus erster Hand VI/3/M3
fish [fɪʃ] fischen, angeln
fish *(pl* **fish)** [fɪʃ] Fisch
fit [fɪt] sich eignen; passen
fit [fɪt] geeignet VI/5/R1
fitting room ['fɪtɪŋ ˌruːm] Umkleide, Anprobe
fizzy drink [ˌfɪzi 'drɪŋk] süßes, kohlensäurehaltiges Getränk V/4/4
flag [flæg] Fahne; Flagge
flame [fleɪm] Flamme
flammable ['flæməbl] leicht entflammbarer/entzündlicher Stoff VI/3/4
flat [flæt] Wohnung
flatten ['flætn] zerdrücken, dem Erdboden gleich machen VI/4/2
flea market ['fliː ˌmɑːkɪt] Flohmarkt, Trödelmarkt VI/3/5
flexibility [ˌfleksə'bɪləti] Flexibilität, Anpassungsfähigkeit V/5/M1
flexible ['fleksəbl] flexibel, anpassungsfähig V/5/3
flight [flaɪt] Flug VI/3/3
flood [flʌd] Überschwemmung, Hochwasser VI/4/1
flood [flʌd] überschwemmen, (über)fluten VI/4/M1
floor [flɔː] Boden; Stockwerk
flour ['flaʊə] Mehl
flower ['flaʊə] Blume
fluent ['fluːənt] fließend VI/2/M6
fly [flaɪ] fliegen
fog [fɒg] Nebel
foggy ['fɒgi] neblig
fold [fəʊld] (zusammen)falten
folder ['fəʊldə] Mappe, Schnellhefter
follow ['fɒləʊ] folgen
follower ['fɒləʊə] Anhänger/in, Follower VI/6/LG1

following ['fɒləʊɪŋ] folgende(r, s)
VI/1/4
be fond of sth/doing sth
[bi: 'fɒnd‿əv ˌsʌmθɪŋ, ˌdu:ɪŋ
ˌsʌmθɪŋ] etw gerne mögen/
machen
food *(no pl)* [fu:d] Essen
foot *(pl feet)* [fʊt, fi:t] Fuß
foot *(pl foot or feet)* [fʊt, fi:t] Fuß
(= 0,3048 Meter)
football ['fʊt‚bɔ:l] Fußball
for [fɔ:] für; nach; seit
for ages *(informal)* [fər‿'eɪdʒɪz]
ewig, seit Ewigkeiten VI/2/3
for example [ˌfɔ:r‿ɪg'za:mpl] zum
Beispiel
for free [fə 'fri:] gratis, umsonst
V/4/M2
for the better [fə ðə 'betə] zum
Besseren, zum Guten VI/3/M9
forbidden [fə'bɪdn] verboten,
nicht zulässig VI/3/4
force sb (to do sth)
['fɔ:s‿sʌmbədi] jdn zwingen
(etw zu tun) V/1/12
forced labour [ˌfɔ:st 'leɪbə]
Zwangsarbeit VI/2/8
forecast ['fɔ:kɑ:st] vorhersagen
VI/4/6
(in the) foreground ['fɔ:ˌgraʊnd]
(im) Vordergrund VI/1/9
foreign ['fɒrɪn] ausländisch, fremd
foreign country [ˌfɒrɪn 'kʌntri]
Ausland
foreigner ['fɒrɪnə] Ausländer/in
forest ['fɒrɪst] Wald
forever [fər'evə] ewig V/1/5
forget [fə'get] vergessen
fork [fɔ:k] Gabel
form [fɔ:m] (sich) bilden,
formen; Form; Formular
formal ['fɔ:ml] formal; formell
VI/2/CIO
former ['fɔ:mə] ehemalige(r, s),
frühere(r, s) VI/1/5
fortune-teller ['fɔ:tʃən ˌtelə]
Wahrsager/in
forum ['fɔ:rəm] Forum VI/4/M7
forward ['fɔ:wəd] nach vorn(e)
look forward to sth [ˌlʊk
'fɔ:wəd‿tə sʌmθɪŋ] sich auf etw
freuen V/1/5

found [faʊnd] gründen VI/3/11
founder ['faʊndə] Gründer/in
V/5/M11
fountain ['faʊntɪn] Brunnen
V/6/M2
(four-)day [('fɔ:)deɪ] (vier)tägig
VI/3/M3
France [frɑ:nts] Frankreich
free [fri:] frei; gratis, umsonst
for free [fri:] gratis, umsonst
V/4/M2
° **free sb** ['fri: ˌsʌmbədi] jdn
freilassen VI/3/PP
free time [ˌfri: 'taɪm] Freizeit
freedom *(no pl)* ['fri:dəm]
Freiheit, Unabhängigkeit
freely ['fri:li] ungehindert; offen;
frei VI/6/R2
freeze [fri:z] gefrieren,
einfrieren, zufrieren
French [frentʃ] Franzose/
Französin; französisch
French fries *(AE, npl)* = chips
(BE, pl) [ˌfrentʃ 'fraɪz] Pommes
frites
frequent ['fri:kwənt] häufig,
regelmäßig VI/4/11
fresh [freʃ] frisch, neu
freshman *(AE)* ['freʃmən]
Studienanfänger/in VI/4/10
Friday ['fraɪdeɪ] Freitag
fridge *(informal)* [frɪdʒ]
Kühlschrank
fried chicken [ˌfraɪd‿'tʃɪkɪn]
Brathähnchen
fried egg [ˌfraɪd‿'eg] Spiegelei
friend [frend] Freund/in
friend request ['frend rɪˌkwest]
Freundschaftsanfrage VI/4/10
friendly ['frendli] freundlich
friendly match [ˌfrendli 'mætʃ]
Freundschaftsspiel
make friends (with sb) [meɪk
'frendz] sich (mit jdm)
anfreunden, einen Freund
gewinnen
friendship ['frendʃɪp]
Freundschaft
be frightened [bi 'fraɪtnd] sich
fürchten
frightening ['fraɪtnɪŋ] Furcht
erregend, beängstigend

frog [frɒg] Frosch V/1/M1
from [frəm] von, aus
° **from ... onwards** [frəm 'ɒnwədz]
von ... an VI/1/PP
from rags to riches [frəm ˌrægz tə
'rɪtʃɪz] vom Tellerwäscher zum
Millionär VI/2/M10
in front [ɪn 'frʌnt] vorn(e)
at the front of [ət ðə 'frʌnt‿əv]
vorne in
in front of [ɪn 'frʌnt‿əv] vor
frown [fraʊn] die Stirn runzeln
fruit [fru:t] Frucht; Obst
frustration [frʌ'streɪʃn]
Niedergeschlagenheit;
Frustration VI/4/M2
fry [fraɪ] frittieren, braten
V/4/M2
full [fʊl] voll
full-time ['fʊlˌtaɪm] Ganztags-,
Vollzeit-
fun [fʌn] Spaß; lustig, witzig,
spaßig V/3/4
be fun [bi 'fʌn] Spaß machen
funeral ['fju:nrəl] Beerdigung,
Begräbnis VI/1/6
funny ['fʌni] lustig, witzig,
komisch
fur [fɜ:] Fell; Pelz V/1/9
furniture *(no pl)* ['fɜ:nɪtʃə] Möbel
further ['fɜ:ðə] weiter VI/4/13
further ['fɜ:ðə] zusätzlich, noch
mehr VI/2/M6
future ['fju:tʃə] Zukunft;
zukünftig, später VI/2/3

G

gadget ['gædʒɪt] Gerät
° **Gaelic** ['geɪlɪk] Gälisch; gälisch
VI/1/CIO
gain [geɪn] erwerben, erlangen,
sammeln, gewinnen V/5/M1
gallery ['gæləri] Galerie,
Ausstellung
game [geɪm] Spiel
game *(no pl)* [geɪm] Wild
VI/3/M3
gaming *(no pl)* ['geɪmɪŋ] Spielen
(am Computer) VI/4/I
gap [gæp] Lücke VI/5/L2
garage ['gærɑ:ʒ] Garage;
(Kfz-)Werkstatt V/5/8

garden ['gɑːdn] Garten

gardener ['gɑːdnə] Gärtner/in

garlic ['gɑːlɪk] Knoblauch

gas [gæs] Gas V/6/M1

GCSE *(= General Certificate of Secondary Education)* [ˌdʒiː siːˌesˌiː] britische Schulabschlussprüfung VI/2/3

in general [ɪn 'dʒenrəl] im Allgemeinen, generell VI/3/2

generate ['dʒenəreɪt] erstellen, erzeugen, generieren VI/6/R2

generation [ˌdʒenə'reɪʃn] Generation V/1/M5

gentleman ['dʒentlmən] (vornehmer) Herr V/4/M8

geography [dʒiː'ɒgrəfi] Erdkunde, Geographie

German ['dʒɜːmən] Deutsche/r; deutsch

German-speaking ['dʒɜːmən ˌspiːkɪŋ] deutschsprachig VI/6/W3

Germany ['dʒɜːməni] Deutschland

get [get] erhalten, bekommen; gelangen; werden; holen; kapieren, verstehen

get (a week) off [ˌget (ˌə ˌwiːk) 'ɒf] (eine Woche) freibekommen VI/3/3

get along (with sb) [get ə'lɒŋ] sich (mit jdm) verstehen

get back [get 'bæk] zurückbekommen; zurückkommen

get in touch with sb [ˌget ɪn 'tʌtʃ wɪð ˌsʌmbədi] mit jdm in Kontakt treten VI/4/10

get into debt [ˌget ɪntə 'det] Schulden machen, sich verschulden V/5/13

get lost [get 'lɒst] sich verirren; sich verlaufen

get married [get 'mærid] heiraten V/2/5

get on [get 'ɒn] einsteigen (in); aufsteigen (auf)

get rid of sth [get 'rɪd əv ˌsʌmθɪŋ] etw loswerden V/3/M8

get sb sth ['get sʌmbədi ˌsʌmθɪŋ] jdm etw bringen

get sb to do sth [ˌget ˌsʌmbədi tə 'duː ˌsʌmθɪŋ] jdn dazu bringen, etw zu tun VI/1/2

get (to) [get] (an)kommen

get to know sb [get tə 'nəʊ ˌsʌmbədi] jdn kennenlernen V/2/M2

get together [get tə'geðə] sich treffen

get up [get 'ʌp] aufstehen

get used to sth [get 'juːsd tə ˌsʌmθɪŋ] sich an etw gewöhnen

get well [get 'wel] gesund werden

get well card [get 'wel ˌkɑːd] Genesungskarte

Get well soon! [ˌget wel 'suːn] Gute Besserung!

ghost [gəʊst] Geist, Gespenst

giant ['dʒaɪənt] Riese; riesig

gig *(informal)* [gɪg] Auftritt, Konzert, Gig VI/4/M5

giraffe [dʒə'rɑːf] Giraffe VI/3/M4

girl [gɜːl] Mädchen

girlfriend ['gɜːlˌfrend] Freundin *(eines Jungen)* VI/1/M4

give [gɪv] geben

give a presentation [ˌgɪv ə ˌprezn'teɪʃn] eine Präsentation halten VI/3/I

give a talk [ˌgɪv ə 'tɔːk] einen Vortrag halten VI/1/M6

give directions [ˌgɪv dɪ'rekʃnz] den Weg beschreiben

give in [ˌgɪv 'ɪn] nachgeben VI/2/10

give sb a hard stare [ˌgɪv sʌmbədi ə hɑːd 'steə] jdm einen bösen Blick zuwerfen

give up for adoption [ˌgɪv ˌʌp fər ə'dɒpʃn] zur Adoption freigeben VI/1/10

glacier ['glæsiə] Gletscher

glad [glæd] glücklich, froh

glamorous ['glæmərəs] glamourös V/3/M7

glass [glɑːs] Glas

glasses *(npl)* ['glɑːsɪz] Brille

global ['gləʊbl] global, weltweit VI/5/MD2

global warming *(no pl)* [ˌgləʊbl 'wɔːmɪŋ] Erwärmung der Erdatmosphäre V/6/M1

globe [gləʊb] die Erde; Globus

go [gəʊ] gehen; werden

go abroad [ˌgəʊ ə'brɔːd] ins Ausland gehen/reisen VI/1/CIO

go ahead [ˌgəʊ ə'hed] loslegen VI/4/M5

° go by [ˌgəʊ 'baɪ] vergehen; vorbeigehen VI/2/1

go for a walk [ˌgəʊ fər ə 'wɔːk] spazieren gehen

go in [gəʊ 'ɪn] hineingehen

go on [gəʊ 'ɒn] weitergehen; weitermachen; passieren

go on (seventeen) [ˌgəʊ ˌɒn ˌsevn'tiːn] (schon) fast (siebzehn) sein VI/1/2

go on strike [ˌgəʊ ɒn 'straɪk] streiken, in (den) Streik treten VI/2/10

go out [gəʊ 'aʊt] (hinaus)gehen; ausgehen

go quiet [gəʊ 'kwaɪət] ruhig/still werden VI/1/M8

° go to plan [ˌgəʊ tə 'plæn] nach Plan verlaufen VI/2/1

go with ['gəʊ wɪð] gehören zu

goal [gəʊl] Tor

score a goal [ˌskɔːr ə 'gəʊl] ein Tor schießen

goalkeeper ['gəʊlˌkiːpə] Tormann/Torfrau

god [gɒd] Gott

goggles *(npl)* ['gɒglz] (Schutz)brille VI/2/10

gold *(no pl)* [gəʊld] Gold VI/4/M6

° golden ['gəʊldn] golden VI/3/12

goldfish ['gəʊldˌfɪʃ] Goldfisch

good [gʊd] gut

be good at sth [bi 'gʊd æt ˌsʌmθɪŋ] gut in etw sein

good luck [gʊd 'lʌk] Glück

Good luck! [gʊd 'lʌk] Viel Glück!

have a good time [ˌhæv ə gʊd 'taɪm] sich amüsieren

good-looking [ˌgʊd'lʊkɪŋ] gut aussehend

Goodbye! [ˌgʊd'baɪ] Auf Wiedersehen!

government ['gʌvənmənt] Regierung V/4/5

governor ['gʌvənə] Gouverneur VI/4/2

grade [greid] Klasse(nstufe) V/5/2; Note V/5/3

graduate ['grædʒueit] die Abschlussprüfung bestehen V/5/2

° graduate ['grædʒuət] Schulabgänger/in; Absolvent/in VI/2/CIO

graduation [ˌgrædʒu'eiʃn] Schulabschluss, Studienabschluss V/5/M2

graffer *(informal)* ['græfə] Graffitikünstler

grammar ['græmə] Grammatik

grandchild *(pl grandchildren)* ['græn,tʃaild] Enkelkind V/5/13

grandfather ['græn,fɑːðə] Großvater V/1/12

grandma ['græn,mɑː] Oma, Omi

grandmother ['græn,mʌðə] Großmutter V/1/12

grandpa ['græn,pɑː] Opa, Opi

grandparents *(pl)* ['græn,peərənts] Großeltern

graphic artist [ˌgræfɪk‿'ɑːtɪst] Grafiker/in

graphics *(pl)* ['græfɪks] Grafik(en), grafische Darstellung(en) VI/4/M5

grass [grɑːs] Gras

grateful ['greitfl] dankbar V/4/M8

° grave [greiv] Grab VI/4/M2

graveyard ['greiv,jɑːd] Friedhof

greasy ['griːsi] fettig VI/1/M8

great [greit] groß, riesig; großartig, wunderbar

Great Britain [ˌgreit 'britn] Großbritannien

Greece [griːs] Griechenland V/1/4

green [griːn] grün; umweltfreundlich, ökologisch V/6/2

greenhouse gas ['griːn,haus gæs] Treibhausgas V/6/M1

greet [griːt] (be)grüßen V/4/M8

grey [grei] grau

grid [grɪd] Gitter; Tabelle

grill [grɪl] grillen

ground [graund] (Erd)boden, Erde; Gelände

group [gruːp] Gruppe

grow [grəʊ] wachsen

grow up [grəʊ‿'ʌp] erwachsen werden

guarantee [ˌgærən'tiː] garantieren VI/3/M3

guard [gɑːd] bewachen

guess [ges] (er)raten; vermuten

have a guess [ˌhəv‿ə 'ges] raten, schätzen

Guess what! [ges 'wɒt] Stell dir vor!

guest [gest] Gast

guide [gaid] Führer/in VI/3/2

guided ['gaidid] geführt VI/3/M3

guilty ['gɪlti] schuldig

guitar [gɪ'tɑː] Gitarre

Gulf of Mexico [ˌgʌlf‿əv 'meksɪkəʊ] Golf von Mexiko VI/4/M1

gun [gʌn] (Schuss)waffe VI/4/M5

guy *(informal)* [gai] Kerl, Typ

gym (= gymnasium) [dʒɪm, dʒɪm'neiziəm] Turnhalle

gymnastics *(npl)* [dʒɪm'næstɪks] Turnen

H

habit ['hæbɪt] Gewohnheit VI/4/M9

hacking skills ['hækɪŋ ˌskɪlz] Hacker-Fähigkeiten VI/4/13

hair *(no pl)* [heə] Haar(e)

hair stylist ['heə ˌstailɪst] Friseur/Friseuse

haircut ['heə,kʌt] Haarschnitt, Frisur V/5/M3

hairdresser ['heə,dresə] Friseur/Friseuse VI/2/3

hairdressing course ['heə,dresɪŋ ˌkɔːs] Ausbildung zum Friseur/zur Friseuse VI/2/3

hairdressing salon ['heə,dresɪŋ ˌsælɒn] Friseur(geschäft) VI/2/3

hairstyle ['heə,stail] Frisur VI/4/M5

Haitian ['heiʃn] Haitianer/in; haitisch, haitianisch VI/5/R3

Haitian-born ['heiʃn,bɔːn] auf Haiti geboren VI/5/R3

half [hɑːf] halb

half past (eight) ['hɑːf ˌpɑːst] halb (neun)

half *(pl halves)* [hɑːf, hɑːvz] Hälfte

half-price [ˌhɑːf 'prais] zum halben Preis VI/5/MD3

hall [hɔːl] Korridor; Halle

ham [hæm] Schinken

hammer ['hæmə] Hammer VI/2/5

hand [hænd] Hand

on the one hand [ɒn ðə 'wʌn ˌhænd] einerseits V/2/2

on the other hand [ɒn ðɪ‿'ʌðə ˌhænd] andererseits V/2/2

handle ['hændl] mit etw umgehen; bewältigen, regeln VI/1/10

handmade [ˌhænd'meid] handgemacht VI/6/R3

hang [hæŋ] hängen

hang out *(informal)* [hæŋ‿'aut] Zeit verbringen, abhängen

hang up [ˌhæŋ‿'ʌp] auflegen, einhängen

hang up sth ['hæŋ‿ʌp ˌsʌmθɪŋ] etw aufhängen

happen ['hæpən] geschehen, passieren

happy ['hæpi] glücklich; zufrieden; fröhlich

Happy birthday! [ˌhæpi 'bɜːθdei] Alles Gute zum Geburtstag!

harbour ['hɑːbə] Hafen VI/1/7

hard [hɑːd] hart; angestrengt

hard [hɑːd] schwierig VI/5/R4

try hard to do sth [ˌtrai 'hɑːd‿tə du: sʌmθɪŋ] sich sehr bemühen, etw zu tun V/5/13

hardly ['hɑːdli] kaum VI/2/3

° harp [hɑːp] Harfe VI/1/CIO

harvest ['hɑːvɪst] Ernte; Ertrag

hat [hæt] Hut

hate [heit] hassen, nicht ausstehen können

hate *(no pl)* [heit] Hass

have [hæv] haben; essen

have a guess [ˌhəv‿ə 'ges] raten, schätzen

have a barbecue [ˌhæv‿ə ˈbɑːbɪˌkjuː] grillen, eine Grillparty feiern V/1/5

have a meal [ˌhæv‿ə ˈmiːl] eine Mahlzeit zu sich nehmen

have got [hæv ˈɡɒt] haben

have sb around [ˌhæv ˌsʌmbədi‿əˈraʊnd] jdn in der Nähe haben VI/1/M2

have sth [ˈhæv ˌsʌmθɪŋ] etw zu sich nehmen, etw bestellen

have sth in common [hæv ˌsʌmθɪŋ‿ɪn ˈkɒmən] etwas gemein haben VI/2/7

have tea [hæv ˈtiː] Tee trinken

have to [ˈhæv tə] müssen

Hawaiian [həˈwaɪən] Hawaiianer/in; hawai(an)isch

he [hi] er

head [hed] Kopf

clear one's head [ˌklɪə wʌnz ˈhed] einen klaren Kopf bekommen VI/5/R4

headline [ˈhedˌlaɪn] Schlagzeile

headstrong [ˈhedˌstrɒŋ] eigensinnig, eigenwillig VI/1/2

headteacher [ˌhedˈtiːtʃə] Schulleiter/in, Rektor/in

health [helθ] Gesundheit

health care [ˈhelθ keə] Gesundheitsfürsorge, Gesundheitsversorgung VI/4/M3

healthy [ˈhelθi] gesund

hear [hɪə] hören

heart [ˈhɑːt] Herz

heart attack [ˈhɑːt‿əˌtæk] Herzinfarkt, Herzanfall V/4/M2

heat [hiːt] erhitzen V/6/3

heat *(no pl)* [hiːt] Wärme; Hitze VI/2/5

heating [ˈhiːtɪŋ] Heizung V/6/1

heavy [ˈhevi] schwer; stark VI/4/1

height [haɪt] (Körper)größe; Höhe V/4/9

hell [hel] Hölle V/4/9

hello [həˈləʊ] hallo

say hello to [ˌseɪ həˈləʊ tə] (be)grüßen

helmet [ˈhelmɪt] Helm V/2/5

help [help] helfen; Hilfe

help out [help‿aʊt] (aus)helfen, unterstützen

helper [ˈhelpə] Helfer/in VI/5/R4

helpful [ˈhelpfl] hilfreich, nützlich VI/5/R4

helpless [ˈhelpləs] hilflos

helpline [ˈhelpˌlaɪn] telefonischer Beratungsdienst; Notruf VI/1/14

hen [hen] Henne, Huhn

her [hɜː] sie; ihr(e, n)

herd [hɜːd] Herde, Rudel VI/3/M3

here [hɪə] hier

Here you are. [ˌhɪə juːˈˌɑː] Hier, bitte!, Bitte schön!

hero *(pl -es)* [ˈhɪərəʊ, ˈhɪərəʊz] Held

hers [hɜːz] ihre(r, s)

herself [həˈself] sich (selbst); selbst

hey there [ˈheɪ ðeə] he, hallo VI/1/3

hi guys *(informal)* [haɪ ɡaɪz] hallo Leute VI/5/R4

hide [haɪd] (sich) verstecken

high [haɪ] hoch

high school [ˈhaɪ ˌskuːl] *weiterführende Schule in den USA (Klasse 9-12)*

high-security prison [ˌhaɪ sɪˈkjʊərəti ˌprɪzn] Hochsicherheitsgefängnis VI/6/R2

highway [ˈhaɪˌweɪ] Bundesstraße, Highway

hike [haɪk] wandern

hiking [ˈhaɪkɪŋ] Wandern

hill [hɪl] Hügel

him [hɪm] ihm, ihn

° **Hindi** [ˈhɪndi] Hindi *(Amtssprache in Indien)* VI/2/CIO

hippopotamus [ˌhɪpəˈpɒtəməs] Nilpferd

his [hɪz] sein(e, r)

Hispanic [hɪˈspænɪk] Hispano-Amerikaner/in; hispanisch

historical [hɪˈstɒrɪkl] historisch VI/5/R2

history [ˈhɪstri] Geschichte

hit [hɪt] schlagen (auf); treffen, erschüttern VI/4/2

hold [həʊld] (fest)halten

hold [həʊld] Griff VI/1/6

hold out [ˌhəʊldˌˈaʊt] hinhalten VI/1/7

° **hold peace talks** [ˌhəʊld ˈpiːs tɔːks] Friedensverhandlungen führen VI/1/PP

holiday [ˈhɒlɪdeɪ] Urlaub, Ferien

be on holiday [ˌbiˌɒn ˈhɒlɪdeɪ] Urlaub haben, im Urlaub sein

holy [ˈhəʊli] heilig V/1/2

home [həʊm] zu Hause; nach Hause; Zuhause; Heim V/1/12

home [həʊm] Haus; Wohnung VI/4/2

at home [ət ˈhəʊm] zu Hause

home address [ˈhəʊm‿əˌdres] Privatadresse VI/5/W1

home country [ˌhəʊm ˈkʌntri] Heimatland VI/3/2

home town [ˈhəʊm taʊn] Heimatstadt VI/2/M2

homecoming *(AE)* [ˈhəʊmˌkʌmɪŋ] *Amerikanisches Schulfest mit Ehemaligentreffen*

homeless [ˈhəʊmləs] heimatlos, obdachlos

be homesick [bi ˈhəʊmˌsɪk] Heimweh haben

homework *(no pl)* [ˈhəʊmˌwɜːk] Hausaufgaben

honest [ˈɒnɪst] ehrlich V/6/4

honey [ˈhʌni] Honig

hope [həʊp] hoffen

hope [həʊp] Hoffnung

hopefully [ˈhəʊpfli] hoffentlich VI/3/M4

horizon [həˈraɪzn] Horizont VI/2/M6

horrible [ˈhɒrəbl] schrecklich V/2/2

horse [hɔːs] Pferd

hospital [ˈhɒspɪtl] Krankenhaus

host family [ˈhəʊst ˌfæmli] Gastfamilie VI/5/R2

hostel [ˈhɒstl] (Jugend)herberge VI/5/S4

hot [hɒt] heiß; scharf

hot [hɒt] toll VI/4/M5

hotel [həʊˈtel] Hotel

hour [ˈaʊə] Stunde

house [haʊs] Haus

house music ['haʊs ˌmjuːzɪk] *Musikstil* VI/3/M9

housekeeper ['haʊsˌkiːpə] Haushälter/in VI/1/5

housework *(no pl)* ['haʊsˌwɜːk] Hausarbeit VI/6/W1

how [haʊ] wie

How about ...? [haʊˌəˈbaʊt] Was ist mit ...?, Wie wäre es mit ...?

How are things? [ˌhaʊˌɑ: ˈθɪŋz] Wie geht's?

How are you doing? [ˌhaʊˌə jə ˈduːɪŋ] Wie geht es dir/Ihnen/euch?

How are you? [haʊˌˈɑ: juː] Wie geht es dir/Ihnen/euch?

How much is/are ... ? [ˌhaʊ mʌtʃˈɪz/ɑ:] Was kostet/kosten ...?

how to [haʊ tə] wie man VI/1/1

however [haʊˈevə] aber, jedoch VI/2/3

hug [hʌg] umarmen VI/3/CIO; Umarmung VI/1/M4

huge [hjuːdʒ] riesig, riesengroß

human ['hjuːmən] Mensch V/6/8

human ['hjuːmən] menschlich V/3/M2

° human rights *(npl)* [ˌhjuːmən ˈraɪts] Menschenrechte VI/2/PP

humanitarian [hjuːˌmænɪˈteəriən] humanitär VI/6/R3

humanoid ['hjuːmənɔɪd] menschenartiges Wesen, Humanoid VI/4/M6

humidity *(no pl)* [hjuːˈmɪdəti] (Luft)feuchtigkeit VI/4/6

hundred ['hʌndrəd] Hundert

hundreds of thousands *(pl)* [ˌhʌndrədzˌəv ˈθaʊzndz] Hunderttausende VI/4/M1

hunger ['hʌŋgə] Hunger V/4/M6

hungry ['hʌŋgri] hungrig

hunt [hʌnt] jagen

hurricane ['hʌrɪkən] Orkan, Hurrikan VI/4/1

hurry ['hʌri] sich beeilen; hetzen

hurt [hɜːt] verletzt, verwundet; wehtun, schmerzen; schaden

husband ['hʌzbənd] Ehemann VI/6/R2

hyena [haɪˈiːnə] Hyäne

I

I [aɪ] ich

I'll have ... [aɪl ˈhæv] Ich hätte gern ...; Ich nehme ...

ice [aɪs] Eis

ice cream ['aɪs ˌkriːm] Eiskrem

idea [aɪˈdɪə] Idee

idea [aɪˈdɪə] Vorstellung, Eindruck VI/3/2

ideal [aɪˈdɪəl] ideal V/1/M1

identification (= ID) *(no pl)* [aɪˌdentɪfɪˈkeɪʃn] Identifizierung; Ausweis

idiotic [ˌɪdiˈɒtɪk] idiotisch V/5/M11

if [ɪf] wenn, falls

ignore [ɪgˈnɔː] ignorieren

ill [ɪl] krank

illegal [ɪˈliːgl] rechtswidrig, illegal

illness ['ɪlnəs] Krankheit, Erkrankung V/4/10

image ['ɪmɪdʒ] Bild, Metapher VI/4/M2

imagination [ɪˌmædʒɪˈneɪʃn] Fantasie, Vorstellungskraft; Einbildung V/2/2

imagine [ɪˈmædʒɪn] sich vorstellen

immediately [ɪˈmiːdiətli] sofort V/3/5

immigrant ['ɪmɪgrənt] Einwanderer/in

immigrate ['ɪmɪˌgreɪt] einwandern

immigration [ˌɪmɪˈgreɪʃn] Einwanderung, Immigration

impala [ɪmˈpɑːlə] Impala, Schwarzfersenantilope VI/3/M5

impolite [ˌɪmpəˈlaɪt] unhöflich

importance *(no pl)* [ɪmˈpɔːtns] Bedeutung, Wichtigkeit V/6/M2

important [ɪmˈpɔːtnt] wichtig

imported [ɪmˈpɔːtɪd] importiert VI/6/L4

impossible [ɪmˈpɒsəbl] unmöglich V/6/8

impressive [ɪmˈpresɪv] beeindruckend V/1/M1

improve [ɪmˈpruːv] verbessern V/5/M2

in [ɪn] in; herein V/2/7

in general [ɪn ˈdʒenrəl] im Allgemeinen, generell VI/3/2

in (months) [ɪn ˈmʌnθs] seit (Monaten) VI/1/7

° one in six [ˌwʌnˌɪn ˈsɪks] eine(r,s) von sechs VI/2/CIO

in the end [ˌɪn ðiˈend] letzten Endes; schließlich

in the first place [ɪn ðə ˈfɜːst ˌpleɪs] zunächst (einmal), an erster Stelle VI/1/10

in town [ɪn ˈtaʊn] in der Stadt VI/2/M5

include [ɪnˈkluːd] beinhalten, einschließen VI/2/M7

included [ɪnˈkluːdɪd] inklusive, mitgerechnet V/1/6

including [ɪnˈkluːdɪŋ] einschließlich VI/3/5

incredible [ɪnˈkredəbl] unglaublich

° independence [ˌɪndɪˈpendəns] Unabhängigkeit VI/1/PP

India ['ɪndiə] Indien

Indian ['ɪndiən] Inder/in; Indianer/in; indisch; indianisch

the Indian Ocean [ðiˌɪndiənˌˈəʊʃn] der Indische Ozean VI/3/5

individual [ˌɪndɪˈvɪdʒuəl] Einzelperson

Indonesia [ˌɪndəʊˈniːʒə] Indonesien VI/2/10

indoor(s) [ɪnˈdɔː] drinnen; zu Hause; Innen-

industry ['ɪndəstri] Branche, Gewerbe VI/2/11; Industrie VI/2/M6

influence ['ɪnfluəns] Einfluss VI/6/S3

inform [ɪnˈfɔːm] informieren VI/6/L4

information *(no pl)* [ˌɪnfəˈmeɪʃn] Information

information technology (= IT) *(no pl)* [ˌɪnfəˌmeɪʃn tekˈnɒlədʒi] Informationstechnologie, IT VI/5/R2

ingredient [ɪnˈɡriːdiənt] Bestandteil, Zutat

injure [ˈɪndʒə] verletzen VI/2/10

injured [ˈɪndʒəd] verletzt

° **innocent** [ˈɪnəsnt] unschuldig; unbeteiligt VI/1/PP

insect [ˈɪnsekt] Insekt VI/6/MD2

inside [ˈɪnˌsaɪd] (in ...) hinein; innen; im Inneren

instant messaging [ˌɪnstənt ˈmesɪdʒɪŋ] Instant Messaging *(sofortige Nachrichtenübermittlung)* VI/6/LG1

instead (of) [ɪnˈsted (ˌəv)] stattdessen; (an)statt V/6/3

instruction [ɪnˈstrʌkʃn] Anweisung, Anleitung

instructor [ɪnˈstrʌktə] Lehrer/in; Betreuer/in

instrument [ˈɪnstrʊmənt] Instrument V/1/10

insult [ˈɪnsʌlt] Beleidigung

intelligent [ɪnˈtelɪdʒnt] intelligent

intensive [ɪnˈtensɪv] intensiv VI/5/R2

interaction [ˌɪntərˈækʃn] Interaktion VI/4/M7

interest [ˈɪntrəst] Interesse V/1/M1

interest sb [ˈɪntrəst ˌsʌmbədi] jdn interessieren, bei jdm Interesse wecken VI/3/7

interested (in) [ˈɪntrəstɪd] interessiert (an)

be interested in [biˈɪntrəstɪdˌɪn] sich interessieren für

interesting [ˈɪntrəstɪŋ] interessant

intern *(AE)* = trainee *(BE)* [ˈɪntɜːn] Praktikant/in

international [ˌɪntəˈnæʃnəl] international VI/2/M2

on the Internet [ˌɒn ðiˈɪntənet] im Internet

surf the Internet [ˌsɜːf ðiˌɪntənet] im Internet surfen VI/2/M2

interview [ˈɪntəˌvjuː] befragen

into [ˈɪntʊ] in

be into sth [ˌbiˈɪntʊ ˌsʌmθɪŋ] an etw interessiert sein, auf etw stehen VI/5/MD1

intolerant [ɪnˈtɒlərənt] intolerant V/2/2

introduce [ˌɪntrəˈdjuːs] vorstellen

invent [ɪnˈvent] erfinden

invention [ɪnˈvenʃn] Erfindung

° **inventor** [ɪnˈventə] Erfinder/in VI/4/PP

invitation [ˌɪnvɪˈteɪʃn] Einladung

invite [ɪnˈvaɪt] einladen

involve [ɪnˈvɒlv] beinhalten; betreffen VI/1/14

be involved (in) [biˌɪnˈvɒlvd (ˌɪn)] beteiligt sein, engagiert sein VI/3/11

Ireland [ˈaɪələnd] Irland

Irish [ˈaɪərɪʃ] irisch

° **the Irish** [ðiˌˈaɪərɪʃ] die Iren VI/1/PP

iron [ˈaɪən] bügeln V/5/M4

island [ˈaɪlənd] Insel

issue [ˈɪʃuː] veröffentlichen, aussprechen VI/4/6

it [ɪt] es

(it's) your turn [ɪtsˌjɔːˈtɜːn] du bist dran VI/1/M8

Italian [ɪˈtæljən] Italiener/in; italienisch

Italy [ˈɪtəli] Italien

item [ˈaɪtəm] Gegenstand, Ding VI/5/S2

itself [ɪtˈself] sich (selbst); selbst

J

jacket [ˈdʒækɪt] Jacke

jacuzzi [dʒəˈkuːzi] Jacuzzi, Whirlpool VI/3/M3

January [ˈdʒænjuəri] Januar

° **Japanese** [ˌdʒæpəˈniːz] Japaner/in; Japanisch; japanisch VI/4/CIO

jealous [ˈdʒeləs] eifersüchtig

jelly [ˈdʒeli] Gelee; Marmelade

jerk about [ˌdʒɜːkˌəˈbaʊt] herumruckeln VI/1/M8

jersey *(no pl)* [ˈdʒɜːzi] Jersey *(Stoffart)* VI/6/R3

jewellery *(no pl)* [ˈdʒuːəlri] Schmuck VI/3/5

Jewish [ˈdʒuːɪʃ] jüdisch

jiggle [ˈdʒɪɡl] hin und her wiegen VI/1/M8

job [dʒɒb] Arbeit, Stelle, Tätigkeit, Aufgabe

job counsellor [ˈdʒɒb ˌkaʊnslə] Berufsberater/in VI/2/3

job interview [ˈdʒɒbˌɪntəvjuː] Bewerbungsgespräch, Vorstellungsgespräch VI/2/3

join [dʒɔɪn] mitmachen bei; beitreten; (sich) anschließen

join in [ˌdʒɔɪnˈɪn] sich anschließen, mitmachen V/2/9

joiner [ˈdʒɔɪnə] Tischler/in, Schreiner/in VI/2/M2

joke [dʒəʊk] Witz

be joking [biˈdʒəʊkɪŋ] Spaß machen, scherzen V/2/2

° **journal** [ˈdʒɜːnl] Zeitschrift, Zeitung VI/3/12

journalist [ˈdʒɜːnəlɪst] Journalist/in VI/2/9

journey [ˈdʒɜːni] Reise VI/3/4

judge [dʒʌdʒ] Richter/in V/2/M5

juggler [ˈdʒʌɡlə] Jongleur/in

juice [dʒuːs] Saft

July [dʒʊˈlaɪ] Juli

jump [dʒʌmp] springen

jump up [dʒʌmpˈʌp] aufspringen, hochspringen

jumper [ˈdʒʌmpə] Pullover V/6/4

June [dʒuːn] Juni

junk food [ˈdʒʌŋk fuːd] Schnellgerichte; ungesundes Essen, Fraß V/4/5

just [dʒʌst] gleich; genau; nur; einfach; gerade

just a minute [ˌdʒʌstˌəˈmɪnɪt] einen Augenblick/Moment bitte

K

kangaroo [ˌkæŋɡəˈruː] Känguru V/1/9

keep [kiːp] (be)halten

keep an eye on sb [ˌkiːp ən ˈaɪ ɒn ˌsʌmbədi] ein (wachsames) Auge auf jdn haben, jdn im Auge behalten VI/4/M8

keep fit [ˌkiːp ˈfɪt] sich fit halten

keep in touch with sb [ˌkiːp ɪn ˈtʌtʃ wɪð ˌsʌmbədi] mit jdm in Kontakt bleiben VI/1/14

keep (on) doing sth [kiːp ˈduːɪŋ ˌsʌmθɪŋ] etw weiter tun; etw wiederholt/immer wieder tun V/3/5

keep out [ˌkiːp ˈaʊt] nicht hereinlassen VI/3/M4

keep sb happy [ˌkiːp ˌsʌmbədi ˈhæpi] jdn bei Laune halten VI/1/M4

keep sth going [ˌkiːp ˌsʌmθɪŋ ˈɡəʊɪŋ] etw in Gang halten VI/3/12

key [kiː] Schlüssel

keyword [ˈkiːˌwɜːd] Schlüsselwort

kick [kɪk] treten, schießen, kicken V/3/3

kill [kɪl] töten V/1/2

killer [ˈkɪlə] mörderisch VI/4/2

° **killing** [ˈkɪlɪŋ] Tötung, Mord VI/3/12

kilo [ˈkiːləʊ] Kilo

kind [kaɪnd] Art, Sorte

kind [kaɪnd] nett, freundlich V/4/M8

kindergarten *(AE)* = nursery school *(BE) (no pl)* [ˈkɪndəˌɡɑːtn] Kindergarten; Vorschule

king [kɪŋ] König

kiss [kɪs] küssen VI/4/10

kiss [kɪs] Kuss

kiss sb on the lips [ˌkɪs ˌsʌmbədi ɒn ðə ˈlɪps] jdn auf den Mund küssen VI/1/M4

kitchen [ˈkɪtʃən] Küche

kitten [ˈkɪtn] Kätzchen, junge Katze

knee [niː] Knie

knife *(pl* **knives)** [naɪf, naɪvz] Messer

know [nəʊ] wissen; kennen

know about [ˈnəʊ əˌbaʊt] Bescheid wissen über

get to know sb [ˌɡet tə ˈnəʊ ˌsʌmbədi] jdn kennenlernen V/2/M2

known [nəʊn] bekannt V/4/M2

L

label [ˈleɪbl] Etikett, Label; Marke VI/2/11

labour *(no pl)* [ˈleɪbə] Arbeitskräfte VI/3/M9

lacrosse *(no pl)* [ləˈkrɒs] Lacrosse (Ballsportart)

lady [ˈleɪdi] Frau; Dame

lake [laɪk] See

lamb [læm] Lamm

lamp [læmp] Lampe

land [lænd] (Fest)land

land [lænd] landen

land-based [ˈlændbeɪst] vom Land aus VI/3/5

landline [ˈlændˌlaɪn] Festnetz(anschluss/-telefon) VI/5/W1

landscape [ˈlændˌskeɪp] Landschaft

language [ˈlæŋɡwɪdʒ] Sprache

use bad language [juːz bæd ˈlæŋɡwɪdʒ] Schimpfwörter benutzen

large [lɑːdʒ] groß

last [lɑːst] halten; (an)dauern; (aus)reichen VI/4/6; letzte(r, s)

last but not least [ˌlɑːst bət nɒt ˈliːst] nicht zuletzt

° at last [ət ˈlɑːst] endlich, schließlich VI/2/1

late [leɪt] (zu) spät

lately [ˈleɪtli] kürzlich, in letzter Zeit VI/3/M4

later [ˈleɪtə] später

later on *(informal)* [ˌleɪtər ˈɒn] später VI/5/R4

Latin [ˈlætɪn] Latein; lateinisch VI/6/R4

Latino *(AE)* [læˈtiːnəʊ] Latino; latino

laugh [lɑːf] lachen

laugh at sb [ˈlɑːf ət ˌsʌmbədi] jdn auslachen

laugh at sth [ˈlɑːf ət ˌsʌmθɪŋ] über etw lachen

laughter *(no pl)* [ˈlɑːftə] Lachen, Gelächter VI/1/7

lava *(no pl)* [ˈlɑːvə] Lava VI/4/1

law [lɔː] Gesetz V/4/5

lawnmower [ˈlɔːnˌməʊə] Rasenmäher

lawyer [ˈlɔːjə] Rechtsanwalt/ -anwältin

lazy [ˈleɪzi] faul, träge V/6/8

lead [liːd] (an)führen, leiten V/4/5

leader [ˈliːdə] Leiter/in, Führer/in VI/3/5

leading [ˈliːdɪŋ] führend VI/3/11

leaflet [ˈliːflət] Prospekt

lean [liːn] lehnen VI/1/3

learn [lɜːn] lernen

least [liːst] am wenigsten VI/3/7

at least [ət ˈliːst] mindestens, wenigstens

leave [liːv] verlassen; da lassen; abfahren; hinterlassen; weggehen; zurücklassen; lassen V/6/3

leave out [ˌliːv ˈaʊt] auslassen, weglassen VI/1/M3

left [left] (nach) links; übrig

on the left [ˌɒn ðə ˈleft] links

leg [leg] Bein

legend [ˈledʒənd] Legende, Sage

lemon [ˈlemən] Zitrone

length [leŋθ] Länge, Dauer VI/5/L2

leopard [ˈlepəd] Leopard/in VI/3/M4

less [les] weniger V/4/4

lesson [ˈlesn] Stunde

let [let] lassen

let off [ˌlet ˈɒf] laufen lassen; abfeuern

let sb be [ˌlet ˌsʌmbədi ˈbiː] jdn in Ruhe lassen VI/1/2

let sb down [ˌlet ˌsʌmbədi ˈdaʊn] jdn enttäuschen, jdn im Stich lassen

let's (= let us) [lets, ˈlet əs] lass(t) uns

Let's go! [lets ˈɡəʊ] Los! Los geht's!

letter [ˈletə] Brief; Buchstabe

lettuce [ˈletɪs] Blattsalat; Kopfsalat

levee ['levi] Damm VI/4/M1

level ['levl] Ebene, Stockwerk V/4/M2

library ['laɪbrəri] Bibliothek, Bücherei

licence ['laɪsns] Genehmigung, Erlaubnis

lie [laɪ] lügen; liegen; sich hinlegen

lie down [,laɪ 'daʊn] sich hinlegen VI/6/R4

life imprisonment *(no pl)* [,laɪf_ɪm'prɪznmənt] lebenslängliche Freiheitsstrafe VI/3/11

life *(pl lives)* [laɪf, laɪvz] Leben

lifeguard ['laɪf,ɡɑːd] Rettungsschwimmer/in; Bademeister/in

lifejacket ['laɪf,dʒækɪt] Schwimmweste V/3/M2

of a lifetime [əv_ə 'laɪf,taɪm] des Lebens VI/3/M3

lift [lɪft] (hoch)heben; Aufzug, Lift

lift up [,lɪft_'ʌp] (hoch)heben VI/1/7

light [laɪt] Licht

light bulb ['laɪt ,bʌlb] Glühbirne

like [laɪk] mögen; wie

like this [laɪk 'ðɪs] so; solche(r, s)

I'd like (to) [,aɪd 'laɪk] ich würde gern

What's ... like? [wɒts 'laɪk] Wie ist ...?

likely ['laɪkli] wahrscheinlich VI/4/6

likes *(pl)* [laɪks] Vorlieben

limit ['lɪmɪt] Grenze, Limit VI/4/M7

line [laɪn] Linie; Zeile

° **line** [laɪn] Leitung, Verbindung VI/4/PP

lines *(pl)* [laɪnz] Text

link [lɪŋk] verbinden

lion ['laɪən] Löwe

list [lɪst] Liste

listen in [,lɪsn_'ɪn] mithören; Radio hören VI/3/10

listen (to) ['lɪsn] zuhören

listener ['lɪsnə] (Zu)hörer/in VI/1/M3

literature *(no pl)* ['lɪtrətʃə] Literatur VI/6/R3

litter *(no pl)* ['lɪtə] Müll, Abfall V/6/M2

little ['lɪtl] klein

a little [ə 'lɪtl] ein bisschen

live [lɪv] leben, wohnen

living conditions *(pl)* ['lɪvɪŋ_kən,dɪʃnz] Lebensbedingungen V/4/M6

living room ['lɪvɪŋ ,ruːm] Wohnzimmer

loads (of) *(informal)* [ləʊdz] jede Menge, massenhaft VI/5/R3

local ['ləʊkl] hiesig, örtlich V/5/5

be located [bi: ləʊ'keɪtɪd] sich befinden, liegen, gelegen sein VI/3/M3

location [ləʊ'keɪʃn] Lage V/1/M1

on location [,ɒn ləʊ'keɪʃn] vor Ort, Außenaufnahmen VI/2/M11

locker ['lɒkə] Schließfach, Spind

lodge [lɒdʒ] Lodge, Hütte VI/3/M4

log on [,lɒɡ_'ɒn] sich einloggen, sich anmelden VI/4/9

logical ['lɒdʒɪkl] logisch VI/4/4

lonely ['ləʊnli] einsam

long [lɒŋ] lang

a long time ago [ə ,lɒŋ ,taɪm_ə'ɡəʊ] vor langer Zeit V/1/11

° **long-distance** [,lɒŋ 'dɪstəns] Fern-, Langstrecken- VI/4/PP

long-sleeved ['lɒŋ ,sliːvd] langärm(e)lig VI/6/MD2

not ... any longer [,nɒt_eni 'lɒŋɡə] nicht länger VI/1/6

look [lʊk] sehen, schauen; aussehen; Aussehen; Blick V/3/8

look after [lʊk_'ɑːftə] sich kümmern um

look around [,lʊk_ə'raʊnd] sich umsehen/umschauen (in)

look at ['lʊk_ət] betrachten, sehen

look at sb ['lʊk_ət ,sʌmbədi] jdn anschauen V/2/10

look for ['lʊk ,fə] suchen nach

look forward to sth [,lʊk 'fɔːwəd_tə sʌmbɪŋ] sich auf etw freuen V/1/5

look out (for sth) [,lʊk_'aʊt (fə ,sʌmθɪŋ)] (nach etw) Ausschau halten; auf etw aufpassen VI/4/M7

look up [lʊk_'ʌp] nachschlagen

look up to [lʊk_'ʌp tə] aufblicken zu

lookout ['lʊkaʊt] Aussichtspunkt VI/3/5

lose [luːz] verlieren

a lot (of) [ə 'lɒt] sehr; viele

lots of ['lɒts_əv] viel, jede Menge

loud [laʊd] laut

love [lʌv] Liebe; lieben; sehr gern mögen; herzliche Grüße, alles Liebe

love marriage ['lʌv ,mærɪdʒ] Liebesheirat VI/1/M4

fall in love (with) [,fɔːl_ɪn 'lʌv] sich verlieben (in)

be in love (with sb) [,bi_ɪn 'lʌv] (in jdn) verliebt sein

lovely ['lʌvli] schön, hübsch

low [ləʊ] niedrig

luckily ['lʌkɪli] glücklicherweise VI/3/M4

be lucky [bi 'lʌki] Glück haben

count oneself lucky [,kaʊnt wʌn,self 'lʌki] sich glücklich schätzen VI/5/R4

luggage *(no pl)* ['lʌɡɪdʒ] Gepäck VI/1/7

lunch [lʌntʃ] Mittagessen

lunchtime ['lʌntʃ,taɪm] Mittagszeit; Mittagspause V/4/9

luxury ['lʌkʃəri] Luxus VI/3/M3

lyrics ['lɪrɪks] (Lied)text

M

machine [mə'ʃiːn] Maschine

mad [mæd] böse, wütend, sauer

made-up [,meɪd'ʌp] erfunden, ausgedacht VI/1/M8

magazine [,mæɡə'ziːn] Zeitschrift, Magazin

magic ['mædʒɪk] Magie, Zauber

magic trick [,mædʒɪk 'trɪk] Zaubertrick

magician [mə'dʒɪʃn] Zauberer/Zauberin

DICTIONARY ENGLISH–GERMAN

mail [meɪl] (Briefe/E-Mails)
schreiben
main [meɪn] Haupt-
main dish [meɪn ˈdɪʃ]
Hauptspeise
mainly [ˈmeɪnli] hauptsächlich,
in erster Linie
° **majority** [məˈdʒɒrəti] Mehrheit
VI/1/PP
make [meɪk] machen
make an appointment
[ˌmeɪk ən əˈpɔɪntmənt]
einen Termin ausmachen/
vereinbaren VI/1/10
make friends (with sb) [meɪk
ˈfrendz] sich (mit jdm)
anfreunden, einen Freund
gewinnen
make it [ˈmeɪk ɪt] es schaffen
VI/2/I
make it up with sb [ˌmeɪk ɪt ʌp
wɪð ˈsʌmbədi] sich (wieder) mit
jdm vertragen
make money [meɪk ˈmʌni] Geld
verdienen
make notes (on) [ˌmeɪk ˈnəʊts]
(sich) Notizen machen (zu,
über)
make sb do sth [ˌmeɪk sʌmbədi
ˈduː sʌmθɪŋ] jdn dazu bringen/
veranlassen, etw zu tun
make sure [ˌmeɪk ˈʃɔː] sich
versichern, darauf achten
make to do sth [ˌmeɪk tə ˈduː
ˌsʌmθɪŋ] Anstalten machen,
etw zu tun VI/1/2
make up one's mind [ˌmeɪk ˌʌp
wʌnz ˈmaɪnd] sich entscheiden
VI/5/R4
make up sth [meɪk ˈʌp sʌmθɪŋ]
etw erfinden, (sich)
ausdenken
make-up artist [ˌmeɪkʌp ˈɑːtɪst]
Maskenbildner/in, Visagist/in
male [meɪl] männlich
mall [mɔːl] Einkaufspassage,
Einkaufszentrum
mammal [ˈmæml] Säugetier
VI/3/2
man (*pl* **men**) [mæn, men] Mann
manage [ˈmænɪdʒ] es schaffen
V/6/8

management (*no pl*)
[ˈmænɪdʒmənt] Management,
(Unternehmens)leitung
VI/2/10
manager [ˈmænɪdʒə]
Geschäftsführer/in
many [ˈmeni] viele
map [mæp] (Land)karte
marathon [ˈmærəθn]
Marathon(lauf)
March [mɑːtʃ] März
marine [məˈriːn] Meeres-, See-
VI/3/5
mark [mɑːk] Note
mark [mɑːk] markieren,
kennzeichnen VI/5/W5
market [ˈmɑːkɪt] Markt
marriage [ˈmærɪdʒ] Heirat VI/1/M3
married [ˈmærid] verheiratet
VI/1/M2
get married [get ˈmærid] heiraten
V/2/5
marry [ˈmæri] heiraten
martial arts (*npl*) [ˌmɑːʃl ˈɑːts]
Kampfsport
mashed potatoes [ˌmæʃt
pəˈteɪtəʊz] Kartoffelbrei
match [mætʃ] Streichholz,
Zündholz
match [mætʃ] passen zu VI/6/R1;
Spiel VI/6/R4
match (with) [mætʃ] zuordnen
mate [meɪt] sich paaren VI/3/5
material [məˈtɪəriəl] Material
V/5/4
maths [mæθs] Mathe
do the maths [ˌduː ðə ˈmæθs]
(aus)rechnen VI/6/R3
matter [ˈmætə] Angelegenheit,
Sache VI/1/10
maximum [ˈmæksɪməm]
maximal, Höchst-, Maximal-
VI/5/S4; Maximum VI/5/R2
May [meɪ] Mai
maybe [ˈmeɪbi] vielleicht,
möglicherweise
mayonnaise [ˌmeɪəˈneɪz]
Majonäse
me [miː] mir, mich
meal [miːl] Mahlzeit, Essen
have a meal [ˌhæv ə ˈmiːl] eine
Mahlzeit zu sich nehmen

mealtime [ˈmiːltaɪm] Essenszeit
VI/3/M3
mean [miːn] bedeuten; meinen;
gemein, fies
meaning [ˈmiːnɪŋ] Bedeutung
° **means** (*pl*) [miːnz] Mittel,
Möglichkeit VI/4/PP
measure [ˈmeʒə] messen
VI/4/6
measurement [ˈmeʒəmənt]
Messung VI/4/6
meat (*no pl*) [miːt] Fleisch
mechanic [mɪˈkænɪk]
Mechaniker/in
mediation [ˌmiːdiˈeɪʃn]
Sprachmittlung VI/5/I
° **medical** [ˈmedɪkl] medizinisch,
ärztlich VI/2/PP
medication [ˌmedɪˈkeɪʃn]
Medikament(e) VI/6/MD2
medicine (*no pl*) [ˈmedsn]
Medizin, Medikament(e)
the Mediterranean Sea [ðə
ˌmedɪtəˌreɪniən ˈsiː] das
Mittelmeer VI/2/M6
meet [miːt] (sich) treffen
meeting point [ˈmiːtɪŋ pɔɪnt]
Treffpunkt VI/6/L2
melon [ˈmelən] Melone V/4/9
member [ˈmembə] Mitglied
mention [ˈmenʃn] erwähnen
VI/3/5
menu [ˈmenjuː] Speisekarte;
Menü
mess [mes] Unordnung,
Durcheinander
message [ˈmesɪdʒ] Nachricht
metal [ˈmetl] Metall
meteorologist [ˌmiːtiəˈrɒlədʒɪst]
Meteorologe/Meteorologin
VI/4/6
° **method** [ˈmeθəd] Methode,
Verfahren, System VI/4/PP
metre [ˈmiːtə] Meter
the Metropolitan Police [ðə
ˌmetrəˌpɒlɪtn pəˈliːs] die
Londoner Polizei VI/6/R2
Mexican [ˈmeksɪkən] Mexika-
ner/in, mexikanisch
Mexico [ˈmeksɪˌkəʊ] Mexiko
microwave [ˈmaɪkrəˌweɪv]
Mikrowelle(nherd) V/6/1

the Mid-South [ðə ˌmɪd ˈsaʊθ] der Mittlere Süden VI/4/2
middle [ˈmɪdl] Mitte VI/4/2
the Middle East [ðə ˌmɪdlˈiːst] der Nahe Osten
in the middle of [ˌɪn ðə ˈmɪdlˈəv] mitten in; in der Mitte
middle-class [ˌmɪdlˈklɑːs] Mittelklasse- VI/5/R2
midnight [ˈmɪdˌnaɪt] Mitternacht
might [maɪt] könnte; vielleicht tun
mile [maɪl] Meile
do military service [duː ˌmɪlɪtri ˈsɜːvɪs] Wehrdienst leisten V/5/2
milk [mɪlk] Milch
million [ˈmɪljən] Million
millionaire [ˌmɪljəˈneə] Millionär/in V/5/10
mind [maɪnd] etw dagegen haben VI/1/7
come to sb's mind [kʌm tə ˌsʌmbədiz ˈmaɪnd] jdm einfallen
make up one's mind [ˌmeɪkˌʌp wʌnz ˈmaɪnd] sich entscheiden VI/5/R4
mind one's own business *(informal)* [ˌmaɪnd wʌnzˌəʊn ˈbɪznəs] sich um seinen (eigenen) Kram/seine (eigenen) Angelegenheiten kümmern VI/1/3
mindmap [ˈmaɪndmæp] Wortnetz
mine [maɪn] meine(r, s); mir
mineral [ˈmɪnrəl] Mineral V/4/3
minimum wage [ˌmɪnɪməm ˈweɪdʒ] Mindestlohn VI/2/10
minute [ˈmɪnɪt] Minute
mirror [ˈmɪrə] Spiegel
Miss [mɪs] Fräulein *(Anrede)*
miss [mɪs] versäumen, verpassen; vermissen
miss [mɪs] fehlen VI/5/LG1
missing [ˈmɪsɪŋ] fehlend VI/5/L2
mistake [mɪˈsteɪk] Fehler, Irrtum, Versehen
° mistrust *(no pl)* [mɪsˈtrʌst] Misstrauen, Argwohn VI/1/PP
mix [mɪks] (ver)mischen, anrühren VI/2/5

mix up sb/sth [ˌmɪksˌˈʌp ˌsʌmbədi/ˌsʌmθɪŋ] jdn/etw verwechseln VI/4/M7
mixed dorm [ˌmɪkstˌˈdɔːm] *Schlafsaal, in dem Männer und Frauen übernachten* V/1/6
mixture [ˈmɪkstʃə] Mischung VI/3/M9
MMORPG (= Massively Multiplayer Online Role-Playing Game) [ˌemˌemˌəʊˌɑːˌpiːˌˈdʒiː] *Rollenspiel im Internet mit extrem vielen Spielern* VI/4/M7
mobile [ˈməʊbaɪl] mobil VI/6/R1; Mobiltelefon, Handy VI/5/W1
mobile phone [ˌməʊbaɪl ˈfəʊn] Mobiltelefon, Handy
mock exam [ˈmɒkˌɪgˌzæm] Probeprüfung VI/6/I
model [ˈmɒdl] modeln, Modell stehen VI/6/R3
modern [ˈmɒdən] modern
moment [ˈməʊmənt] Moment, Augenblick
at the moment [ˌæt ðə ˈməʊmənt] im Augenblick, momentan
Monday [ˈmʌndeɪ] Montag
money [ˈmʌni] Geld
make money [meɪk ˈmʌni] Geld verdienen
raise money [reɪz ˈmʌni] Geld aufbringen/auftreiben
monkey [ˈmʌŋki] Affe
month [mʌnθ] Monat
more [mɔː] mehr
more or less [ˌmɔːˌɔː ˈles] mehr oder weniger, ungefähr V/2/2
moreover [mɔːrˈəʊvə] darüber hinaus, zudem, ferner VI/3/M4
morning [ˈmɔːnɪŋ] Morgen
in the morning [ˌɪn ðə ˈmɔːnɪŋ] morgens, am Morgen, vormittags
this morning [ðɪs ˈmɔːnɪŋ] heute Morgen
° Morse Code *(no pl)* [ˌmɔːs ˈkəʊd] Morsezeichen, Morsealphabet VI/4/PP
(the) most [məʊst] am/die meisten

most of all [ˌməʊstˌəvˈˈɔːl] am meisten; vor allem VI/1/10
mother [ˈmʌðə] Mutter
motivated [ˈməʊtɪˌveɪtɪd] motiviert VI/2/M6
motivation *(no pl)* [ˌməʊtɪˈveɪʃn] Motivation VI/6/S3
mountain [ˈmaʊntɪn] Berg
mouth [maʊθ] Mund
move [muːv] sich bewegen; umziehen
° move [muːv] Bewegung; Schritt VI/3/12
° moved [muːvd] bewegt, angetrieben VI/4/PP
movement [ˈmuːvmənt] Bewegung VI/3/11
movie *(AE)* = film *(BE)* [ˈmuːvi] (Kino-, Spiel)film
Mr [ˈmɪstə] Herr *(Anrede)*
Mrs [ˈmɪsɪz] Frau *(Anrede)*
Ms [məz] Frau *(Anrede für verheiratete und unverheiratete Frauen)* VI/3/4
much [mʌtʃ] viel; sehr
mug sb [ˈmʌg ˌsʌmbədi] jdn überfallen und ausrauben VI/3/13
mum *(informal)* [mʌm] Mama, Mutti
murder [ˈmɜːdə] umbringen, ermorden V/5/M11
museum [mjuːˈziːəm] Museum
mushroom [ˈmʌʃruːm] Pilz
music [ˈmjuːzɪk] Musik
° musical instrument [ˌmjuːzɪklˈˈɪnstrəmənt] Musikinstrument VI/1/CIO
must [mʌst] müssen
must not [ˌmʌst ˈnɒt] nicht dürfen
my [maɪ] mein(e)
my name is [maɪ ˈneɪmˌɪz] ich heiße
myself [maɪˈself] mich, mir; selbst

N

name [neɪm] (be)nennen; Name
my name is [maɪ ˈneɪmˌɪz] ich heiße

DICTIONARY *English – German*

DICTIONARY ENGLISH–GERMAN

by the name of [ˌbaɪ ðə ˈneɪm_əv] namens VI/1/3

What's your name? [ˌwɒts jə ˈneɪm] Wie heißt du?, Wie heißen Sie?

call sb names [ˌkɔːl sʌmbədi ˈneɪmz] jdn beschimpfen

nappy [ˈnæpi] Windel VI/1/M8

narrator [nəˈreɪtə] Erzähler/in

nasty [ˈnɑːsti] scheußlich, grässlich, widerlich

nation [ˈneɪʃn] Nation, Land VI/3/I

national [ˈnæʃnəl] national; National-

the National Guard [ðə ˌnæʃnəl ˈgɑːd] die Nationalgarde (USA) VI/4/2

national park [ˌnæʃnəl ˈpɑːk] Nationalpark

° Nationalist [ˈnæʃnəlɪst] Nationalist (Anhänger der Republik Irland) VI/1/PP

nationality [ˌnæʃəˈnæləti] Nationalität; Staatsangehörigkeit V/5/M2

° native [ˈneɪtɪv] Eingeborene/r, Einheimische/r VI/3/PP

Native American [ˌneɪtɪv_əˈmerɪkən] amerikanischer Ureinwohner/ amerikanische Ureinwohnerin; indianisch

native speaker [ˌneɪtɪv ˈspiːkə] Muttersprachler/in VI/5/R2

natural [ˈnætʃrəl] natürlich, naturbelassen

natural disaster [ˌnætʃrəl dɪˈzɑːstə] Naturkatastrophe VI/4/1

natural history museum [ˌnætʃrəl ˌhɪstri mjuːˈziːəm] Naturkundemuseum

nature [ˈneɪtʃə] Natur

navigation system [ˌnævɪˈgeɪʃn ˌsɪstəm] Navigationssystem VI/2/5

near [nɪə] nahe

nearly [ˈnɪəli] fast, beinahe

necessary [ˈnesəsri] nötig, notwendig, erforderlich VI/2/M6

neck [nek] Hals; Nacken

necklace [ˈnekləs] (Hals)kette V/3/10

need [niːd] brauchen

need *(no pl)* [niːd] Notwendigkeit VI/4/13

need to [ˈniːd tə] müssen

needle [ˈniːdl] Nadel VI/2/10

neighbour [ˈneɪbə] Nachbar/in

neighbourhood [ˈneɪbəhʊd] Viertel; Nachbarschaft

nephew [ˈnefjuː] Neffe

get on sb's nerves [ˌget_ɒn sʌmbədiz ˈnɜːvz] jdm auf die Nerven gehen V/5/M10

nervous [ˈnɜːvəs] nervös

net [net] Netz VI/6/MD2

the Netherlands [ðə ˈneðlənz] die Niederlande VI/5/L3

network [ˈnetˌwɜːk] (soziales) Netzwerk VI/6/LG1

never [ˈnevə] nie(mals)

nevertheless [ˌnevəðəˈles] trotzdem, dennoch VI/3/M4

new [njuː] neu

New Year *(no pl)* [ˌnjuː ˈjɪə] Neujahr

New Zealand [njuː ˈziːlənd] Neuseeland V/1/4

° newborn baby [ˌnjuːˌbɔːn ˈbeɪbi] Neugeborene/s VI/1/CIO

the news [ðə njuːz] Nachrichtensendung

news *(no pl)* [njuːz] Neuigkeit; Nachrichten VI/1/7

newsagent [ˈnjuːzˌeɪdʒnt] Zeitschriftengeschäft; Zeitungshändler/in

newspaper [ˈnjuːzˌpeɪpə] Zeitung

next [nekst] dann, gleich darauf; nächste(r, s)

the next day [ðə ˌnekst_ˈdeɪ] am nächsten Tag V/2/10

next to [ˈnekst_tə] neben

nice [naɪs] schön, angenehm; nett, freundlich

Nice to meet you. [ˌnaɪs tə ˈmiːt jə] Es freut mich, Sie/dich kennen zu lernen.

night [naɪt] Nacht; Abend

nightlife *(no pl)* [ˈnaɪtˌlaɪf] Nachtleben VI/5/W5

no [nəʊ] kein(e); nein

no one [ˈnəʊ wʌn] keiner, niemand V/4/M6

no sooner ... than [ˌnəʊ ˈsuːnə ðæn] gerade, kaum ... als, da VI/4/M1

Nobel Peace Prize [nəʊˌbel ˈpiːs praɪz] Friedensnobelpreis VI/3/11

nobody [ˈnəʊbɒdi] niemand

nocturnal [nɒkˈtɜːnl] nachtaktiv; nächtlich VI/3/M4

nod [nɒd] nicken

noise [nɔɪz] Lärm, Krach; Geräusch

noisy [ˈnɔɪzi] laut

non-smoking [ˌnɒnˈsməʊkɪŋ] Nichtraucher- VI/3/4

non-stop [ˌnɒn ˈstɒp] nonstop, ununterbrochen VI/4/M7

non-white [ˌnɒn ˈwaɪt] Farbige/r VI/3/11

noodle [ˈnuːdl] Nudel

normal [ˈnɔːml] normal, üblich

normally [ˈnɔːmli] normalerweise

north [nɔːθ] Norden

North America [ˌnɔːθ_əˈmerɪkə] Nordamerika

north-east [ˌnɔːθˈiːst] Nordosten V/1/7

north-east [ˌnɔːθˈiːst] nordöstlich, Nordost- V/1/M1

north-west [ˌnɔːθˈwest] Nordwesten V/1/7

Northern Ireland [ˌnɔːðn_ˈaɪələnd] Nordirland VI/1/2

nose [nəʊz] Nase

not [nɒt] nicht

not ... any longer [ˌnɒt_eni ˈlɒŋgə] nicht länger VI/1/6

° not at all [ˌnɒt_ət_ˈɔːl] überhaupt nicht VI/3/12

not only ... but also [ˌnɒt_ˌəʊnli ˌbʌt_ˈɔːlsəʊ] nicht nur ... sondern auch VI/4/M1

note [nəʊt] Notiz

note down [nəʊt ˈdaʊn] (sich) notieren

take/make notes (on) [ˌteɪk/ ˌmeɪk ˈnəʊts] (sich) Notizen machen (zu, über)

nothing [ˈnʌθɪŋ] nichts

206

for nothing [fə ˈnʌθɪŋ] umsonst V/4/M8

notice [ˈnəʊtɪs] bemerken

notice [ˈnəʊtɪs] Aushang, Anschlag VI/5/W4

noticeboard [ˈnəʊtɪsˌbɔːd] schwarzes Brett VI/6/MD1

noun [naʊn] Hauptwort, Substantiv

novel [ˈnɒvl] Roman V/4/M6

November [nəʊˈvembə] November

now [naʊ] jetzt

° **now and again** [ˌnaʊ ənd əˈgen] ab und zu VI/3/12

nowhere [ˈnəʊweə] nirgends, nirgendwo V/5/M11

number [ˈnʌmbə] Zahl; Ziffer, Nummer

nurse [nɜːs] (Kranken)schwester, (Kranken)pfleger

nursery teacher [ˈnɜːsəri ˌtiːtʃə] Erzieher/in V/5/2

O

(eight) o'clock [əˈklɒk] (acht) Uhr

object [ˈɒbdʒekt] Objekt, Gegenstand, Sache

observe [əbˈzɜːv] beobachten VI/4/6

ocean [ˈəʊʃn] Meer; Ozean

October [ɒkˈtəʊbə] Oktober

off [ɒf] weg von VI/1/3

off [ɒf] weg von, raus aus V/5/M11

be off [biˈɒf] weggehen

get (a week) off [ˌget (ə ˌwiːk) ˈɒf] (eine Woche) freibekommen VI/3/3

off-road [ˌɒfˈrəʊd] im Gelände VI/3/M4

offence [əˈfens] Straftat V/2/M5

offend sb [əˈfend ˌsʌmbədi] jdn beleidigen; jdn kränken V/2/2

offender [əˈfendə] (Straf)täter/in V/2/M5

offer [ˈɒfə] (an)bieten; Angebot VI/3/3

office [ˈɒfɪs] Büro VI/2/3

office administrator [ˌɒfɪs ədˈmɪnɪˌstreɪtə] Bürokaufmann/Bürokauffrau VI/2/5

official [əˈfɪʃl] offiziell, amtlich

often [ˈɒfn] oft, häufig

Oh dear! [əʊ ˈdɪə] Du meine Güte!

oil [ɔɪl] Öl

be okay with sth [biˌəʊˈkeɪ wɪð ˌsʌmθɪŋ] mit etw einverstanden sein VI/1/10

old [əʊld] alt

in old age [ɪnˌəʊldˈeɪdʒ] im (hohen) Alter VI/1/M4

old style [ˌəʊld ˈstaɪl] im alten Stil VI/3/M4

olive [ˈɒlɪv] Olive

on [ɒn] auf; am, an; über; bei; im

on location [ˌɒn ləʊˈkeɪʃn] vor Ort, Außenaufnahmen VI/2/M11

on one's own [ˌɒn wʌnzˈəʊn] allein(e)

on the one hand [ɒn ðə ˈwʌn ˌhænd] einerseits V/2/2

on the other hand [ɒn ðiˈʌðə ˌhænd] andererseits V/2/2

on the run [ˌɒn ðə ˈrʌn] auf der Flucht VI/6/R2

once [wʌns] einmal

at once [ət ˈwʌns] auf einmal V/4/M3

once and for all [ˌwʌns ənd fərˈɔːl] endgültig, ein für alle Mal VI/4/M5

once more [ˌwʌns ˈmɔː] wieder; noch einmal VI/6/R4

one another [ˌwʌn əˈnʌðə] einander VI/2/7

one day [ˌwʌn ˈdeɪ] eines Tages

onion [ˈʌnjən] Zwiebel

only [ˈəʊnli] nur

only [ˈəʊnli] erst V/3/M2

not only ... but also [ˌnɒt ˈəʊnli ˌbʌt ˈɔːlsəʊ] nicht nur ... sondern auch VI/4/M1

open [ˈəʊpən] (sich) öffnen; offen, geöffnet

open [ˈəʊpən] eröffnet werden

openly [ˈəʊpənli] offen; öffentlich VI/2/10

opinion [əˈpɪnjən] Meinung, Ansicht

in my opinion [ɪn ˈmaɪ əˌpɪnjən] meiner Meinung/Ansicht nach V/1/12

opponent [əˈpəʊnənt] Gegner/in; Gegenspieler/in

opportunity [ˌɒpəˈtjuːnəti] Möglichkeit, Chance; Gelegenheit V/5/M1

opposite [ˈɒpəzɪt] Gegenteil; gegenüber

optimism *(no pl)* [ˈɒptɪˌmɪzəm] Optimismus VI/3/M9

optimistic [ˌɒptɪˈmɪstɪk] optimistisch, zuversichtlich V/3/10

option [ˈɒpʃn] Wahl, Möglichkeit, Option VI/1/14

or [ɔː] oder

orange juice [ˈɒrɪndʒ ˌdʒuːs] Orangensaft

order [ˈɔːdə] bestellen; Ordnung, Reihenfolge; Bestellung VI/2/5

in order to [ɪnˈɔːdə tʊ] um zu V/1/M2

organic [ɔːˈgænɪk] biologisch angebaut VI/6/R3

organise [ˈɔːgənaɪz] organisieren V/2/7

organised [ˈɔːgənaɪzd] organisiert, geplant VI/5/R2

organization [ˌɔːgənaɪˈzeɪʃn] Organisation V/5/14

organizer [ˈɔːgəˌnaɪzə] Organisator/in VI/6/R4

origin [ˈɒrɪdʒɪn] Ursprung, Herkunft VI/3/M9

originally [əˈrɪdʒnəli] ursprünglich VI/5/R3

orphan [ˈɔːfn] Waise, Waisenkind V/4/M8

orphaned [ˈɔːfnd] elternlos V/4/M6

other [ˈʌðər] andere(r, s)

the other day [ðiˌʌðə ˈdeɪ] neulich, vor einigen Tagen VI/3/2

our [aʊə] unser(e)

ours [aʊəz] unsere(r, s)

ourselves [aʊəˈselvz] uns; selbst

out [aʊt] aus VI/1/3

say sth out loud [ˌseɪ ˌsʌmθɪŋ ˌaʊt ˈlaʊd] etw laut sagen VI/3/3

out of [aʊtˈɒv] aus

out of date [ˌaʊt ˌəv ˈdeɪt] überholt, nicht mehr aktuell, nicht mehr zeitgemäß VI/1/M6

outback *(no pl)* [ˈaʊtˌbæk] Hinterland (Australiens) V/1/2

outdoor(s) [ˌaʊtˈdɔː] draußen; im Freien; Outdoor-

outfit [ˈaʊtfɪt] Kleidung, Outfit VI/4/M5

outside [ˌaʊtˈsaɪd] außen, außerhalb; im Freien, draußen

oven [ˈʌvn] (Back)ofen V/6/1

over [ˈəʊvə] hinüber; vorbei; über

over the radio [ˌəʊvə ðə ˈreɪdiəʊ] über Funk V/1/5

overcome [ˌəʊvəˈkʌm] überwinden, bewältigen VI/3/2

do overtime [ˌduː ˈəʊvəˌtaɪm] Überstunden machen VI/2/10

overweight [ˌəʊvəˈweɪt] übergewichtig V/4/5

own [əʊn] eigene(r, s); besitzen V/5/13

on one's own [ɒn wʌnz ˈəʊn] allein(e) V/5/3

owner [ˈəʊnə] Besitzer/in, Eigentümer/in VI/2/10

ozone hole [ˈəʊzəʊn ˌhəʊl] Ozonloch V/1/M3

P

p (= penny, pence) [piː, ˈpeni, pens] Penny, Centstück V/5/11

pack [pæk] packen

packaging [ˈpækɪdʒɪŋ] Verpackung(smaterial) V/6/5

packet [ˈpækɪt] Packung, Schachtel

pad [pæd] -schützer

paddle [ˈpædl] Paddel V/3/M2

page [peɪdʒ] Seite

paint [peɪnt] malen; anstreichen

painter [ˈpeɪntə] Maler/in; Anstreicher/in; Lackierer/in V/5/2

painting [ˈpeɪntɪŋ] Bild, Gemälde

pair [peə] Paar

panic [ˈpænɪk] in Panik geraten

paper [ˈpeɪpə] Papier

paper bank [ˈpeɪpə bæŋk] Altpapiercontainer V/6/M4

parade [pəˈreɪd] Parade, Umzug

paragraph [ˈpærəˌgrɑːf] Absatz, Abschnitt

paramedic [ˌpærəˈmedɪk] Rettungssanitäter/in

° **paramilitary** [ˌpærəˈmɪlɪtri] paramilitärisch VI/1/PP

parent [ˈpeərənt] Elternteil, Erziehungsberechtigte/r VI/4/M7

parenting *(no pl)* [ˈpeərəntɪŋ] Verhalten als Eltern, Kindererziehung VI/1/14

parents [ˈpeərənts] Eltern

park [pɑːk] Park, Parkanlagen

park ranger [ˈpɑːk ˌreɪndʒə] Parkaufseher/in, Ranger/in

part [pɑːt] Teil

part [pɑːt] Rolle

part-time [ˌpɑːtˈtaɪm] Teilzeit-

partner [ˈpɑːtnə] Partner

party [ˈpɑːti] Partei VI/3/11

pass [pɑːs] bestehen VI/5/L3; verabschieden *(Gesetz)* VI/2/CIO

passenger [ˈpæsɪndʒə] Passsagier/in, Fluggast; Fahrgast VI/3/4

passive [ˈpæsɪv] passiv VI/4/2

passport [ˈpɑːspɔːt] (Reise)pass V/2/5

password [ˈpɑːsˌwɜːd] Passwort V/2/9

past [pɑːst] Vergangenheit; vorbei/vorüber an

pasta [ˈpæstə] Nudeln, Teigwaren

path [pɑːθ] Weg, Pfad

patient [ˈpeɪʃnt] geduldig; Patient/in

° **pattern** [ˈpætən] Muster VI/4/PP

pause [pɔːz] innehalten VI/1/6

paw [pɔː] Pfote, Tatze V/1/9

pay [peɪ] bezahlen

pay cash [peɪ ˈkæʃ] bar bezahlen V/5/13

pay *(no pl)* [peɪ] Lohn, Gehalt VI/2/10

PE (= physical education) [ˌpiː ˈiː, ˌfɪzɪkl ˌedjuˈkeɪʃn] Sport(unterricht)

pea [piː] Erbse

peace [piːs] Frieden

° **hold peace talks** [ˌhəʊld ˈpiːs tɔːks] Friedensverhandlungen führen VI/1/PP

peaceful [ˈpiːsfl] friedlich VI/3/11

peanut [ˈpiːˌnʌt] Erdnuss

pear [peə] Birne

pen [pen] Feder, Stift

pencil [ˈpensl] Bleistift

pencil case [ˈpensl ˌkeɪs] Federmäppchen

penguin [ˈpeŋgwɪn] Pinguin

people *(pl)* [ˈpiːpl] Leute, Menschen

pepper [ˈpepə] Pfeffer; Paprika

per [pɜː] pro V/1/6

per cent [pəˈsent] Prozent

perfect [ˈpɜːfɪkt] perfekt VI/5/W5

perfectly [ˈpɜːfɪktli] vollkommen VI/4/M7

perform [pəˈfɔːm] vorführen; aufführen

perform [pəˈfɔːm] auftreten VI/5/R3

perhaps [pəˈhæps] vielleicht

period [ˈpɪəriəd] Periode, Zeitraum VI/3/M9

person [ˈpɜːsn] Person, Mensch

personal [ˈpɜːsnəl] persönlich; privat V/2/9

personality [ˌpɜːsəˈnæləti] Persönlichkeit, Charakter V/3/10

pet [pet] Haustier

the Philippines [ðə ˈfɪləpiːnz] die Philippinen V/1/4

phone [fəʊn] anrufen; Telefon

answer the phone [ˌɑːnsə ðə ˈfəʊn] ans Telefon gehen, einen Anruf entgegennehmen VI/4/CIO

phone card [ˈfəʊn kɑːd] Telefonkarte VI/5/MD2

phone-in [ˈfəʊnɪn] *Sendung, bei der sich das Publikum telefonisch beteiligen kann* VI/5/R3

photo [ˈfəʊtəʊ] Foto

take photos [ˌteɪk ˈfəʊtəʊz] Bilder machen, fotografieren

phrase [freɪz] Satz; Ausdruck, (Rede)wendung

phrase book ['freɪz bʊk] Sprachführer VI/2/M8

physical ['fɪzɪkl] körperlich, physisch V/3/M2

pick [pɪk] pflücken, sammeln V/5/M1

pick on sb ['pɪk ˌɒn ˌsʌmbədi] auf jdm herumhacken

pick pockets ['pɪk ˌpɒkɪts] Taschendiebstahl begehen V/4/M10

pick up [ˌpɪk ˈʌp] aufheben VI/6/4

pick up [ˌpɪk ˈʌp] abholen; aufheben; hochheben VI/1/M8

picnic ['pɪknɪk] Picknick

picture ['pɪktʃə] Bild, Foto

picture sth ['pɪktʃə ˌsʌmθɪŋ] sich etw vorstellen VI/3/9

take pictures [ˌteɪk 'pɪktʃəz] Bilder machen, fotografieren VI/1/M1

pie [paɪ] Pastete; Kuchen

pie chart ['paɪ tʃɑːt] Tortendiagramm VI/4/M9

pie-eating contest [ˌpaɪ iːtɪŋ 'kɒntest] Kuchenwettessen

piece [piːs] Stück

piece of paper [ˌpiːs əv 'peɪpə] Blatt Papier, Zettel

pig [pɪg] Schwein

pile into (the car) [ˌpaɪl 'ɪntʊ] sich in (das Auto) zwängen VI/3/M4

The Pilgrims *(pl)* [ðə 'pɪlgrɪms] die Pilger(väter)

pilot ['paɪlət] Pilot/in

pink [pɪŋk] rosa, pink

pistol ['pɪstl] Pistole VI/4/M5

pizza ['piːtsə] Pizza

place [pleɪs] Ort; Platz

at someone's place [ət 'sʌmwʌnz ˌpleɪs] bei jdm zu Hause VI/1/5

in the first place [ɪn ðə 'fɜːst ˌpleɪs] zunächst (einmal), an erster Stelle VI/1/10

placemat ['pleɪsˌmæt] Set, Platzdeckchen VI/3/M1

plan [plæn] Plan; planen

° **go to plan** [ˌgəʊ tə 'plæn] nach Plan verlaufen VI/2/1

plane [pleɪn] Flugzeug

planet ['plænɪt] Planet V/6/3

plant [plɑːnt] Pflanze; pflanzen V/6/8

plastic ['plæstɪk] Plastik, Kunststoff V/6/3

plastic bottle bank ['plæstɪk ˌbɒtl bæŋk] Plastikflaschencontainer V/6/M4

plate [pleɪt] Teller

platform ['plætˌfɔːm] Plattform; Bahnsteig

play [pleɪ] Spiel; (Theater)stück; spielen

player ['pleɪə] Spieler/in

playful ['pleɪfl] spielerisch, scherzhaft; verspielt

playground ['pleɪˌgraʊnd] Spielplatz

playing field ['pleɪŋ ˌfiːld] Sportplatz; Spielfeld

please [pliːz] bitte

Pleased to meet you. [ˌpliːzd tə 'miːt jʊ] Freut mich, dich/euch/Sie kennen zu lernen.

plenty ['plenti] mehr als genug

plot [plɒt] Handlung VI/1/M7

plumber ['plʌmə] Klempner/in, Sanitärinstallateur/in VI/2/3

pm (= post meridiem) [ˌpiː 'em, ˌpəʊst məˌrɪdiəm] nachmittags, abends *(nur hinter Uhrzeit zwischen 12 Uhr mittags und Mitternacht)*

pocket ['pɒkɪt] Tasche

pocket money ['pɒkɪt ˌmʌni] Taschengeld V/5/13

poem ['pəʊɪm] Gedicht

poetry *(no pl)* ['pəʊtri] Lyrik, Dichtung VI/4/M2

point [pɔɪnt] Punkt

point of view [ˌpɔɪnt əv 'vjuː] Standpunkt, Gesichtspunkt VI/1/M9

point out sth [ˌpɔɪnt 'aʊt ˌsʌmθɪŋ] auf etw hinweisen/zeigen VI/3/8

I can see your point. [ˌaɪ kən ˌsiː jɔː 'pɔɪnt] Ich weiß, was du sagen willst. VI/5/S2

police *(npl)* [pə'liːs] Polizei

police officer [pə'liːs ˌɒfɪsə] Polizeibeamter/-beamtin

policeman/-woman [pə'liːsmən, pə'liːsˌwʊmən] Polizist/in

polite [pə'laɪt] höflich

political [pə'lɪtɪkl] politisch VI/3/5

politician [ˌpɒlə'tɪʃn] Politiker/in VI/3/13

pollute [pə'luːt] verschmutzen V/6/13

polluted [pə'luːtɪd] verschmutzt V/6/8

pollution [pə'luːʃn] (Umwelt)verschmutzung V/6/3

pony ['pəʊni] Pony

poor [pɔː] arm

poor man *(informal)* [ˌpɔː 'mæn] der Arme VI/2/M5

the poor *(pl)* [ðə pɔː] die Armen VI/4/M1

popsicle ['pɒpsɪkl] Eis am Stiel

popular ['pɒpjʊlə] beliebt

popularity *(no pl)* ['pɒpjʊˌlærəti] Beliebtheit, Popularität VI/4/M5

population [ˌpɒpjʊ'leɪʃn] Bevölkerung

pornography *(no pl)* [pɔː'nɒgrəfi] Pornografie VI/2/8

portable ['pɔːtəbl] tragbar VI/2/5

portfolio [pɔːt'fəʊliəʊ] (Akten)mappe VI/1/6

portion ['pɔːʃn] Portion V/4/M2

portrait ['pɔːtrɪt] Porträt, Darstellung VI/2/M10

position [pə'zɪʃn] Position, Stelle VI/2/3

positive ['pɒzətɪv] positiv VI/4/M7

possible ['pɒsəbl] möglich V/4/4

post office ['pəʊst ˌɒfɪs] Postamt

post sth ['pəʊst ˌsʌmθɪŋ] etw ins Internet stellen

post- [pəʊst] nach-/Nach-, post-/Post- VI/3/M9

postcard ['pəʊstˌkɑːd] Postkarte

potato *(pl -es)* [pə'teɪtəʊ, pə'teɪtəʊz] Kartoffel

pound (£) [paʊnd] Pfund

poverty ['pɒvəti] Armut VI/3/2

power [ˈpaʊə] Kraft, Stärke V/3/M2; Macht; Einfluss VI/4/M5

° **come into power** [ˌkʌm ˌɪntə ˈpaʊə] an die Macht kommen VI/3/PP

powerful [ˈpaʊəfl] mächtig; leistungsfähig VI/4/13; stark, heftig VI/4/1

practical [ˈpræktɪkl] praktisch VI/2/3

practice [ˈpræktɪs] Übung; Training

practise [ˈpræktɪs] üben

practise [ˈpræktɪs] praktizieren, ausüben

Prague [prɑːg] Prag VI/6/R2

° **preacher** [ˈpriːtʃə] Geistliche/r, Pfarrer/in VI/3/12

predator [ˈpredətə] Raubtier VI/3/5

prefer [prɪˈfɜː] vorziehen, bevorzugen

pregnancy [ˈpregnənsi] Schwangerschaft VI/1/10

pregnant [ˈpregnənt] schwanger V/5/13

prejudice [ˈpredʒʊdɪs] Vorurteil

prepaid [ˌpriːˈpeɪd] im Voraus bezahlt VI/5/MD2

prepare [prɪˈpeə] vorbereiten

present [ˈpreznt] Geschenk

present [ˈpreznt] Gegenwart VI/3/I

present [prɪˈzent] darstellen VI/3/4

present (to) [prɪˈzent] bieten; präsentieren

presentation [ˌpreznˈteɪʃn] Präsentation

give a presentation [ˌgɪv ə ˌpreznˈteɪʃn] eine Präsentation halten VI/3/I

president [ˈprezɪdənt] Präsident/in; Vorsitzende/r

press [pres] drücken

° **pressure** [ˈpreʃə] Druck VI/3/12

pretty [ˈprɪti] hübsch; ziemlich

previous experience [ˌpriːviəs ɪkˈspɪəriəns] Vorkenntnisse VI/2/M6

price [praɪs] Preis

pride [praɪd] Stolz

primary school [ˈpraɪməri ˌskuːl] Grundschule V/5/4

prince [prɪns] Prinz

print (out) [prɪnt] (aus)drucken V/2/9

printer cartridge [ˈprɪntə ˌkɑːtrɪdʒ] Druckerpatrone V/6/M2

prison [ˈprɪzn] Gefängnis V/1/12

prisoner [ˈprɪznə] Gefangene/r

privacy *(no pl)* [ˈprɪvəsi] Privatsphäre VI/4/13

private [ˈpraɪvət] privat; vertraulich V/2/10

private room [ˌpraɪvət ˈruːm] Einzelzimmer V/1/6

prize [praɪz] Preis, Gewinn

probably [ˈprɒbəbli] wahrscheinlich

problem [ˈprɒbləm] Problem

process [ˈprəʊses] Prozess, Vorgang VI/2/M11

Prod *(informal)* [prɒd] Protestant/in VI/1/3

produce [prəˈdjuːs] herstellen, erzeugen, produzieren VI/2/5

producer [prəˈdjuːsə] Produzent/in; Hersteller

product [ˈprɒdʌkt] Produkt, Erzeugnis

production assistant [prəˈdʌkʃn əˌsɪstnt] Produktionsassistent/in VI/2/M11

production *(no pl)* [prəˈdʌkʃn] Produktion, Herstellung VI/2/11

professional [prəˈfeʃnəl] professionell, Profi-; Profi V/3/5

profile [ˈprəʊfaɪl] Profil VI/4/10

program *(AE)* = programme *(BE)* [ˈprəʊgræm] Programm VI/5/R4

programme [ˈprəʊgræm] Programm; Sendung

programmed [ˈprəʊgræmd] programmiert V/6/8

programmer [ˈprəʊgræmə] Programmierer/in VI/2/3

project [ˈprɒdʒekt] Projekt

promise [ˈprɒmɪs] versprechen

properly [ˈprɒpəli] korrekt, richtig VI/2/10

prostitute [ˈprɒstɪtjuːt] Prostituierte/r VI/2/10

prostitution *(no pl)* [ˌprɒstɪˈtjuːʃn] Prostitution VI/2/8

protect [prəˈtekt] schützen

protection [prəˈtekʃn] Schutz VI/4/M3

protein [ˈprəʊtiːn] Eiweiß, Protein V/4/3

protest [ˈprəʊtest] Protest(kundgebung) VI/2/11

protest (against sth) [prəˈtest (əˌgenst ˌsʌmθɪŋ)] (gegen etw) protestieren VI/6/R4

Protestant [ˈprɒtɪstənt] Protestant/in; protestantisch VI/1/2

proud [praʊd] stolz

provide [prəˈvaɪd] zur Verfügung stellen, sorgen für VI/4/M3

provide [prəˈvaɪd] bieten, geben, sorgen für VI/3/5

provided [prəˈvaɪdɪd] sofern, vorausgesetzt VI/1/M4

provoke [prəˈvəʊk] provozieren V/3/10

psychologist [saɪˈkɒlədʒɪst] Psychologe/Psychologin V/4/9

pub [pʌb] Kneipe

public [ˈpʌblɪk] öffentlich V/3/5

publish [ˈpʌblɪʃ] veröffentlichen V/4/M6

pull [pʊl] ziehen

° **pulse** [pʌls] (Im)puls VI/4/PP

punctual [ˈpʌŋktʃuəl] pünktlich V/5/3

punish [ˈpʌnɪʃ] bestrafen V/2/M5

pupil [ˈpjuːpl] Schüler/in

puppy [ˈpʌpi] junger Hund, Welpe

pure [pjʊə] rein, pur V/4/M2

purpose [ˈpɜːpəs] Zweck VI/5/R2

push [pʊʃ] schieben; drücken; stoßen

put [pʊt] setzen, legen, stellen

put on [pʊt ˈɒn] anziehen; sich eincremen mit

put on sth [ˌpʊtˌˈɒn ˌsʌmθɪŋ]
etw einschalten/anmachen
VI/1/M8

put on weight [ˌpʊtˌˈɒn ˌweɪt]
zunehmen V/4/9

put out sth [pʊtˌˈaʊt ˌsʌmθɪŋ] etw
löschen; etw ausmachen

put sb in touch with sb [ˌpʊt
ˌsʌmbədiˌɪn ˈtʌtʃ wɪð ˌsʌmbədi]
jdm helfen, mit jdm Kontakt
aufzunehmen VI/1/14

put up [pʊtˌˈʌp] aufhängen

pyjamas *(pl)* [pəˈdʒɑːməz]
Pyjama, Schlafanzug V/1/5

Q

quake *(informal)* [kweɪk]
(Erd)beben VI/5/R3

qualification [ˌkwɒlɪfɪˈkeɪʃn]
Qualifikation; Abschluss
V/5/M2

qualified [ˈkwɒlɪfaɪd] qualifiziert,
kompetent, ausgebildet
VI/5/R2

quality [ˈkwɒləti] Qualität, Güte
V/5/M1

quarter (past/to) [ˈkwɔːtə] Viertel
(nach/vor)

queen [kwiːn] Königin

question [ˈkwestʃn] Frage

question sth [ˈkwestʃn ˌsʌmθɪŋ]
etw in Frage stellen, etw
hinterfragen VI/3/M9

ask questions [ɑːskˌˈkwestʃnz]
Fragen stellen

queue [kjuː] Schlange, Reihe

quick [kwɪk] schnell

quiet [ˈkwaɪət] leise, ruhig

quite [kwaɪt] ziemlich

quite [kwaɪt] ganz, völlig
VI/5/R4

quiz sb [ˈkwɪzˌsʌmbədi] jdn
befragen/prüfen VI/1/CIO

quotation [kwəʊˈteɪʃn] Zitat
VI/4/10

R

rabbit [ˈræbɪt] Kaninchen

race [reɪs] Rennen

race [reɪs] Rasse V/2/M1

racial [ˈreɪʃl] rassisch, Rassen-
VI/3/11

racism *(no pl)* [ˈreɪˌsɪzm]
Rassismus VI/3/13

racist [ˈreɪsɪst] Rassist/in;
rassistisch V/2/M1

radar [ˈreɪdɑː] Radar VI/4/6

radio [ˈreɪdiəʊ] Radio

radio station [ˈreɪdiəʊ ˌsteɪʃn]
Radiosender VI/1/M3

radioactive [ˌreɪdiəʊˈæktɪv]
radioaktiv VI/3/4

raft [rɑːft] Floß

from rags to riches [frəm ˌrægz tə
ˈrɪtʃɪz] vom Tellerwäscher zum
Millionär VI/2/M10

rail [reɪl] Geländer V/3/5

railroad *(AE)* = railway *(BE)*
[ˈreɪlˌrəʊd] Schienen;
(Eisen)bahn

rain [reɪn] Regen; regnen

rainbow [ˈreɪnˌbəʊ] Regenbogen
VI/3/13

rainforest [ˈreɪnˌfɒrɪst]
Regenwald

rainy [ˈreɪni] regnerisch

raise [reɪz] großziehen,
aufziehen VI/1/M3

raise money [reɪz ˈmʌni] Geld
aufbringen/auftreiben

ramp [ræmp] Rampe V/3/5

rand [rænd] Rand *(Währung in
Südafrika)* VI/5/MD3

range [reɪndʒ] Bereich, Spektrum
VI/6/W1; Reihe, Sortiment,
Kollektion VI/6/R3

rank [ræŋk] einstufen; anordnen

rat [ræt] Ratte

rate [reɪt] Rate, Quote VI/5/L3

rather [ˈrɑːðə] lieber VI/2/3

raven [ˈreɪvn] Rabe

reach [riːtʃ] greifen; erreichen
VI/1/7

react [riˈækt] reagieren
V/4/10

reaction (to) [riˈækʃn] Reaktion
(auf) V/4/5

read [riːd] lesen

read [riːd] lauten VI/6/R2

read along [ˌriːdˌəˈlɒŋ]
mitlesen

read out [ˌriːdˌˈaʊt] (laut)
vorlesen VI/3/3

ready [ˈredi] fertig

(Are you) ready to order? [ˌredi
təˌˈɔːdə] Möchten Sie schon
bestellen?

real [rɪəl] wirklich; echt

realise sth [ˈrɪəlaɪz] sich einer
Sache bewusst werden
V/2/M2

realistic [ˌrɪəˈlɪstɪk] realistisch
VI/2/2

really [ˈrɪəli] wirklich

reason [ˈriːzn] Grund

reassure [ˌriːəˈʃʊə] beruhigen
VI/1/M4

rebuild [ˌriːˈbɪld] wieder
aufbauen VI/4/2

receipt [rɪˈsiːt] Beleg; Kassenbon

receive [rɪˈsiːv] empfangen,
erhalten VI/5/W3

reception *(no pl)* [rɪˈsepʃn]
Empfang, Rezeption VI/2/M6

receptionist [rɪˈsepʃnɪst]
Empfangschef/in V/1/6

recipe [ˈresəpi] Rezept

recognize [ˈrekəgnaɪz]
(wieder)erkennen VI/1/5

recruit sb [rɪˈkruːt ˌsʌmbədi] jdn
einstellen VI/2/M6

recycle [riːˈsaɪkl]
wiederverwerten, recyclen
V/6/3

recycled [riːˈsaɪkld]
wiederverwertet, recycelt
VI/6/R3

red [red] rot

the Red Cross [ðə ˌred ˈkrɒs] das
Rote Kreuz VI/4/2

reduce [rɪˈdjuːs] verringern,
reduzieren, verkleinern V/6/3

reef [riːf] Riff V/1/M1

referee [ˌrefəˈriː] Schiedsrich-
ter/in

referee [ˌrefəˈriː] Referenz
VI/2/M7

refill [riːˈfɪl] auffüllen, nachfüllen
V/6/M2

refresher course [rɪˈfreʃə ˌkɔːs]
Auffrischungskurs VI/5/R2

refuse [rɪˈfjuːz] ablehnen, sich
weigern VI/2/10

register [ˈredʒɪstə] sich
(an)melden, sich eintragen
VI/6/R1

registered ['redʒɪstəd] registriert, eingetragen VI/6/LG1

regular ['regjʊlə] regelmäßig; üblich, normal

relationship [rɪ'leɪʃnʃɪp] Beziehung VI/4/10

relative ['relətɪv] Verwandte/r, Angehörige/r

relative pronoun [ˌrelətɪv 'prəʊnaʊn] Relativpronomen VI/1/M3

relax [rɪ'læks] sich entspannen VI/5/R2

relaxing [rɪ'læksɪŋ] entspannend V/1/10

release [rɪ'liːs] herausbringen, veröffentlichen V/3/M8

reliable [rɪ'laɪəbl] verlässlich, zuverlässig V/5/3

religion [rɪ'lɪdʒn] Religion; Glaube

religious [rə'lɪdʒəs] religiöse(r, s), Religions-

rely on [rɪ'laɪ ˌɒn] sich verlassen auf VI/4/6

remain [rɪ'meɪn] bleiben, anhalten VI/3/13

remember [rɪ'membə] sich erinnern (an)

remove [rɪ'muːv] entfernen

rent [rent] Miete

repair [rɪ'peə] reparieren

repair [rɪ'peə] Reparatur VI/2/3

repeat [rɪ'piːt] Wiederholung

repeat [rɪ'piːt] wiederholen V/4/M6

replace [rɪ'pleɪs] ersetzen

report [rɪ'pɔːt] Bericht; berichten; (sich) melden

reporter [rɪ'pɔːtə] Reporter/in

reporting *(no pl)* [rɪ'pɔːtɪŋ] Berichterstattung VI/4/3

° Republic of Ireland [rɪˌpʌblɪk ˌəv ˈaɪələnd] Republik Irland VI/1/PP

reputation *(no pl)* [ˌrepjʊ'teɪʃn] Ruf, Ansehen VI/3/11

request [rɪ'kwest] Bitte, Anfrage; Wunsch; bitten (um); (sich) wünschen

require sb to do sth [rɪˌkwaɪə ˌsʌmbədi tə 'duː, ˌsʌmθɪŋ] von jdm verlangen, etw zu tun VI/1/14

required [rɪ'kwaɪəd] erforderlich VI/2/M6

rescue ['reskjuː] retten

rescue worker ['reskjuː ˌwɜːkə] Rettungskraft VI/4/2

do research [duː rɪ'sɜːtʃ] recherchieren VI/4/M9

research *(no pl)* [rɪ'sɜːtʃ] Forschung, Erforschung, Recherche VI/2/M13

reservation [ˌrezə'veɪʃn] Reservierung; Reservat *(= ein den Indianern vorbehaltenes Gebiet)*

resistance *(no pl)* [rɪ'zɪstns] Widerstand VI/3/11

respect [rɪ'spekt] Respekt, Achtung; respektieren, anerkennen

responsibility [rɪˌspɒnsə'bɪləti] Verantwortlichkeit, Zuständigkeit; Verantwortung V/2/5

responsible [rɪ'spɒnsəbl] verantwortungsbewusst VI/6/W3

be responsible for sth [biː rɪ'spɒnsəbl fə ˌsʌmθɪŋ] für etw verantwortlich sein; für etw haften V/2/5

rest [rest] Rest V/2/2

rest [rest] (Ruhe)pause; Erholung VI/6/L2

restaurant ['restrɒnt] Restaurant

restore [rɪ'stɔː] wiederherstellen VI/4/M3

result [rɪ'zʌlt] Folge; Ergebnis

return [rɪ'tɜːn] zurückkehren V/6/8

return (ticket) [rɪ'tɜːn] Hin- und Rückfahrkarte

reuse [riː'juːz] wiederverwenden V/6/3

review [rɪ'vjuː] Kritik, Rezension VI/1/10

reviewer [rɪ'vjuːə] Rezensent/in, Kritiker/in VI/1/12

reward [rɪ'wɔːd] Belohnung VI/5/W4

rhino (= rhinocerus) ['raɪnəʊ, raɪ'nɒsrəs] Nashorn, Rhinozeros VI/3/M4

rhythm ['rɪðəm] Rhythmus, Takt V/1/10

rice [raɪs] Reis

rich [rɪtʃ] reich

from rags to riches [frəm ˌrægz tə 'rɪtʃɪz] vom Tellerwäscher zum Millionär VI/2/M10

get rid of sth [get 'rɪd ˌəv ˌsʌmθɪŋ] etw loswerden V/3/M8

ride [raɪd] fahren; reiten

ride [raɪd] Fahrt VI/5/R3

rider ['raɪdə] Reiter/in

riding ['raɪdɪŋ] Reiten

right [raɪt] (nach) rechts; Recht; richtig

right [raɪt] genau, direkt VI/4/2

be right [bi 'raɪt] Recht haben

on the right [ˌɒn ðə 'raɪt] rechts, auf der rechten Seite

right from the start [ˌraɪt frəm ðə 'stɑːt] von vornherein, von Beginn/Anfang an VI/2/CIO

ring [rɪŋ] klingeln, läuten; Ring VI/4/M6

rise [raɪz] (auf)steigen VI/4/2

risk [rɪsk] Risiko, Gefahr V/3/5

river ['rɪvə] Fluss

road [rəʊd] Straße

roar [rɔː] brüllen VI/1/2

robot ['rəʊbɒt] Roboter V/6/8

rock [rɒk] Stein, Fels(en)

rocket ['rɒkɪt] (Marsch)flugkörper, Rakete(ngeschoss) VI/4/M5

role [rəʊl] Rolle

roll [rəʊl] Brötchen

Roman ['rəʊmən] Römer/in; römisch VI/4/M5

romance [rəʊ'mæns] Romanze; Liebesfilm

romantic [rəʊ'mæntɪk] romantisch V/6/8

Rome [rəʊm] Rom VI/4/M5

roof [ruːf] Dach VI/1/2

° rooftop ['ruːfˌtɒp] (Haus)dach VI/4/M2

room [ruːm] Zimmer

root [ruːt] Wurzel VI/3/M3
rope [rəʊp] Seil
rotate [rəʊˈteɪt] rotieren, sich drehen VI/5/MD3
rotating [rəʊˈtaɪtɪŋ] rotierend VI/4/1
round [raʊnd] um VI/5/R3
route [ruːt] Route, Strecke, Verlauf VI/2/5
° row [rəʊ] Reihe VI/4/M2
royal [ˈrɔɪəl] königlich VI/3/11
rubber *(BE)* [ˈrʌbə] Gummi; Radiergummi
rubbish [ˈrʌbɪʃ] Müll
rude [ruːd] unhöflich
ruin [ˈruːɪn] ruinieren, zerstören VI/1/M3
rule [ruːl] Regel
ruler [ˈruːlə] Lineal
ruling [ˈruːlɪŋ] herrschend, regierend VI/3/11
run [rʌn] laufen, rennen
run [rʌn] etw leiten/betreiben/führen VI/6/R2; regieren VI/3/12
on the run [ˌɒn ðə ˈrʌn] auf der Flucht VI/6/R2
run after [ˌrʌn ˈɑːftə] hinterherlaufen
run away [ˌrʌn əˈweɪ] weglaufen VI/1/6
run into [ˌrʌn ˈɪntʊ] in jdn/etw hineinrennen; jdm über den Weg laufen
runaway [ˈrʌnəˌweɪ] Ausreißer/in V/5/M11

S

sad [sæd] traurig
safe [seɪf] sicher
safety [ˈseɪfti] Sicherheit
sail [seɪl] segeln
salad [ˈsæləd] Salat
be on sale [bɪ ˌɒn ˈseɪl] reduziert sein; im Angebot sein
salesperson [ˈseɪlzˌpɜːsn] Verkäufer/in
salt [sɔːlt] Salz
the same [ðə ˈseɪm] der-/die-/dasselbe
same here [seɪm ˈhɪə] ich/wir auch

Saturday [ˈsætədeɪ] Samstag
sauce [sɔːs] Soße
sausage [ˈsɒsɪdʒ] Wurst, Würstchen
save [seɪv] retten; sparen V/5/13; speichern, sichern V/2/9
save up for sth [ˌseɪv ˈʌp fə ˌsʌmθɪŋ] auf/für etw sparen V/5/15
say [seɪ] sagen
say hello to [ˌseɪ həˈləʊ tə] (be)grüßen
say sth out loud [ˌseɪ ˌsʌmθɪŋ ˌaʊt ˈlaʊd] etw laut sagen VI/3/3
saying [ˈseɪɪŋ] Sprichwort
sb cannot wait to do sth [ˌsʌmbədi ˌkænɒt ˈweɪt tə duː ˌsʌmθɪŋ] jmd kann es kaum erwarten, etw zu tun VI/2/3
Scandinavia [ˌskændɪˈneɪviə] Skandinavien VI/2/M2
scare [skeə] Angst machen, erschrecken
scared [skeəd] verängstigt
be scared [bɪ ˈskeəd] Angst haben
scarf *(pl -s or* scarves*)* [skɑːf, skɑːvz] Schal
scary [ˈskeəri] Furcht erregend; unheimlich
scene [siːn] Szene
scenery *(no pl)* [ˈsiːnəri] Landschaft VI/5/MD3
school [skuːl] Schule
schoolbag [ˈskuːlbæg] Schultasche
schooling *(no pl)* [ˈskuːlɪŋ] Schulbildung; Ausbildung VI/2/9
schoolwork *(no pl)* [ˈskuːl ˌwɜːk] Schularbeiten V/1/5
science [ˈsaɪəns] Naturwissenschaft
scientist [ˈsaɪəntɪst] Wissenschaftler/in
(pair of) scissors [ˈsɪzəz] Schere
scooter [ˈskuːtə] (Tret)roller
score [skɔː] Punktestand
score [skɔː] einen Punkt machen, punkten

score a goal [ˌskɔːr ə ˈgəʊl] ein Tor schießen
Scotland [ˈskɒtlənd] Schottland
Scottish [ˈskɒtɪʃ] schottisch
scratch [skrætʃ] (zer)kratzen
scream [skriːm] schreien; kreischen
screen [skriːn] Leinwand VI/1/13
screw [skruː] Schraube V/3/5
script [skrɪpt] Drehbuch, Skript VI/1/10
sea [siː] Meer
search [sɜːtʃ] (durch)suchen; Suche VI/4/2
search engine [ˈsɜːtʃ ˈendʒɪn] Suchmaschine
seasick [ˈsiːˌsɪk] seekrank
seaside [ˈsiːˌsaɪd] Küste VI/3/5
seat [siːt] (Sitz)platz VI/3/4
second [ˈsekənd] Sekunde
° the Second World War [ðə ˌsekənd ˌwɜːld ˈwɔː] der Zweite Weltkrieg VI/2/PP
secondary school [ˈsekəndri ˌskuːl] höhere/weiterführende Schule
secret [ˈsiːkrət] geheim; Geheimnis
secretary [ˈsekrətri] Sekretär/in
secretly [ˈsiːkrətli] heimlich, im Stillen VI/2/10
section [ˈsekʃn] Bereich, Teil VI/5/I
sector [ˈsektə] Bereich, Sektor VI/4/M7
° secure [sɪˈkjʊə] sichern, garantieren VI/2/PP
security camera [sɪˈkjʊərəti ˌkæmrə] Überwachungskamera
security *(no pl)* [sɪˈkjʊərəti] Sicherheit; Sicherheitsdienst
see [siː] sehen
see [siː] einsehen, verstehen
° see [siː] (mit)erleben VI/1/PP
see sb off [ˌsiː ˌsʌmbədi ˈɒf] jdn verabschieden VI/1/7
See you! *(informal)* [ˈsiː jʊ] Bis bald!
seem [siːm] scheinen V/5/13
seize sb (by the shoulder) [ˈsiːz ˌsʌmbədi baɪ ðə ˈʃəʊldə] jdn (an der Schulter) packen VI/1/3

DICTIONARY   English–German

self-confidence (no pl) [selfˈkɒnfɪdns] Selbstvertrauen VI/3/M9

selfish [ˈselfɪʃ] egoistisch, selbstsüchtig VI/1/M4

sell [sel] verkaufen

seller [ˈselə] Verkäufer/in

semi-tunnel [ˈsemiˌtʌnl] Halbtunnel VI/3/5

semifinal [ˌsemiˈfaɪnl] Halbfinale

send [send] (zu)schicken

send out sth [ˌsendˌaʊt ˈsʌmθɪŋ] etw aussenden, etw abgeben VI/4/1

sensible [ˈsensəbl] vernünftig VI/4/10

sensitive [ˈsensətɪv] sensibel VI/4/10

sentence [ˈsentəns] Satz

sentence [ˈsentəns] Urteil, Strafe V/2/M5

sentence sb to sth [ˈsentənsˌsʌmbədi təˌsʌmθɪŋ] jdn zu etw verurteilen VI/3/11

separate [ˈseprət] getrennt, separat VI/3/13

separate [ˈsepəreɪt] trennen VI/3/11

September [sepˈtembə] September

serious [ˈsɪəriəs] ernst

seriously [ˈsɪəriəsli] ernst(lich), schwer VI/4/2

servant [ˈsɜːvnt] Diener/in, Dienstmädchen, Bedienstete/r V/1/M5

serve [sɜːv] servieren V/4/6

serve [sɜːv] dienen V/2/M5

serve [sɜːv] verbüßen, absitzen VI/6/R2

service [ˈsɜːvɪs] Service; Bedienung; Dienst VI/2/M2

set [set] festgefahren VI/1/M4

be set somewhere [biː ˌset ˈsʌmweə] irgendwo spielen/ stattfinden VI/1/CIO

set the table [ˌset ðə ˈteɪbl] den Tisch decken

set up [ˌsetˈʌp] aufbauen, einrichten VI/4/2

settle [ˈsetl] sich niederlassen

settle on sb [ˈsetlˌɒn ˌsʌmbədi] sich für jdn entscheiden, sich auf jdn einigen VI/2/M11

settlement [ˈsetlmənt] Siedlung V/1/M5

settler [ˈsetlə] Siedler/in

several [ˈsevrəl] einige V/1/M1

sew [səʊ] nähen VI/2/9

sex [seks] Geschlecht VI/4/10

shake [ʃeɪk] beben VI/4/1

shame [ʃeɪm] Schande; Scham VI/1/M4

° **shape** [ʃeɪp] Form; Art VI/3/12

share [ʃeə] teilen

shark (pl -s or -) [ʃɑːk, ʃɑːks] Hai(fisch)

sharp [ʃɑːp] scharf

she [ʃiː] sie

shed [ʃed] Schuppen

shed [ʃed] Regendach, Wartehäuschen VI/1/7

sheep (pl sheep) [ʃiːp] Schaf

shelf (pl shelves) [ʃelf, ʃelvz] Regal

shell [ʃel] Schale V/1/M1

shelter [ˈʃeltə] Schutz, Zuflucht VI/4/M1

shift [ˈʃɪft] Schicht V/5/2

shift work (no pl) [ˈʃɪft ˌwɜːk] Schichtarbeit, Schichtdienst

ship [ʃɪp] Schiff

shirt [ʃɜːt] Hemd V/5/M4

shit (informal) [ʃɪt] Kacke, Scheiße VI/1/M8

shock [ʃɒk] Schock VI/1/10

shock wave [ˈʃɒk weɪv] Stoßwelle, Druckwelle VI/4/1

shocked [ʃɒkt] schockiert, entsetzt

shocking [ˈʃɒkɪŋ] schockierend VI/4/M1

shoe [ʃuː] Schuh

shoot-out [ˈʃuːtˌaʊt] Schießerei VI/4/M5

shop [ʃɒp] Geschäft, Laden

shop assistant [ˈʃɒpˌəˌsɪstnt] Verkäufer/in

shopping mall [ˈʃɒpɪŋ mɔːl] Einkaufszentrum VI/3/5

short [ʃɔːt] kurz

shortly after [ˈʃɔːtliˌɑːftə] kurz nachdem VI/6/R4

should [ʃʊd] sollte/müsste

shoulder [ˈʃəʊldə] Schulter

shout [ʃaʊt] schreien, rufen

shove [ʃʌv] schieben, schubsen VI/1/3

show [ʃəʊ] zeigen

take a shower [teɪk əˈʃaʊə] duschen V/6/3

shy [ʃaɪ] schüchtern

sick [sɪk] krank V/4/9

sb feels sick [ˌsʌmbədi fiːlzˈsɪk] jdm ist schlecht/übel VI/3/M4

be sick of sth [biː ˈsɪkˌəvˌsʌmθɪŋ] etw satt haben, von etw genug haben VI/1/3

side [saɪd] Seite

side order [ˈsaɪdˌɔːdə] Beilage

sigh [saɪ] seufzen

sight [saɪt] Sehleistung; Sehenswürdigkeit

sign [saɪn] unterschreiben; signieren; Zeichen; (Straßen-/ Verkehrs)schild

sign up [ˌsaɪnˈʌp] sich anmelden VI/4/10

signal [ˈsɪgnl] Signal V/3/M2

signature [ˈsɪgnətʃə] Unterschrift

silly [ˈsɪli] albern, dumm

similar [ˈsɪmɪlə] ähnlich V/4/9

simple [ˈsɪmpl] einfach

since [sɪns] da, weil; seit V/3/4

since then [sɪns ˈðen] seitdem, seit damals VI/5/R2

sing [sɪŋ] singen

singer [ˈsɪŋə] Sänger/in

single [ˈsɪŋgl] einzelne(r, s) V/5/M11

single mother [ˌsɪŋgl ˈmʌðə] allein erziehende Mutter VI/3/M9

single room [ˈsɪŋgl ˌruːm] Einzelzimmer V/1/6

single (ticket) [ˈsɪŋgl] Einzelfahrkarte

° **single wire telegraph** [ˌsɪŋgl ˌwaɪə ˈtelɪˌgrɑːf] Eindrahttelegraf, Schreibtelegraf VI/4/PP

sink [sɪŋk] untergehen, sinken

sister [ˈsɪstə] Schwester

sit [sɪt] sitzen

sit down [sɪt ˈdaʊn] sich (hin)setzen

site *(informal)* [saɪt] Website
VI/4/9

situation [ˌsɪtʃuˈeɪʃn] Situation,
Lage

six-year [ˈsɪks jɪə] sechsjährig
VI/6/R2

sixth form *(BE)* [ˈsɪksθ fɔːm] *die
letzten zwei Schuljahre für
Schüler zwischen 16 und 18*
VI/2/3

size [saɪz] Größe

skate [skeɪt] Schlittschuh;
Skate-Veranstaltung; skaten,
Skateboard fahren V/3/5

skeleton [ˈskelɪtn] Skelett

ski [skiː] Ski V/3/4

skill [skɪl] Fähigkeit;
Geschick(lichkeit) V/3/4

skin [skɪn] Haut V/1/M3

skinny [ˈskɪni] dünn, mager
V/4/9

skirt [skɜːt] Rock

sky [skaɪ] Himmel V/1/11

skyline [ˈskaɪˌlaɪn] Skyline,
Horizont

skyscraper [ˈskaɪˌskreɪpə]
Wolkenkratzer

slap [slæp] schlagen VI/1/M4

slave [sleɪv] Sklave/Sklavin

sled [sled] Schlitten V/3/4

sleep [sliːp] schlafen

sleep [sliːp] Schlaf VI/1/M8

sleep suit [ˈsliːp ˌsuːt] (Baby-)
Schlafanzug VI/1/M8

sleepless [ˈsliːpləs] schlaflos
VI/1/M8

slice [slaɪs] Scheibe V/4/9

slim [slɪm] schlank, schmal,
dünn

slow [sləʊ] langsam

slum [slʌm] Slum, Elendsviertel
VI/2/M10

small [smɔːl] klein

smell [smel] Geruch; Duft;
Gestank; riechen

smile [smaɪl] lächeln

smoke [sməʊk] Rauch; rauchen

snack bar [ˈsnæk ˌbɑː]
Imbissstube

snake [sneɪk] Schlange

° sneak [sniːk] schleichen VI/3/12

snow [snəʊ] Schnee

so [səʊ] also, so

so far [ˈsəʊ fɑː] bisher, bis jetzt
V/3/M2

so what? *(informal)* [ˌsəʊ ˈwɒt] na
und? VI/1/3

so-called [ˌsəʊˈkɔːld] so genannt
VI/3/M4

soap (opera) [ˈsəʊpˌɒprə]
Seifenoper

soccer *(AE)* = football *(BE)*
[ˈsɒkə] Fußball

social [ˈsəʊʃl] gesellschaftlich,
sozial VI/3/M9

social network [ˌsəʊʃl ˈnetˌwɜːk]
soziales Netzwerk VI/4/10

social networking [ˌsəʊʃl
ˈnetˌwɜːkɪŋ] soziales
Netzwerken VI/4/9

social worker [ˌsəʊʃl ˈwɜːkə]
Sozialarbeiter/in

society [səˈsaɪəti] Gesellschaft
VI/3/11

sock [sɒk] Socke

sofa [ˈsəʊfə] Sofa, Couch

soft [sɒft] weich

soldier [ˈsəʊldʒə] Soldat/in
VI/2/10

solution [səˈluːʃn] Lösung
V/2/7

solve [sɒlv] lösen, klären
V/5/M11

some [sʌm] einige; etwas

somebody [ˈsʌmbədi] jemand

somehow [ˈsʌmhaʊ] irgendwie
VI/5/R4

someone [ˈsʌmwʌn] jemand

something [ˈsʌmθɪŋ] etwas

sometimes [ˈsʌmtaɪmz]
manchmal

somewhere [ˈsʌmweə] irgendwo

son [sʌn] Sohn

song [sɒŋ] Lied

soon [suːn] bald

no sooner ... than [ˌnəʊ ˈsuːnə
ðæn] gerade, kaum ... als, da
VI/4/M1

sore [sɔː] schlimm, weh; wund

feel sorry for sb [ˌfiːl ˈsɒri fə
sʌmbədi] Mitleid mit jdm
haben V/2/2

Sorry. [ˈsɒri] Verzeihung!,
Entschuldigung!; Wie bitte?

I'm sorry. [aɪm ˈsɒri] Das tut mir
leid.

sort [sɔːt] sortieren

sound [saʊnd] Geräusch, Klang;
Ton; klingen, sich anhören

soup [suːp] Suppe

south [saʊθ] Süden

South Africa [saʊθ ˈæfrɪkə]
Südafrika VI/3/1

South African [saʊθ ˈæfrɪkən]
Südafrikaner/in;
südafrikanisch VI/3/2

South America [ˌsaʊθ əˈmerɪkə]
Südamerika

south-east [ˌsaʊθˈiːst] Südosten
V/1/7

south-west [ˌsaʊθˈwest]
Südwesten V/1/7

° southern [ˈsʌðən] südlich, Süd-
VI/1/PP

Southern Right Whale [ˌsʌðən
ˌraɪt ˈweɪl] Südlicher Glattwal
VI/3/5

space [speɪs] Raum, Weltraum

space [speɪs] Platz,
Zwischenraum VI/6/LG1

spaceship [ˈspeɪsˌʃɪp]
Raumschiff

Spain [ˈspeɪn] Spanien

Spanish [ˈspænɪʃ] Spanier/in;
spanisch; Spanisch

speak [spiːk] sprechen

speak up [spiːkˈʌp] lauter
sprechen

special [ˈspeʃl] besondere(r, s)

specialist [ˈspeʃəlɪst] Spezia-
list/in, Fachmann/-frau VI/5/R2

spectacular [spekˈtækjʊlə]
fantastisch, sensationell
VI/3/5

speech [spiːtʃ] Rede VI/4/2

speed [spiːd] Geschwindigkeit,
Tempo VI/4/2

spell [spel] buchstabieren

spelling [ˈspelɪŋ]
Rechtschreibung

spend [spend] ausgeben *(Geld)*;
verbringen *(Zeit)*

spicy [ˈspaɪsi] würzig; scharf

spider [ˈspaɪdə] Spinne

spin (a)round [ˌspɪn (ə)ˈraʊnd]
(um)drehen VI/1/3

spirit *(no pl)* [ˈspɪrɪt] Stimmung, Geist VI/3/M9

spit out [ˌspɪt ˈaʊt] ausspucken V/1/M2

split up [ˌsplɪt ˈʌp] sich teilen; sich trennen

spoken [ˈspəʊkən] gesprochen VI/5/R2

spokesman/spokeswoman [ˈspəʊksmən, ˈspəʊksˌwʊmən] Sprecher/in VI/4/2

sponsor [ˈspɒnsə] sponsern, als Sponsor finanzieren

sponsored walk [ˌspɒnsəd ˈwɔːk] Wohltätigkeitslauf

sponsorship *(no pl)* [ˈspɒnsəʃɪp] finanzielle Förderung, Sponsoring, Unterstützung VI/5/R3

spooky *(informal)* [ˈspuːki] schaurig; unheimlich

spoon [spuːn] Löffel

sport [spɔːt] Sport; Sportart

sports field [ˈspɔːts ˌfiːld] Spielfeld, Sportplatz

sports programme [ˈspɔːts ˌprəʊgræm] Sportsendung

sportsmanship *(no pl)* [ˈspɔːtsmənʃɪp] Fairness

sportsperson [ˈspɔːtsˌpɜːsn] Sportler/in

spot [spɒt] entdecken

spotter [ˈspɒtə] *Person, die Extremwetterlagen aufspürt und meldet* VI/4/6

spray [spreɪ] (be)sprühen

spread [spred] verbreiten, ausbreiten VI/3/M9

spring [sprɪŋ] Frühling

spy [spaɪ] Spion/in V/3/M2

square [skweə] Quadrat; Platz

squeeze [skwiːz] drücken VI/1/M4

stability *(no pl)* [stəˈbɪləti] Stabilität; Gleichgewicht VI/4/6

stable [ˈsteɪbl] Stall, Box

stadium *(pl* -s *or* -ia) [ˈsteɪdɪəm, ˈsteɪdɪəmz, ˈsteɪdɪə] Stadion

staff *(no pl)* [stɑːf] Mitarbeiter, Personal, Belegschaft VI/2/M6

stage [steɪdʒ] Bühne

stairs *(npl)* [steəz] Treppe

stall [stɔːl] (Verkaufs)stand

stamp [stæmp] Stempel; Briefmarke

stand [stænd] stehen; ertragen, aushalten

stand up [ˌstænd ˈʌp] aufstehen

star [stɑː] Stern

star [stɑː] in einem Film/ Theaterstück auftreten V/3/M8

star sb [ˈstɑː ˌsʌmbədi] jdn in einer Hauptrolle zeigen VI/6/R4

stare at sb/sth [ˈsteə ət ˌsʌmbədi, ˌsʌmθɪŋ] jdn/etw anstarren V/3/10

start [stɑːt] anfangen; eröffnen, ins Leben rufen V/2/7

start [stɑːt] Anfang, Beginn

right from the start [ˌraɪt frəm ðə ˈstɑːt] von vornherein, von Beginn/Anfang an VI/2/CIO

start off (with sth) [ˌstɑːt ˈɒf (wɪð ˌsʌmθɪŋ)] (mit etw) anfangen VI/5/R3

starter [ˈstɑːtə] Vorspeise

starve [stɑːv] (ver)hungern V/4/M3

state [steɪt] (Bundes)staat

state [steɪt] aussprechen VI/1/10

state of emergency [ˌsteɪt əv ɪˈmɜːdʒnsi] Ausnahmezustand VI/4/2

° state sth [steɪt] etw nennen, etw angeben VI/2/PP

statement [ˈsteɪtmənt] Aussage; Äußerung

station [ˈsteɪʃn] Bahnhof; Station

statistics *(npl)* [stəˈtɪstɪks] Statistik VI/2/8

the Statue of Liberty [ðə ˈstætʃuː əv ˌlɪbəti] die Freiheitsstatue

status update [ˈsteɪtəs ˌʌpˌdeɪt] Aktualisierung des Status VI/4/10

stay [steɪ] bleiben; untergebracht sein, wohnen

stay [steɪ] Aufenthalt VI/5/R2

steal [stiːl] stehlen

step [step] Stufe; treten

° take a first step [ˌteɪk ə ˌfɜːst ˈstep] einen ersten Schritt machen/unternehmen VI/3/PP

stereo [ˈsteriəʊ] (Stereo)anlage

stick [stɪk] kleben; Stock

still [stɪl] (immer) noch, noch immer

still [stɪl] Standfoto VI/1/9

stomach ache [ˈstʌmək ˌeɪk] Magenschmerzen, Bauchschmerzen

stone [stəʊn] Stein

stop [stɒp] aufhören, beenden; anhalten

° stop [stɒp] (Zwischen)halt; Anlegestelle VI/3/PP

Stop it! [ˈstɒp ɪt] Hör(t) auf (damit)!

store [stɔː] (Lebensmittel)laden, Geschäft VI/6/R2

storm [stɔːm] Sturm

story [ˈstɔːri] Geschichte, Erzählung

straight [streɪt] gerade(aus)

straight [streɪt] glatt *(Haar)* V/3/M8

straight [streɪt] sofort VI/5/R4

strange [streɪndʒ] sonderbar; ungewöhnlich; fremd

stranger [ˈstreɪndʒə] Fremde/r

strategic thinking [strəˌtiːdʒɪk ˈθɪŋkɪŋ] strategisches Denken VI/4/M7

strawberry [ˈstrɔːbri] Erdbeere V/5/M1

street [striːt] Straße

streetside [ˈstriːtsaɪd] an der Straße gelegen VI/3/5

strength [streŋθ] Stärke, Kraft VI/6/R4

stress [stres] betonen, hervorheben VI/2/M11

stressed [ˈstrest] gestresst V/1/M2

stressful [ˈstresfl] stressig, anstrengend V/2/M2

stretch [stretʃ] (sich) dehnen

strict [strɪkt] streng V/1/12

strike [straɪk] angreifen, treffen, zuschlagen VI/4/2; Streik VI/2/10

go on strike [ˌgəʊ‿ɒn ˈstraɪk] streiken, in (den) Streik treten VI/2/10

stroke [strəʊk] streicheln

strong [strɒŋ] stark; robust, stabil V/5/8

structure [ˈstrʌktʃə] Gefüge, Struktur VI/3/M10

struggle [ˈstrʌgl] sich abmühen VI/3/M9

student [ˈstjuːdnt] Student/in, Studierende/r; Schüler/in

studio [ˈstjuːdiəʊ] Studio VI/2/M11

study [ˈstʌdi] studieren; lernen

stunt performer [ˈstʌnt pəˌfɔːmə] Stuntman, Stuntgirl

stupid [ˈstjuːpɪd] dumm, blöd

style [staɪl] Stil VI/3/M9

subject [ˈsʌbdʒɪkt] Thema; (Schul)fach

° **subjection** *(no pl)* [səbˈdʒekʃn] Unterwerfung; Abhängigkeit VI/3/12

° **subtitle** [ˈsʌbˌtaɪtl] Untertitel VI/2/CIO

subway *(AE)* = underground *(BE)* [ˈsʌbˌweɪ] U-Bahn

success *(no pl)* [səkˈses] Erfolg V/2/M5

successful [səkˈsesfl] erfolgreich

such as [ˈsʌtʃ‿əz] wie (zum Beispiel)

suddenly [ˈsʌdnli] plötzlich, auf einmal

sugar [ˈʃʊgə] Zucker

suggest [səˈdʒest] vorschlagen V/5/M10

suggestion [səˈdʒestʃn] Vorschlag VI/5/S3

suit [suːt] passen, recht sein; stehen

suitcase [ˈsuːtˌkeɪs] Koffer VI/1/7

suite [swiːt] Suite, Apartment, Wohnung VI/3/M3

sum [sʌm] Summe, Betrag VI/5/R3

summer [ˈsʌmə] Sommer

summer camp [ˈsʌmə ˌkæmp] Ferienlager

sun [sʌn] Sonne

sunbeam [ˈsʌnˌbiːm] Sonnenstrahl V/6/M1

Sunday [ˈsʌndeɪ] Sonntag

sunny [ˈsʌni] sonnig

sunscreen [ˈsʌnˌskriːn] Sonnencreme

sunset [ˈsʌnˌset] Sonnenuntergang VI/3/5

supermarket [ˈsuːpəˌmɑːkɪt] Supermarkt

support [səˈpɔːt] (unter)stützen VI/1/10

support *(no pl)* [səˈpɔːt] Unterstützung VI/2/M6

° **supporter** [səˈpɔːtə] Anhänger/in, Unterstützer/in VI/3/12

suppose [səˈpəʊz] denken, annehmen, vermuten V/4/M8

sure [ʃɔː] sicher

make sure [ˌmeɪk ˈʃɔː] sich versichern, darauf achten

surf the Internet [ˌsɜːf ði‿ˈɪntənet] im Internet surfen VI/2/M2

surname [ˈsɜːˌneɪm] Familienname, Nachname

surprise [səˈpraɪz] Überraschung; überraschen VI/3/2

surprised [səˈpraɪzd] überrascht

surprising [səˈpraɪzɪŋ] überraschend

surrounded (by) [səˈraʊndɪd] umgeben (von) VI/4/M1

survey [ˈsɜːveɪ] Untersuchung, Umfrage

survival [səˈvaɪvl] Überleben

survive [səˈvaɪv] überleben

survivor [səˈvaɪvə] Überlebende/r VI/4/2

swallow [ˈswɒləʊ] schlucken VI/1/6

swap [swɒp] tauschen

sweater [ˈswetə] Pullover, Sweater

sweatshop [ˈswetʃɒp] Ausbeuterbetrieb VI/6/R1

Sweden [ˈswiːdn] Schweden VI/2/M6

sweet [swiːt] süß; Süßigkeit(en)

sweetie paper [ˈswiːti ˌpeɪpə] Süßwaren-Einwickelpapier VI/6/R3

swim [swɪm] schwimmen

swimming [ˈswɪmɪŋ] Schwimmen

° swing opinions [ˌswɪŋ‿əˈpɪnjənz] Meinungen manipulieren VI/3/12

switch off [ˌswɪtʃ‿ˈɒf] ausschalten, abschalten VI/6/R1

symbol [ˈsɪmbl] Symbol, Zeichen

system [ˈsɪstəm] System VI/3/11

T

table [ˈteɪbl] Tisch

set the table [ˌset ðə ˈteɪbl] den Tisch decken

Table Mountain [ˈteɪbl ˌmaʊntɪn] Tafelberg VI/3/5

tackle sb [ˈtækl ˌsʌmbədi] jdn angreifen

take [teɪk] (mit)nehmen; dauern

° take [teɪk] brauchen VI/3/PP

take a bath [ˌteɪk‿ə ˈbɑːθ] baden V/6/3

° take a first step [ˌteɪk‿ə ˌfɜːst ˈstep] einen ersten Schritt machen/unternehmen VI/3/PP

take a shower [ˌteɪk‿ə ˈʃaʊə] duschen V/6/3

take a tour [ˌteɪk‿ə ˈtʊə] eine Tour/Führung machen VI/3/2

take action [ˌteɪk‿ˈækʃn] handeln, etw unternehmen V/6/3

take advantage of sth [ˌteɪk‿ədˈvɑːntɪdʒ‿əv ˌsʌmθɪŋ] etw (aus)nutzen VI/4/13

take care of [ˌteɪk‿ˈkeər‿əv] sich kümmern um, versorgen

take down [ˌteɪk ˈdaʊn] abnehmen, abmachen, entfernen VI/6/R2

take notes (on) [ˌteɪk ˈnəʊts] (sich) Notizen machen (zu, über)

take off [ˌteɪk‿ˈɒf] abnehmen; ausziehen

take oneself off [ˌteɪk wʌnˌself‿ˈɒf] sich davonmachen VI/1/3

take out [ˌteɪk‿ˈaʊt] herausnehmen

take part (in) [ˌteɪk ˈpɑːt] teilnehmen (an)

take photos [ˌteɪk ˈfəʊtəʊz] Bilder machen, fotografieren

take pictures [ˌteɪk ˈpɪktʃəz]
 Bilder machen, fotografieren
 VI/1/M1
take place [teɪk ˈpleɪs]
 stattfinden
take seriously [teɪk ˈsɪəriəsli]
 ernst nehmen VI/1/M8
take time off [ˌteɪk ˌtaɪm‿ˈɒf] sich
 freinehmen VI/5/R4
take time out [ˌteɪk ˌtaɪm‿ˈaʊt]
 sich eine Auszeit nehmen
 VI/5/W6
take turns [ˌteɪk ˈtɜːnz] sich
 abwechseln
takeaway [ˈteɪkəˌweɪ] Essen zum
 Mitnehmen
talk [tɔːk] Gespräch,
 Unterhaltung; Referat
give a talk [ˌgɪv‿ə ˈtɔːk] einen
 Vortrag halten VI/1/M6
talk (to) [tɔːk] sprechen/reden
 (mit)
tall [tɔːl] hoch; groß
tank [tæŋk] (Wasser)becken
 VI/3/5
tank [tæŋk]
 (Flüssigkeits)behälter,
 (Wasser)tank VI/6/M2
tap [tæp] Wasserhahn V/6/M2
task [tɑːsk] Aufgabe
taste [teɪst] schmecken
tasty [ˈteɪsti] schmackhaft,
 lecker
taxi [ˈtæksi] Taxi VI/2/5
tea [tiː] Tee
have tea [hæv ˈtiː] Tee trinken
teach [tiːtʃ] unterrichten,
 beibringen
teacher [ˈtiːtʃə] Lehrer/in
teammate [tiːmmeɪt]
 Teammitglied, Teamkollege/
 Teamkollegin V/5/M2
teamwork [ˈtiːmˌwɜːk] Teamarbeit
 V/5/4
be in tears [ˌbiː‿ɪn ˈtɪəz] weinen
 VI/5/R3
technique [tekˈniːk] Technik,
 Verfahren, Methode VI/6/R3
technology [tekˈnɒlədʒi] Technik,
 Technologie VI/4/13
teenage [ˈtiːneɪdʒ] jugendlich;
 Teenager-

telegraph *(no pl)* [ˈtelɪˌgrɑːf]
 Telegraf VI/4/13
telephone [ˈtelɪˌfəʊn] anrufen;
 Telefon
television [ˈtelɪˌvɪʒən] Fernseher;
 Fernsehen
tell [tel] erzählen; sagen
tell sb to do sth [ˌtel ˌsʌmbədi
 tə ˈduː: ˌsʌmθɪŋ] jdm etw
 vorschreiben/befehlen
 VI/1/M2
temperature [ˈtemprɪtʃə]
 Temperatur VI/4/6
° **tempt sb** [ˈtempt ˌsʌmbədi] jdn in
 Versuchung führen; jdn locken
 VI/3/12
tent [tent] Zelt VI/5/R3
term [tɜːm] Ausdruck VI/3/M10
terrible [ˈterəbl] schrecklich,
 furchtbar
test [test] Prüfung, Test;
 Klassenarbeit V/5/3
test [test] prüfen, testen VI/1/15
testing format [ˈtestɪŋ ˌfɔːmæt]
 Aufgabenformat VI/5/I
text [tekst] SMS verschicken
 VI/3/3
text message [ˈtekst ˌmesɪdʒ]
 SMS (Short Message Service)
textbook [ˈtekstˌbʊk] Lehrbuch
 VI/3/M9
Thai [taɪ] Thai, Thailänder/in;
 thailändisch
than [ðæn] als
thank [θæŋk] danken
Thank goodness! [ˌθæŋk ˈgʊdnəs]
 Gott sei Dank!
thank you [ˈθæŋk juː] danke
thanks [θæŋks] danke
Thanks a lot! [ˌθæŋks‿ə ˈlɒt]
 Vielen Dank!
Thanksgiving [ˈθæŋksˌgɪvɪŋ]
 Thanksgiving *(amerikanisches
 Erntedankfest)*
that [ðæt] das; der/die/das
that [ðæt] so VI/2/3
That'll be ... *(informal)* [ðætl
 ˈbiː] Das macht dann ... ; Das
 beläuft sich auf ...
that's why [ðæts waɪ] das ist der
 Grund, warum V/5/8
the [ðə] der/die/das

the same age [ðə ˌseɪm‿ˈeɪdʒ]
 gleichaltrig V/3/4
theatre [ˈθɪətə] Theater
their [ðeə] ihr(e)
theirs [ðeəz] ihr(e, es)
them [ðem] sie, ihnen
theme [θiːm] Thema; Lektion,
 Kapitel VI/3/I
theme park [ˈθiːm ˌpɑːk]
 Themenpark; Freizeitpark
themselves [ðəmˈselvz] sich
 (selbst); selbst
then [ðen] damals; dann
therapist [ˈθerəpɪst] Thera-
 peut/in V/4/9
therapy [ˈθerəpi] Therapie,
 Behandlung V/4/8
there [ðeə] dort(hin)
there are [ðeər‿ˈɑː] es gibt, da
 sind
there is [ðeər‿ˈɪz] es gibt
therefore [ˈðeəfɔː] deshalb,
 daher V/3/M8
these (*pl of* **this**) [ðiːz] diese
they [ðeɪ] sie
thick [θɪk] dick V/4/13
thief (*pl* **thieves**) [θiːf] Dieb
 V/3/M2
thigh [θaɪ] (Ober)schenkel
 VI/1/M4
thin [θɪn] dünn
thing [θɪŋ] Ding, Gegenstand
think [θɪŋk] denken, glauben,
 meinen; nachdenken
think about (sb/sth)
 [ˈθɪŋk‿əˌbaʊt] an (jdn/etw)
 denken; sich (etw) überlegen
think of [ˈθɪŋk‿əv] denken an;
 sich ausdenken
third [θɜːd] Drittel
° **thirst** [θɜːst] Durst VI/4/M2
this [ðɪs] diese(r, s)
this afternoon [ðɪs‿ˌɑːftəˈnuːn]
 heute Nachmittag
this morning [ðɪs ˈmɔːnɪŋ] heute
 Morgen
those (*pl of* **that**) [ðəʊz] diese;
 jene
though [ðəʊ] trotzdem, dennoch
 VI/3/13
as though [əz ˈðəʊ] als ob
 VI/1/M8

thousand [ˈθaʊzənd] Tausend
thousands *(pl)* [ˈθaʊzndz] Tausende
threaten sb [ˈθretn] jdn bedrohen V/2/M5
threaten to do sth [ˌθretn tə ˈduː ˌsʌmθɪŋ] damit drohen, etw zu tun VI/1/M4
through [θruː] durch
throughout [θruːˈaʊt] während, im Laufe VI/4/8
throw [θrəʊ] werfen
Thursday [ˈθɜːzdeɪ] Donnerstag
tick [tɪk] abhaken, ankreuzen VI/5/L3
ticket [ˈtɪkɪt] Karte
ticket counter [ˈtɪkɪt ˌkaʊntə] Fahrkartenschalter
° **tide** [taɪd] Gezeiten; (öffentliche) Meinung VI/3/12
tidy [ˈtaɪdi] ordentlich
tidy up [ˌtaɪdi ˈʌp] aufräumen
tiger [ˈtaɪgə] Tiger
tighten [ˈtaɪtn] verstärken VI/1/6
till [tɪl] bis
time [taɪm] (Uhr)zeit; Mal
(just) in time [ɪn ˈtaɪm] (gerade noch) rechtzeitig
have a good time [ˌhæv ə gʊd ˈtaɪm] sich amüsieren
on time [ɒn ˈtaɪm] pünktlich; rechtzeitig V/5/5
a long time ago [ə ˌlɒŋ ˌtaɪm əˈgəʊ] vor langer Zeit V/1/11
What time (is it)? [wɒt ˈtaɪm (ˌɪz ɪt)] Wie spät/Wie viel Uhr (ist es)?
take time off [ˌteɪk ˌtaɪm ˈɒf] sich freinehmen VI/5/R4
time out [ˌtaɪm ˈaʊt] Auszeit
take time out [ˌteɪk ˌtaɪm ˈaʊt] sich eine Auszeit nehmen VI/5/W6
What's the time? [ˌwɒts ðə ˈtaɪm] Wie viel Uhr ist es?
timeline [ˈtaɪmˌlaɪn] Zeitstrahl VI/3/11
at all times [ət ˌɔːl ˈtaɪmz] stets, jederzeit VI/3/4
timetable [ˈtaɪmˌteɪbl] Stundenplan; Fahrplan

tin [tɪn] Büchse, Dose
tiny [ˈtaɪni] winzig V/1/M1
tip [tɪp] Tipp VI/1/3
tirade [taɪˈreɪd] Tirade (Redeschwall) VI/1/2
tired [ˈtaɪəd] müde
title [ˈtaɪtl] Titel
to [tə] in, nach, zu, an; vor
today [təˈdeɪ] heute
toe [təʊ] Zeh(e)
together [təˈgeðə] zusammen, gemeinsam
toilet [ˈtɔɪlət] Toilette, Klo
tolerance [ˈtɒlərəns] Toleranz V/2/M2
tolerant [ˈtɒlərənt] tolerant VI/1/10
toll-free [ˌtəʊlˈfriː] gebührenfrei VI/1/14
tomato *(pl -es)* [təˈmɑːtəʊ, təˈmɑːtəʊz] Tomate
tomorrow [təˈmɒrəʊ] morgen
tonight [təˈnaɪt] heute Abend
too [tuː] zu; auch
too bad [ˌtuː ˈbæd] zu schade
tool [tuːl] Werkzeug
tooth *(pl teeth)* [tuːθ, tiːθ] Zahn
top [tɒp] oberes Ende, Spitze
on top [ɒn ˈtɒp] oben
topic [ˈtɒpɪk] Thema V/6/M2
tornado *(pl -es)* [tɔːˈneɪdəʊ, tɔːˈneɪdəʊz] Tornado VI/4/1
total [ˈtəʊtl] Gesamt-; völlig
total [ˈtəʊtl] Gesamtsumme VI/2/8
totally [ˈtəʊtəli] völlig, total V/4/M3
totem pole [ˈtəʊtəm ˌpəʊl] Totempfahl
touch [tʌʃ] berühren
touch down [ˌtʌʃ ˈdaʊn] aufsetzen, landen, niedergehen VI/4/2
get in touch with sb [ˌget ɪn ˈtʌʃ wɪð ˌsʌmbədi] mit jdm in Kontakt treten VI/4/10
keep in touch with sb [ˌkiːp ɪn ˈtʌʃ wɪð ˌsʌmbədi] mit jdm in Kontakt bleiben VI/1/14
put sb in touch with sb [ˌpʊt ˌsʌmbədi ɪn ˈtʌʃ wɪð ˌsʌmbədi] jdm helfen, mit jdm Kontakt aufzunehmen VI/1/14

take a tour [ˌteɪk ə ˈtʊə] eine Tour/Führung machen VI/3/2
tour guide [ˈtʊə gaɪd] Reiseführer/in, Reiseleiter/in
tourism *(no pl)* [ˈtʊərɪzm] Tourismus VI/3/14
toward(s) [təˈwɔːd(z)] in Richtung
tower [ˈtaʊə] Turm
town [taʊn] Stadt
in town [ɪn ˈtaʊn] in der Stadt VI/2/M5
township [ˈtaʊnʃɪp] Township *(von Schwarzen bewohnte, abseits der Stadt gelegene Siedlung)* VI/3/2
toy [tɔɪ] Spielzeug
tradition [trəˈdɪʃn] Tradition, Brauch
traditional [trəˈdɪʃnəl] traditionell
traffic [ˈtræfɪk] Verkehr
trafficked [ˈtræfɪkt] verschleppt VI/2/8
° **tragic** [ˈtrædʒɪk] tragisch VI/4/PP
trail [treɪl] Weg, Pfad
train [treɪn] trainieren; Zug
train for a job [ˌtreɪn fər ə ˈdʒɒb] eine Ausbildung machen VI/2/M2
train ride [ˈtreɪn ˌraɪd] Zugfahrt
train sb [ˈtreɪn ˌsʌmbədi] jdn ausbilden V/1/12
trainee [ˌtreɪˈniː] Auszubildende/r; Praktikant/in VI/2/3
trainer *(BE)* [ˈtreɪnə] Turnschuh
training [ˈtreɪnɪŋ] Ausbildung; Schulung V/5/2
training on the job [ˌtreɪnɪŋ ɒn ðə ˈdʒɒb] *Ausbildung am Arbeitsplatz* VI/5/R4
traitor [ˈtreɪtə] Verräter VI/1/4
° **transcontinental** [ˌtrænzkɒntɪˈnentl] transkontinental VI/4/PP
translate [trænsˈleɪt] übersetzen
transport [ˈtrænspɔːt] Transport, Beförderung
transport *(no pl)* [ˈtrænspɔːt] öffentlicher Personennahverkehr VI/6/L3
travel [ˈtrævl] reisen
travel guide [ˈtrævl gaɪd] Reiseführer

traveller ['trævlə] Reisende/r
VI/5/R4

travels *(pl)* ['trævlz] Reise
VI/5/R4

treatment ['tri:mənt]
Behandlung VI/3/M3

tree [tri:] Baum

tribe [traɪb] Stamm

trip [trɪp] Ausflug; Reise, Fahrt

trolley ['trɒli] Einkaufswagen

trouble ['trʌbl] Schwierigkeiten,
Ärger

° the Troubles [ðə 'trʌblz] *Zeit der
Unruhen in Nordirland* VI/1/PP

trousers *(npl)* ['traʊzəz] Hose

truck [trʌk] Last(kraft)wagen,
Laster VI/4/2

true [tru:] wahr

come true [ˌkʌm 'tru:] wahr
werden VI/3/2

truth [tru:θ] Wahrheit V/3/10

try [traɪ] versuchen; probieren

try hard to do sth [ˌtraɪ 'hɑːd‿tə
du: sʌmθɪŋ] sich sehr
bemühen, etw zu tun V/5/13

try on [traɪ‿'ɒn] anprobieren

the tube [ðə 'tjuːb] die
(Londoner) U-Bahn

Tuesday ['tjuːzdeɪ] Dienstag

tug-of-war [ˌtʌg‿əv 'wɔː]
Tauziehen

turkey ['tɜːki] Truthahn/-henne,
Pute/r

turn [tɜːn] sich drehen;
abbiegen; umblättern

° turn [tɜːn] umschlagen VI/3/12

(it's) your turn [ɪts jɔː 'tɜːn] du
bist dran VI/1/M8

° turn into sth [ˌtɜːn‿ˈɪntə sʌmθɪŋ]
zu etw werden VI/2/1

turn off [ˌtɜːn‿'ɒf] ausmachen,
ausschalten V/6/2

turn on [ˌtɜːn‿'ɒn] einschalten

turn over [tɜːn‿'əʊvə] (sich)
umdrehen

turn round [tɜːn 'raʊnd] (sich)
umdrehen

turn sb against sb [ˌtɜːn
ˌsʌmbədi‿ə'genst ˌsʌmbədi] jdn
gegen jdn aufbringen VI/1/2

turn to sth ['tɜːn tʊ ˌsʌmθɪŋ] sich
etw zuwenden VI/4/M2

turn up [ˌtɜːn‿'ʌp] aufdrehen,
höher stellen V/6/4

take turns [ˌteɪk 'tɜːnz] sich
abwechseln

turtle ['tɜːtl] Meeresschildkröte
VI/3/5

watch TV [ˌwɒtʃ tiː'viː] fernsehen

TV (= television) [ˌtiː'viː, 'telɪˌvɪʒn]
Fernseher; Fernsehen

TV guide [tiːˌviː 'gaɪd]
Fernsehzeitschrift

TV studio [tiː viː ˌstjuːdiəʊ]
Fernsehstudio

twice [twaɪs] zweimal V/4/5

twin city [ˌtwɪn 'sɪti] Partnerstadt
VI/3/M8

twin room [ˌtwɪn 'ruːm]
Zweibettzimmer VI/5/S4

twister *(informal)* ['twɪstə]
Tornado VI/4/2

type [taɪp] Art; Typ; Maschine
schreiben, tippen

typewriter ['taɪpˌraɪtə]
Schreibmaschine VI/2/5

typical ['tɪpɪkl] typisch

U

ugly ['ʌgli] hässlich

UK (= United Kingdom) [ˌjuː 'keɪ,
juːˌnaɪtɪd 'kɪŋdəm] Vereinigtes
Königreich

unbutton [ʌn'bʌtn] aufknöpfen
VI/1/M8

uncle ['ʌŋkl] Onkel

unconquered [ˌʌn'kɒŋkəd]
unbesiegt, nicht erobert
VI/6/R4

undefeated [ˌʌndɪ'fiːtɪd]
unbesiegt, ungeschlagen
VI/6/R4

under ['ʌndə] unter

underground ['ʌndəˌgraʊnd]
U-Bahn

underline [ˌʌndə'laɪn]
unterstreichen

understand [ˌʌndə'stænd]
verstehen

understanding [ˌʌndə'stændɪŋ]
verständnisvoll VI/1/10

understanding *(no pl)*
[ˌʌndə'stændɪŋ] Verständnis
VI/5/LG1

undertaker ['ʌndəˌteɪkə]
Leichenbestatter/in;
Bestattungsinstitut V/4/M7

° unemployment rate
[ˌʌnɪm'plɔɪmənt reɪt]
Arbeitslosenrate,
Arbeitslosenzahl VI/3/PP

unfair [ʌn'feə] unfair, ungerecht
V/2/2

unfortunately [ʌn'fɔːtʃnətli]
leider, unglücklicherweise
V/6/4

unfriendly [ʌn'frendli]
unfreundlich

unhappy [ʌn'hæpi] unglücklich

unhealthy [ʌn'helθi] kränklich,
ungesund

uniform ['juːnɪˌfɔːm] Uniform

° Unionist ['juːnjənɪst] Unionist
(Anhänger der Union) VI/1/PP

unique [juː'niːk] einzigartig
V/3/M7

unite [juː'naɪt] vereinen,
vereinigen VI/6/R4

° the United Nations
Organization [ðə juːˌnaɪtɪd
'neɪʃnzˌɔːgənaɪˌzeɪʃn] die
Vereinten Nationen
VI/2/PP

the United States [ðə juːˌnaɪtɪd
'steɪts] die Vereinigten Staaten

universal [ˌjuːnɪ'vɜːsl] universell
VI/6/R4

university [ˌjuːnɪ'vɜːsəti]
Universität

unpaid [ʌn'peɪd] unbezahlt

unrealistic [ˌʌnrɪə'lɪstɪk]
unrealistisch VI/1/10

unskilled worker [ˌʌnˌskɪld 'wɜːkə]
Hilfsarbeiter VI/1/2

until [ən'tɪl] bis

unusual [ʌn'juːʒʊəl]
ungewöhnlich

up [ʌp] (nach) oben; hinauf
VI/1/2

up to [ʌp tʊ] bis zu VI/4/2

° uphill [ˌʌp'hɪl] bergauf (führend)
VI/4/CIO

uproot [ʌp'ruːt] entwurzeln
VI/4/2

upset [ʌp'set] aufgeregt,
aufgebracht

upside down [ˌʌpsaɪdˈdaʊn] verkehrt herum V/6/M6

upstairs [ʌpˈsteəz] (nach) oben

us [ʌs] uns

the US (= United States) [ðə ˌjuː ˈes, juːˌnaɪtɪd ˈsteɪts] die USA

USA [ˌjuː es ˈeɪ] USA (= Vereinigte Staaten von Amerika)

usage ['juːsɪdʒ] Verbrauch V/6/M2

usage ['juːsɪdʒ] Benutzung, Gebrauch VI/4/M9

use [juːz] benutzen

use [juːs] Verwendung, Gebrauch V/6/M2

use bad language [juːz bæd 'læŋgwɪdʒ] Schimpfwörter benutzen

**used to ... ** *(+ infinitive)* ['juːsd̮tə] früher ...

get used to sth [get 'juːsd̮tə ˌsʌmθɪŋ] sich an etw gewöhnen

useful ['juːsfl] nützlich, brauchbar

useless ['juːsləs] zu nichts zu gebrauchen V/3/5

user ['juːzə] Benutzer/in, Anwender/in VI/6/LG1

usually ['juːʒʊəli] gewöhnlich, normalerweise

V

vacation *(AE)* = holiday *(BE)* [vəˈkeɪʃn] Ferien, Urlaub

vaccination [ˌvæksɪˈneɪʃn] (Schutz)impfung VI/6/MD2

valley ['væli] Tal

value *(no pl)* ['væljuː] Wert VI/5/W1

vandalism ['vændəˌlɪzm] Vandalismus, Sachbeschädigung

vegetable ['vedʒtəbl] Gemüse

vegetarian [ˌvedʒəˈteəriən] Vegetarier/in

vending machine ['vendɪŋ məˌʃiːn] Automat

verb [vɜːb] Verb VI/4/2

version ['vɜːʃn] Version VI/4/M5

very ['veri] sehr

vest [vest] Unterhemd VI/1/M8

vet [vet] Tierarzt/-ärztin

via ['vaɪə] per, über, via VI/6/LG1

victim ['vɪktɪm] Opfer VI/4/2

view [vjuː] Sicht; (Aus)blick, Aussicht

view [vjuː] Ansicht, Meinung VI/1/M3

village ['vɪlɪdʒ] Dorf

vinegar ['vɪnɪgə] Essig

violence ['vaɪələns] Gewalt, Gewalttätigkeit VI/3/2

violent ['vaɪələnt] brutal, gewalttätig V/2/M1

violent ['vaɪələnt] brutal, gewalttätig; heftig VI/4/1

virtual ['vɜːtʃʊəl] virtuell VI/4/M7

visa ['viːzə] Visum VI/5/R4

° **visible** ['vɪzəbl] sichtbar VI/4/PP

visit ['vɪzɪt] Besuch; besuchen

visitor ['vɪzɪtə] Besucher/in

vitamin ['vɪtəmɪn] Vitamin V/4/3

vocational school [vəˈkeɪʃnəl ˌskuːl] Berufsschule VI/2/M2

do vocational training [duː vəʊˌkeɪʃnəl ˈtreɪnɪŋ] eine Berufsausbildung machen V/5/2

voice [vɔɪs] Stimme V/4/M8

volcanic eruption [vɒlˌkænɪkˌɪˈrʌpʃn] Vulkanausbruch VI/4/1

volcano *(pl* **-oes** *or* **-os)** [vɒlˈkeɪnəʊ, vɒlˈkeɪnəʊz] Vulkan

volunteer [ˌvɒlənˈtɪə] freiwillig, ehrenamtlich VI/3/2; Freiwillige/r VI/5/R3

do volunteer work [duː 'vɒləntɪə ˌwɜːk] Freiwilligenarbeit leisten VI/5/R4

vote [vəʊt] wählen V/2/5

W

wage(s) [weɪdʒ(ɪz)] Lohn VI/2/10

Wait a second! [ˌweɪt̮əˈsekənd] Moment mal!

wait (for) [weɪt] warten (auf)

sb cannot wait to do sth [ˌsʌmbədi ˌkænɒt ˈweɪt̮tə duː ˌsʌmθɪŋ] jmd kann es kaum erwarten, etw zu tun VI/2/3

waiter/waitress ['weɪtə/'weɪtrəs] Bedienung, Kellner/in

waiting room ['weɪtɪŋ ˌruːm] Wartezimmer

wake up [ˌweɪk̮'ʌp] aufwecken; aufwachen

walk [wɔːk] (zu Fuß) gehen; Gehen; Spaziergang

go for a walk [ˌgəʊ fərˌə ˈwɔːk] spazieren gehen

walk up [wɔːk̮'ʌp] hinaufgehen

wall [wɔːl] Wand

wallet ['wɒlɪt] Brieftasche

want [wɒnt] wünschen; wollen

war [wɔː] Krieg VI/2/8

wardrobe ['wɔːdrəʊb] Kleiderschrank

warlike ['wɔːˌlaɪk] kriegerisch VI/2/8

warm [wɔːm] warm

warm [wɔːm] warmherzig, herzlich VI/3/CIO

warm up [wɔːm̮'ʌp] sich aufwärmen

warm-up exercise ['wɔːmˌʌp eksəsaɪz] Aufwärmübung

warmth *(no pl)* [wɔːmθ] Wärme VI/5/LG1

warn [wɔːn] warnen VI/4/4

warning ['wɔːnɪŋ] Warnung VI/4/5

warthog ['wɔːtˌhɒg] Warzenschwein VI/3/M5

wash [wɒʃ] (sich) waschen

wash up [wɒʃ̮'ʌp] abspülen, abwaschen

washing machine ['wɒʃɪŋ məˌʃiːn] Waschmaschine V/6/1

waste *(no pl)* [weɪst] Verschwendung VI/4/10

waste [weɪst] verschwenden V/4/M3

waste *(no pl)* [weɪst] Abfall, Müll V/6/5

waste of time [ˌweɪstˌəv ˈtaɪm] Zeitverschwendung

watch [wɒtʃ] beobachten; zusehen, zuschauen; anschauen; Uhr

watch TV [ˌwɒtʃ tiːˈviː] fernsehen

water ['wɔːtə] Wasser

water ['wɔːtə] gießen V/6/M2

water ['wɔːtə] Gewässer VI/3/5

waterfall ['wɔːtəˌfɔːl] Wasserfall

wave [weɪv] winken; schwenken
wave [weɪv] Welle
wax [wæks] Wachs
way [weɪ] Weg; Art, Weise
along the way [əˌlɒŋ ðə ˈweɪ]
  unterwegs, auf dem Weg
  VI/5/R4
by the way [baɪ ðə ˈweɪ] übrigens
  V/1/5
way of life [ˌweɪ ˌəv ˈlaɪf]
  Lebensweise
we [wiː] wir
weapon [ˈwepən] Waffe
  VI/4/M5
wear [weə] tragen
wearily [ˈwɪərəli] müde; lustlos
  VI/1/3
weather [ˈweðə] Wetter
wedding [ˈwedɪŋ] Hochzeit
  VI/1/M1
° wedding costume [ˈwedɪŋ
  ˌkɒstjuːm] Hochzeitskleidung
  VI/1/CIO
° wedding ring [ˈwedɪŋ rɪŋ]
  Ehering, Trauring VI/1/CIO
Wednesday [ˈwenzdeɪ] Mittwoch
week [wiːk] Woche
weekend [ˌwiːkˈend]
  Wochenende
weekly [ˈwiːkli] wöchentlich
weigh [weɪ] wiegen V/4/9
weight [weɪt] Gewicht
put on weight [ˌpʊt ˌɒn ˌweɪt]
  zunehmen V/4/9
weird *(informal)* [wɪəd]
  merkwürdig, seltsam, komisch
  VI/1/M8
welcome [ˈwelkəm] willkommen
  heißen, begrüßen VI/3/M3
You're welcome. [ˌjɔː ˈwelkəm]
  Gern geschehen.
weld [weld] schweißen VI/2/5
welder [ˈweldə] Schweißer/in
  VI/2/5
well [wel] nun (ja), tja
do well [duː ˈwel] gut
  abschneiden VI/2/3
Well done! [ˌwel ˈdʌn] Gut
  gemacht!
well-known [ˌwelˈnəʊn] berühmt,
  (allgemein) bekannt V/5/M11
Welsh [welʃ] walisisch

west [west] westlich, West-;
  Westen V/1/7
the West Indies *(npl)* [ðə
  ˌwest ˌɪndiz] die Westindischen
  Inseln
Western Europe [ˌwestən ˈjʊərəp]
  Westeuropa VI/3/CIO
wet [wet] nass
whale [weɪl] Wal VI/3/5
what [wɒt] was; welche(r, s)
What about …? *(informal)*
  [ˌwɒt ˌəˈbaʊt] Was ist mit …?,
  Wie wäre es mit …?
What time (is it)? [wɒt ˌtaɪm (ˌɪz
  ɪt)] Wie spät/Wie viel Uhr (ist
  es)?
What's … like? [wɒts ˈlaɪk] Wie
  ist …?
What's on? [wɒts ˌɒn] Was
  gibt's?; Was läuft?
What's the time? [ˌwɒts ðə ˈtaɪm]
  Wie viel Uhr ist es?
What's up? *(informal)* [wɒts ˌʌp]
  Wie geht's?; Was geht?
  VI/2/CIO
What's your name? [ˌwɒts jə
  ˈneɪm] Wie heißt du?, Wie
  heißen Sie?
whatever [wɒtˈevə] was (auch
  immer) VI/1/10
wheel [wiːl] Rad
wheelchair [ˈwiːlˌtʃeə] Rollstuhl
when [wen] als; wann; wenn
whenever [wenˈevə] immer
  wenn, wann (auch) immer
  VI/2/M2
where [weə] wo(hin)
Where are you from? [ˌweərˌaː jə
  ˈfrɒm] Wo kommst du her?
wherever [werˈevə] wo(hin) auch
  immer V/3/10
whether [ˈweðə] ob
which [wɪtʃ] welche(r, s); der/
  die/das
while [waɪl] während
while *(no pl)* [waɪl] Weile
  VI/1/M4
whirl (a)round [ˈwɜːl (ə)ˌraʊnd]
  herumwirbeln VI/1/7
whisper [ˈwɪspə] flüstern
whistle [ˈwɪsl] pfeifen
white [waɪt] weiß

who [huː] wer; wen; wem; der/
  die/das
° **whoever** [huːˈevə] wer (auch
  immer) VI/2/1
whole [həʊl] ganz
the whole of [ðə ˈhəʊl ˌəv] ganz
  VI/5/MD3
whose [huːz] wessen
why [waɪ] warum
wide [waɪd] breit VI/4/2
wife *(pl wives)* [waɪf, waɪvz]
  Ehefrau
wild [waɪld] wild
wildebeest *(pl - or -s)*
  [ˈvɪldəˌbiːst] Gnu
wildfire [ˈwaɪldˌfaɪə] Lauffeuer,
  nicht zu kontrollierender
  (Großflächen)brand
wildlife [ˈwaɪldˌlaɪf] Tier- und
  Pflanzenwelt
wildlife reserve [ˈwaɪldˌlaɪf rɪˌzɜːv]
  Naturschutzgebiet VI/5/R1
will [wɪl] werden
be willing [ˌbiː ˈwɪlɪŋ] bereit sein
  VI/6/W1
win [wɪn] gewinnen
wind [wɪnd] Wind
wind [wɪnd] ein Bäuerchen
  machen VI/1/M8
window [ˈwɪndəʊ] Fenster
windy [ˈwɪndi] windig
wing [wɪŋ] Flügel
winner [ˈwɪnə] Gewinner/in,
  Sieger/in
winter [ˈwɪntə] Winter
wipe [waɪp] (ab)wischen,
  (ab)putzen VI/1/M8
° **wire** [ˈwaɪə] Draht; Leitung, Kabel
  VI/4/PP
wish [wɪʃ] (sich) wünschen;
  Wunsch V/5/13
best wishes [ˌbest ˈwɪʃɪz] viele/
  beste Grüße
with [wɪð] mit
within [wɪðˈɪn] innerhalb V/4/9
without [wɪðˈaʊt] ohne
woman *(pl women)* [ˈwʊmən,
  ˈwɪmɪn] Frau
wonder [ˈwʌndə] sich fragen
  V/2/2
no wonder [ˌnəʊ ˈwʌndə] kein
  Wunder V/2/10

wonderful [ˈwʌndəfl] wunderbar, wundervoll

wood [wʊd] Holz

wooden [ˈwʊdn] hölzern, Holz- V/3/M2

word [wɜːd] Wort

wordbank [ˈwɜːdbæŋk] Wortfeld VI/1/3

work [wɜːk] Arbeit; arbeiten; funktionieren

out of work [aʊt‿əv ˈwɜːk] arbeitslos V/5/13

work experience *(no pl)* [ˈwɜːk‿ɪkˌspɪəriəns] Praktikum; Berufserfahrung V/5/5

work out [ˌwɜːk‿ˈaʊt] ausrechnen V/5/15

work out [ˌwɜːk‿ˈaʊt] funktionieren, klappen

work out [ˌwɜːk‿ˈaʊt] entwickeln, ausarbeiten VI/5/R3

workbook [ˈwɜːkˌbʊk] Arbeitsbuch

worker [ˈwɜːkə] Arbeiter/in, Angestellte/r VI/2/10

working hours [ˈwɜːkɪŋ‿aʊəz] Arbeitszeit

working life [ˈwɜːkɪŋ laɪf] Arbeitsleben VI/2/6

world [wɜːld] Welt, Erde

World Cup [ˌwɜːld ˈkʌp] Weltmeisterschaft VI/6/R4

World Heritage Site [ˌwɜːld ˈherɪtɪdʒ ˌsaɪt] Weltkulturerbe, Weltkulturdenkmal VI/3/5

world record [wɜːld ˈrekɔːd] Weltrekord

worldwide [ˌwɜːldˈwaɪd] weltweit VI/2/8

worm [wɜːm] Wurm V/1/M1

worried [ˈwʌrid] beunruhigt, besorgt

worry [ˈwʌri] sich Sorgen machen

worry [ˈwʌri] Sorge

be worth sth [bi: ˈwɜːθ ˌsʌmθɪŋ] etw wert sein V/3/5

would [wʊd] würde(st/n/t)

wrap [ræp] einpacken, (ein)wickeln

write [raɪt] schreiben

write down [raɪt ˈdaʊn] aufschreiben

writing paper *(no pl)* [ˈraɪtɪŋ ˌpeɪpə] Schreibpapier V/6/5

wrong [rɒŋ] falsch

be wrong [bi ˈrɒŋ] nicht stimmen; sich irren V/3/10

Y

yard [jɑːd] Yard (= 0,91 Meter) VI/1/7

yeah *(informal)* [jeə] ja VI/1/M8

year [jɪə] Jahr

yearbook [ˈjɪəˌbʊk] Jahresausgabe; Jahrbuch

yellow [ˈjeləʊ] gelb

yes [jes] ja

yesterday [ˈjestədeɪ] gestern

yet [jet] bis jetzt; schon

not yet [nɒt ˈjet] noch nicht

yo *(informal)* [jəʊ] hi VI/2/CIO

you [juː] du, dich, dir, Sie, Ihnen; ihr, euch

you lot *(informal)* [ju ˈlɒt] ihr VI/2/3

You're welcome. [ˌjɔː ˈwelkəm] Gern geschehen.

young [jʌŋ] jung

young [jʌŋ] Junge(s) VI/3/5

your [jɔː] dein(e); euer/eure; Ihr(e)

yours [jɔːz] deine(r, s); eure(r, s); Ihre(r, s)

yours sincerely [ˌjɔːz‿sɪnˈsɪəli] mit freundlichen/herzlichen Grüßen VI/2/M7

yourself *(pl yourselves)* [jəˈself, jəˈselvz] dich, dir; selbst/ihr, euch; selbst

youth [juːθ] Jugend; Jugendliche/r; Jugend- VI/2/M2

youth centre [ˈjuːθ ˌsentə] Jugendzentrum

youth hostel [ˈjuːθ ˌhɒstl] Jugendherberge

Z

zebra [ˈzebrə] Zebra VI/3/M4

zoo [zuː] Zoo

A

abbiegen turn
abbrennen burn down
(ab)bürsten brush
Abend evening; night
Abendessen dinner
abends in the evening;
  pm (= post meridiem) *(nur hinter Uhrzeit)*
Abenteuer adventure
aber but; however
abfahren depart, leave
Abfall waste *(no pl)*, litter *(no pl)*
abfeuern let off
abhängen hang out *(informal)*
abhängig (von) addicted (to)
abholen collect, pick up
(ab)holen come for
das Abitur machen do one's A levels
ablehnen refuse
sich abmühen struggle
abnehmen take off
Abneigungen dislikes *(pl)*
... der Aboriginals Aboriginal
Aborigine Aborigine
(ab)putzen wipe
Absatz paragraph
Abschluss qualification
die Abschlussprüfung bestehen graduate
Abschnitt paragraph
abschreiben copy
absolut absolutely
abspülen wash up
Abtreibung abortion
abwaschen wash up
sich abwechseln take turns
(ab)wischen wipe
darauf achten make sure
Achtung respect
Adjektiv adjective
adoptieren adopt
Adoption adoption
zur Adoption freigeben give up for adoption
Adresse address
Affe monkey
Afrika Africa
Afrikaner/in African
afrikanisch African

Afroamerikaner/in African American
afroamerikanisch African American
aggressiv aggressive
ähnlich similar
Aktion action; campaign
aktiv active
Aktivität activity
Akzent accent
akzeptieren accept
albern silly
(Musik)album album
Alkohol alcohol
alle everybody, everyone
allein alone
allein erziehende Mutter single mother
allein(e) on one's own
alle(s) all
alles everything; anything
Alles Gute zum Geburtstag! Happy birthday!
alles in allem all in all
alles Liebe love
im Allgemeinen in general
alltäglich everyday
Alphabet alphabet
als as, than *(Vergleich)*, when
also so
alt old
Alter age
Alternative alternative
Altglascontainer bottle bank
Altpapiercontainer paper bank
am on
am Abend in the evening
am besten best
am liebsten best
am meisten best; most
am Nachmittag in the afternoon
am nächsten Tag the next day
am wenigsten least
Amerikaner/in American
amerikanisch American
amisch Amish
die Amischen the Amish
amtlich official
Amtsgewalt authority
sich amüsieren have a good time
an on, to, at

(an)bieten offer
(an)dauern last
andere(r, s) other; different
ein anderer/anderes, eine andere another
andererseits on the other hand
anders different
(sich) (ver)ändern change
(Ver)änderung change
anerkennen respect
Anfang beginning, start
anfangen start, begin
anfangs at first
anfeuern cheer
Anfrage request
sich (mit jdm) anfreunden make friends (with sb)
(an)führen lead
(persönliche) Angaben data *(pl)*
Angebot offer
im Angebot sein be on sale
Angehörige/r relative
angeln fish
angenehm nice
Angestellte/r worker
angestrengt hard
angreifen attack, strike, tackle
Angriff attack
Angst fear
Angst haben be scared, be afraid
Angst machen scare
anhalten stop
sich anhören sound
Animationsfilm animated film
(an)klicken click
ankommen arrive, get (to)
Ankunft arrival
Anleitung instruction
Anmache chat-up line *(informal)*
Anmeldeformular entry form
sich anmelden log on
annehmen accept; suppose
anonym anonymous
anordnen rank
Anorexie anorexia *(no pl)*
anpassungsfähig flexible
Anpassungsfähigkeit flexibility
anprobieren try on
(Telefon)anruf call
anrufen phone, telephone, call
Anrufer/in caller

anrühren mix
anschauen watch, look at
sich anschließen join (in)
anschließend afterwards
Ansicht opinion, view
meiner Ansicht nach in my
   opinion
jdn/etw anstarren stare at
   sb/sth
(an)statt instead (of)
anstreichen paint
Anstreicher/in painter
anstrengend stressful
Antwort answer
(be)antworten answer
Anweisung instruction
Anzeige advert
   (= advertisement)
anziehen put on
sich anziehen dress
Anziehung(skraft) attraction
Apfel apple
gedeckter Apfelkuchen apple
   pie
Appetit appetite
April April
Aquarium aquarium
Arbeit work, job
arbeiten work
Arbeiter/in worker
Arbeitgeber/in employer
Arbeitsbuch workbook
arbeitslos out of work
arbeitsreich busy
Arbeitszeit working hours
Ärger trouble
ärgern annoy
Argument argument
argumentieren argue
Arm arm
arm poor
die Armen the poor *(pl)*
Armee army
Armut poverty
arrangierte Hochzeit arranged
   marriage
Art kind; way; type
Artikel article
Arzt/Ärztin doctor
Asiat/in Asian
asiatisch Asian
Asien Asia

Ast branch
Astronaut/in astronaut
atemlos breathless
Athlet/in athlete
der Atlantische Ozean the
   Atlantic Ocean
Atmosphäre atmosphere
Attraktion attraction
auch also, as well, too
auf on, at
auf einmal at once; suddenly
auf Englisch in English
Auf Wiedersehen! Goodbye!
aufbauen set up; establish
aufblicken zu look up to
aufdrehen turn up
aufführen perform
auffüllen refill
Aufgabe task; job
aufgebracht upset
aufgeregt excited; upset
aufhängen put up, hang up
aufheben pick up
aufhören stop, finish
aufknöpfen unbutton
auflegen *(Telefon)* hang up
aufmuntern cheer up
(auf etw) aufpassen look out
   (for sth)
aufräumen tidy up
aufregend exciting
aufschreiben write down
aufspringen jump up
aufstehen get up, stand up
aufsteigen (auf) get on
(in einem Film) auftreten star
Auftritt gig *(informal)*
aufwachen wake up
sich aufwärmen warm up
Aufwärmübung warm-up
   exercise
aufwecken wake up
aufziehen raise
Aufzug lift
Auge eye
Auge in Auge face to face
Augenblick moment
einen Augenblick bitte just a
   minute
im Augenblick at the moment
August August
aus out (of); from

aus erster Hand first-hand
aus Versehen by accident
jdn ausbilden train sb
(Aus)bildung education
Ausbildung apprenticeship,
   training
(Aus)blick view
sich ausdenken think of,
   make up
Ausdruck phrase
ausdrücken express
(aus)drucken print (out)
Äußerung statement
Ausflug trip
ausfüllen fill out, fill in
Ausgang exit
ausgeben *(Geld)* spend
ausgedacht made-up
ausgehen go out
ausgezeichnet excellent
aushalten stand
(aus)helfen help out
jdn auslachen laugh at sb
Ausland foreign country
im Ausland abroad
Ausländer/in foreigner
ausländisch foreign
ausmachen turn off, put out
etw (aus)nutzen take advantage
   of sth
ausrechnen work out, figure out
(aus)reichen last
ausreichend enough
Ausreißer/in runaway
Ausrüstung equipment
Aussage statement
ausschalten turn off
(nach etw) Ausschau halten look
   out (for sth)
aussehen look
Aussehen look
außen outside
außerhalb outside
Aussicht view
ausspucken spit out
Ausstattung equipment
Ausstellung exhibition; gallery
Australien Australia
Australier/in Australian
australisch Australian
australische/r Ureinwohner/in
   Aborigine

austrinken finish
auswählen choose
Ausweis identification (= ID) *(no pl)*
(Aus)wirkung effect
Auszeichnung award
Auszeit time out
ausziehen take off
Auszubildende/r intern *(AE)*, trainee *(BE)*
Auto car
Autogramm autograph
Automat vending machine
Autor/in author

B

Backe cheek
backen bake
Bäcker/in baker
(Back)ofen oven
Bademeister/in lifeguard
baden take a bath
(Bade)wanne bath
Bad(ezimmer) bath(room)
(Eisen)bahn railroad *(AE)*, railway *(BE)*
Bahnhof station
Bahnsteig platform
bald soon
Ball ball
Ballon balloon
Banane banana
Bank bench
Bär bear
bar bezahlen pay cash
Bargeld cash *(no pl)*
Batterie battery
Bau building
Bauarbeiter/in builder
Bauchschmerzen stomach ache
bauen build
Bauer/Bäuerin farmer
Bauernhof farm
Baum tree
beängstigend frightening
(be)antworten answer
(Land) bebauen farm (land)
beben shake
(Wasser)becken tank
bedeckt cloudy
bedeuten mean

Bedeutung meaning; importance *(no pl)*
Bedienstete/r servant
Bedienung waiter/waitress; service
Bedingungen conditions *(npl)*
jdn bedrohen threaten sb
sich beeilen hurry
beeindruckend impressive
(be)enden end, stop
beenden finish, stop
beendet finished
sich befassen mit deal with
sich befinden be located
Beförderung transport
befragen interview
befürchten fear
begehen *(Verbrechen)* commit
Beginn start
beginnen begin
(be)grüßen greet, say hello to
begrüßen welcome
(be)halten keep
(Flüssigkeits)behälter tank
Behandlung therapy
behindert disabled
Behörde authority
bei by, at
beibringen teach
beide both
beifügen enclose
Beilage side order
beilegen enclose
Bein leg
beinahe almost, nearly
beinhalten include
Beispiel example
zum Beispiel for example
beißen bite
beitreten join
bekannt known
(allgemein) bekannt well-known
sich beklagen complain
Bekleidung clothes *(npl)*
bekommen get
jdn belästigen bother sb
Beleg receipt
Belegschaft staff *(no pl)*
jdn beleidigen offend sb
Beleidigung insult
beliebt popular
Beliebtheit popularity *(no pl)*

bellen bark
bemerken notice; detect
Bemerkung comment
sich sehr bemühen, etw zu tun try hard to do sth
jdn benachteiligen discriminate against sb
Benehmen behavior *(AE)*, behaviour *(BE)*
sich benehmen behave
(be)nennen name
benutzen use
beobachten observe, watch
bequem comfortable
(be)raten advise
Berg mountain
Bericht report
berichten report
Beruf career
eine Berufsausbildung machen do vocational training
Berufserfahrung work experience *(no pl)*
Berufsschule vocational school
berühmt famous, well-known
berühren touch
(be)schädigen damage
beschäftigt busy
Bescheid wissen über know about
jdn beschimpfen call sb names
beschließen decide
beschreiben describe
Beschreibung description
besiegen beat
besitzen own
Besitzer/in owner
besondere(r, s) special
besonders especially, extra
besorgt worried
besprechen discuss
(be)sprühen spray
Bestandteil ingredient
Bestattungsinstitut undertaker
(ein Flugzeug) besteigen board (a plane)
(etw) bestellen order; have sth
Bestellung order
beste(r, s) best
bestimmte(r, s) certain
bestrafen punish
Besuch visit

besuchen visit
Besucher/in visitor
betrachten look at
betreten enter
Betreuer/in instructor
Bett bed
betteln beg
Bettler/in beggar
beunruhigt worried
Bevölkerung population
bevor before
bevorzugen prefer
bewachen guard
etw bewältigen cope with sth
sich bewegen move
sich bewerben (um/für) apply
  (for/to)
Bewerber/in candidate
Bewerbungsformular
  application form
Bewerbungsgespräch job
  interview
Bewerbung(sschreiben) (letter
  of) application
bewölkt cloudy
sich einer Sache bewusst sein
  be aware of sth
sich einer Sache bewusst
  werden realise sth
bezahlen pay
bezaubernd charming
Bibliothek library
(sich) biegen bend
Bier beer
(an)bieten offer
bieten present (to)
Bild picture, painting
(sich) bilden form
Bilder machen take photos, take
  pictures
(Aus)bildung education
billig cheap
Biologie biology
Birne pear
bis till, until
(spätestens) bis by
Bis bald! See you! *(informal)*
bis jetzt yet, so far
bis zu up to
bisher so far
bitte please
Bitte request

bitten (um) request, ask
Bitte schön! Here you are.
blasen blow
Blatt Papier piece of paper
Blattsalat lettuce
blau blue
bleiben stay
Bleistift pencil
Blick look
jdm einen bösen Blick zuwerfen
  give sb a hard stare
(Aus)blick view
blockieren block
blöd stupid
blond blonde
Blume flower
Boden floor; bottom
(Erd)boden ground
Bohne bean
Bombe bomb
Boot boat
böse mad
braten fry
Brathähnchen fried chicken
Brauch custom, tradition
brauchbar useful
brauchen need
braun brown
(zer)brechen break
breit wide
brennen be on fire
(ver)brennen burn
Brett board
Brief letter
Briefmarke stamp
Brieftasche wallet
Briefumschlag envelope
Brille glasses *(npl)*
jdm etw bringen get sb sth
jdn dazu bringen, etw zu tun
  make sb do sth
die Briten the British *(pl)*
britische(r, s) British
Broschüre brochure
Brot bread
Brötchen roll
Brücke bridge
Bruder brother
brüllen roar
Brunnen fountain
Brust(korb) chest
brutal violent

Buch book
buchen book
Bücherei library
Büchse tin
Buchstabe letter
buchstabieren spell
Büffel buffalo
bügeln iron
Bühne stage
Bulle bull
(Bundes)staat state
Bundesstraße highway
Burg castle
(Staats)bürger/in citizen
Büro office
(ab)bürsten brush
Bus bus
Busch bush
Bushaltestelle bus stop
Bußgeld fine
Butter butter

C

Cafeteria cafeteria
Campingplatz campsite
Cent(münze) cent
Center centre
Centstück p (= penny, pence)
Chance chance, opportunity
Chaos chaos *(no pl)*
Charakter personality
Chef boss
Chemikalie chemical
China China
Chinese/Chinesin Chinese
chinesisch Chinese
Chips crisps *(npl)*
Clan clan
Couch sofa
Cousin/e cousin
Curry(gericht) curry

D

da since
da lassen leave
Dach roof
etw dagegen haben mind
daher therefore
dahinter behind
damals then
Dame lady
Damm causeway; levee

danach afterwards
dankbar grateful
danke thank you, thanks
danken thank
dann then; next
Darf es noch etwas sein? Anything else?
darüber hinaus moreover
das the; that; which
Das beläuft sich auf ... That'll be ... *(informal)*
Das macht dann ... That'll be ... *(informal)*
Das tut mir leid. I'm sorry.
dasselbe the same
Daten data *(pl)*
Datenschutz data protection *(no pl)*
Datum date
dauern take
(an)dauern last
dauernd all the time; constantly
Definition definition
definitiv definitely
(sich) dehnen stretch
dein(e) your
deine(r, s) yours
Delphin dolphin
Demokratie democracy
demokratisch democratic
denken think, suppose
denken an think of, think about
dennoch nevertheless
deprimiert depressed
der the; that; which
derselbe the same
deshalb therefore
Dessert dessert
Detail detail
(Privat)detektiv/in detective
deutsch German
Deutsche/r German
Deutschland Germany
Dezember December
Dialog dialogue
Diamant diamond
Diät diet
dich you; yourself
dick thick, fat
die the; that; which
Dieb thief *(pl thieves)*
dienen serve

Diener/in servant
Dienst service
Dienstag Tuesday
Dienstmädchen servant
diese these *(pl of this)*, those *(pl of that)*
dieselbe the same
diese(r, s) this
Ding thing
Dingo dingo *(pl -es)*
Dinosaurier dinosaur
dir yourself *(pl yourselves)*, you
direkt direct
jdn diskriminieren discriminate against sb
Diskussion discussion
Dokumentarfilm documentary
Dokumentation documentary
Donnerstag Thursday
Doppelzimmer double room
Dorf village
dort(hin) there
Dose can, tin
Dosencontainer can bank
Drache dragon
drangsalieren bully
draußen outdoor(s), outside
dreckig dirty
drehen film
sich drehen turn
(um)drehen spin (a)round
dringend desperately
drinnen indoor(s)
Drittel third
Droge drug
damit drohen, etw zu tun threaten to do sth
(aus)drucken print (out)
drücken press, push, squeeze; click
Druckerpatrone printer cartridge
du bist dran (it's) your turn
Du meine Güte! Oh dear!
du you
Duft smell
dumm stupid, silly
dunkel dark
dünn thin, skinny, slim
durch through
durcheinander confused
Durcheinander mess, chaos *(no pl)*

durcheinanderbringen disturb
durchqueren cross
(durch)suchen search
etw tun dürfen be allowed to do sth
Dürre(periode) drought
duschen take a shower

E

Ebene level
echt real
Ecke corner
jdm ist es egal sb does not care
egoistisch selfish
Ehefrau wife *(pl wives)*
ehemalige(r, s) former
ehrlich honest
Ei egg
eifersüchtig jealous
eigene(r, s) own
eigentlich actually
Eigentümer/in owner
sich eignen fit
ein bisschen a bit, a little
einander each other
Einbildung imagination
einchecken check in
sich eincremen mit put on
eindeutig clear; definitely
ein(e) a/an; one
einerseits on the one hand
eines Tages one day
einfach easy, simple; just
jdm einfallen come to sb's mind
Einfluss effect; power
einfrieren freeze
einführen establish
etw eingestehen admit sth
einhängen hang up
einige (a) few, several, some
sich einigen auf agree on
Einkaufspassage mall
Einkaufswagen trolley
Einkaufszentrum (shopping) mall
einladen invite
Einladung invitation
sich einloggen log on
einmal once
einpacken wrap
einrichten set up
einsam lonely

einschalten turn on
einschlafen fall asleep
einschließen include
einsehen see
einsetzen fill in
einsteigen (in) get on
einstufen rank
Einwanderer/in immigrant
einwandern immigrate
Einwanderung immigration
(ein)wickeln wrap
Einzelfahrkarte single (ticket)
Einzelheit detail
einzelne(r, s) single
Einzelperson individual
Einzelzimmer single room,
   private room
einzigartig unique
Eis ice
Eis am Stiel popsicle
(Eisen)bahn railroad *(AE)*,
   railway *(BE)*
Eiskrem ice cream
Eiweiß protein
Elefant elephant
elegant elegant
Elektriker/in electrician
elektrisch electrical
(elektrischer) Strom (electric)
   power
Elektrizität electricity
Elektro- electrical
Elektrogerät electrical appliance
Elektronik electronics *(npl)*
Elendsviertel slum
Ellbogen elbow
Eltern parents
elternlos orphaned
Elternteil parent
emotional emotional
Empfang reception *(no pl)*
Empfangschef/in receptionist
Ende end, ending
enden end up
(be)enden end, stop
endgültig final
endlich finally
Energie energy
energiesparend energy-saving
energisch aggressive
England England
englisch English

auf Englisch in English
Enkelkind grandchild *(pl*
   grandchildren)
entdecken discover; detect; spot
Entdecker/in explorer
Ente duck
entfernen remove
(ent)fliehen escape
entkommen escape
entlang along
sich entscheiden decide
Entscheidung decision
Entschluss decision
sich entschuldigen apologize
Entschuldigen Sie bitte! Excuse
   me!
Entschuldigung apology; excuse
Entschuldigung! Sorry!
entsetzt shocked
entspannend relaxing
jdn enttäuschen let sb down
enttäuscht disappointed
entweder ... oder ... either ...
   or ...
entwerfen design
(sich) entwickeln develop
Entwicklung development
Entwicklungsland developing
   country
entwurzeln uproot
Episode episode
er he
Erbse pea
Erdatmosphäre atmosphere
Erdbeben earthquake
Erdbeere strawberry
(Erd)boden ground
dem Erdboden gleich machen
   flatten
Erde ground
die Erde earth, globe
Erdkunde geography
Erdnuss peanut
Erdteil Kontinent
erfahren experience
Erfahrung experience
erfinden invent, make up
Erfindung invention
Erfolg success *(no pl)*
erfolgreich successful
erforderlich necessary
erfunden made-up

Ergebnis result
erhalten get
erhitzen heat
sich erinnern (an) remember
Erkältung cold
(wieder)erkennen recognize
erklären explain
Erklärung definition
Erkrankung illness
erlangen gain
Erlaubnis license
erleben experience
Erlebnis adventure
ermorden murder
Ernährung diet
ernst serious
ernst nehmen take seriously
ernst(lich) seriously
Ernte harvest
eröffnen start
eröffnet werden open
Erörterung discussion
(er)raten guess
erreichen reach
erschaffen create
erscheinen appear
erschöpft exhausted
erschrecken scare
erschüttern hit
ersetzen replace
erst only
erste(r, s) first
als Erstes (at) first
Ertrag harvest
ertragen stand
erwachsen werden grow up
Erwachsene/r adult
Erwärmung der Erdatmosphäre
   global warming *(no pl)*
erwarten expect
erwerben gain
erzählen tell
Erzähler/in narrator
Erzählung story
erzeugen produce
Erzeugnis product
Erzieher/in nursery teacher
Erziehungsberechtigte/r parent
es it
Es freut mich, Sie/dich kennen
   zu lernen. Nice to meet you.
es gibt there is, there are

essen eat; have
Essen food *(no pl)*, meal
Essen zum Mitnehmen takeaway
zu essen geben feed
Essgewohnheiten eating habits *(npl)*
Essig vinegar
Esszimmer dining room
etwas something, anything; some
euch you; yourselves
euer/eure your
eure(r, s) yours
Europa Europe
Europäer/in European
europäisch European
ewig forever
existieren exist
Expedition expedition
explodieren explode
extrem extreme

F

Fabrik factory
(Schul)fach subject
Fähigkeit skill, ability
Fahne flag
Fähre ferry
fahren drive, ride
Fahrer/in driver
Fahrgast passenger
Fahrkartenschalter ticket counter
Fahrplan timetable
Fahrrad bicycle
(Fahr)rad bike
Fahrt trip
Fairness sportsmanship *(no pl)*
Fakt fact
Fall case
fallen fall
fallen lassen drop
fällen cut down
falls if
falsch false, wrong
(zusammen)falten fold
Familie family; clan
Familienname surname
fangen catch
Fantasie fantasy, imagination
fantastisch fantastic *(informal)*
Farbe colour

färben dye
farbenfroh colourful
farbenprächtig colourful
farbig coloured
Farbige/r Coloured
fast almost, nearly
faszinieren fascinate
faszinierend fascinating
faul lazy
Favorit/in favourite
Februar February
Feder feather; pen
Federmäppchen pencil case
Fehler mistake, fault
Feier celebration
feiern celebrate
Feigling coward
Feld field
Fell fur
Fels(en) rock
Fenster window
Ferien vacation *(AE)*, holiday *(BE)*
Ferienlager summer camp
fernsehen watch TV
Fernsehen, Fernseher television, TV
Fernsehstudio TV studio
Fernsehwerbung commercial
Fernsehzeitschrift TV guide
fertig ready, finished
mit etw fertig werden cope with sth
(fest)halten hold
(Fest)land land
festnehmen catch
fett fat
Fett fat
fettig greasy
fettreduziert fat-reduced
Feuer fire
jdn feuern fire sb *(informal)*
Feuerwehrmann/-frau firefighter
Feuerwerk firework
fies mean
(Kino)film movie *(AE)*, film *(BE)*
filmen film
Filmstudio film studio
finden find
Finger finger
Firma firm, company
Fisch fish *(pl fish)*

fischen fish
sich fit halten keep fit
Flagge flag
Flamme flame
in Flammen stehen be on fire
Flasche bottle
Fleisch meat *(no pl)*
Fleischer/in butcher
flexibel flexible
Flexibilität flexibility
fliegen fly
(ent)fliehen escape
fließend fluent
Flohmarkt flea market
Floß raft
Flug flight
Flügel wing
Fluggast passenger
Flughafen airport
Flugzeug plane
Fluss river
(Flüssigkeits)behälter tank
flüstern whisper
(über)fluten flood
Folge result; consequence; episode
folgen follow
Form form
formen form
Formular form
Forscher/in explorer
Forschungsreise expedition
Foto photo, picture
Fotoapparat camera
fotografieren take photos, take pictures
Frage question
Fragen stellen ask questions
fragen ask
sich fragen wonder
Frankreich France
französisch French
Fraß junk food
Frau woman *(pl women)*, lady
Frau *(Anrede)* Mrs
Fräulein *(Anrede)* Miss
frei free
im Freien outdoor(s)
Freiheit freedom *(no pl)*
die Freiheitsstatue the Statue of Liberty
Freitag Friday

Freizeit free time
Freizeitpark theme park
fremd foreign, strange
Fremde/r stranger
sich auf etw freuen look forward
    to sth
Freund *(eines Mädchens)*
    boyfriend
Freund/in friend
Freundin *(eines Jungen)*
    girlfriend
freundlich friendly, kind, nice
Freundschaft friendship
Freundschaftsspiel friendly
    match
Freut mich, dich/euch/Sie
    kennen zu lernen. Pleased to
    meet you., Nice to meet you.
Frieden peace
Friedhof graveyard
friedlich peaceful
frisch fresh
Frischkäse cream cheese
Friseur/Friseuse hair stylist,
    hairdresser
Frisur hairstyle, haircut
frittieren fry
froh glad
fröhlich happy
Frosch frog
Frucht fruit
früh early
früher ... used to ... *(+ infinitive)*
frühere(r,s) former
Frühling spring
Frühstück breakfast
Frühstückszerealien cereal
(sich) fühlen feel
(an)führen lead
führend leading
Führer/in guide, leader; chief
füllen fill
Fünftel fifth
funktionieren work (out)
für for
Furcht fear
Furcht erregend frightening,
    scary
furchtbar awful, terrible
fürchten fear
sich fürchten be frightened, be
    afraid

Fuß foot *(pl* feet)
Fuß (= 0,3048 Meter) foot
    (pl foot *or* feet)
(zu Fuß) gehen walk
Fußball soccer *(AE)*,
    football *(BE)*
füttern feed
Fütterungszeit feeding time

G

Gabel fork
Galerie gallery
ganz whole; completely; all
den ganzen Tag all day
Ganztags- full-time
Garage garage
garantieren guarantee
Garten garden
Gärtner/in gardener
Gas gas
Gast guest
Gebäude building
geben give
Gebiet area
geboren born
Gebrauch use
Geburt birth
Geburtsdatum date of birth
Geburtstag birthday
Gedicht poem
geduldig patient
Gefahr risk
(Lebens)gefahr danger
gefährlich dangerous
Gefangene/r prisoner
Gefängnis prison
gefrieren freeze
Gefühl feeling
geführt guided
gegen against
Gegensatz contrast
Gegenspieler/in opponent
Gegenstand object, thing
Gegenteil opposite
gegenüber opposite
einander gegenüber face to face
Gegner/in opponent
Gehalt pay *(no pl)*
geheim secret
Geheimnis secret
gehen go, walk
(zu Fuß) gehen walk

mit jdm gehen date sb
    (informal)
Gehirn brain
gehören zu go with
Geist ghost
gekocht boiled
Gelächter laughter *(no pl)*
Gelände ground
Geländer rail
gelangen get
gelassen calm
gelb yellow
Geld money
Geld aufbringen raise money
Geld verdienen make money
Geldautomat cash machine
Geldstrafe fine
Geldstück coin
Gelee jelly
Gelegenheit opportunity
gelegen sein be located
Gemälde painting
gemein mean
Gemeinde community
gemeinsam together
Gemeinschaft community
gemischtrassig coloured
Gemüse vegetable
genannt called
genau exactly, just
(genau)so ... wie ... as ... as ...
Genehmigung licence
Generation generation
generell in general
Genesungskarte get well card
genießen enjoy
genug enough
von etw genug haben be sick
    of sth
genügend enough
geöffnet open
Geographie geography
Gepäck luggage *(no pl)*
geprellt bruised
gerade just; no sooner ... than
(gerade noch) rechtzeitig (just)
    in time
gerade(aus) straight
Gerät gadget
Geräusch sound, noise
Gericht court; dish *(pl* -es)
Gern geschehen. You're welcome.

Geruch smell
Gesamt- total
Geschäft shop
Geschäftsführer/in manager
geschehen happen
gescheit clever
Geschenk present
Geschichte history; story
Geschick(lichkeit) skill
geschieden divorced
Geschirrspülmaschine
   dishwasher
Geschwindigkeit speed
Geschwister brothers and
   sisters
Gesellschaft society; company
gesellschaftlich social
Gesetz law
Gesicht face
Gespenst ghost
Gespräch dialogue, talk
gesprächig communicative
gestalten create
Gestank smell
gestern yesterday
gestresst stressed
gesund healthy
gesund werden get well
Gesundheit health
Gesundheitsfürsorge health
   care
Gesundheitsversorgung health
   care
Getränk drink
Getreide corn
Getreide(sorte) cereal
getrennt separate
Gewalt violence
gewalttätig violent
Gewalttätigkeit violence
Gewicht weight
Gewinn prize
gewinnen win; gain
Gewinner/in winner
gewisse(r, s) certain
sich an etw gewöhnen get used
   to sth
Gewohnheit habit
gewöhnlich usually
gießen water
Giraffe giraffe
Gitarre guitar

Gitter grid
glamourös glamorous
Glas glass
glatt *(Haar)* straight
Glaube religion
glauben think
glauben (an) believe (in)
gleich just; equal
jdm ist es gleich sb does not
   care
gleich darauf next
gleichaltrig the same age
gleichberechtigt equal
Gleichberechtigung equality
Gleichheit equality
Gletscher glacier
Globus globe
Glück good luck
Glück haben be lucky
glücklich glad, happy
glücklicherweise luckily
Glückwunsch congratulations
   (npl)
Glückwünsche congratulations
   (npl)
Glühbirne light bulb
Gnu wildebeest *(pl - or -s)*
Gold gold *(no pl)*
Goldfisch goldfish
Gott god
Gott sei Dank! Thank goodness!
Graffitikünstler graffer
   (informal)
Grafiker/in graphic artist
Grammatik grammar
Gras grass
grässlich nasty
gratis (for) free
grau grey
grausam cruel
greifen reach
Grenze border; limit
Griechenland Greece
grillen grill; have a barbecue
eine Grillparty feiern have a
   barbecue
groß big, large, tall, great
großartig great
Großbritannien Britain, Great
   Britain
Größe size
(Körper)größe height

Großeltern grandparents *(pl)*
nicht zu kontrollierender
   (Großflächen)brand wildfire
Großmutter grandmother
(Groß)stadt city
Großvater grandfather
jdn großziehen bring up sb,
   raise sb
grün green
Grund reason; excuse; cause
das ist der Grund, warum that's
   why
gründen found
Gründer/in founder
gründlich careful
Grundschule primary school
Gruppe group
beste Grüße best wishes
herzliche Grüße love
mit herzlichen Grüßen yours
   sincerely
mit freundlichen Grüßen yours
   sincerely
viele Grüße best wishes
(be)grüßen greet, say hello to
Gummi rubber
(Salat)gurke cucumber
gut good, fine
gut aussehend good-looking
Gut gemacht! Well done!
gut in etw sein be good at sth
Gute Besserung! Get well soon!
Guten Appetit! Enjoy your meal!

H

Haar(e) hair *(no pl)*
Haarschnitt haircut
haben have (got)
für etw haften be responsible
   for sth
Hai(fisch) shark *(pl -s or -)*
halb half
halb (neun) half past (eight)
Halbfinale semifinal
Hälfte half *(pl halves)*
Halle hall
hallo hello
Hals neck
Halskette necklace
halten last
(be)halten keep
(fest)halten hold

Hammer hammer
Hand hand
handeln take action; act
handeln von be about, deal with
Handlung action
Handy mobile phone
hängen hang
hart hard
Hass hate *(no pl)*
hassen hate
hässlich ugly
häufig frequent, often
Haupt- main
Häuptling chief
hauptsächlich mainly
Hauptspeise main dish
Hauptstadt capital
Hauptwort noun
Haus house
Hausaufgaben homework *(no pl)*
nach Hause home
zu Hause at home, indoor(s)
bei jdm zu Hause at someone's place
Haustier pet
Haut skin
hawai(an)isch Hawaiian
Hawaiianer/in Hawaiian
(hoch)heben lift (up)
Heer army
Heft exercise book
heftig powerful
heilig holy
Heim home
Heimatland home country
heimatlos homeless
Heimatstadt home town
heimlich secretly
Heimweh haben be homesick
Heirat marriage
heiraten get married, marry
heiß hot
ich heiße my name is
Wie heißt du?/Wie heißen Sie? What's your name?
Heizung heating
Held hero *(pl -es)*
helfen help
hell bright
Helm helmet

Hemd shirt
Henne hen
herausbringen release
herausfinden find out, discover; figure out
Herausforderung challenge
herauskommen come out
herausnehmen take out
sich herausputzen dress up
Herbst fall *(AE)*, autumn *(BE)*
Herde herd
herein in
hereinkommen come in
Herkunft background
Herr *(Anrede)* Mr
(vornehmer) Herr gentleman
herstellen produce
Hersteller producer
(her)überkommen come over
auf jdm herumhacken pick on sb
herunterfallen fall off
hervorragend excellent
Herz heart
Herzanfall heart attack
Herzinfarkt heart attack
hetzen hurry
heute today
heute Abend tonight
heute Morgen this morning
heute Nachmittag this afternoon
hier here
Hier, bitte! Here you are.
hiesig local
Hilfe help
hilflos helpless
Himmel sky
Hin- und Rückfahrkarte return (ticket)
hinab down
hinauf up
hinaufgehen walk up
(hinauf)klettern climb
(hinauf)steigen climb
hinausgehen go out
(in ...) hinein inside
hineingehen go in
in jdn/etw hineinrennen run into sb/sth
sich hinlegen lie (down)
sich (hin)setzen sit down
hinten in at the back of
hinter behind

(im) Hintergrund (in the) background
hinterherlaufen run after
Hinterland (Australiens) outback *(no pl)*
hinterlassen leave
hinüber over
hinunter down
hinzufügen add
hispanisch Hispanic
Hispano-Amerikaner/in Hispanic
Hitze heat *(no pl)*
hoch high, tall
(hoch)heben lift (up)
hochheben pick up
Hochschule college
hochspringen jump up
Hochwasser flood
Hochzeit wedding
hoffen hope
hoffentlich hopefully
Hoffnung hope
höflich polite
Höhe height
höhere Schule secondary school
holen get
Hölle hell
Holz wood
Holz- wooden
hölzern wooden
Honig honey
hören hear
(Zu)hörer/in listener
Horizont horizon, skyline
Hör(t) auf (damit)! Stop it!
Hose trousers *(npl)*
Hotel hotel
hübsch pretty, lovely
Hügel hill
Huhn chicken, hen
Hund dog
junger Hund puppy
Hundert hundred
Hunderttausende hundreds of thousands *(pl)*
Hunger hunger
(ver)hungern starve
hungrig hungry
Hurrikan hurricane
Hut hat
Hyäne hyena

DICTIONARY *German–English*

DICTIONARY GERMAN–ENGLISH

I

ich I
Ich hätte gern ... I'll have ...
Ich nehme ... I'll have ...
ich würde gern I'd like (to)
ich/wir auch same here
ideal ideal
Idee idea
Identifizierung identification (= ID) *(no pl)*
idiotisch idiotic
ignorieren ignore
ihm him
ihn him
ihnen them
Ihnen you
ihr you
Ihr(e) your
ihr(e) their
ihr(e, es) theirs
ihr(e, n) her
ihre(r, s) hers
ihre(r, s) yours
illegal illegal
Imbissstube snack bar
immer always
(immer) noch still
immer wenn whenever
etw immer wieder tun keep (on) doing sth
Immigration immigration
Imperator emperor
in in, into, at, to; around
(in ...) hinein inside
in Ordnung fine
Ist alles in Ordnung? Are you all right?
in Richtung toward(s)
Inder/in Indian
Indianer/in Indian, Native American
indianisch Indian, Native American
Indien India
indisch Indian
der Indische Ozean the Indian Ocean
Information information *(no pl)*
inklusive included
innen inside, indoor(s)
im Inneren inside
innerhalb within

Insel island
Inserat advert (= advertisement)
Instrument instrument
intelligent intelligent
Interaktion interaction
interessant interesting
Interesse interest
bei jdm Interesse wecken interest sb
jdn interessieren interest sb
sich interessieren für be interested in
interessiert (an) interested (in)
Internat boarding school
international international
im Internet on the Internet
im Internet surfen surf the Internet
etw ins Internet stellen post sth
intolerant intolerant
irgendein(e) any
irgendwo somewhere
irisch Irish
Irland Ireland
sich irren be wrong
Irrtum mistake
Italien Italy
Italiener/in Italian
italienisch Italian

J

ja yes
Jacke jacket
jagen hunt
Jahr year
Jahrbuch yearbook
Jahresausgabe yearbook
Jahrhundert century
Januar January
jedenfalls anyway
jede/r anyone, everyone, everybody
jede(r, s) each, every; any
jedoch however
jemals ever
jemand somebody, someone, anyone
jene those *(pl of* that)
jetzt now
Jongleur/in juggler
jubeln cheer
jüdisch Jewish

Jugend youth
Jugendherberge youth hostel
jugendlich teenage
Jugendliche/r youth
Jugendzentrum youth centre
Juli July
jung young
Junge boy
Juni June

K

Kaffee coffee
Kaiser/in emperor
Kalender calendar
Kalorie calorie
kalt cold, cool
Kälte cold
Kamera camera
Kameramann/-frau cameraman/-woman
Kamm comb
Kampagne campaign
Kampf battle, fight
kämpfen (um) fight (for), compete (for)
Kämpfer/in fighter
Kampfsport martial arts *(npl)*
Kanada Canada
Kanal channel
Kandidat/in candidate
Känguru kangaroo
Kaninchen rabbit
Kantine canteen
kapieren get
Kapitän/in captain
Kappe cap
kaputt broken
kaputtgehen break down
die Karibik the Caribbean (Sea)
karibisch Caribbean
das Karibische Meer the Caribbean Sea
die Karibischen Inseln the Caribbean
Karneval carnival
Karotte carrot
Karriere career
Karte ticket; card
(Land)karte map
Kartoffel potato *(pl* -es)
Kartoffelbrei mashed potatoes
(Papp)karton card(board) *(no pl)*

234

Käse cheese
Kasse *(im Kino, Theater)* box office
Kassenbon receipt
Katastrophe disaster
Katholik/in Catholic
katholisch Catholic
Kätzchen kitten
Katze cat
junge Katze kitten
kaufen buy
Käufer/in buyer
Kaufhaus department store
Kaugummi chewing gum *(no pl)*
kaum hardly
kaum ... als no sooner ... than
kein Wunder no wonder
kein(e) no
keiner no one
Keks biscuit
Keller cellar, basement
Kellner/in waiter/waitress
kennen know
jdn kennenlernen get to know sb
Kerl guy *(informal)*
Kerze candle
Kette chain
(Kfz-)Werkstatt garage
kicken kick
Kilo kilo
Kind child *(pl children)*
Kinderarbeit child labour
Kindergarten kindergarten *(AE)*, nursery school *(BE)*
Kino cinema
(Kino)film movie *(AE)*, film *(BE)*
Kirche church
Kirsche cherry
Kissen cushion
klagen complain
Klang sound
klappen work out
klar clear
klären solve
(Schul)klasse class
Klassenarbeit test
Klassenkamerad/in classmate
Klasse(nstufe) grade
Klassenzimmer classroom
kleben stick
Kleid dress
sich kleiden dress

Kleider clothes *(npl)*
Kleiderschrank wardrobe
Kleidung clothing *(no pl)*, outfit
klein little, small
Klempner/in plumber
(hinauf)klettern climb
klingeln ring
klingen sound
Klo toilet
Kloß dumpling
Klub club
klug clever
Kneipe pub
Knie knee
Knoblauch garlic
Knochen bone
Knödel dumpling
Koch/Köchin chef, cook
kochen cook
Koffer suitcase
Kohle(n)hydrat carbohydrate
Kollege/Kollegin colleague
Kolonie colony
komisch funny
kommen come
kommen wegen come for
Kommentar comment
Kommode chest of drawers
Komm(t) jetzt! Come on!
Kommunikation communication
kommunizieren communicate
Komödie comedy
Komposttonne compost bin
Konferenz conference
König king
Königin queen
können can
könnte might
Konrektor deputy head
Konsequenz consequence; effect
Kontakt contact
mit jdm in Kontakt bleiben keep in touch with sb
mit jdm in Kontakt treten get in touch with sb
jdn kontaktieren contact sb
Kontext context
Kontinent continent
Konto account
Kontrast contrast
Kontrolle control

kontrollieren check
Konzert concert, gig *(informal)*
Kopf head
Kopf hoch! Cheer up!
Kopfsalat lettuce
kopieren copy
Koralle coral
Korallenriff coral reef
Korb basket
Korn corn
Körper body
(Körper)größe height
körperlich physical
korrekt correct; properly
Korridor hall
korrigieren correct
kosten cost
Kosten cost
köstlich delicious
Kostüm fancy dress; costume
Krach noise
Kraft power, energy
krank ill, sick
jdn kränken offend sb
Krankenhaus hospital
(Kranken)pfleger nurse
(Kranken)schwester nurse
Krankheit disease, illness
kränklich unhealthy
(zer)kratzen scratch
kreativ creative
Krebs *(Krankheit)* cancer
Kreditkarte credit card
Kreide chalk *(no pl)*
Kreis circle
kreischen scream
Kreuzfahrt cruise
Kreuzfahrtschiff cruise ship
Krieg war
kriegen get; catch
Kriminelle/r criminal
Krokodil crocodile
Krone crown
Küche kitchen
Kuchen cake, pie
Kugelschreiber ballpoint
Kuh cow
kühl cool
Kühlschrank fridge *(informal)*
Kultur culture
sich kümmern um look after, take care of, care for

Kunde/Kundin customer
Kunst art
Künstler/in artist
Kunststoff plastic
Kurs course
kurz short
kürzlich lately
Kuss kiss
küssen kiss
Küste coast, seaside
Kuvert envelope

L

lächeln smile
lachen laugh
Lachen laughter *(no pl)*
über etw lachen laugh at sth
Lackierer/in painter
Laden shop
Lage location; situation
Lamm lamb
Lampe lamp
Land country
(Fest)land land
(Land) bebauen farm (land)
landen land
(Land)karte map
Landschaft landscape
lang long
langsam slow
sich langweilen be bored
langweilig boring
Lärm noise
Lass (doch) den Kopf nicht hängen! Cheer up!
lassen let; leave
lass(t) uns let's (= let us)
latino Latino *(AE)*
Latino Latino *(AE)*
laufen run
laufen lassen let off
Lauffeuer wildfire
laut loud, noisy; aloud
läuten ring
lauter sprechen speak up
leben live, be alive
Leben life *(pl lives)*
am Leben sein be alive
ins Leben rufen start
Lebensbedingungen living conditions *(pl)*
(Lebens)gefahr danger

Lebenslauf CV (= curriculum vitae)
Lebensweise way of life
lecker tasty, delicious
leer empty
legen put
Legende legend
lehnen lean
Lehnstuhl armchair
Lehre apprenticeship
Lehrer/in teacher, instructor
Leichenbestatter/in undertaker
leicht easy
Das tut mir leid. I'm sorry.
leider unfortunately
leihen borrow
leise quiet
sich leisten afford
leistungsfähig powerful
leiten lead
Leiter/in leader
Leopard/in leopard
lernen learn; study
lesen read
letzten Endes in the end
letzte(r, s) last, final
Leute people *(pl)*
Licht light
Liebe love
alles Liebe love
lieben love
liebe(r) *(Anrede)* dear
Liebesfilm romance
Liebesheirat love marriage
Liebling favourite
Lieblings- favourite
Lied song
(Lied)text lyrics
Lieferant/in für Speisen und Getränke caterer
liegen be located, lie
Lineal ruler
Linie line
links on the left
Liste list
Löffel spoon
Lohn wage(s), pay *(no pl)*
die (Londoner) U-Bahn the tube
Los!; Los geht's! Let's go!
etw löschen put out sth
lösen solve
Lösung solution
etw loswerden get rid of sth

Löwe lion
Luft air
lügen lie
lustig fun, funny
Luxus luxury

M

machen make, do
Macht power
Mach(t) schon! Come on!
mächtig powerful
Mädchen girl
Magazin magazine
Magenschmerzen stomach ache
mager skinny
Magersucht anorexia *(no pl)*
magersüchtig anorexic
Magie magic
mähen cut
Mahlzeit meal
eine Mahlzeit zu sich nehmen have a meal
Mai May
Majonäse mayonnaise
Mal time
malen paint
Maler/in painter
Mama mum *(informal)*
manchmal sometimes
Mann man *(pl men)*
männlich male
Mappe folder
Marathon(lauf) marathon
Markt market
Marmelade jelly
März March
Maschine machine, engine
Maschine schreiben type
Maskenbildner/in make-up artist
Material material
Mathe maths
Mechaniker/in mechanic
Medikament drug, medicine *(no pl)*
Medizin medicine *(no pl)*
Meer sea, ocean
Meeresschildkröte turtle
Mehl flour
mehr more
mehr als genug plenty
mehr oder weniger more or less

Meile mile
mein(e) my
meinen think; mean
meine(r, s) mine
Meinung opinion, view
einer Meinung sein über agree on
meiner Meinung nach in my opinion
Meisterschaft championship
(sich) melden report
Melone melon
Menge amount
jede Menge lots of
Mensa canteen
Mensch human, person
Menschen people *(pl)*
(Menschen)menge crowd
menschlich human
Menü menu
messen measure
Messer knife *(pl* knives*)*
Metall metal
Meteorologe/Meteorologin meteorologist
Meter metre
Metzger/in butcher
Mexikaner/in Mexican
mexikanisch Mexican
Mexiko Mexico
mich myself; me
Miete rent
Mikrowelle(nherd) microwave
Milch milk
Milchprodukt dairy food
Million million
Millionär/in millionaire
mindestens at least
Mineral mineral
Minute minute
mir me; mine; myself
(ver)mischen mix
Mischung mixture
mit with; by
Mitarbeiter staff *(no pl)*
Mitarbeiter/in colleague
mitgerechnet included
(mit)bringen bring
Mitglied member
Mitleid mit jdm haben feel sorry for sb
mitlesen read along

mitmachen join (in)
(mit)nehmen take
Mitschüler/in classmate
Mittagessen lunch; dinner
Mittagspause lunchtime
Mittagszeit lunchtime
Mitte middle
in der Mitte in the middle of
mitteilsam communicative
das Mittelmeer the Mediterranean Sea
mitten in in the middle of
Mitternacht midnight
Mittwoch Wednesday
Mobbing bullying
Möbel furniture *(no pl)*
Mobiltelefon mobile phone
Möchten Sie schon bestellen? (Are you) ready to order?
modern modern
mögen like, fancy *(informal)*
etw gerne mögen be fond of sth
sehr gern mögen love
möglich possible
möglicherweise maybe
Möglichkeit opportunity, chance
Möhre carrot
Mohrrübe carrot
Moment moment
Moment mal! Wait a second!
einen Moment bitte just a minute
momentan at the moment
Monat month
Montag Monday
Morgen morning
morgen tomorrow
am Morgen in the morning
morgens in the morning; am (= ante meridiem) *(nur hinter Uhrzeit)*
motiviert motivated
Motor engine
müde tired
Müll rubbish *(no pl)*, waste *(no pl)*, litter *(no pl)*
Mülleimer bin
Mülltonne bin
Mund mouth
Münze coin
Museum museum
Musik music

(Musik)album album
müssen have to, must, need to
müsste should
mutig brave
Mutter mother
Muttersprache first language
Mutti mum *(informal)*
Mütze cap

N

nach after; for, to
(nach) links left
(nach) oben upstairs, up
(nach) rechts right
nach vorn(e) forward
Nachbar/in neighbour
Nachbarschaft neighbourhood
nachdem after
nachdenken think
nachfüllen refill
Nachmittag afternoon
nachmittags in the afternoon; pm (= post meridiem) *(nur hinter Uhrzeit)*
Nachname surname
Nachricht message
Nachrichten news *(no pl)*
Nachrichtensendung the news
nachschlagen look up
nachspielen act out
nächste(r, s) next
Nacht night
Nachtisch dessert
Nacken neck
Nadel needle
nah(e) near; close
der Nahe Osten the Middle East
nähen sew
Nahrung diet
Name name
Nase nose
Nashorn rhino (= rhinocerus)
nass wet
national national
National- national
Nationalität nationality
Nationalpark national park
Natur nature
naturbelassen natural
Naturkatastrophe natural disaster

Naturkundemuseum natural history museum
natürlich of course; natural
Naturwissenschaft science
Nebel fog
neben next to
neblig foggy
Neffe nephew
(mit)nehmen take
nein no
nennen call
(be)nennen name
nerven annoy
jdm auf die Nerven gehen get on sb's nerves
nervös nervous
nett kind, nice
neu new, fresh
neugierig curious
Neuigkeit news *(no pl)*
Neujahr New Year *(no pl)*
neulich the other day
Neuseeland New Zealand
nicht not
nicht dürfen must not
nicht einverstanden sein disagree
nicht länger not … any longer
nicht mehr not anymore
nicht mehr aktuell out of date
nicht mehr zeitgemäß out of date
nicht nur … sondern auch not only … but also
nicht stimmen be wrong
nicht übereinstimmen disagree
nicht zuletzt last but not least
nichts nothing
zu nichts zu gebrauchen useless
nicken nod
niederbrennen burn down
niederländisch Dutch
sich niederlassen settle
niedlich cute
niedrig low
nie(mals) never
niemand nobody, no one
Nilpferd hippopotamus
nirgends nowhere
nirgendwo nowhere
noch ein(e, r, s) another

noch (ein)mal again
noch immer still
noch nicht not yet
Nordamerika North America
Norden north
Nordirland Northern Ireland
Nordost- north-east
Nordosten north-east
nordöstlich north-east
Nordwesten north-west
normal normal; regular; common
normalerweise normally, usually
Note mark, grade
Notfall emergency
(sich) notieren note down
nötig necessary
Notiz note
(sich) Notizen machen (zu, über) make/take notes (on)
Notunterkunft emergency shelter
notwendig necessary
November November
Nudel noodle
Nudeln pasta
Nummer number
nun (ja) well
nur only, just
etw (aus)nutzen take advantage of sth
nützlich useful

O

ob whether
obdachlos homeless
oben on top
oberes Ende top
Oberhaupt chief
(Ober)schenkel thigh
obgleich although
Objekt object
Obst fruit
obwohl although
oder or
(Back)ofen oven
offen open
öffentlich public
offiziell official
(sich) öffnen open
oft often
ohne without

ohnmächtig werden faint
Ohr ear
Ohrring earring
ökologisch green
Oktober October
Öl oil
Olive olive
Oma grandma
Omi grandma
Onkel uncle
Opa grandpa
Opfer victim
Opi grandpa
Optimismus optimism *(no pl)*
optimistisch optimistic
Orangensaft orange juice
ordentlich tidy
Ordnung order
in Ordnung fine
Ist alles in Ordnung? Are you all right?
Organisation organization
organisieren organise
Orkan hurricane
Ort place
orten detect
örtlich local
Ost- east, eastern
Osten east
Osterfest Easter
Ostern Easter
östlich east, eastern
Ozean ocean
Ozonloch ozone hole

P

Paar pair; couple
packen pack
Packung packet
Paddel paddle
in Panik geraten panic
Papa dad *(informal)*
Papier paper
Pappe card, cardboard *(no pl)*
(Papp)karton cardboard *(no pl)*
Paprika pepper
Parade parade
Park(anlagen) park
Parkaufseher/in park ranger
Partei party

Partner partner
Partyservice caterer
(Reise)pass passport
passen suit; fit
passieren happen, go on
Passsagier/in passenger
Passwort password
Pastete pie
Patient/in patient
Pause break
peinlich embarrassing
peinlich berührt embarrassed
Pelz fur
Person person
Personal staff *(no pl)*
persönlich personal
Persönlichkeit personality
Pfad path, trail
Pfeffer pepper
pfeifen whistle
Pferd horse
Pflanze plant
pflanzen plant
(Kranken)pfleger nurse
pflücken pick
Pfote paw
Pfund pound (£)
die Philippinen the Philippines
physisch physical
Picknick picnic
die Pilger(väter) the Pilgrims *(pl)*
Pilot/in pilot
Pilz mushroom
Pinguin penguin
pink pink
Pizza pizza
Plan plan
planen plan
Planet planet
Plastik plastic
Plastikflaschencontainer plastic
  bottle bank
Plattform platform
Platz place; square
(Sitz)platz seat
plötzlich suddenly
Politiker/in politician
politisch political
Polizei police *(npl)*
Polizeibeamter/-beamtin police
  officer
Polizist/in policeman/-woman

Pommes frites French fries *(AE,
  npl)*, chips *(BE, pl)*
Pony pony
Popularität popularity *(no pl)*
Portion portion
Position position
positiv positive
Postamt post office
Postkarte postcard
Praktikant/in intern *(AE)*, trainee
  (BE)
Praktikum work experience
  (no pl)
praktisch practical
praktizieren practise
präsentieren present (to)
Präsentation presentation
Präsident/in president
Preis price; cost; prize; award
preiswert cheap
Prinz prince
privat private, personal
(Privat)detektiv/in detective
pro per, a
probieren try
Problem problem, difficulty
Produkt product
Produzent/in producer
produzieren produce
professionell professional
Profi professional
Programm programme; channel
Programmierer/in programmer
programmiert programmed
Projekt project
Prospekt leaflet
Protein protein
Protestant/in Protestant
protestantisch Protestant
provozieren provoke
Prozent per cent
Prüfung exam (= examination),
  test
Psychologe/Psychologin
  psychologist
Pullover jumper, sweater
Punkt point
einen Punkt machen score
punkten score
Punktestand score
pünktlich punctual, on time
Puppe doll

pur pure
Pute/r turkey
putzen clean (up); brush
(ab)putzen wipe
Pyjama pyjamas *(pl)*

Q

Quadrat square
Qualifikation qualification
Qualität quality

R

Rabauke bully
Rabe raven
Rad wheel
(Fahr)rad bike
Rad fahren cycle
Radar radar
Radeln cycling
Radfahren cycling
Radfahrer/in cyclist
Radiergummi rubber *(BE)*
Radio radio
Radiosender radio station
Radiowerbung commercial
Rampe ramp
Rasenmäher lawnmower
Rasse race
rassisch racial
Rassismus racism *(no pl)*
Rassist/in racist
rassistisch racist
Rat advice *(no pl)*
raten (have a) guess
(be)raten advise
Ratte rat
Rauch smoke
rauchen smoke
Raum space
Raumschiff spaceship
raus aus off
jdn rausschmeißen fire sb
  (informal)
reagieren react
Reaktion (auf) reaction (to)
Rechnung bill
Recht right
Recht haben be right
recht sein suit
rechts right, on the right
Rechtsanwalt/-anwältin lawyer
Rechtschreibung spelling

rechtswidrig illegal
rechtzeitig on time
(gerade noch) rechtzeitig (just) in time
recyclen recycle
reden (mit) talk (to)
Redewendung phrase
reduzieren reduce
reduziert sein be on sale
Referat talk
Regal shelf (*pl* shelves)
Regel rule
regelmäßig regular, frequent
Regen rain
Regenbogen rainbow
Regenwald rainforest
Regierung government
Region area
regnen rain
regnerisch rainy
reich rich
(aus)reichen last
Reihe queue
Reihenfolge order
rein pure
reinigen clean (up)
Reis rice
Reise journey, trip
Reiseführer travel guide
Reiseführer/in tour guide
Reiseleiter/in tour guide
reisen travel
(Reise)pass passport
reiten ride
Reiten riding
Reiter/in rider
reizend charming
Rektor/in headteacher
Religion religion
religiöse(r, s) religious
Rendezvous date
rennen run
Rennen race
reparieren repair
Reporter/in reporter
Reservat (= *ein den Indianern vorbehaltenes Gebiet*) reservation
Reservierung reservation
Respekt respect
respektieren respect
Rest rest

Restaurant restaurant
retten save, rescue
Rettungskraft rescue worker
Rettungssanitäter/in paramedic
Rettungsschwimmer/in lifeguard
Rezept recipe
Rezeption reception (*no pl*)
Rhinozerus rhino (= rhinocerus)
Rhythmus rhythm
Richter/in judge
richtig right, correct; properly
Richtung direction
riechen smell
Riese giant
riesengroß huge
riesig huge, giant, great
Riff reef
Ring ring
Risiko risk
Roboter robot
robust strong
Rock skirt
Rolle role; part
(Tret)roller scooter
Rollstuhl wheelchair
Rolltreppe escalator
Roman novel
romantisch romantic
Romanze romance
rosa pink
rot red
Rücken back
Rückenschmerzen backache
Rückseite back
Rudel herd
Ruf cry
rufen shout
jdn in Ruhe lassen leave sb alone
ruhig calm, quiet
ruinieren ruin
Rüpel bully

S

Sachbeschädigung vandalism
Sache thing, object
Saft juice
Sage legend
sagen say, tell
Sahne cream
Salat salad

(Salat)gurke cucumber
Salz salt
sammeln collect; pick; gain
Samstag Saturday
Sänger/in singer
Sanitärinstallateur/in plumber
Sarg coffin
etw satt haben be sick of sth
Satz sentence, phrase
sauber clean
sauber machen clean (up)
sauer mad
Schach(spiel) chess
Schachtel packet
zu schade too bad
schaden hurt
Schaden damage
(be)schädigen damage
Schaf sheep (*pl* sheep)
es schaffen manage
Schal scarf (*pl* -s *or* scarves)
Schale dish (*pl* -es); shell
Scham shame
sich schämen be ashamed
Schande shame
scharf sharp; spicy, hot
schätzen have a guess
schauen look
schaurig spooky (*informal*)
Schauspieler/in actor/actress
Schauspielerei drama (*no pl*)
Scheibe slice
scheinen seem
(Ober)schenkel thigh
Schere (pair of) scissors
scherzen be joking
scherzhaft playful
scheußlich nasty
Schicht shift
Schichtarbeit shift work (*no pl*)
Schichtdienst shift work (*no pl*)
(zu)schicken send
schieben push
Schiedsrichter/in referee
Schienen railroad (*AE*), railway (*BE*)
schießen kick
Schiff ship
Schimpanse chimpanzee
Schimpfwörter benutzen use bad language
Schinken ham

(Schinken)speck bacon
Schlacht battle
Schlaf sleep
Schlafanzug pyjamas *(pl)*
schlafen sleep, be asleep
Schlafsaal *(in dem Männer und Frauen übernachten)* mixed dorm
Schlafzimmer bedroom
schlagen (auf) hit, slap, beat
Schlagzeile headline
Schlange snake; queue
schlank slim
schlau clever
schlecht bad
jdm ist schlecht sb feels sick
schließen close
Schließfach locker
schließlich finally, in the end
schlimm bad; sore
Schlitten sled
Schlittschuh skate
Schloss castle
schlucken swallow
Schluss ending
Schlüssel key
Schlüsselwort keyword
schmackhaft tasty
schmal slim
schmecken taste
schmerzen hurt
Schmuck jewellery *(no pl)*
schmücken decorate
schmutzig dirty
Schnee snow
schneiden cut
schnell fast, quick
Schnellgerichte junk food
Schnellhefter folder
Schnupfen cold
Schock shock
schockierend shocking
schockiert shocked
Schokolade chocolate
schon already; yet
schön beautiful, nice, lovely
schottisch Scottish
Schottland Scotland
Schrank cupboard
Schraube screw
schrecklich horrible, awful, terrible

Schrei cry
schreiben write
(Briefe/E-Mails) schreiben mail
Schreibpapier writing paper *(no pl)*
Schreibtisch desk
schreien cry, shout, scream
Schriftsteller/in author
schüchtern shy
Schuh shoe
Schulabschluss graduation
Schularbeiten schoolwork *(no pl)*
Schuld fault
Schulden machen get into debt
schuldig guilty
Schule school
weiterführende Schule secondary school
Schüler/in pupil, student
(Schul)fach subject
(Schul)klasse class
Schulleiter/in headteacher
Schultasche schoolbag
Schulter shoulder
Schulung training
Schuppen shed
Schüssel bowl
(Schuss)waffe gun
Schutz protection, shelter
schützen protect
-schützer pad
schwanger pregnant
Schwangerschaft pregnancy
Schwangerschaftsabbruch abortion
schwarz black
Schweden Sweden
Schwein pig
schwenken wave
schwer heavy; difficult; seriously
Schwester sister
(Kranken)schwester nurse
schwierig difficult
Schwierigkeit difficulty
Schwierigkeiten trouble
Schwimmen swimming
schwimmen swim
Schwimmweste lifejacket
See lake
seekrank seasick

segeln sail
sehen see, look (at)
Sehenswürdigkeit sight
Sehleistung sight
sehr very, much, a lot (of)
Seifenoper soap (opera)
Seil rope
sein be
sein(e, r) his
seit since, for
Seite page, side
Sekretär/in secretary
Sekunde second
selbst even; myself, yourself, herself, himself, itself, ourselves, yourselves, themselves
selbstsüchtig selfish
Selbstvertrauen self-confidence *(no pl)*
Sendung programme
sensibel sensitive
separat separate
September September
Service service
servieren serve
Sessel armchair
setzen put
sich (hin)setzen sit down
seufzen sigh
sicher safe; sure, certain
Sicherheit safety *(no pl)*, security *(no pl)*
Sicherheitsdienst security *(no pl)*
sichern save
Sicht view
sie she, they, them, her
Siedler/in settler
Siedlung settlement
Sieger/in winner
Signal signal
signieren sign
singen sing
sinken sink
Sippe clan
Sitte custom
Situation situation
sitzen sit
(Sitz)platz seat
Skate-Veranstaltung skate
Skateboard fahren skate

skaten skate
Skelett skeleton
Ski ski
Sklave/Sklavin slave
Slum slum
SMS *(Handy)* text message
SMS verschicken text
so so, like this
so genannt so-called
(genau)so ... wie ... as ... as ...
sobald as soon as
Socke sock
Sofa sofa
sofort immediately
sogar even
Sohn son
solche(r, s) like this
Soldat/in soldier
sollte should
Sommer summer
sonderbar strange
Sonne sun
Sonnencreme sunscreen
Sonnenstrahl sunbeam
sonnig sunny
Sonntag Sunday
Sorge worry, fear
sich Sorgen machen (um) worry, be concerned (about)
sorgen für provide
sorgfältig careful
Sorte kind
sortieren sort
Soße sauce
sowieso anyway
sozial social
Sozialarbeiter/in social worker
soziales Netzwerk social network
soziales Netzwerken social networking
Spanien Spain
Spanier/in Spanish
spanisch Spanish
spannend exciting
sparen save
für etw sparen save up for sth
Spaß fun
Spaß machen be fun; be joking
spaßig fun, funny
(zu) spät late
später later, afterwards; future

Spaziergang walk
spazieren gehen go for a walk
(Schinken)speck bacon
speichern save
Speisekarte menu
spenden donate
Spiegel mirror
Spiegelei fried egg
Spiel game, play
spielen play
Spieler/in player
spielerisch playful
Spielfeld sports field, playing field
Spielplatz playground
Spielzeug toy
Spind locker
Spinne spider
Spion/in spy
Spitze top
sponsern sponsor
als Sponsor finanzieren sponsor
Sport(art) sport
Sportler/in sportsperson
Sportplatz playing field, sports field
Sportsendung sports programme
Sport(unterricht) PE (= physical education)
Sprache language
sprechen speak, talk (to)
Sprichwort saying
springen jump
(be)sprühen spray
(Bundes)staat state
Staatsangehörigkeit nationality
(Staats)bürger/in citizen
stabil strong
Stadion stadium *(pl -s or -ia)*
Stadt town
in der Stadt in town
(Groß)stadt city
Stall stable
Stamm *(Volk)* tribe, clan
(Verkaufs)stand stall
ständig all the time, constantly
stark strong; powerful; heavy
Stärke power
Station station
(an)statt instead (of)
stattdessen instead (of)

stattfinden take place
Staub dust *(no pl)*
Steckbrief fact file
stehen stand; suit
stehlen steal
(hinauf)steigen climb
Stein stone, rock
Stell dir vor! Guess what!
Stelle position; job
stellen put
Stempel stamp
sterben die
Stereoanlage stereo
Stern star
jdn im Stich lassen let sb down
Stiefel boot
Stier bull
Stift pen
Stil style
im Stillen secretly
Stimme voice
Stimmung atmosphere
die Stirn runzeln frown
Stock stick
Stockwerk floor, level
Stolz pride
stolz proud
stören disturb, bother
stoßen push
Strafe sentence
Straftat offence
(Straf)täter/in offender
Strand beach
Straße road, street
Straßenmusikant/in busker
(Straßen)schild sign
streicheln stroke
Streichholz match
Streik strike
in (den) Streik treten go on strike
streiken go on strike
Streit fight
(sich) streiten argue, fight
streng strict
stressig stressful
Strom electricity
(elektrischer) Strom (electric) power
Stück piece, bit
Stückchen bit
Student/in student

Studienabschluss graduation
studieren study
Studierende/r student
Studio studio
Stufe step
Stuhl chair
Stunde hour, lesson
Stundenplan (class) schedule *(AE)*, timetable *(BE)*
Stuntgirl/Stuntman stunt performer
Sturm storm
stürzen fall
stützen support
Substantiv noun
Suche search
(durch)suchen search
suchen nach look for
Suchmaschine search engine
süchtig (nach) addicted (to)
Südafrika South Africa
Südafrikaner/in South African
südafrikanisch South African
Südamerika South America
Süden south
Südosten south-east
Südwesten south-west
Supermarkt supermarket
Suppe soup
süß sweet; cute
süßes, kohlensäurehaltiges Getränk fizzy drink
Süßigkeit(en) sweet
Symbol symbol
System system
Szene scene

T

Tabelle grid
Tafel blackboard
Tag day
Tagebuch diary
(vier)tägig (four-)day
täglich daily
Tagung conference
Takt rhythm
Tal valley
Talent ability
Tante aunt
Tanz dance
tanzen dance
Tanzen dancing

Tänzer/in dancer
Tasche bag, pocket
Taschendiebstahl begehen pick pockets
Taschengeld pocket money
Tasse cup
(Straf)täter/in offender
Tätigkeit job
Tatsache fact
Tatze paw
tauschen swap
Tausend thousand
Tausende thousands *(pl)*
Tauziehen tug-of-war
Taxi taxi
Teamarbeit teamwork
Teamkollege/Teamkollegin teammate
Teammitglied teammate
Technik technology
Technologie technology
Tee tea
Tee trinken have tea
Teenager- teenage
Teigwaren pasta
Teil part
teilen share
sich teilen split up
teilnehmen (an) take part (in)
Teilzeit- part-time
Telefon (tele)phone
(Telefon)anruf call
Teller plate
Temperatur temperature
Tempo speed
Teppich carpet
Termin date
einen Termin vereinbaren make an appointment
Test test
teuer expensive
Text lines *(pl)*
(Lied)text lyrics *(pl)*
Thai Thai
Thailänder/in Thai
thailändisch Thai
Theater theatre; drama *(no pl)*
(Theater)stück play
Thema topic, subject
Themenpark theme park
Therapeut/in therapist
Therapie therapy

tief deep
Tier animal
Tier- und Pflanzenwelt wildlife
Tierarzt/-ärztin vet
Tiger tiger
tippen type
Tisch table
den Tisch decken set the table
Titel title
tja well
Tochter daughter
Tod death
Toilette bathroom *(AE)*, toilet *(BE)*
tolerant tolerant
Toleranz tolerance
Tomate tomato *(pl -es)*
Ton sound
Tor goal
ein Tor schießen score a goal
Tormann/Torfrau goalkeeper
Tornado tornado *(pl -es)*
tot dead
total totally
Totempfahl totem pole
töten kill
Tracht costume
Tradition tradition
traditionell traditional
träge lazy
tragen carry; wear
Trainer coach
trainieren train; exercise
Training practice
Transport transport
sich trauen dare
Traum dream
träumen dream
traurig sad
treffen hit, strike
sich treffen meet, get together
Treibhausgas greenhouse gas
trennen separate
sich trennen split up
Treppe stairs *(npl)*
treten step; kick
(Tret)roller scooter
trinken drink
trocken dry
Trockenheit drought
Trödelmarkt flea market

trotzdem nevertheless; anyway
Truthahn/-henne turkey
Tschüss! Bye! *(informal)*, Byebye! *(informal)*
tun do
tun können be able to do
Tür door
Türglocke doorbell
Türklingel doorbell
Turm tower
Turnen gymnastics *(npl)*
Turnhalle gym (= gymnasium)
Turnschuh trainer *(BE)*
Typ type; guy *(informal)*
typisch typical
Tyrann bully
tyrannisieren bully

U

U-Bahn subway *(AE)*, underground *(BE)*
die (Londoner) U-Bahn the tube
jdm ist übel sb feels sick
üben practise
über about, above, across, over
über Funk over the radio
überall everywhere
überall in/auf all over
(über)fluten flood
übergewichtig overweight
überholt out of date
Überleben survival
überleben survive
Überlebende/r survivor
sich (etw) überlegen think about (sth)
überprüfen check
überqueren cross
überraschen surprise
überraschend surprising
überrascht surprised
Überraschung surprise
überschwemmen flood
Überschwemmung flood
übersetzen translate
Überstunden machen do overtime
übertreten *(Vorschrift)* break
Überwachungskamera security camera
üblich common, normal, regular

übrig left
übrigens by the way
Übung exercise; practice
Uhr clock, watch
(acht) Uhr (eight) o'clock
(Uhr)zeit time
um at; around
um zu in order to
umblättern turn
umbringen murder
(um)drehen spin (a)round
(sich) umdrehen turn over, turn round
Umfrage survey
umgeben (von) surrounded (by)
Umgebung environment
umhauen cut down
Umkleide fitting room
sich umschauen (in) look around
sich umsehen (in) look around
umsonst (for) free; for nothing
Umwelt environment
umweltfreundlich green
(Umwelt)verschmutzung pollution
umziehen move
Umzug parade
Unabhängigkeit freedom *(no pl)*
unbezahlt unpaid
und and
unerschrocken brave
unfair unfair
Unfall accident
unfreundlich unfriendly
ungefähr about, more or less
ungerecht unfair
ungesund unhealthy
ungesundes Essen junk food
ungewöhnlich unusual, strange
unglaublich incredible
Unglück disaster
unglücklich unhappy
unglücklicherweise unfortunately
unheimlich spooky *(informal)*, scary
unhöflich impolite, rude
Uniform uniform
Universität university, college
unmöglich impossible
Unordnung mess
unrealistisch unrealistic

uns us, ourselves
unser(e) our
unsere(r, s) ours
unten below
unter under, among
unteres Ende bottom
untergebracht sein stay
untergehen sink
Untergeschoss basement
Unterhaltung talk
Unternehmen firm, company
Unterricht class
unterrichten teach
Unterschied difference
unterschreiben sign
Unterschrift signature
Unterseite bottom
unterstreichen underline
unterstützen support, help out
Untersuchung survey
amerikanischer Ureinwohner/ amerikanische Ureinwohnerin Native American
australische/r Ureinwohner/in Aborigine
Urlaub vacation *(AE)*, holiday *(BE)*
Urlaub haben be on holiday
im Urlaub sein be on holiday
Ursache cause
Urteil sentence
die USA the US (= United States)
USA (= Vereinigte Staaten von Amerika) USA

V

Vandalismus vandalism
Vater father
Vati dad *(informal)*
Vegetarier/in vegetarian
sich mit jdm verabreden ask sb out, date sb *(informal)*
Verabredung date
(sich) (ver)ändern change
(Ver)änderung change
verängstigt scared
für etw verantwortlich sein be responsible for sth
Verantwortlichkeit responsibility
Verantwortung responsibility
verärgert angry

Verband bandage
verbessern improve
etw verbieten ban sth
verbinden connect, link
sich mit jdm in Verbindung setzen contact sb
verboten forbidden
Verbrauch usage
Verbrechen crime
(ver)brennen burn
verbringen *(Zeit)* spend
verdammen damn
verdienen earn
Verein club
die Vereinigten Staaten the United States
Vereinigtes Königreich UK (= United Kingdom)
Verfasser/in author
jdm zur Verfügung stehen be at sb's disposal
zur Verfügung stellen provide
Vergangenheit past
vergessen forget
vergleichen compare
vergnügt(er) werden cheer up
jdn verhaften arrest sb
Verhalten behavior *(AE)*, behaviour *(BE)*
sich verhalten behave, act
Verhältnisse conditions *(npl)*; background
verheiratet married
(ver)hungern starve
sich verirren get lost
verkaufen sell
Verkäufer/in salesperson, seller, shop assistant
(Verkaufs)stand stall
Verkehr traffic
(Verkehrs)schild sign
verkehrt herum upside down
sich verkleiden dress up
Verkleidung fancy dress
verkleinern reduce
verlassen leave
sich verlassen auf rely on
verlässlich reliable
sich verlaufen get lost
verlegen embarrassed
verletzen injure
verletzt injured, hurt

sich verlieben (in) fall in love (with)
(in jdn) verliebt sein be in love (with sb)
verlieren lose
(ver)mischen mix
vermissen miss
vermuten guess, suppose
vernichten devastate
vernünftig sensible
veröffentlichen publish, release; issue
Verpackung(smaterial) packaging
verpassen miss
verprügeln beat up
Verräter traitor
verringern reduce
verrückt crazy
versäumen miss
verschieden different
verschmutzen pollute
verschmutzt polluted
(Umwelt)verschmutzung pollution
sich verschulden get into debt
verschwenden waste
Verschwendung waste *(no pl)*
verschwinden disappear
Versehen mistake
sich versichern make sure
Version version
versorgen take care of
den Weg versperren block
verspielt playful
versprechen promise
Verstand brain
sich verständigen communicate
verständnisvoll understanding
(sich) verstecken hide
verstehen understand, see, get, figure out
sich (mit jdm) verstehen get along (with sb)
verstellen block
verstoßen break
versuchen try
verteidigen defend
sich (wieder) mit jdm vertragen make it up with sb
vertraulich private
verurteilen damn

jdn zu etw verurteilen sentence sb to sth
vervollständigen complete
Verwandte/r relative
(jdn/etw) verwechseln mix up (sb/sth)
Verwendung use
verwirrt confused
verwundet hurt
verwüsten devastate
Verzeihung! Sorry.
verzweifelt desperate
Viel Glück! Good luck!
viel much, a lot (of), lots of
viele many, a lot (of)
Vielen Dank! Thanks a lot!
vielleicht perhaps, maybe
vielleicht tun might
(vier)tägig (four-)day
Viertel (nach/vor) quarter (past/to)
Viertel neighbourhood
virtuell virtual
Visagist/in make-up artist
Vitamin vitamin
Vogel bird
Volksfest carnival
voll full
völlig completely; absolutely; totally; all; total
volljährig werden come of age
Vollzeit- full-time
von from; by
von weit her far
vor before; in front of; to
vor (zwei Tagen) (two days) ago
vor einigen Tagen the other day
vor langer Zeit a long time ago
vorbei over
vorbei an past
vorbereiten prepare
sich vorbeugen bend over
(im) Vordergrund (in the) foreground
vorführen perform
Vorhang curtain
vorher before
vorhersagen forecast
Vorkenntnisse previous experience
vorkommen exist
Vorlieben likes *(pl)*

vormittags in the morning; am (= ante meridiem) *(nur hinter Uhrzeit)*
Vorname first name
vorn(e) in front
vorne in at the front of
(vornehmer) Herr gentleman
vorschlagen suggest
Vorschule kindergarten *(AE)*, nursery school *(BE)*
vorsichtig careful
Vorsingen audition
Vorsitzende/r president
Vorspeise starter
Vorspielen audition
Vorsprechen audition
vorstellen introduce
sich vorstellen imagine
Vorstellungsgespräch job interview
Vorstellungskraft imagination
Vortanzen audition
Vorteil advantage
vorüber an past
Vorurteil prejudice
vorziehen prefer
Vulkan volcano *(pl -oes or -os)*
Vulkanausbruch volcanic eruption

W

wach awake
Wachs wax
wachsen grow
Wachstum development
Waffe weapon
(Schuss)waffe gun
wagen dare
Wahl choice, election
wählen elect, vote
Wahlfach elective *(AE)*
Wahlkurs elective *(AE)*
wahr true
wahr werden come true
während during, while
Wahrheit truth
Wahrsager/in fortune-teller
wahrscheinlich probably
Waise orphan
Waisenkind orphan
Wal whale
Wald forest

walisisch Welsh
Wand wall
wandern hike
Wandern hiking
Wange cheek
wann when
wann (auch) immer whenever
warm warm
Wärme heat *(no pl)*
warnen warn
Warnung warning
warten (auf) wait (for)
Wartezimmer waiting room
warum why
was what
Was gibt's? What's on?
Was ist mit ...? How about ...?, What about ...? *(informal)*
Was kostet/kosten ...? How much is/are ...?
Was läuft? What's on?
was man tun und was man nicht tun sollte dos and don'ts
(sich) waschen wash
Waschmaschine washing machine
Wasser water
(Wasser)becken tank
Wasserfall waterfall
Wasserhahn tap
Wechselgeld change
wechseln change
Wecker alarm clock
weg away
Weg way, path, trail
den Weg beschreiben give directions
den Weg versperren block
jdm über den Weg laufen run into sb
weg von off
wegen because of; about
weggehen leave, be off
weglaufen run away
weh sore
wehen blow
Wehrdienst leisten do military service
wehtun hurt
weiblich female
weich soft
Weide field

sich weigern refuse
Weihnachten Christmas
weil because, since
Weile while *(no pl)*
Weinen cry
weinen cry
Weise way
weiß white
weit far
weiter further
etw weiter tun keep (on) doing sth
weiterführende Schule secondary school
weitergehen go on
weitermachen go on
welche(r, s) what; which
Welle wave
Welpe puppy
Welt world
Weltraum space
Weltrekord world record
weltweit worldwide
wenige (a) few
weniger less
wenigstens at least
wenn if; when
wer who
Werbespot commercial
Werbung advert (= advertisement)
werden become; go; will; get
werfen throw
Werk factory
(Kfz-)Werkstatt garage
Werkzeug tool
etw wert sein be worth sth
wessen whose
West- west
Westen west
die Westindischen Inseln the West Indies *(npl)*
westlich west
Wettbewerb competition, contest
wetteifern (um) compete (for)
wetten bet
Wetter weather
wichtig important
Wichtigkeit importance *(no pl)*
(ein)wickeln wrap
widerlich disgusting, nasty

wie how, like
Wie geht es dir/Ihnen/euch? How are you doing?, How are you?
Wie geht's? How are things?
Wie heißt du?/Wie heißen Sie? What's your name?
Wie ist ...? What's ... like?
Wie spät (ist es)? What time (is it)?
Wie viel Uhr ist es? What's the time?, What time is it?
Wie wäre es mit ... ? How about ...?, What about ...? *(informal)*
wie (zum Beispiel) such as
wieder again
wieder aufbauen rebuild
(wieder)erkennen recognize
wiederherstellen restore
wiederholen repeat
Wiederholung repeat
wiederverwenden reuse
wiederverwerten recycle
wiegen weigh
Wiese field
Wild game *(no pl)*
wild wild
Wildnis bush *(no pl)*
willkommen heißen welcome
Wind wind
Windel nappy
(australischer) Windhund dingo
windig windy
Windpocken chickenpox
winken wave
Winter winter
winzig tiny
wir we
wirklich real; really
(Aus)wirkung effect
Wirtschaft economy
(ab)wischen wipe
wissen know
Wissenschaftler/in scientist
Witz joke
witzig fun, funny
Wo kommst du her? Where are you from?
Woche week
Wochenende weekend
Wochentage days of the week

wöchentlich weekly
wo(hin) where
wo(hin) auch immer wherever
wohltätige Zwecke charity
Wohltätigkeitslauf sponsored walk
Wohltätigkeitsveranstaltung charity
wohnen live; stay
Wohnung apartment *(AE)*, flat *(BE)*
Wohnzimmer living room
Wolke cloud
Wolkenkratzer skyscraper
wollen want, fancy *(informal)*
Wort word
Wörterbuch dictionary
Wortnetz mindmap
wund sore
wunderbar wonderful, great
wundervoll wonderful
Wunsch wish; request
(sich) wünschen wish; want; request
würde(st/n/t) would
Wurm worm
Wurst sausage
Würstchen sausage
Wurzel root
würzig spicy
Wüste desert
wütend angry, mad

Z

Zahl number
zählen count
Zahn tooth *(pl teeth)*
Zauber magic
Zauberer/Zauberin magician
Zaubertrick magic trick
Zaun fence
Zebra zebra
Zeh(e) toe
Zeichen sign, symbol
(Zeichen)trickfilm animated film, cartoon
zeichnen draw
zeigen show
Zeile line
(Uhr)zeit time
Zeit verbringen hang out *(informal)*

Zeitschrift magazine
Zeitschriftengeschäft newsagent
Zeitung newspaper
Zeitungshändler/in newsagent
Zeitverschwendung waste of time
Zeltplatz campsite
Zentrum centre
(zer)brechen break
zerbrochen broken
zerdrücken flatten
(zer)kratzen scratch
zerstören destroy, ruin, devastate
Zerstörung destruction *(no pl)*
Zettel piece of paper
ziehen pull
Ziel finish
ziemlich pretty, quite
Ziffer number
Zimmer room
Zitrone lemon
Zivildienst leisten do civilian service
Zoo zoo
zornig angry
zu too; to
(zu Fuß) gehen walk
zu Hause (at) home
zu nichts zu gebrauchen useless
zu schade too bad
Zucker sugar
zudem moreover
zuerst (at) first
zufällig by accident
Zuflucht shelter
zufrieden happy
zufrieren freeze
Zug train
etw zugeben admit sth
Zugfahrt train ride
Zuhause home
zuhören listen (to)
(Zu)hörer/in listener
zuknöpfen button
Zukunft future
zukünftig future
zumachen close
Zündholz match
zunehmen put on weight
zuordnen match (with)
zurück back

zurückbekommen get back
zurückkehren return
zurückkommen get back
zurücklassen leave
zusammen together
zusammenbrechen break down
Zusammenhang context
(zusammen)falten fold
zusammenschlagen beat up
zusätzlich extra

zuschauen watch
Zuschauermenge crowd
(zu)schicken send
zuschlagen strike
zusehen watch
Zuständigkeit responsibility
zustimmen agree (with)
Zutat ingredient
zuverlässig reliable
zuversichtlich optimistic

zuvor before
Zweig branch
zweimal twice
ein(e) zweite(r, s) another
Zwiebel onion
jdn zwingen (etw zu tun) force
   sb (to do sth)
zwischen between

NAMES

Girls/Women
Alicia [ə'lɪʃə]
Alisha [ə'lɪʃə]
Amy ['eɪmi]
Annie ['æni]
Bernie ['bɜːni]
Brede ['briːd]
Dawn [dɔːn]
Emily ['eməli]
Emma ['emə]
Gemma ['dʒemə]
Golda ['gəʊldə]
Gustava [gʊ'staːvə]
Hermione [hɜː'maɪəni]
Jacky ['dʒæki]
Jasmine ['dʒæzmɪn]
Juno ['dʒuːnəʊ]
Kate [keɪt]
Kathrin ['kæθrɪn]
Katie ['keɪti]
Katrina [kə'triːnə]
Kendra ['kendrə]
Kirsty ['kɜːsti]
Latika ['laːtɪkaː]
Leah [ˌliːə]
Leonora [ˌliːə'nɔːrə]
Lisa ['liːsə]
Maria [mə'riːə]
Melinda [mə'lɪndə]
Michelle [mɪ'ʃel]
Mira ['maɪrə]
Pat [pæt]
Phumzile ['pʌmzaɪl]
Rachel ['reɪtʃl]
Sadie ['seɪdi]
Sashi ['sæʃi]
Tessa ['tesə]
Vanessa [və'nesə]
Wendy ['wendi]
Zoe ['zəʊi]

Boys/Men
Aaron ['eərən]
Albert ['ælbət]
Ali ['æli]
Baruti [baː'ruːtɪ]
Ben [ben]
Bert [bɜːt]
Brad [bræd]
Brian ['braɪən]
Charlie ['tʃaːli]
Colin ['kɒlɪn]
Craig [kreɪg]
Darren ['dærən]
Fergus ['fɜːgəs]
Fred [fred]
Jamal [dʒə'maːl]
Jamie ['dʒeɪmi]
Jason ['dʒeɪsən]
Jim [dʒɪm]
Jordan ['dʒɔːdn]
Kevin ['kevɪn]
Liam ['liːəm]
Luke [luːk]
Manjit ['mʌndʒɪt]
Manny ['mæni]
Marc [maːk]
Mark [maːk]
Martin ['maːtɪn]
Matthew ['mæθjuː]
Mnqobi ['nkəʊbi]
Moloko [mə'lɒkəʊ]
Neil [niːl]
Paulie ['pɔːli]
Peter ['piːtə]
Rob [rɒb]
Robert ['rɒbət]
Roof [ruːf]
Salim [saː'liːm]
Sam [sæm]
Sean [ʃɔːn]
Stephen ['stiːvn]
Thabo ['taːbəʊ]
Tom [tɒm]
Yassir ['jæsə]

Families
Akbar ['ækbaː]
Barinski [bə'rɪnski]
Bennett ['benɪt]
Blake [bleɪk]
Bleeker ['bliːkə]
Boons [buːnz]
Burrus ['bɜːrəs]
Carroll ['kærəl]
Deaton ['diːtən]
Denton ['dentən]
Doyle [dɔɪl]
Fox [fɒks]
Go [gəʊ]
Gunn [gʌn]
Henry ['henri]
Lynch [lɪntʃ]
Malakalaka [ˌmæləkə'lækə]
Malik ['mælɪk]
Mayor [meə]
McCoy [mə'kɔɪ]
McGuff [mə'gʌf]
McHoggart [mək'hɒgət]
O'Brian [əʊ'braɪən]
Rafferty ['ræfəti]
Reddy ['redi]
Robertson ['rɒbətsən]
Roper ['rəʊpə]
Sheen [ʃiːn]
Simmonds ['sɪməndz]
Simpson ['sɪmpsən]
Stephens ['stiːvənz]
Taylor ['teɪlə]
Thembu ['tembuː]
Wedderspoon ['wedəspuːn]
Weinstein ['waɪnstaɪn]
Zwane ['zweɪn]

Other Names

African National Congress [ˌæfrɪkən‿ˈnæʃnəl ˈkɒŋgres]

Alice in Wonderland [ˌælɪs‿ɪn ˈwʌndəˌlænd]

the All Blacks [ðiˌ‿ɔːl ˈblæks]

the ANC (= African National Congress) [ðiˌ‿eɪˌen siː]

Bali Rai [ˌbaːli ˈraɪ]

The Beatles [ðə ˈbiːtlz]

Beyoncé [biˈjɒntseɪ]

Bristol Airport [ˌbrɪstl‿ˈeəpɔːt]

Britannia [brɪˈtænjə]

Buddy Holly [ˌbʌdi ˈhɒli]

Clint Eastwood [ˌklɪnt‿ˈiːstwʊd]

Clock Tower [ˈklɒk ˌtaʊə]

Convention on the Rights of the Child [kənˌvenʃn‿ɒn ðə raɪts‿əv ðə ˈtʃaɪld]

CSIRAC (= Council for Scientific and Industrial Research Automatic Computer) [ˌsiːˌes‿aɪˌaːr‿eɪ ˈsiː]

Danny Boyle [ˌdæni ˈbɔɪl]

Democratic Party [ˌdeməˈkrætɪk ˌpaːti]

Desmond Tutu [ˌdezmənd ˈtuːtuː]

Eddie Grant [ˌedi ˈgraːnt]

Ellen Page [ˌelən ˈpeɪdʒ]

Emma Watson [ˌemə ˈwɒtsən]

Esmile [ˌezˈmaɪəl]

Facebook [ˈfeɪsbʊk]

François Pienaar [ˌfrɒnswaː pieˈnaː]

Fried Green Tomatoes [ˌfraɪd ˌgriːn təˈmaːtəʊz]

Friendster [ˈfrendstə]

Glebe Point Road [ˌgliːb‿ˌpɔɪnt ˈrəʊd]

Glebe Village Backpackers [ˌgliːb ˌvɪlɪdʒ ˈbækˌpækəz]

Hannibal [ˈhænɪbəl]

Harry Potter [ˌhæri ˈpɒtə]

Harvard [ˈhaːvəd]

Heathrow Airport [ˌhiːθrəʊ‿ˈeəpɔːt]

Hollesley Bay Prison [ˌhɒləsli beɪ ˈprɪzn]

ICQ [ˌaɪ ˌsiː ˈkjuː]

Imbali Safari Lodge [ɪmˌbaːli səˈfaːri lɒdʒ]

Invictus [ɪnˈvɪktəs]

Jersey Zoo [ˌdʒɜːzi ˈzuː]

Jesus [ˈdʒiːzəs]

Jo'anna [dʒəʊˈænə]

Joan Lingard [ˌdʒəʊn ˈlɪŋgaːd]

Kenilworth Road [ˌkenlwɜːθ ˈrəʊd]

Khoka Moya [ˌkəʊkə ˈmɔɪə]

Kruger National Park [ˌkruːgə ˌnæʃnəl ˈpaːk]

kwaito [ˈkwaɪtəʊ]

Les Augrés Manor [leːzˌ‿əʊgreɪ ˈmænə]

Lone Grove Post [ˌləʊn ˌgrəʊv ˈpəʊst]

Mad Men [ˌmæd ˈmen]

Madonna [məˈdɒnə]

Malva Pudding [ˌmælvə ˈpʊdɪŋ]

Mardi Gras [ˌmaːdi ˈgraː]

Mark Zuckerberg [ˌmaːk ˈzʌkəbɜːg]

Matt Damon [ˌmæt ˈdeɪmən]

Michael Cera [ˌmaɪkl ˈsɪərə]

Morgan Freeman [ˌmɔːgən ˈfriːmən]

MySpace [ˈmaɪspeɪs]

National Weather Service [ˌnæʃnəl ˈweðə ˌsɜːvɪs]

Nelson Mandela [ˌnelsn mænˈdelə]

New England College [njuː‿ˌɪŋglənd ˈkɒlɪdʒ]

Nick Hornby [ˌnɪk ˈhɔːnbi]

Oklahoma Emergency Management [ˌəʊkləˌhəʊmə‿ɪˈmɜːdʒnsi ˌmænɪdʒmənt]

People Tree [ˈpiːpl triː]

PowerPoint [ˈpaʊəpɔɪnt]

Predator Exhibit [ˈpredətə ɪgˌzɪbɪt]

Psych [saɪk]

Queen Elizabeth [ˌkwiːn‿ɪˈlɪzəbəθ]

Queen Victoria [ˌkwiːn vɪkˈtɔːriə]

Samuel Morse [ˌsæmjuəl ˈmɔːs]

Shipandane Sleepover Hide [ˌʃɪpənˌdaːni ˈsliːpˌəʊvə haɪd]

Slam [slæm]

Slumdog Millionaire [ˌslʌmdɒg ˈmɪljəˌneə]

South African Airways [saʊθˌ‿æfrɪkən‿ˈeəweɪz]

the Springboks [ðə ˈsprɪŋbɒks]

the Superdome [ðə ˈsuːpədəʊm]

Table Mountain Aerial Cableway [ˌteɪbl ˌmaʊntɪnˌ‿eəriəl ˈkeɪblweɪ]

Teenage Bride [ˌtiːneɪdʒ ˈbraɪd]

Twilight [ˈtwaɪlaɪt]

Twitter [ˈtwɪtə]

Two Oceans Aquarium [ˌtuːˌ‿əʊʃnzˌ‿əˈkweəriəm]

the UN (= United Nations Organization) [ðə ˌjuːˌˈen]

UNICEF (= United Nations International Children's Emergency Fund) [ˈjuːnisef]

V&A Waterfront [ˌviːˌ‿ənˌeɪ ˈwɔːtəˌfrʌnt]

Vitamin C [ˌvɪtəmɪn ˈsiː]

Web 2.0 [ˌweb ˌtuː pɔɪntˌ‿əʊ]

Wii box [ˈwiː bɒks]

William Ernest Henley [ˌwɪljəmˌˌɜːnɪst ˈhenli]

Wyclef Jean [ˌwaɪklɪf ˈʒɒn]

Geographical Names

Africa [ˈæfrɪkə]

Arkansas [ˈaːkənsɔː]

the Atlantic Ocean [ðiˌ‿ətˌlæntɪk ˈəʊʃn]

Australia [ɒˈstreɪliə]

Baltimore [ˈbɔːltɪmɔː]

Bangladesh [ˌbæŋgləˈdeʃ]

Bangor [ˈbæŋgə]

Belfast [ˌbelˈfaːst]

Berlin [ˌbɜːˈlɪn]

Bombay [ˌbɒmˈbeɪ]

Bristol [ˈbrɪstl]

Cambridge [ˈkeɪmbrɪdʒ]

Cape Town [ˈkeɪptaʊn]

the Caribbean Sea [ðə ˌkærɪˌbiən ˈsiː]

Carter County [ˌkaːtə ˈkaʊnti]

Carthage [ˈkaːθɪdʒ]

Cave Hill [ˌkeɪv ˈhɪl]

Chatsworth [ˈtʃætswəθ]

Copenhagen [ˌkəʊpənˈheɪgən]

the Czech Republic [ðə ˌtʃek rɪˈpʌblɪk]

Denmark [ˈdenmaːk]

Dublin [ˈdʌblɪn]

Durban [ˈdɜːbən]

Eastern Cape [ˌiːstən ˈkeɪp]

Edinburgh [ˈedɪnbərə]

England ['ɪŋglənd]
Europe ['jʊərəp]
France [frɑːnts]
Fulham ['fʊləm]
Gauteng ['gaʊteŋ]
Germany ['dʒɜːməni]
Glebe [gliːb]
Gulf of Mexico [ˌgʌlf‿əv
  'meksɪkəʊ]
Haiti ['heɪti]
Hermanus [hɜːm'eɪnəs]
Hillcrest ['hɪlkrest]
India ['ɪndiə]
the Indian Ocean
  [ði‿ˌɪndiən‿'əʊʃn]
Indonesia [ˌɪndəʊ'niːʒə]
Ireland ['aɪələnd]
Italy ['ɪtəli]
Jackson ['dʒæksən]
Jakarta [dʒə'kɑːtə]
Jersey ['dʒɜːzi]
Johannesburg [dʒə'hænɪsbɜːg]
Jones [dʒəʊnz]
Kent [kent]
Korea [kə'rɪə]
KwaMashu [ˌkwɑː'mɑːʃuː]
KwaZulu-Natal [kwɑːˌzuːlu:
  nə'tæl]

Lake Pontchartrain [ˌleɪk
  'pɒntʃətreɪn]
Lancashire ['læŋkəʃə]
Leeds [liːdz]
Liverpool ['lɪvəpuːl]
London ['lʌndən]
Lone Grove [ˌləʊn 'grəʊv]
Louisiana [luˌiːzi'ænə]
Malta ['mɔːltə]
the Mediterranean Sea [ðə
  ˌmedɪtəˌreɪniən 'siː]
Mexico ['meksɪˌkəʊ]
Mississippi [ˌmɪsɪ'sɪpi]
the Mississippi River [ðə
  ˌmɪsɪˌsɪpi 'rɪvə]
Missouri [mɪ'zʊəri]
Mopani ['məʊpɑːni]
Mpumalanga [əmˌpuːmə'læŋgə]
Muckanaghederdauhaulia
  [ˌmwɪkænɒkɪðɪrgɔː'hɔːljɑː]
Mumbai [ˌmʊm'baɪ]
Nelspruit [nels'pruːɪt]
Nepal [nɪ'pɔːl]
the Netherlands [ðə 'neðləndz]
New Haven [njuː 'heɪvən]
New Orleans [ˌnjuː‿'ɔːliənz]
New York City [ˌnjuː jɔːk 'sɪti]
New Zealand [njuː 'ziːlənd]

Northern Ireland [ˌnɔːðn‿'aɪələnd]
Oklahoma [ˌəʊklə'həʊmə]
Pakistan [ˌpɑːkɪ'stɑːn]
Paris ['pærɪs]
Polokwane [ˌpɒlək'wɑːni]
Port-au-Prince [ˌpɔːt‿əʊ 'prɪnts]
Prague [prɑːg]
Robben Island [ˌrɒbɪn‿'aɪlənd]
Rome [rəʊm]
Scandinavia [ˌskændɪ'neɪviə]
Scotland ['skɒtlənd]
South Africa [saʊθ‿'æfrɪkə]
Soweto [sə'wetəʊ]
Spain [speɪn]
Stirling ['stɜːlɪŋ]
Suffolk ['sʌfək]
Sweden ['swiːdn]
Sydney ['sɪdni]
Table Mountain ['teɪbl ˌmaʊntɪn]
Texas ['teksəs]
the Transvaal [ðə 'trænzvɑːl]
Trinity ['trɪnəti]
Tsendze River [ˌtenzə 'rɪvə]
Washington, D. C. [ˌwɒʃɪŋtən
  ˌdiː'siː]
Wentworth ['wentwəθ]
Western Europe [ˌwestən 'jʊərəp]
Winchester ['wɪntʃɪstə]

Numbers

0	oh, zero, nil [əʊ, ˈzɪərəʊ, nɪl]	21	twenty-one [ˌtwenti ˈwʌn]	1st	first [fɜːst]
1	one [wʌn]	22	twenty-two [ˌtwenti ˈtuː]	2nd	second [ˈsekənd]
2	two [tuː]	↓	↓	3rd	third [θɜːd]
3	three [θriː]	30	thirty [ˈθɜːti]	4th	fourth [fɔːθ]
4	four [fɔː]	40	forty [ˈfɔːti]	5th	fifth [fɪfθ]
5	five [faɪv]	50	fifty [ˈfɪfti]	6th	sixth [sɪksθ]
6	six [sɪks]	60	sixty [ˈsɪksti]	7th	seventh [ˈsevnθ]
7	seven [ˈsevn]	70	seventy [ˈsevnti]	8th	eighth [eɪtθ]
8	eight [eɪt]	80	eighty [ˈeɪti]	9th	ninth [naɪnθ]
9	nine [naɪn]	90	ninety [ˈnaɪnti]	10th	tenth [tenθ]
10	ten [ten]	100	a/one hundred [ə/wʌn ˈhʌndrəd]	11th	eleventh [ɪˈlevnθ]
11	eleven [ɪˈlevn]			12th	twelfth [twelfθ]
12	twelve [twelv]	101	one hundred and one [wʌn ˌhʌndrəd ən ˈwʌn]	13th	thirteenth [ˌθɜːˈtiːnθ]
13	thirteen [ˌθɜːˈtiːn]	102	one hundred and two [wʌn ˌhʌndrəd ən ˈtuː]	↓	↓
14	fourteen [ˌfɔːˈtiːn]			20th	twentieth [ˈtwentiəθ]
15	fifteen [ˌfɪfˈtiːn]	↓	↓	21st	twenty-first [ˌtwenti ˈfɜːst]
16	sixteen [ˌsɪksˈtiːn]	1,000	a/one thousand [ə/wʌn ˈθaʊznd]	22nd	twenty-second [ˌtwenti ˈsekənd]
17	seventeen [ˌsevnˈtiːn]	↓	↓	30th	thirtieth [ˈθɜːtiəθ]
18	eighteen [ˌeɪˈtiːn]	100,000	a/one hundred thousand [ə/wʌn ˌhʌndrəd ˈθaʊznd]	40th	fortieth [ˈfɔːtiəθ]
19	nineteen [ˌnaɪnˈtiːn]			50th	fiftieth [ˈfɪftiəθ]
20	twenty [ˈtwenti]	↓	↓	60th	sixtieth [ˈsɪkstiəθ]
		1,000,000	a/one million [ə/wʌn ˈmɪljən]	70th	seventieth [ˈsevntiəθ]
		↓	↓	80th	eightieth [ˈeɪtiəθ]
		1,000,000,000	a/one billion [ə/wʌn ˈbɪljən]	90th	ninetieth [ˈnaɪntiəθ]
				100th	hundredth [ˈhʌndrədθ]

1/2	a/one half [ə/wʌn ˈhɑːf]
1/3	a/one third [ə/wʌn ˈθɜːd]
1/4	a/one quarter [ə/wʌn ˈkwɔːtə]
1/8	a/one eighth [ən/wʌn ˈeɪtθ]
3/4	three quarters [θriː ˈkwɔːtəz]

Months

January [ˈdʒænjuəri]	May [meɪ]	September [sepˈtembə]
February [ˈfebruəri]	June [dʒuːn]	October [ɒkˈtəʊbə]
March [mɑːtʃ]	July [dʒʊˈlaɪ]	November [nəʊˈvembə]
April [ˈeɪprəl]	August [ˈɔːgəst]	December [dɪˈsembə]

infinitive	simple past	participle	
be [biː]	was/were [wɒz/wɜː]	been [biːn]	sein
beat [biːt]	beat [biːt]	beaten [biːtn]	schlagen; besiegen
become [bɪˈkʌm]	became [bɪˈkeɪm]	become [bɪˈkʌm]	werden
begin [bɪˈgɪn]	began [bɪˈgæn]	begun [bɪˈgʌn]	anfangen, beginnen
bend [bend]	bent [bent]	bent [bent]	(sich) biegen
bet [bet]	bet/betted [bet/ˈbetɪd]	bet/betted [bet/ˈbetɪd]	wetten
bite [baɪt]	bit [bɪt]	bit/bitten [bɪt/ˈbɪtn]	beißen
blow [bləʊ]	blew [bluː]	blown [bləʊn]	wehen, blasen
break [breɪk]	broke [brəʊk]	broken [ˈbrəʊkən]	(zer)brechen
bring [brɪŋ]	brought [brɔːt]	brought [brɔːt]	(mit)bringen
broadcast [ˈbrɔːdˌkɑːst]	broadcast [ˈbrɔːdˌkɑːst]	broadcast [ˈbrɔːdˌkɑːst]	senden, ausstrahlen
build [bɪld]	built [bɪlt]	built [bɪlt]	bauen
burn [bɜːn]	burnt/burned [bɜːnt/bɜːnd]	burnt/burned [bɜːnt/bɜːnd]	(ver)brennen
buy [baɪ]	bought [bɔːt]	bought [bɔːt]	kaufen
catch [kætʃ]	caught [kɔːt]	caught [kɔːt]	fangen; kriegen; festnehmen
choose [tʃuːz]	chose [tʃəʊz]	chosen [ˈtʃəʊzn]	auswählen
come [kʌm]	came [keɪm]	come [kʌm]	kommen
cost [kɒst]	cost [kɒst]	cost [kɒst]	kosten
cut [kʌt]	cut [kʌt]	cut [kʌt]	schneiden; mähen
deal with [ˈdiːl wɪð]	dealt with [ˈdelt wɪð]	dealt with [ˈdelt wɪð]	handeln von; sich befassen mit
do [duː]	did [dɪd]	done [dʌn]	machen, tun
draw [drɔː]	drew [druː]	drawn [drɔːn]	zeichnen
dream [driːm]	dreamt/dreamed [dremt/driːmd]	dreamt/dreamed [dremt/driːmd]	träumen
drink [drɪŋk]	drank [dræŋk]	drunk [drʌŋk]	trinken
drive [draɪv]	drove [drəʊv]	driven [ˈdrɪvn]	fahren
eat [iːt]	ate [eɪt]	eaten [ˈiːtn]	essen
fall [fɔːl]	fell [fel]	fallen [ˈfɔːlən]	fallen; stürzen
feed [fiːd]	fed [fed]	fed [fed]	zu essen geben, füttern
feel [fiːl]	felt [felt]	felt [felt]	(sich) fühlen
fight [faɪt]	fought [fɔːt]	fought [fɔːt]	kämpfen, streiten
find [faɪnd]	found [faʊnd]	found [faʊnd]	finden
fit [fɪt]	fit/fitted [fɪt/ˈfɪtɪd]	fit/fitted [fɪt/ˈfɪtɪd]	sich eignen; passen
fly [flaɪ]	flew [fluː]	flown [fləʊn]	fliegen
forecast [ˈfɔːkɑːst]	forecast [ˈfɔːkɑːst]	forecast [ˈfɔːkɑːst]	vorhersagen
forget [fəˈget]	forgot [fəˈgɒt]	forgotten [fəˈgɒtn]	vergessen
freeze [friːz]	froze [frəʊz]	frozen [ˈfrəʊzn]	gefrieren, einfrieren, zufrieren
get [get]	got [gɒt]	got/gotten (AE) [gɒt/ˈgɒtn]	erhalten, bekommen; gelangen; werden; holen; verstehen
give [gɪv]	gave [geɪv]	given [ˈgɪvn]	geben
go [gəʊ]	went [went]	gone [gɒn]	gehen; werden
grow [grəʊ]	grew [gruː]	grown [grəʊn]	wachsen
hang [hæŋ]	hung [hʌŋ]	hung [hʌŋ]	hängen
have [hæv]	had [hæd]	had [hæd]	haben; essen
hear [hɪə]	heard [hɜːd]	heard [hɜːd]	hören
hide [haɪd]	hid [hɪd]	hid/hidden [hɪd/ˈhɪdn]	(sich) verstecken
hit [hɪt]	hit [hɪt]	hit [hɪt]	schlagen (auf); treffen, erschüttern
hold [həʊld]	held [held]	held [held]	(fest)halten
hurt [hɜːt]	hurt [hɜːt]	hurt [hɜːt]	wehtun, schmerzen
keep [kiːp]	kept [kept]	kept [kept]	(be)halten
know [nəʊ]	knew [njuː]	known [nəʊn]	wissen; kennen
lead [liːd]	led [led]	led [led]	(an)führen, leiten

IRREGULAR VERBS

infinitive	simple past	participle	
learn [lɜːn]	learnt/learned [lɜːnt/lɜːnd]	learnt/learned [lɜːnt/lɜːnd]	lernen
leave [liːv]	left [left]	left [left]	verlassen; da lassen; hinterlassen; abfahren; weggehen
let [let]	let [let]	let [let]	lassen
lose [luːz]	lost [lɒst]	lost [lɒst]	verlieren
make [meɪk]	made [meɪd]	made [meɪd]	machen
mean [miːn]	meant [ment]	meant [ment]	bedeuten; meinen
meet [miːt]	met [met]	met [met]	(sich) treffen
pay [peɪ]	paid [peɪd]	paid [peɪd]	bezahlen
put [pʊt]	put [pʊt]	put [pʊt]	setzen, legen, stellen
read [riːd]	read [red]	read [red]	lesen
rebuild [ˌriːˈbɪld]	rebuilt [ˌriːˈbɪlt]	rebuilt [ˌriːˈbɪlt]	wieder aufbauen
ride [raɪd]	rode [rəʊd]	ridden [ˈrɪdn]	fahren; reiten
ring [rɪŋ]	rang [ræŋ]	rung [rʌŋ]	klingeln, läuten
rise [raɪz]	rose [rəʊz]	risen [ˈrɪzn]	(auf)steigen
run [rʌn]	ran [ræn]	run [rʌn]	laufen, rennen; regieren
say [seɪ]	said [sed]	said [sed]	sagen
see [siː]	saw [sɔː]	seen [siːn]	sehen; einsehen, verstehen; (mit)erleben
sell [sel]	sold [səʊld]	sold [səʊld]	verkaufen
send [send]	sent [sent]	sent [sent]	(zu)schicken
set up [ˌsetˈʌp]	set up [ˌsetˈʌp]	set up [ˌsetˈʌp]	aufbauen, einrichten
sew [səʊ]	sewed [səʊd]	sewn [səʊn]	nähen
shake [ʃeɪk]	shook [ʃʊk]	shaken [ˈʃeɪkən]	schütteln; beben
show [ʃəʊ]	showed [ʃəʊd]	shown [ʃəʊn]	zeigen
sing [sɪŋ]	sang [sæŋ]	sung [sʌŋ]	singen
sink [sɪŋk]	sank [sæŋk]	sunk [sʌŋk]	untergehen, sinken
sit [sɪt]	sat [sæt]	sat [sæt]	sitzen
sleep [sliːp]	slept [slept]	slept [slept]	schlafen
smell [smel]	smelt/smelled [smelt/smeld]	smelt/smelled [smelt/smeld]	riechen
speak [spiːk]	spoke [spəʊk]	spoken [ˈspəʊkən]	sprechen
spell [spel]	spelt/spelled [spelt/speld]	spelt/spelled [spelt/speld]	buchstabieren
spend [spend]	spent [spent]	spent [spent]	ausgeben (Geld); verbringen (Zeit)
spin (a)round [ˌspɪn (ə)ˈraʊnd]	spun (a)round [ˌspʌn (ə)ˈraʊnd]	spun (a)round [ˌspʌn (ə)ˈraʊnd]	(um)drehen
split up [ˌsplɪtˈʌp]	split up [ˌsplɪtˈʌp]	split up [ˌsplɪtˈʌp]	sich teilen; sich trennen
spread [spred]	spread [spred]	spread [spred]	verbreiten, ausbreiten
stand [stænd]	stood [stʊd]	stood [stʊd]	stehen; ertragen, aushalten
steal [stiːl]	stole [stəʊl]	stolen [ˈstəʊlən]	stehlen
stick [stɪk]	stuck [stʌk]	stuck [stʌk]	kleben
strike [straɪk]	struck [strʌk]	struck [strʌk]	angreifen, treffen, zuschlagen
swim [swɪm]	swam [swæm]	swum [swʌm]	schwimmen
take [teɪk]	took [tʊk]	taken [ˈteɪkən]	(mit)nehmen; dauern
teach [tiːtʃ]	taught [tɔːt]	taught [tɔːt]	unterrichten, beibringen
tell [tel]	told [təʊld]	told [təʊld]	erzählen; sagen
think [θɪŋk]	thought [θɔːt]	thought [θɔːt]	denken, glauben, meinen; nachdenken
throw [θrəʊ]	threw [θruː]	thrown [θrəʊn]	werfen
understand [ˌʌndəˈstænd]	understood [ˌʌndəˈstʊd]	understood [ˌʌndəˈstʊd]	verstehen
wake up [ˌweɪkˈʌp]	woke up [ˌwəʊkˈʌp]	woken up [ˌwəʊkənˈʌp]	aufwecken; aufwachen
wear [weə]	wore [wɔː]	worn [wɔːn]	tragen (Kleidung)
win [wɪn]	won [wʌn]	won [wʌn]	gewinnen
write [raɪt]	wrote [rəʊt]	written [ˈrɪtn]	schreiben

QUELLENVERZEICHNIS

Bildquellen

|(c) die-bildbeschaffer.de, Hamburg: Alamy images 98 A; AP Photo / Johnson Lin 19 o. l.; F1 Online RF 67 u. r.; fotofinder RM 130 o.; image100 69 m. l.; imagebroker 10 m. l.; istockphoto microstock 69 l., 69 r.. |alamy images, Abingdon/Oxfordshire: Roger Bamber 87 o.; © Juice Images 50 m. r.; © Nicosan 50 l.; © The Art Gallery Collection 46 u.. |Ellert, Mario, Bremen: 16, 17. |Getty Images, München: 44 D; AFP 29 E, 44 C; Bambu Productions 54 o. l.; Dianne Christie 39 B, 44; Digital Vision 25; dpa 19 o. m.; Fraser Hall 42 o. l.; Hulton Archive 28 o. l.; InterNetwork Media 53 u. r., 54; Jean Claude Chapon 30 r.; Jose Luis Pelaez 28 Nr. 4; Per-Anders Petterson 42 o., 46, 47; Tom Stoddart 48 u.; © Greg James 10 o. r.; © Warren Faidley 54 u. m.. |Hammersen, Bettina, Braunschweig: 28 Nr. 3. |Interfoto, München: Ronald Grant Archive / Mary Evans 36 u.; Science & Society 61 o.. |iStockphoto.com, Calgary: Roger Jegg 53, 58. |Kletterwald Niederrhein: 107. |Kohn, Klaus G., Braunschweig: 10 m. r., 98 C. |Kunze, Claudia (bei Elisabeth Badelt), Nürnberg: 41. |Mass, Dirk, Oetze: 28 Nr. 1, 28 Nr. 5. |mauritius images GmbH, Mittenwald: age 29 F; Alamy 34 r., 36 o., 42 u. l., 53 o. l., 58 E, 62 o. r., 62 u. l.; Boris Lehner 58 D; Cuboimages 48 m. r.; Image Source 87 r.; imagebroker / Florian Kopp 50 m. l.; imagebroker / NielsDK 58 A; imagebroker/jspix 43; imagebroker/Stephan Gabriel 32 l.; imagebroker/U. Niehoff 29 D; Jutta Ulmer 83 u. l.; Kerstin Layer 49; NIKKY NEON 69 m. r.; Peter Enzinger 67 u. l.; Pixtal 67 l.; Prisma 29 B; Schöttger-Munich 48 o.; Wolfgang Weinhäupl 11 m. r., 12. |Mohm, Julia, Braunschweig: 59. |OKAPIA KG - Michael Grzimek & Co., Frankfurt/M.: 53 o., 54 u. l., 57. |Otfried Börner, Hamburg: 15, 21, 23, 28 u., 57 u., 109; Diercke Weltatlas (Karte); getty images/AFP (Tonschalen); mauritius/ Candelier (Teppichknüpferei); getty images/Per-Anders Pettersson (Müll sammeln) 31 u.. |Penguin Books (UK) Ltd, Essex: (c) Nick Hornby 2007 11 o. r.. |Penguin Books Ltd., London: Reproduced by permission of Penguin Books Ltd. (c) Joan Lingard, 1973 / (c) 2003 126. |Penguin Random House UK, London: Reprinted by permission of The Random House Group Limited. (c) 2001 11, 20. |photoplexus, Dortmund: Koelsche 70. |Picture-Alliance GmbH, Frankfurt/M.: africamediaonline 3; akg-images 29 C, 58 B; Augenklick / KUNZ 44 E; dpa 10 o. l., 19, 19 u. r., 44 A, 48 m. l., 54 o. m., 54 o. r., 83 o., 102 o. r.; dpa / DB Kathrin Streckenbach 32 r.; dpa / epa 29 A, 44 F, 45 r.; dpa / epa AFP Casella 54 m. r.; dpa / Frank Leonhardt 28 Nr. 2; dpa / Guido Meisenheimer 30 l.; dpa / Larry W. Smith 55, 56; empics / David Davies 39 o. r., 42; epa Hrusa 39 l., 45; Golden Pixels LLC 18; Helga Lade GmbH, Germany 83 u. r.; newscom / Picture History 61 u.; Photoshot 34 l.; ZB 10 u. r., 11 u. l., 19; ZB / Nestor Bachmann 28 Nr. 6; ZB / Wolfgang Schmidt 98 B; ZB/ Patrick Pleul 27. |Scholastic Inc., New York: 129. |Shutterstock.com, New York: 248885077 53, 58; Antonio Jorge Nunes 128; Daxiao Productions 47; Hans Wagemaker 48; Jorg Hackemann 11, 12; Lopolo 128; rvlsoft 53, 58; vystekimages 47, 47. |ullstein bild, Berlin: africanpictures.net 39, 51; CHROMORANGE 39 u. l., 40. |UNICEF Deutschland, Köln: 31 m. r.. |vario images, Bonn: 28 o. l., 50 r.. |Visum Foto GmbH, Hannover: Tom Hoenig 107.

QUELLENVERZEICHNIS

Textquellen

12-15   Auszüge aus: „Across the Barricades", Joan Lingard (Hamish Hamilton, 1972) © Joan Lingard, 1972, S. 41 - 174. Reproduced by permission of Penguin Books Ltd.

20   Auszug aus: "(Un)arranged marriage", Bali Rai, published by Corgi. Reprinted by permission of the Random House Group Ltd.

22   Auszug aus: "SLAM", Nick Hornby (Puffin Books 2007) © Nick Hornby 2007, S. 281 - 285. Reproduced by permission of Penguin Books Ltd.

26   "The start of something new", © Zoe Carroll

46   "Gimme hope Jo'anna", Text und Musik: Eddie Grant,
© Greenheart Music Ltd.

51   Adaptierter Auszug aus: "Kwaito: the voice of youth", Grant Clark © BBC World Service, von: http://www.bbc.co.uk/worldservice/africa/features/rhythms/southafrica.shtml

63   "Only the Rooftops", © Dawn Fox

65   "Computer usage", © 2005-2008, Pew Research Center

126   "Into Exile", Joan Lingard (first published by Hamish Hamilton, 1973, Puffin Books 1974). Copyright © Joan Lingard, 1973, S. 41 - 174. Reproduced by permission of Penguin Books Ltd.

127   Auszug aus: "love & betrayal & hold the mayo", Francine Pascal, published by Simon Pulse 2003, © Francine Pascal, 1985

128   Adaptierter Auszug aus: "My African Dream", © Sarah Gaehwiler

1329   Auszug aus: "TOP 8", Katie Finn. Scholastic Inc./Point. Copyright ©2008 by Katie Finn. Reprinted by permission of Scholastic Inc.

130   "The Player", Naomi Alderman, aus: The Guardian,
7 January 2010, p. 17, © Guardian News & Media Ltd. 2010

World Ma

Abbreviations:

A	= Austria	**DK**	= Denmark
B	= Belgium	**EST**	= Estonia
BG	= Bulgaria	**GR**	= Greece
BIH	= Bosnia and	**H**	= Hungary
	Herzegovina	**HR**	= Croatia
CH	= Switzerland	**LT**	= Lituania
CZ	= Czech Republic	**LUX**	= Luxembourg
D	= Germany	**LV**	= Latvia

• Capital

— National border